ABOUT THE AUTHOR

Kevin D. Randle has studied the UFO phenomena in all its various incarnations for more than forty years. Training with the U.S. Army as a helicopter pilot, intelligence officer, and military policeman, and with the U.S. Air Force as both an intelligence officer and a public affairs officer, provided Randle with a keen insight into the operations and protocols of the military, their investigations into UFOs, and into a phenomenon that has puzzled people for more than a century. He retired from the army and the Iowa National Guard as a lieutenant colonel in 2009.

Randle's educational background is as diverse as his military experience. As an undergraduate at the University of Iowa, he studied anthropology. Graduate work included journalism, psychology, and military science at the University of Iowa, California Coast University, and the American Military University. He has both a master's degree and a doctorate in psychology, as well as a second master's degree in the art of military science.

During his investigations, Randle has traveled the United States to interview hundreds of witnesses who were involved in everything from the Roswell, New Mexico, crash of 1947 to the repeated radar sightings of UFOs over Washington, D.C., in 1952 to the latest of the abduction cases. He was among the first writers to review the declassified Project Blue Book files, and to report on animal mutilations, alien abductions and home invasions, and to suggest that humans are working with the aliens.

Randle has published many books about UFOs, including *The UFO Casebook, Crash: When UFOs Fall from the Sky,* and *Reflections of a UFO Investigator.* He hosts the blog www.KevinRandle.blogspot.com.

ALSO FROM VISIBLE INK PRESS

"Real Nightmares" Ebooks

Please visit us at visibleinkpress.com.

ALIEN
MYSTERIES,
CONSPIRACIES
AND COVER-UPS

KEVIN D. RANDLE

VISIBLE
INK
PRESS

Detroit

ALIEN MYSTERIES, CONSPIRACIES AND COVER-UPS

Visible Ink Press®
43311 Joy Rd., #414
Canton, MI 48187-2075

Visible Ink Press is a registered trademark of Visible Ink Press LLC.

Most Visible Ink Press books are available at special quantity discounts when purchased in bulk by corporations, organizations, or groups. Customized printings, special imprints, messages, and excerpts can be produced to meet your needs. For more information, contact Special Markets Director, Visible Ink Press, www.visibleinkpress.com, or 734-667-3211.

Managing Editor: Kevin S. Hile
Art Director: Mary Claire Krzewinski
Typesetting: Marco Di Vita
Proofreaders: Shoshana Hurwitz and Chrystal Rosza
Indexing: Shoshana Hurwitz
Cover images: Shutterstock.

Library of Congress Cataloging-in-Publication Data

Randle, Kevin D., 1949–
  Alien mysteries and conspiracies / by Kevin Randle.
    pages cm
  Includes bibliographical references and index.
  ISBN 978-1-57859-418-4 (pbk. : alk. paper)
  1. Unidentified flying objects—Sightings and encounters—History. I. Title.
  TL789.R32328 2013
  001.942—dc23
                                                                2012047277

Printed in the United States of America

10 9 8 7 6 5 4 3 2

Contents

Ezekiel, His Wheel, and the Ancient Astronauts
[1]

Those Out of Place Things (OOPTHs)
[17]

The Great Airship of 1897
[35]

The Modern Era Begins, June 1947
[59]

The Cover-Up Begins
[81]

Alien Bodies
[93]

Aztec, New Mexico

The Robertson Panel

The MJ-12 Conspiracy

The UFO Projects

The Levelland, Texas, UFO Sightings in 1957

Disappearing Aircraft and Missing Pilots

The Condon Committee

UFO Conspiracy Today

PHOTO CREDITS

Bill Oliver: 50.

Brad Steiger: 13.

Brattarb: 31.

Don Burleson: 235, 238, 239, 241.

Jerome Clark: 74.

Kevin Randle: 44, 80, 82, 103, 106, 108, 110, 112, 144, 163, 165, 234, 260, 264, 320.

Mary Evans Picture Library: 7, 42, 60, 70, 79, 153, 156, 159, 195, 196, 197, 198, 203, 207, 218, 222, 223, 236, 247, 276, 303.

Nick Redfern: 152, 209.

Paul Kimball: 136, 137, 147, 149.

Philip Mantel: 114, 116, 119, 124, 126, 128, 129, 130, 131.

Robert Schaeffer: 180.

Shutterstock: 27, 40, 48, 67, 95, 139, 187, 199, 227, 272, 294, 321.

Therese Clutario: 25.

William Rhodes: 85, 86.

All other images are in the public domain.

ACKNOWLEDGMENTS

This book would not have been possible without the help of the librarians at the Library of the Chathams, part of the Morris County, New Jersey, library system. They helped with loans of more than 100 DVDs and VHS tapes, though I'm sure they were often horrified by the titles I had requested. (I certainly was.)

Just as importantly, during two sustained power outages, the library was a place where I could plug in the computer, watch DVDs, take notes, write, recharge my phone, and get warm. I can't imagine what I would have done without the people and the place. They have my most sincere thanks.

INTRODUCTION

The dictionary definition of a conspiracy is two or more acting in concert with either an evil or criminal intent.

In the modern world, the idea of a conspiracy has expanded beyond the traditional and legal definitions. Today, it can mean the government acting to keep national secrets, to hide information that it would find detrimental to the operations of various departments, or to keep the public in the dark about what some of those working for the government know. In other words, the government is involved with many conspiracies from who shot President John Kennedy to the idea that no one ever landed on the moon.

To take this a step further, it might be said that some of those involved in UFO research are also involved in conspiracies to hide the truth. It might be a continued to support of the Majestic-Twelve, or the Allende Letters, or any of the faked photographs that have been published as the real thing. It might be said that a conspiracy exists to push out information to convince others that alien creatures have visited Earth.

Or, it might be said that the government, along with debunkers, have conspired to keep the best information from the public. Was the Condon Committee, the "scientific" study of UFOs at the University of Colorado in the late 1960s, a conspiracy to hide the truth about UFOs?

In other words, there are conspiracies all over the world regarding the UFO phenomenon. Some are government-sanctioned, some are government-sponsored, and more than a few can be laid at the feet of UFO witnesses and UFO investigators. It is a world that is confusing, obscure, and hidden, overshadowing the serious research.

Now is the time to try to untangle some of this. We have access to information that had long been hidden. We have confessions by those who were involved in some of those conspiracies. We have new science that helps us untangle some of the knots that fooled us in the past. We have what we need to understand much of what has happened in the last half century if we are smart enough to see it.

Here is the latest information, provided by many of those who were involved from the very beginning. Here are their words, telling us what they observed, what they did, and why they did it. Here, finally, is an opportunity to remove some of the conspiracy notions from the world of the UFO, to understand how other rumors began, and to sort it all out so that we can understand what happened.

Now, with inside sources, with new information, and with candid interviews, some of the theories of conspiracy can be eliminated... but in other cases, the conspiracy can be defined so that we understand it a little better.

Here are some answers… and more than a few questions.

Ezekiel, His Wheel, and the Ancient Astronauts

The current ufological thinking is that visitation by alien creatures didn't begin in 1947 with the sightings in the United States and the crash outside of Roswell, New Mexico, or with the massive foo fighter sightings of the Second World War, or even as far back as the Great Airship sightings in 1897. Some believe that such visitation might have begun early in the history of human civilization, while others suggest such visitation began before there were even written records. Research of the records available, limited though they might be, and in drawings and artifacts left behind by those ancient people, hint that our human ancestors were seeing things in the sky that they could not identify and that they did not understand. They would invent some interesting explanations for these apparitions, including the idea that the creatures associated with the apparitions were gods that lived far above the Earth.

That meant, simply, there were sightings, or rather, descriptions of events that suggest something unusual and possibly extraterrestrial was seen in the sky at the very dawn of human history. A look at ancient texts, hieroglyphics, and even cave paintings suggest there were sightings by the Egyptians, Romans, Greeks, Sumerians, Babylonians, and Chinese, and the peoples who preceded them. There is a rich history of UFO sightings in the ancient past, and it is only in the last fifty years that such information has been recovered and understood.

Prehistoric UFO Sightings

There is a report, circulated for more than a half century now, that the remnants of an ancient and mysterious people had been found on the Chinese–Tibetan border in 1938. The tale came from a Chinese scientist, Dr. Chi Pu Tei, when he found what are now called the Dropa discs. He had led an ex-

This prehistoric wall painting in a cave in Val Camonica, Italy, seems to depict two people wearing space helmets.

pedition into an unexplored part of the Himalayan Mountains when he and his team stumbled into a series of interconnected caves. Examination by these scientists suggested that the caves had been artificially created as some kind of underground storage or burial complex in the distant past.

They discovered neat rows of graves that contained small skeletons with big heads and fragile bodies, according to some of the available information. Found in the area of the graves was a disc described as about nine inches in diameter, a half-inch thick with a hole in the center, making it look like an old-fashioned phonograph record. Archaeological dating techniques suggested the disc was ten to twelve thousand years old.

Eventually 716 such discs were uncovered. Each was etched with a groove, adding to the suggestion it was some kind of record. They were taken back to Beijing University for study. Curiously, none of the skeletons were collected at the time for further research and no photographs of them have ever been located.

The discs, along with other finds from the expedition, were filed away at Beijing University for about twenty years. There, Dr. Tsum Um Nui, who began to examine them, discovered that the grooves were not just lines carved into the stone, but hieroglyphics that were so small and so fine that he needed a magnifying glass to see them clearly. He claimed that he was able to decipher them after long study.

According to his research, he learned that "The Dropas came down from the clouds in their aircraft. Our men, women, and children hid in the caves ten times before sunrise. When at last they understood the sign language of the Dropas, they realized that the newcomers had peaceful intentions."

Another section of the nearly microscopic etchings suggested that the Dropas had "crash-landed" in a remote area that was inaccessible. Given that they were so isolated, they were unable to repair their craft, or to build a new one. They could not return to their home world.

Tsum supposedly wrote a journal article about his research, but was denied permission to publish it, either by the university or by the journal editors. Another source, however, suggested that he did publish his article, "The Grooved Script concerning Spaceships which, as recorded on Discs, landed on Earth 12,000 years ago," in 1962. His theories, however, were ridiculed by the established anthropological and archaeological communities. He was called a liar and worse by his colleagues and fled to Japan, where he died some time later.

There was further research on these discs conducted in the former Soviet Union. According to Dr. Vyatcheslav Saizev, they scraped the discs, removing a layer of dirt and other debris, and then subjected them to chemical analysis. He said that the discs seemed to vibrate or "hum" when an electrical current was introduced.

In 1974, an Austrian engineer, Ernst Wegerer, photographed two of the discs that were displayed in the Banpo Museum in Xian. He said that he could see the hole in the center and could see some of the hieroglyphics on them, but his photographs didn't show the writing.

He said that he held the discs, which were fairly light, weighing but a couple of pounds. His guide, or the manager of the museum as he called her, didn't know much about the discs. She said that they were some sort of cult objects. Wegerer reported that a couple of days after his visit, the manager was called away and the discs had vanished from the museum displays.

Like so much else, these discs are still wrapped in controversy. Skeptics say that the man who made the discovery, Chi Pu Tei, seems not to have existed, and that there is no reliable record of an expedition in 1938 to the area claimed. There is no Peking Academy of Prehistory.

The real problem is that there are no known cases of someone translating a new language without decades of work and some sort of major clue. The Egyptian hieroglyphics were only understood after nearly a century of study and the discovery of the Rosette Stone, which contained three versions of the same statement, two of which were known languages and the third being the hieroglyphics. Even with that, it still took years of patient work to understand and decipher the hieroglyphics.

Other ancient writings have remained undeciphered because there was no connection to a modern language and no clues found in ancient texts. In other words, without some sort of hint, without someone or something to assist in the translation, there is no way for an unknown written language to be translated. It is not similar to the deciphering of a code, but a completely new written language.

While it is claimed there are 716 discs, there are only pictures of two, and neither of them fit the descriptions offered for the majority of them. When chased to its source, the information about the discs seems to vanish and that makes it difficult to substantiate the existence of the discs, or the translations that have supposedly come from them, or even the tale as handed down since the 1930s.

Indian Cave Paintings

Much more recently, the *Rajasthan Times* (though the newspaper is listed in various databases as *Rajasthan Patrika*), in February 2010, reported that anthropological groups working in a remote part of India had found prehistoric cave paintings that seemed to show both alien ships and the creatures from inside them.

UFO researcher Stanton Friedman has said that he and author-researcher William Moore interviewed at least 130 individuals who have firsthand knowledge of the UFO crash at Roswell.

The newspaper reported, "Local archaeologist Mr. Wassim Khan has personally seen the images. He claims that the objects and creatures seen in them are totally anomalous and out of character when compared to other already discovered examples of prehistoric cave art depicting ancient life in the area. As such he believes that they might suggest beings from other planets have been interacting with humans since prehistoric times, adding weight to the 'ancient astronaut theory' which postulates that human civilization was established with the assistance of benevolent space-faring aliens."

No follow-up stories have been found, and the *Rajasthan Times* is a newspaper printed in Hindi, which makes it difficult to verify the story. The last paragraph seems to be too good to be true, since it quotes an anthropologist who claims that this discovery is "adding weight to the 'ancient astronaut theory.'"

Both these tales, the Dropa discs and the Indian cave paintings, seem to have a basis in fact, but follow-up information and corroboration have not been found. That suggests, to the careful researcher, that these might be stories invented by others to further their own beliefs, their careers, or to thrust them into the international spotlight. Without more in the way of evidence, these are just stories that cannot be substantiated or trusted.

The Ancient Historical Written Record

The written record of UFO sightings in ancient times suffers from the same sort of trouble that plagues cave art, petroglyphs, and other stylized representations from prehistory. That is, the interpretation of the symbols and the exact meaning is often open to question. What is one man's alien creature or extraterrestrial spacecraft is another man's religious icon. Descriptions of events are written in the language of those ancient times, which often makes them confusing if not misleading.

In about 100 B.C.E., Pliny wrote in his *Natural History, Volume II*, for example, about a "burning shield scattering sparks across the sky at sunset from east to west." While that suggests a disc-shaped object, it could also refer to a bright meteor that looked more or less disc-shaped.

Jacques Vallee, writing in *Anatomy of a Phenomenon*, reported that in 213 B.C.E., "In Hadria an 'altar' was seen in the sky, accompanied by the form of a man in white clothing. A total of a dozen such sightings between 222 and 90 B.C.E. can be listed…."

Brinsley Le Poer Trench wrote in the *Flying Saucer Story* that in 218 B.C.E., "In Amiterno district many places were seen the appearance of men in white garments from far away. The orb of the sun grew smaller. At Praeneste glowing lamps from heaven. At Arpi a shield in the sky. The Moon contended with the sun and during the night two moons were seen. Phantom ships appeared in the sky."

For a little more information, and maybe a slightly different interpretation of the Trench work, there is Harold T. Wilkins' *Flying Saucers on the Attack*. He wrote, "In B.C.E. 216: At Praeneste (65 Roman miles from Rome), burning lamps fell from the sky, and at Arpinium (42 Roman miles east of Praeneste), a thing *like a round shield* [emphasis in the original] was seen in the sky."

Wilkins also wrote that in 170 B.C.E., "At Lanupium (on the Appian Way 16 miles from Rome) a remarkable spectacle of a fleet of ships seen in the air (*classis magna species in coelo visae*)."

What is interesting is that the information provided by Trench is just slightly different than that provided by Wilkins. It means one of three things and that is that both were working from primary sources and translated the Latin themselves, which could give the variations, or that Trench used Wilkins as the base and his reporting style was slightly different, meaning he rewrote the sentences to his taste, or that Wilkins wrote originally in English and Trench in French so there would be some slight variations in the way they related the material. It can also be suggested that these slight variations are of little real importance.

But translations can lead researchers astray. In the 1980s, a corporation that was opening trade with Russia conducted an experiment. They translated one of their technical papers into Russian and then had it translated back into English to find out how well the translations held up. The most interesting example was that Hydraulic Rams came back as water lambs, not exactly the same thing. In fact, in the context of the paper (and about any context imaginable) it meant nothing. Just what is a water lamb anyway?

Such observations might not be important, except that later, the variations become important to those studying the ancient sightings. They provide some hints as to what has been going on in ancient times, at least as they relate to UFO sightings.

These sorts of sightings, of strange manifestations, continued on and moved around the European continent. Wilkins wrote that in 80 C.E., "When the Roman Emperor, Agricola, was in Scotland (Caledonia), wondrous flames were seen in the skies over Caledon wood, all one winter night. Everywhere the air burned, and on many nights, when the weather was serene, a ship was seen in the air, moving fast."

In 230 C.E., "Armies of footmen and horses were seen in the air over London and other places in England. They were fighting. This was the time of the Roman emperor Alexander Severus."

There were sightings that predate the few listed here. The story of Ezekiel and his wheel predates them all and has been discussed in UFO circles almost from the beginning of the modern era.

Ezekiel Saw the Wheel

Nearly everyone has heard about Ezekiel and his wheel almost from the moment they first learned about flying saucers and could understand the Bible. Being part of the Bible provides the sighting with an authenticity that many other ancient reports cannot claim, not to mention giving the story access to millions of people around the world. But the problem with lumping Ezekiel's wheel in with modern UFO reports is that the tale, as it has been translated and retranslated and reinterpreted so many times by so many people, becomes difficult to know what is the truth about it and what is a translator's interpretation. Many of those doing the translation had their own ideas and their own agendas, so modern UFO researchers might not have a good idea about what Ezekiel saw, if he saw anything at all. The modern interpretation, that Ezekiel had an encounter with extraterrestrials, here meaning creatures from another planet, isn't necessarily the correct one, or even the only such interpretation. Those who believe other things have used the sighting to advance their causes as well.

Ezekiel, according to nearly everything that has been written about him, was a Hebrew prophet who lived about twenty-five hundred years ago. He was among several thousand captives taken from Jerusalem (in what is now Israel) to Babylon by Nebuchadnezzar after he attacked the city. Ezekiel lived at Tel-abib on the Grand Canal that ran near Nippur from Babylon to Uruk in what is now modern-day Iraq.

It might be said that Ezekiel re-established his ministry in Babylon after his capture because his fellow Israelites felt they were out of touch with Yahweh, who it was believed resided in the temple in Jerusalem. By telling his flock that

Yahweh could be worshipped anywhere, he gave them hope and restored their faith while they were held captive in that foreign land; because of this, Ezekiel became their prophet.

It was while he was in Babylon that he reported his experience that was eventually recorded in the Bible. According to the King James version of the Bible, Ezekiel wrote:

> (4) And I looked, and behold a whirlwind came out of the north, a great cloud, and a fire infolding itself, and a brightness was about it, and out of the midst thereof as the color of amber, out of the midst of the fire.... (5) Also out of the midst thereof came the likeness of four living creatures … they had the likeness of man.... (6) And every one had four faces, and every one had four wings.... (13) Their appearance was like burning coals of fire and like the appearance of lamps: it went up and down among the living creatures.... (15) Now as I beheld the living creatures, behold one wheel upon the earth by the living creatures, with his four faces … the appearance of the wheels and their work was like unto the color of beryl; and the four had one likeness; and their appearance and their work was as if it were a wheel in the middle of a wheel....

A depiction of the prophet Ezekiel's sighting of a UFO.

UFO researchers, looking at these words in a modern world as people begin to break away from their religious heritage, have interpreted them in the context of the extraterrestrial, meaning, of course, coming from another planet. And if the creatures described are of an extraterrestrial origin, then the wheel refers, of course, to their spacecraft, a flying saucer.

But all of this is filtered through modern eyes, putting a modern spin on it. If we look further and deeper, we begin to see things that do suggest the religious aspect to the report. Ezekiel, a religious man of the ancient world, quite naturally saw this as a religious experience. That is the spin he put on it, and we might want to consider what the witness himself thought about his experience rather than what we would like to believe about it now.

Examination of the text reveals some of the trouble might be found with the interpretation or the translation of the ancient words made by so many others long after Ezekiel was gone and who are now long gone themselves. In the

This fifteenth-century painting (believed to be by artist Domenico Ghirlandaio), when inspected closely, appears to include a UFO flying in the background and observed by a man on a ledge. Sightings of UFOs in the past may have been interpreted as religious experiences by our ancestors.

King James version of the Bible, the color of the wheel, for example, is said to be beryl, which, unfortunately, doesn't do much to define it. According to the dictionary definition, beryl is "a vitreous, green, light blue, yellow, pink, or white silicate of aluminum."

In the standard revised version of the Bible as opposed to the King James version, it says, "(16) As for the appearance of the wheels and their construction: their appearance was like the gleaming of a chrysolite; and the four had the same likeness, their construction being as a wheel within a wheel."

Chrysolite is defined as a variety of olivine. And that, in turn, is defined as "a vitreous, orthorhombic, often transparent, olive-green, magnesium-iron silicate."

So, in the various translations we have a variety of color for the wheels that does little to define it. It was either green, light blue, yellow, pink, white, or olive green. Of course this problem is not that of Ezekiel but of those translating his original words, or a translation of a translation as it has come down through history, which is the whole point.

There are many other areas of conflict that can be discovered with very little effort. For example, in the King James version, in chapter 13 it says that "… their appearance was like burning coals of fire and like the appearance of lamps: it went up and down among the living creatures.…"

In the standard revised version, it says, "In the midst of the living creatures there was something that looked like burning coals of fire, like torches moving to and fro among the living creatures."

Nothing there changes the actual meaning of the words. Each suggests something glowing, whether a lamp or coals, but they are not exactly the same thing. All this demonstrates is that those making the translations have interpreted the words as best they could so that we see minor discrepancies. In fact, it might be suggested that some of the translators changed the words to make them more understandable to the audience of those very translations. But all of this is trivial in nature and more playing with words than looking at the totality of the sighting.

An ancient Egyptian text, *Annals of Thutmose III*, written about a thousand years before Ezekiel, told of Thutmose's wheel in the sky....

There is another problem, and what some consider the major problem with Ezekiel's tale, and that is plagiarism. Ezekiel, according to many writers, was not the first to make the claim of wheels in the sky, or that there were strange creatures associated with them. An ancient Egyptian text, *Annals of Thutmose III*, written about a thousand years before Ezekiel, told of Thutmose's wheel in the sky, containing a similar story using many of the same images and descriptions that were attributed to Ezekiel.

Published reports now suggest that Prince Boris de Rachewiltz said that all this, Ezekiel's wheel, came from a translation of a papyrus that was among the papers of Professor Alberto Tulli, formerly the director of the Egyptian Vatican Museum. Somehow, after Tulli's death, his papers and the original papyrus were scattered among his living relatives and eventually lost. However, the translation remained and according to it:

> In the year 22, third month of winter, sixth hour of the day.... The scribes of the House of Life found it was a circle of fire that was coming in the sky ... it had no head, the breath of its mouth ... a foul odour. Its body was 1 rod long and 1 rod large. It had no voice.... They went to the King ... to report it. His Majesty ordered ... as to all which is written in the House of Life of His Majesty was meditating upon what happen. Now, after some days had passed over those things, Lo! They were more numerous than anything. They were shining in the sky more than the sun to the limits of the four supports of heaven.... Powerful position of the fire circles.... The army of the king looked on and His Majesty was in the midst of it.... Thereupon [the fire circles] went up higher.... Fishes and volatiles fell down from the sky....

But what is one of these ancient stories of alien contact without additional controversy? The Condon Committee, the scientific study of UFOs conducted at the University of Colorado in the late 1960s (and examined in depth later) and paid for by the Air Force, was led by American physicist Edward Uhler Condon (1902–1974), who helped develop radar and was a pioneer of quantum mechanics. His committee investigated the papyrus story because of its association with Ezekiel, his association with UFOs, and an alleged connection to the Vatican and de Rachewiltz. Samuel Rosenberg wrote in the Condon Committee's final report, *Scientific Study of Unidentified Flying Objects*, that de Rachewiltz was an amateur Egyptologist and that the papyrus, if it had ever existed, was now missing, which he thought suspicious. Without the original papyrus, they were unable to ascertain the validity of the story or even the existence of the original document.

In the end it makes little difference if de Rachewiltz was an amateur Egyptologist or not. Many amateurs provide useful service in various scientific fields. Amateur astronomers, for example, provide a huge network of eyes trained in astronomy to perform tasks that the professionals would rather not do because they can become tedious. Sometimes these amateurs, because of their love for the topic, are simply better at it than the professionals who are obligated to produce results and publish their findings on a regular basis. While they choose the profession originally for its appeal to them, they often have lost their love of it while the amateurs work in the field because they love doing it. It's not unlike the Little League baseball player who struggles to play while the major leaguer seems to be more interested in his salary, his product endorsements, and looking good on the sports shows than he is in playing the game.

Other researchers, such as Jacques Bergier in his book, *Extraterrestrial Intervention: The Evidence,* followed the path created by the Condon Committee and Rosenberg and obtained different results which, again, is no real surprise. He found no evidence that the Tulli papyrus was a fraud or a hoax, which is not to say that it isn't. He was merely suggesting that the case wasn't quite as cut and dried as Rosenberg had claimed it to be when he finished his research for the Condon Committee and the Air Force. Bergier thought the question of the translation and the papyrus validity was still open. I'm not sure that the question matters at this point unless you're a biblical scholar. For the UFO researcher, the source of this story, because of its age and its ambiguities, is irrelevant.

In the end, whether researchers accept the more ancient story written on Egyptian papyrus or that of Ezekiel written some time later, the case is still a single witness sighting that the witness himself suggested was of a religious nature and termed it in the words of a religious experience. It could be nothing more than a hallucination, it could be a confabulation, it could be the accurate description of a religious experience, or it could be some sort of interaction with alien creatures from another world. Given the passage of time and the somewhat vague and even contradictory nature of the descriptions, there isn't much that can be said about Ezekiel and his wheel other than it could have come from a more ancient story and that it could refer to alien visitation—even if Ezekiel had plagiarized it.

More Ancient Sightings

Then, a couple of thousand years later there are other sightings that are of interest to researchers. In 577 C.E., for example, an object described as a lance crossed the

A wood print by Samuel Coccius depicts a scene in Basle, Switzerland, in which witnesses said they saw numerous globes apparently fighting each other at fast speeds.

sky. And four hundred years after that, in 919, a flaming torch was seen, and two hundred years later, in 1168, a globe of fire was seen moving "to and fro."

These are just a few of the examples of ancient UFO reports that dot the literature. Each of these sightings could be explained by meteors. While a burning shield suggests something other than a meteor, it could also refer to a bolide, a large, bright meteor that could easily be called a burning shield and would be easily visible in the daylight. Flaming torches and a globe of fire certainly could be meteors or other natural phenomena that the ancient observer didn't understand. Each would suggest something spectacular simply because meteors were surely seen frequently and while not understood for what they were, would be considered a natural event. If the meteor was large enough or bright enough, then special note might have been made of it by the observer.

Meteors do not explain a sighting made on March 3, 1557, when, according to the old sources, a "thunderbolt pierced the bridal chamber of Francois Montmorency and Diane de France, running into every corner of the tent before it exploded harmlessly." That sounds suspiciously like ball lightning, a natural phenomenon that has only recently been accepted by modern science and something that would have easily startled someone living in the sixteenth century.

Jacques Vallee wrote, in *Anatomy of a Phenomenon*, that Edmund Halley, in 1716, saw a bright object that stayed in the sky for two hours. He said that it was so bright that he could read a printed text. Clearly this was not some kind of meteor or comet, which Halley understood. It was not ball lightning either. It was something else. Something strange enough that Halley made note of it.

Alien Beings in Ancient Times

And there are descriptions, or rather tales, of beings from these craft. W.R. Drake, in his *Spacemen in the Middle Ages*, reported, "Agobard, Archbishop of Lyons, wrote in *De Grandine et Tonitrua* how, in 840 C.E., he found the mob in Lyons lynching three men and a woman accused of landing from a cloudship from the aerial region of Magonia. The Archbishop halted the execution and freed the victims."

Brad Steiger, in his book *The Fellowship*, also claimed contact between aliens and humans was made in 840 C.E. using the same account of the Archbishop as his source. He suggested that the French referred to the aliens as sky people because they descended from the upper reaches of the atmosphere in spacecraft. The locals called the spacecraft "ships from the clouds."

The description of the aliens offered by Steiger was of creatures with large heads, pointed ears, and bulging eyes, which isn't all that different from some of the descriptions of the gray aliens said to be responsible for modern abductions. Steiger also wrote, as have others, that these aliens told the French that their home was a place called Magonia. These creatures interacted with the local peasants and tradesmen, making them sound more like sailors or merchants than alien creatures from some kind of a spacecraft.

For some reason, according to Steiger, a dispute erupted between the French and the four aliens, who were then seized and bound with chains. Steiger said that after being held for several days in jail, the prisoners were paraded before a mob, which suddenly went berserk and stoned them to death.

The Archbishop, according to still another variation of the story, which was offered in still another UFO book, was an eyewitness to the alien's execution. This all was revealed by Hayden Hewes, a fellow from Oklahoma who, with Steiger, coauthored the *UFO Missionaries Extraordinary*, which was published in 1976. Yes, the same Brad Steiger who had a slightly different interpretation in a different book. This, of course, is in conflict with still other accounts, including that of Vallee, who said that the mob was attempting to lynch the men and woman but apparently were stopped by the Archbishop.

Text, written originally in Latin and available in various libraries today, actually reads (as translated into English):

We have seen and heard many men plunged in such great stupidity, sunk in such depths of folly, as to believe that there is a certain region, which they call Magonia, whence ships sail in the clouds, in order to carry back to that region those fruits of the earth which are destroyed by hail and tempests; sailors paying rewards to the storm wizards, and themselves receiving corn and other produce.

Out of the number of those whose blind folly was deep enough to allow them to believe these things possible, I saw several exhibitions in a certain concourse of people, four persons in bonds—three men and a woman who said they had fallen from these same ships; after keeping them for some days in captivity they had brought them before the assembled multitude, as we have said in our presence, to be stoned. But truth prevailed.

Brad Steiger

So, now it is a tale of four people who came from ships that travel in the clouds, as opposed to "cloudships" and who, according to the original text, were about to be stoned. The Archbishop, apparently, was able to stop the execution with the truth. There is no description in the original that matches modern-day aliens, and only a reference to a ship that sails in clouds suggests the reason for making this some sort of UFO report. The description could refer to many things, and none of them require an alien spacecraft.

Somewhat less controversial is the story of demon ships in the skies above Ireland, which here means that there aren't many different interpretations of the sighting. According to the information contained in *Flying Saucers on the Attack*:

There happened in the borough of Cloera, one Sunday, while the people were at Mass, a marvel.... It befell that an anchor was dropped from the sky with a rope attached to it and one of the flukes caught in the arch above the church door. The people rushed out of the church and saw in the sky a ship with men on board, floating before the anchor-cable, and they saw a man leap overboard ... as to release it....

Each of these sightings, including reports of beings or creatures from them, could not only refer to a classical UFO, but it could also mean sightings of natural phenomena or terrestrial-built craft crewed by humans rather than alien creatures. There is simply not enough information for us to draw any kind of specific conclusion or to suggest this is a flying saucer sighting and actually, no reason to believe it so. It is a matter of interpretation.

Ancient Sightings Continue

There are other writings in which the object is not something vague that could easily be a misidentified natural phenomenon, but in which the descriptions are very interesting and detailed enough for us to eliminate the mundane. Most of these cases come from the nineteenth century and most are here in the United States, but a few are from the more distant past and from a variety of foreign lands.

On August 12, 1133, in Japan, it was reported that a large, silvery disc approached the ground. In 1361, a flying object described as being "shaped like a drum, about twenty feet in diameter" emerged from the Inland Sea off western Japan. On January 2, 1458, a bright object resembling the full moon was seen in the sky, and its apparition was followed by "curious signs" in heaven and earth. On March 17, 1458, five stars appeared, circling the moon. They changed color three times and vanished suddenly. Japanese rulers were horrified and believed that the sign announced the coming of a great disturbance. The people in Kyoto were expecting disasters to follow, and the emperor himself was very upset.

> On March 17, 1458, five stars appeared, circling the moon. They changed color three times and vanished suddenly.

Researchers believe that the sightings are real because they have been recorded in ancient works, or rather, they have been told they were. But then there is the tale of "Brother John's Saucer," which was spotted in 1250 C.E., or 1290 according to Jacques Vallee in his *Anatomy of a Phenomenon*. No matter what the exact date, it is a report that is more than 750 years old and fits into the pattern of ancient sightings in ancient texts.

According to the documents:

As the brothers assembled for their evening meal, they heard a noise in the doorway. Brother John stood in the doorway with a terror-stricken look on his face.

"What happened, Brother John," inquired the abbot.

"I was walking towards the abbey from the fields and thinking about the roast mutton dinner. A strange noise overhead scared me. I looked up in the sky. A large silver plate is up there in the sky."

The monks forgot their dinners and dashed into the yard.… Henry the Abbot and Brother John stepped from the dining room. A giant flying disc hovered in the sky and drifted slowly in the clouds.…

There is, of course, the expected controversy about the sighting. This is, after all, a report of a disc in the sky, hovering over a church, observed by the brothers of the abbey. UFO researchers as distinguished as Jacques Vallee and Brinsley Le Poer Trench, as sloppy as Frank Edwards and Morris K. Jessup, and as radical as George Adamski and Desmond Leslie have reported on the sighting. But, as is the case in so much of UFO research, they failed to go to the original sources, often because access to those sources is strictly limited. Rosenberg, of the Condon Committee who worried about Ezekiel, checked to see if the abbey existed, learned that it did, and cabled (for those of the younger generation, think emailed) John Haggerty to check on the validity of the document and to investigate the story in the original sources. The reply from Haggerty was that the document was a hoax created by two students in a letter to the *London Times*. This just shows that something that is suggested to be ancient and that has been printed in the newspaper isn't necessarily the truth.

Finally, the Flying Saucers

It wasn't until the nineteenth century that descriptions became detailed enough for investigators to understand them completely and rule out many natural phenomena. The language used is, of course, our language, and the people had a better understanding of meteors, comets, and even weather phenomena that still inspires some UFO reports today. But as researchers move into an arena where there are lots of records and lots of witness statements, they are able to remove many natural phenomena from listings. At least the records are there for those who wish to see them, and sometimes that is the only way to understand what has been happening.

John Martin, who lived near Dennison, Texas, reported that on January 22, 1878, he saw an orange object high in the morning sky. It approached him, and when it was nearly overhead, he said that it appeared to be about the size of a large saucer.

The *Dennison Daily News* reported on January 25, 1878:

Mr. John Martin, a farmer who lives some six miles south of this city, we learn the following strange story: Tuesday morning while out hunting, his attention was directed to a dark object high up in the northern sky. The peculiar shape and velocity with which the object seemed to approach riveted his attention and he strained his eyes to discover its character. When first noticed, it appeared to be about the size of an orange, which continued to grow in size.

After gazing at it for some time Mr. Martin became blind from long looking and left off viewing it for a time in order to rest his eyes. On resuming his view, the object was almost overhead and had increased considerably in size, and appeared to be going through space at wonderful speed.

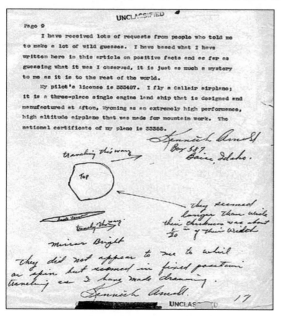

The letter Kenneth Arnold wrote to Army Air Force Intelligence on July 12, 1947, describing a UFO.

When directly over him it was about the size of a large saucer and was evidently at great height. Mr. Martin thought it resembled, as well as he could judge, a balloon. It went as rapidly as it had come and was soon lost to sight in the heavenly skies. Mr. Martin is a gentleman of undoubted veracity and this strange occurrence, if it was not a balloon, deserves the attention of our scientists.

He wasn't really talking about its motion as that of a saucer, or that it was even saucer shaped, but that it was the size of a saucer in the sky, but he did say saucer in relation to the sighting. Some seventy years later, a newsman would report the words of Kenneth Arnold about the motion of the objects he saw, and the world would be introduced to flying saucers. Arnold's report then was no more descriptive of the object than Martin's words—but when have things like that ever gotten in the way of a good story.

On May 15, 1879, sailors on the *Vultur*, sailing in the Persian Gulf, saw two large, glowing wheels that were slowly descending and spinning. They were about 120 feet in diameter and separated by nearly 500 feet. These were more like flying saucers than most of what we have read about in so many of those ancient accounts.

The ship's crew talked of wheels, just as did Ezekiel so many centuries earlier. So maybe there is a connection with UFOs and the past. Maybe we're just looking too hard but the problem is that we don't have any physical evidence. We are left with written records that have been misinterpreted by writers who wish for ancient confirmation of our modern sightings, or writers who borrowed from one another, assuming that the first had checked the source but did no checking him- or herself. Myths, exaggerations, half-truths, and hoaxes are perpetuated by one writer after another simply because he or she didn't attempt to find the original sources. In the end, we are left with some interesting tales but no real confirmation of them and no evidence that UFOs as we know them today have been sighted for centuries.

There is, however, an area where there are claims of physical evidence. These are the "Out of Place Artifacts," and they just might give us the physical evidence of those ancient UFOs for which we search. If nothing else, they are an interesting side issue to our human history.

Those Out of Place Things (OOPTHs)

There is a form of evidence for UFOs that goes beyond the sightings recorded by our ancestors and that suggests that we might not have been alone during our long climb from nomadic creatures who could barely be classified as human to our modern civilizations. This physical evidence is available for study and could supply some clues about the validity of an interpretation of those ancient writings and UFO reports. It can always be said that the ancient writers were unfamiliar with the natural world around them and jumped to conclusions based on their ignorance. A glowing shield or a flaming spear giving off sparks can just as easily be a meteor as it can an alien spacecraft. It all depends on the interpretation and the knowledge of the natural world by those making the observations.

Physical artifacts seem to support the idea of ancient technological civilization or alien visitation and can validate the importance of those earlier writings. Ancient artifacts are a form of corroboration that can be seen, felt, and tested in today's world. It is physical evidence that provides proof without interpretation.

These ancient artifacts, such as iron nails found in solid rock, a delicate gold chain found in a lump of coal in the 1890s, or an ornate bell-shaped vessel inlaid with silver blasted from solid rock in a Massachusetts quarry in 1852, are called "Out of Place Artifacts," known popularly as OOPARTs. They seem to suggest that someone had been manufacturing objects millions of years before the human race was capable of such fine and precise work or even before humans in any form existed on this planet. These artifacts are, in essence, a form of proof that another intelligence had once walked the Earth, maybe before the dinosaurs disappeared, and that those sophisticated beings probably originated in outer space, given the fossil and geological records relied on by our modern-day scientists. It is circumstantial evidence that, if accurate and properly dated, provides us with the proof that some ancient UFO sightings were of alien spacecraft.

These OOPARTs, or Out of Place Things (OOPTHs; the origin of both terms seem to belong to Ivan T. Sanderson), break nicely into two categories. First are the gold chains found inside rock, suggesting manufacture millions of years ago. The second group is those inventions or creations that seem too advanced for the society that produced them, such as electric batteries made in Babylon thousands of years before anyone had a need for electricity or any kind of storage cell, and a working, gear-driven model of the solar system made by the ancient Greeks and found just over a century ago. This model is, in essence, a type of mechanical, astronomical computer used to predict the movement of the then-known planets, the sun, and the moon.

OOPTHs

One of the first of that former group was referenced in several UFO books (and some of the creationist materials) and refers to some sort of "bell-shaped vessel" discovered during blasting in a quarry in Massachusetts in the mid-nineteenth century. According to those writers and researchers, the object, based on the geological formation from which it came, is somewhere around half a billion years old. Other sources suggested it was a mere one hundred thousand years old. Either way, it is something that shouldn't have existed at the time it was made or in the rock strata in which it was found.

According to some of those UFO books, the original source for this story was the *Scientific American* in 1851, a periodical that was a little less scientifically oriented then than it is today. The story was headlined "A relic of a by-gone age," although some suggested it was labeled simply as "A Curiosity."

The story, as reported in those UFO books, was that the blasting in the quarry "threw an immense mass of rock … in all directions." Among the shattered debris, the workmen found a small metallic vessel in two pieces that when re-assembled formed a "bell shape" about four and a quarter inches high and about six inches wide at the top. The whole thing was something like an eighth of an inch thick and it was clearly something that required a knowledge of metalworking because of the fine detail on it.

The report continued, saying that it was made of zinc with "a considerable portion of silver." The sides were inlaid with silver, and the carving was "exquisitely done by the art of some cunning workman." The magazine concluded, again according to all those UFO books, that the find was worthy of additional investigation because the vessel was extremely old, predating the first inhabitants of the continent, including all of the native tribes.

The University of Iowa library, in its bound periodical section, holds the entire run of *Scientific American*. It would be easy enough to check the primary source of the story. So I did. To my disappointment, but not great surprise, there was nothing in the 1851 issues about anything like the metal vessel being found. True, there were a number of things labeled as "curiosities," but nothing that told of manufactured items coming out of solid rock from a quarry.

But research isn't always that simple, and there is always the chance that someone had written down a date wrong and it was then copied by all those others who failed to do primary research but who believed the others had checked. So, I decided to look in both 1850 and 1852, and being somewhat compulsive about such things, I quite naturally started in 1850 because it came before 1852.

> **According to ... writers and researchers, the object, based on the geological formation from which it came, is somewhere around half a billion years old.**

The article appeared in the June 5, 1852 edition of the *Scientific American,* on page 298. The details as listed in most of the UFO books were substantially correct, though they do leave out some important and interesting information.

That *Scientific American* article said, "On the sides there are six figures of a flower or bouquet, beautifully inlaid with pure silver, and around the lower part of the vessel a vine, or wreath, inlaid also with silver. The chasing, carving, and inlaying are exquisitely done by the art of some cunning workman."

The entry continues, noting, "There is no doubt that this curiosity was blown out of the rock ... but will ... some other scientific man please tell us how it came there?"

While I had been at the mercy of those other writers in the past, until I began to roam the stacks in the bound periodicals section of the University of Iowa library, researchers today aren't so restricted (and I wouldn't be surprised to learn that some of them have never seen the inside of a library, let alone bound periodicals). I typed "*Scientific American* 1852" into a search engine and in seconds was looking at a complete listing for *Scientific American* available online. Since I already knew the date, I could easily pull up what I wanted. Anyone with access to a computer and an online service could do the same (and therefore stay out of the library).

Tubal Cain

Like so much else in the UFO field, there is always something left out of the stories in all those UFO books. What is rarely mentioned is a paragraph at the end of the article in which it is suggested that Tuba Cain, one of the first residents of the area (from seventeenth century America), had made the vessel.

But sometimes UFO research takes off on strange tangents. On closer examination of the *Scientific American,* it begins to look as if the mark at the end of the sentence that I thought originally was an artifact caused by the microfilm process, and right after the word Tuba, is an "L" that slipped out of alignment and into the margin. This means the name is a reference to Tubal Cain, and Tubal Cain probably wasn't a reference to one of the first residents of Dorchester County, Massachusetts, but was a descendant of Adam and Eve. Tubal Cain refers to blacksmiths from antiquity, and the original Tubal Cain supposedly worked with bronze and iron in the far distant past and nowhere near the New World. In fact, according to the Bible (Genesis 4:22), "Zillah also had a son, Tubal-Cain, who forged all kinds of tools out of bronze and iron. Tubal-Cain's sister was Naaman."

> In the end, we're left with many unanswered questions, including that of the placement of the vessel....

Here is something else from outside the UFO field: Tubal Cain is a secret Masonic phrase, something that certainly wasn't well known in 1852. So now the question becomes: Is this tale of a metallic vessel found in solid rock true, or does it have some significance to the Masons and the use of Tubal Cain is the clue? I confess that I don't know. I am more than a little disturbed to learn of the history of Tubal Cain and the reference to it, or him, in this particular article. There is no reason for those other writers to have made anything out of the reference, unless they themselves were Masons and knew the code. Without an Internet connection and search engines, I certainly would not have made the connection, nor would I have known to ask the question.

Ignoring that little bit of diversion, we find that if we are going to look at the rest of the case with a scientific detachment, we must ask a couple of other questions. First, did they find anything to suggest the vessel had been embedded in the rock? Did they find bits of rock that matched the contours of the vessel? If we were to date the "vessel" according to standard archaeological methodology, would we be forced to conclude that the vessel was millions of years old because that was the age of the material in which it was found?

Second, they suggest that a scientific man should take a look at the vessel and name Professor Agassiz as someone to study the find. The *Scientific American* wondered what Agassiz's credentials were to make any sort of study. I confess that in today's world, I'm a little curious about the man's credentials as well, though there is nothing to suggest that he ever looked at the vessel or rendered an opinion about its authenticity, so this is really a dead issue.

But, of course, it is possible to learn who, exactly, Agassiz is, with the same Internet that provided the information on Tubal Cain. He was a Swiss-born paleontologist, glaciologist, and geologist who studied the Earth's natural history. He was a professor at Harvard, and in 1852 he accepted a medical professorship of comparative anatomy in Charleston, Massachusetts, which suggests that if he had examined the vessel, he would have been able to render a professional assessment of it. There is no indication that he ever looked at it, or that he was even aware of its existence.

In the end, we're left with many unanswered questions, including that of the placement of the vessel and if it was actually embedded in the stone as originally suggested. It is always possible that it was not embedded in the stone but was associated with it. That means, simply, that the vessel was hidden in the dirt on top of the stone, maybe lost in it, but had not been embedded in the stone.

Keith Fitzpatrick-Matthews and James Doeser, two professional archaeologists who run the Bad Archaeology website, wrote this about the vessel: "… it is difficult to understand why anyone might take this report seriously." They suggest that the object is a candlestick in the Victorian style. They don't understand why anyone in 1852 would think the object was more than a few years old.

And we all now wonder if there was a hidden meaning in this article that was meant for the Masons because of the use of Tubal Cain. Does that mean the story is untrue and placed there for some now forgotten reason, or is the rest of the article accurate? In a world filled with speculations about a da Vinci code, Templars, and a bloodline related to Christ, it is not difficult to believe that the Masons of the nineteenth century planted the article for some probably trivial, but certainly unknown, reason.

More OOPTHS

There are, however, other incidents, not unlike this report, but where the manufactured objects were taken out of what looked to be solid rock or coal. In an account given before the British Association for the Advancement of Science, Sir David Brewster said that a nail had been found embedded in solid rock. About an inch of the nail was protruding and the rest was lying along the stone and projecting into a layer of ground, where it had rusted. The report suggested that the nail was partially in the stone but had not been driven into it. In other words, the nail was part of the sedimentary material that had congealed into granite so that it was part of the rock. That would mean that the nail had been manufactured millions of years earlier, if all aspects of the report were true and the observations about it accurate.

Similarly, there is a story about a rock hammer that was found embedded in rock in June, 1934 near London, Texas. According to the story, members of the Hahn family found a bit of wood that seemed to be protruding from the rock. When they broke it open, they found the hammer head and just a bit of the handle.

The whole area, on the Red Creek, is part of the Edwards Plateau, which is made up of Cretaceous rock. Upstream there is an area with many fossils of dinosaurs, which according to one dating method means the hammer is about 140 million years old. Analysis of the hammer suggests that it is made out of a strange iron mix with chlorine as some kind of an additive. That is not a common mixture today.

Many more such objects seem to have been found in coal. Brad Steiger, in *Mysteries of Time & Space*, reported that Wilbert H. Rusch, Sr., Professor of Biology, Concordia College, Ann Arbor, Michigan, quoted a letter a friend had received from Frank J. Kenwood, who said that he had been a fireman at the Municipal Electric Plant in Thomas, Oklahoma, in 1912 when he split a large piece of coal and found an iron pot encased inside.

Quoting from the letter, Steiger wrote, "This iron pot fell from the center leaving the impression or mold of the pot in this piece of coal. I traced the source of the coal and found that it came from the Wilburton, Oklahoma, mines."

Others have made similar discoveries in lumps of coal. Mrs. S. W. Culp, according to the Morrisonville, Illinois *Times*, published on June 11, 1891, found an artifact when she broke a lump of coal as she was preparing to toss it in a stove. According to the story, "Mrs. Culp thought the chain had been dropped accidentally in the coal, but as she undertook to lift the chain up, the idea of its having been recently dropped was at once fallacious, for as the lump of coal broke, the middle of the chain became loosened while each end remained fastened to the coal."

The coal was identified as coming from mines in southern Illinois. Steiger suggests that the coal is from the Carboniferous era.

> The hard stone had surrounded the screw so that its contours had been preserved but the metal itself was gone.

In 1869, miners working the Abbey Mine near Treasure City, Nevada, claimed they had found a screw, or rather the remnants of a screw, embedded in a piece of feldspar. They could see the screw's taper and the way the threads had lined up. The hard stone had surrounded the screw so that its contours had been preserved but the metal itself was gone.

I queried the Smithsonian about this and several other like reports a number of years ago. They suggested, "… manufactured items … would not normally be found in rocks or coal since the latter were formed before the advent of man. The only such inclusion [meaning here that it has become mixed in with other debris] would be if the rock material had been broken and the artifacts had gotten lost among it, and then moss had recemented it by sedimentary action."

This is certainly a convenient explanation and is, of course, quite possible. It is also possible, as in the case of the metal vessel from Dorchester, that it had not been embedded in the rock, but was associated with material around the rock. That means, simply, that it could have been something buried in softer ground that was uprooted by the explosion and fell in among the debris of the quarry where it was found, giving the impression that it was blown out of solid rock.

Some support for that conclusion comes from the study of the history of OOPARTs. *Info Journal* (No. 59) reported that around 1900 an Englishman found a coin embedded in a lump of coal. The coin was clearly dated 1397. So, we have an artifact that was found in coal that was clearly dated long after the coal was formed, unless we are willing to believe that some ancient, unknown, or alien civilization used a numbering system just like ours. We have seen, since the beginning of written history, a variety of numbering systems, so why believe the ancients would use the same system we do today? Why wouldn't they have invented their own?

There is further information that sheds additional light on this, and we don't need philosophic discussions of numbering systems to understand it. After Mount St. Helens blew up a group of scientists discovered that peat deposits had developed in an unexpectedly short time at the bottom of a lake. It suggested that some coal beds could theoretically form in far less time than conventionally believed.

What all this tells us is that there are some interesting enigmas out there and that there seem to be some rational explanations for some of these strange finds. But, and this is critical, those explanations rely partly on speculation. Further study is required on this before we can either accept the data as proved or reject it as flawed.

Out of Place Inventions

But now we move into the arena of inventions that seem out of place for the time in which they were created. Books and magazines are filled with examples of inventions that seem to be ahead of their time, and they have used these inventions to postulate alien intervention in human history. Some writers, however, suggest these super inventions, such as the steam engine created by the ancient Egyptian Hero, are little more than curiosities that had no practical use in their worlds, at least none that were obvious to others. Some, however, created out of the cultural elements of the time, are certainly the things of speculation and conjecture.

Many of those books and magazines often refer to batteries that were made in ancient Babylon some two or three thousand years ago. They were discovered by German archaeologist Wilhelm König working near Baghdad in 1938.

These were a number of small clay jars with necks covered in asphalt and containing iron rods encased in copper. König thought, based on his observations, that these were some form of storage battery. When filled with an electrolyte (like citrus fruit juice), each of the jars could generate an electrical current, though the liquid for the electrolyte had long ago escaped from the jars he found.

König came to this conclusion because a number of very fine silver objects had been discovered in Iraq that had been plated with a thin layer of gold. Electroplating requires electricity, and the batteries would provide the current to do it. *Mythbusters*, which airs on The Discovery Channel, showed that similar batteries, when hooked up in series, could produce a current of sufficient strength to electroplate objects. It might take a while, but it could be done.

Of course, the fact that similar batteries constructed today have that capability doesn't mean that the ancient batteries were used for that purpose. Others, such as Dr. Arne Eggebrecht, showed that the Babylon Batteries weren't very effective at electroplating. Besides, it's now believed that the objects that König thought had been electroplated might have been fire-guilded instead.

Then, other information found by other archaeologists suggests the batteries might be only fifteen hundred years old, not two to three thousand years. Not that a change in the date from two thousand to fifteen hundred matters all that much. The questions that remain—since the jars obviously exist and were, until recently, on display in Baghdad—are who made them and why would they do that?

It is clear, however, that the elements used to construct these batteries, meaning the material for the jars, the copper, iron, and electrolyte, all existed in the region at the time of their creation. This isn't actually an out-of-place invention, it is more of an anomaly in time. But the question about the use for such devices is the one that remains unanswered.

The Antikythera Computer

Another such anomaly is the Antikythera computer that could display with great accuracy the movements of the sun, moon, and the five planets known to the Greeks. The computer was discovered at the beginning of the last century when a sponge diver, Elisa Stadiatos, found the wreck of an ancient cargo ship. Lying on the seabed near the wreck were a number of statues, and those are what he remembered most when interviewed about his find some time later. Inside the ship were luxury items that included jewelry, wine, pottery, and bronze that dated to something like two thousand years earlier.

Also found were some green lumps that were extremely difficult to identify. Whatever they were, they had been housed in a wooden case that wasn't much larger than a shoebox. There seemed to be dials on the outside of the box and bronze gears on the inside. X rays showed a complex design of thirty or more gears. Analysis suggested that the device was a computer that could predict the position of the sun, moon, and known planets on any given date in the past and project those positions into the future.

There has been some controversy about that. Derek Price, described as a science historian at Yale, used a number of X rays and reconstruction to come up with the initial claim that the device would calculate the position of the sun and moon. It was Michael Wright, at the Science Museum in London, who realized

Fragments of the Antikythera machine, which is believed to be an ancient computer, are on display at the National Archeological Museum in Athens, Greece.

the overall potential of the calculator. But he also said that it appeared that Price had been overly generous as he calculated the number of teeth on some of the gears, and that in turn set up the proper ratios to move the various parts.

The device, as it was found, seemed to provide for the orbits of the sun and moon, that is, using the Ptolemy system which put the Earth at the center of the solar system. It also seemed to have been built so that the orbits of both Mercury and Venus could be predicted as well. This seems to make little sense. Why build such a device when there are another three planets in the Greek world: Mars, Jupiter, and Saturn?

Speculation is that there was another level that added these to the mix. In fact, there have been Greek writings that suggest such things did exist in Greece at the time. Cicero told of his friend Poseidonius who had created just such a device that simulated the motion of the sun, moon, and the five planets. It is also claimed that Archimedes had built a small planetarium that could do this as well. This means, simply, that there is a written record to go along with the speculations of Wright and others about the purpose of the Antikythera computer.

In the end, what this seems to prove is that the ancient Greeks had the knowledge to build the computer. That it used the Ptolemy system rather than the Copernican system seems to suggest that it predates Copernicus, which is consistent with other dating criterion. Copernicus, remember, said that the sun, not the Earth, was the center of the solar system, but then Copernicus was born centuries after the Antikythera computer was built and that knowledge wasn't available to the Greeks.

The Plains of Nasca and Other Strange Markings

Before we move on, we need to address the huge stone buildings and the bizarre markings the ancients left for us all around the world. I believe that in today's world, we understand that the pyramids were built by the Egyptians using primitive and ingenious techniques that we do understand. Recent discoveries in Egypt, along with experimentation, have shown that they had the ability to build the pyramids. It is an impressive technological feat given the state of their civilization, but one that was within their capability and their knowledge. There is no need to postulate alien intervention to explain the pyramids.

If we look beyond those monolithic stone structures (figuratively), we can see markings made on the ground around the world that are quite large and often visible only from above. These huge drawings suggest an advanced knowledge of geometry and an understanding of the environment in which they were created. But do they suggest something that is alien to Earth?

On the Peruvian Plains of Nasca, a desolate plateau that is still difficult to reach, are a set of lines that at ground level look almost random, but from above show stylized creatures and shapes. Two parallel lines run for quite a distance, never wavering. Another set of the lines look remarkably like a modern airport, though the lines were laid down hundreds of years ago by a people who had never heard of airplanes or airports. It is an accomplishment that suggests to some that they had help, and in this particular case that means extraterrestrial help.

These sorts of displays gave rise in the late 1960s and through the 1970s to the idea that ancient astronauts, meaning alien creatures, had interacted with humans just as we were beginning to build our civilizations. Many of these structures or lines, the reasoning went, were beyond the ability of the people of that time, so they had some kind of external help. That help arrived on spaceships.

The research in the area has provided an answer for the lines and that the people who lived in the area a thousand years ago had the ability to create the lines. It is a remarkable feat, but there is nothing about the lines that suggest an alien presence. That the nature of the drawings are visible only from the air above does not remove the religious nature of the symbols. In other words, modern scientists believe that the lines were created to please the gods that resided high above the Earth.

It could be argued that those gods were in spaceships and were alien creatures. But the fact remains that the lines were created by humans, on the ground, without guidance from above. In other words, the lines do not represent a technological advance that was beyond the people in the area and if you are going to argue for alien creatures, then you need to produce some evidence of them.

The Nasca lines in Peru form pictures, like this whale, that can only be seen clearly from the sky, which is why some believe them to be alien-created. Archeologists maintain, though, that the Nasca culture (400–650 C.E.) made them.

Nasca suggests nothing more than clever humans working with the materials available to them.

Archaeological research, much of it completed after the first of the ancient astronaut theories was advanced, has provided us with a few answers. The pyramids, for example, would have required a relatively large population to construct them and now, on the Giza Plateau, the remains of the city where those thousands of workers lived (and some archaeologists believe they were Egyptian workers rather than Jewish slaves) have been discovered. Evidence about the methods used to construct the pyramids has also been uncovered. Nothing to suggest an intervention by aliens has been found. The evidence suggests an ancient people who understood engineering and construction and used the materials available to them.

The real argument today concerns the age of the Sphinx located near the pyramids. Some believe it was the first object built and that evidence near it suggests it is thousands of years older than the rest of the structures on the Giza Plateau. Even with that, there is no real suggestion that ancient astronauts had a hand in any of the construction there. Just clever humans who were able to cre-

Pyramid strutures can be found from Central America to Africa. The Giza pyramids in Egypt, shown here, are among the most impressive. Some people speculate the engineering involved to build the pyramids is too advanced for ancient peoples to accomplish, so they speculate aliens may have been involved in building them.

ate something that has lasted thousands of years utilizing the materials they had available to them at the time of the construction.

In fact, there is a hint about the evolution of the pyramid form and why the Egyptians settled on constructing them the way they did. First, is the step pyramid that gives an impression that the pyramid wasn't the original form, but that the Egyptians began with building a large square structure for the tombs and then just added more and smaller squares on top of it. The final building was the step pyramid.

Second, is the bent pyramid. This was a larger structure with steep sides. It has been suggested that the Egyptians, as they worked on the bent pyramid, realized the structure would be unstable. They decreased the angle of the sides, resulting in the bent look. From there they began building the massive pyramids that we see in Giza and scattered around modern Egypt today.

It would seem that alien creatures would have been aware of the inherent instability of such a steep-sided pyramid and warned the Egyptians about it before they made their error. It would also seem that alien creatures would have a good working knowledge of metallurgy, yet when they arrived, whether in Egypt, Mexico, Easter Island, South America (or anywhere else that proponents of the ancient astronauts claim they landed) the only material they could find to work with was the local stone. They didn't provide our ancient ancestors with a knowledge of metallurgy. They didn't give them a good knowledge of the solar system, which the space travelers would have had, but rather provided them only with a knowledge that the humans could have discovered for themselves with careful terrestrial observation without instrumentation. The point here is that the extraordinary knowledge that would have been a by-product of extraterrestrial contact simply isn't in evidence anywhere.

The Egyptian OOPTHs

There are a number of things found in the Egyptian tombs, or representations drawn on the walls of those tombs, that suggest a technology that was advanced, even for the Egyptians of the ancient world. One of these, known as the Dendera Light, is an image that seems to mimic lightbulbs in the modern world. It has a rounded front with what seems to be a slender filament passing through the center of a long, clear structure that might be the glass of the bulb.

Egyptologists have said that the carving is a mythological depiction of a Djed pillar and a lotus flower giving birth to a snake in the center. It is a religious symbol that links fertility to the annual Nile floods and is not really a lightbulb at all. And there is no physical artifact to go with it. Just the illustration that some, from their modern perspective, believe might be a lightbulb. Without that physical evidence there is no reason to assume that it is a lightbulb.

The Saqqara Bird is another example of this same thinking. This is a bird-shaped, wooden artifact found in 1898 during the excavation of the Pa-di-Imen Tomb. It is, according to the various dating techniques, at least 2,200 years old and is made of sycamore.

According to traditional archaeologists, the Saqqara Bird is a religious or ceremonial object that was created in a form that represented the most important of the Egyptian gods, including Ra and Horus. There are other suggestions

The Saqqara Bird was discovered by Dr. Khalil Messiha, who believed it to be a working model of a glider.

about its purpose, including a weather vane and a toy. It should be remembered that when no obvious answer presents itself, the conclusion drawn by modern scientists is that the artifact had a religious or ceremonial significance.

Dr. Khalil Messiha, a physician, an archaeologist, and a parapsychologist, thought that the Saqqara Bird was some sort of monoplane or glider. He believed that it would fly and that the vertical stabilizer (tail) had been broken off the rear of the plane sometime in the past. He built a model of it that was six times larger than the original and added a stabilizer. He insisted that he made his model fly.

Martin Gregorie, who designed and built gliders, also made a model of the Saqqara Bird out of balsa. He couldn't duplicate the results claimed by Messiha, even when he added a tail section and experimented with the design. He thought the object was probably a toy of some kind rather than a religious artifact.

Peruvian Dinosaurs (The Ica Stones)

The Ica stones are a collection of andesite stones (basically an igneous rock) that range in size from the very small to what some have described as boulders. Carved on them are Inca and Aztec warriors riding and attacking dinosaurs (Tyrannosaurus rex and stegosaurs), extinct animals, scientists, medical doctors performing brain and heart surgery, and both land and star maps. They have not been carbon dated because they contain no organic materials that would allow such testing.

The best-known collection of these stones is owned by Javier Cabrera Darquea. He is said to have started his collection when he was presented with stone that held the image that he recognized as an extinct fish. According to the story, Cabrera also began to supplement the collection that had been begun in the 1930s by his father, who had found the original stones in the fields of the family plantation. With the help of a farmer, Basilo Uschuya, Cabrera gathered additional samples and his collection eventually reached more than 10,000 specimens.

The whole case becomes muddied in 1996 when Cabrera stopped practicing medicine and opened a museum to display his stones. While serving as a doctor, as a professor, and as the chief of the Department of Medicine at the University of Lima, he kept his interest in the Ica stones secret. But when he retired, he opened a museum displaying all the various stones he had gathered, grouped by subject.

Another man, Santiago Aguuto Calvo, an architect by trade, also bought many of the stones and began excavating pre-Inca tombs near Ocucaje in 1966, according to what he claimed. He wrote an article about the artifacts he was finding, believing that the Ica stones were part of a prehistory burial ritual that predated the Inca.

This "Ica stone" from Peru has a drawing that appears to be some kind of dinosaur.

Add to this the fact that something like the Ica stones were found by the Spanish in the mid-fifteenth century. In other words, stones similar to those being displayed by Cabrera in his museum had been found by the Spanish and described in their literature. This seemed to suggest the Ica stones were not a modern hoax.

Some of Calvo's collection was displayed in the Ica museum, but were labeled as pre-Inca burial art. Eventually the curator of that museum withdrew the stones from display when Cabrera's ideas about the antiquity of his collection began to gain notoriety. The curator said that he now believed that the stones were the work of grave-robbers, or, in other words, faked. The curator would no longer display them.

As if the story couldn't become more convoluted, Uschuya, who had provided many of the stones to Cabrera (or more precisely sold them to him), said that he had created them. Part of it was to inspire writers like Erich von Daniken, and part of it was to make money. But now, after the stones had been featured in a BBC documentary and Uschuya was in trouble for selling Peru's cultural history, he said that he had created them himself. He said that he used school texts and comic books as inspiration for the etchings on the Ica stones.

One of them clearly shows a T-rex, but it is a version of the animal as it existed in the 1960s. That is, the tail dragging on the ground with the animal standing nearly upright. In today's world, scientists have changed their minds, believing the tail was a counterbalance used in hunting, and the posture was anything but upright. This suggests that the confession of a hoax is accurate because the stone etchings reflected the image of the animals that is now outdated.

And because nothing is ever easy, Cabrera explained part of this by saying that many of the original stones had been copied, but that was so the copies could be sold legally to tourists. Everyone agreed that there was no harm in creating replicas as long as it was understood that they were replicas and they were marked as such. Cabrera continues to claim that the original stones are not faked in any way and depict a world in which humans existed with dinosaurs, hunted them, and that the scientists of that long-ago era did perform brain surgery and understood the cosmos nearly as well as we do today.

What Have We Learned?

Fortunately, in our modern world, many of the questions we once asked about these ancient marvels can now be answered. While proponents of the ancient astronauts ask their same old tired questions, we have new answers for them. The people around when those marvels were created did have the capability and the technical ability to build the pyramids, or Stonehenge, or the statues on Easter Island. And when they ask why there were pyramids in Egypt and the New World, which implies communication among the various cultures, all we have to do is suggest that the Mayan pyramids look nothing like the Egyptian pyramids other than in a basic form. The connection simply isn't there.

What we are left with here are ancient peoples who created the lines on Nasca because it amused them to do so and they had the ability to do it. The Egyptians built the pyramids because they could and because their leaders ordered it done. None of what we see in these objects from our distant past requires the intervention of alien creatures, and there is no real evidence for this type of intervention.

There are literally dozens of artifacts that have been linked to ancient and unknown civilizations or to alien races in the distant past. The truth here, however, is that some of the Out of Place Artifacts have easy explanations. They aren't relics out of the dawn of time, but objects that have somehow become mixed into strata, or areas like seams of coal, that suggest great antiquity. The explanation for many of them are just as the Smithsonian told me in that letter a couple of decades ago.

Others are artifacts that show a sophisticated understanding of the world by our ancestors, which tells us they knew more about the world around them than we had believed. Their observations of the world were precise and, while some of their theories explaining nature were more imagination than reality, they were able to deduce quite a bit that was right.

That's not to say that there are easy explanations for everything we find mysterious. It means that sometimes we have underestimated the abilities of the ancient Greeks, Romans, or Egyptians. They understood more than we give them credit for and were far more technologically advanced than we sometimes believe them to be.

But there is something else and that comes out of the anomaly reported in the *Scientific American*. It's a little thing, just a tilted "L," that makes a name into a secret Masonic sign. It might be that this tale of a metal, bell-shaped vessel from solid rock had some significance to a small and selected portion of the population. For whatever reason, an editor inserted Tubal Cain into that article and we might never know the reason for that.

But there are still anomalies that we cannot explain. There are nails pulled from solid rock and we don't know how they got there. We have seen, as we study all these things, that sometimes we have no answer and there are some things that we might never know. All we can do is look at the clues and try to understand the world around us.

The Great Airship of 1897

The Great Airship sightings, as they are usually reported, took place in late 1896 and early 1897 and foreshadowed, to a great extent, the modern UFO era. All categories of sightings from occupant reports, abductions, cattle mutilations, and landings to crashes were reported during this first acknowledged UFO wave. This is an observation that is sometimes frightening to the modern UFO researcher for more than one reason, which we'll examine as we work our way through all these reports.

The Beginning

This wave began, semi-officially, on the evening of November 17, 1896, when, according to the *Sacramento Evening Bee*, a light like an "electric arc lamp propelled by some mysterious force" passed over Sacramento, California, and touched off the first of the reports of what would become known as the Great Airship. Once the story had been printed, other newspapers started to make their own announcements and print their own stories about the growing airship controversy, often taking contrary views simply because they couldn't say anything positive about their competitors. The name of the game then, as it always is, was circulation, and no one wanted to help the enemy build his circulation while his own decreased.

So, early on the *San Francisco Chronicle* claimed that the Sacramento airship was a hoax, but also noted that those who had made reports were quite sincere. The implication here was that the good citizens of the area, who might buy the *Chronicle*, were not the perpetrators of the hoax. They were just fooled by it, whatever *it* might have been, and those other individuals who were perpetrating the hoax.

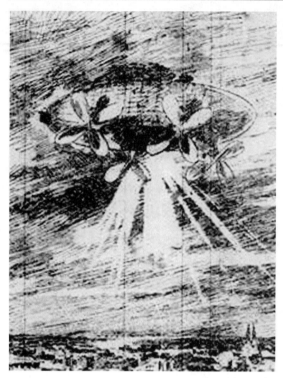

A drawing of the mysterious airship that appeared over Sacramento, California, was printed in the *Daily Record-Union* on November 18, 1896.

Then, on November 20, just three days after the original sighting, the *Chronicle* quoted Professor George Davidson who believed the whole episode was the result of "a sort of free masonry [remember Tubal Cain of the last chapter] of liars. Half a dozen fellows got together, sent up a balloon with some sort of an electric light attached, and imagination has done the rest. It is a pure fake." (Are there any parallels here to what we have seen time and again in the modern era? Hot-air balloons filled with candles launched in the 1960s sparked hundreds of UFO reports.)

Even so, the airship returned to Sacramento on November 20 and then appeared over San Francisco on November 21. Passengers on a streetcar in Oakland saw something that was described as a "peculiar-looking contrivance."

As the one newspaper, the *San Francisco Call*, was reporting these events, the other, the *Chronicle*, was suggesting that a lawyer, George D. Collins, had met with the inventor of the airship. Collins, according to the newspaper, had seen the machine, which he described as being 150 feet long with two canvas wings and a rudder like the tail of a bird. The airship had been built in Oroville, California, by a wealthy man who had moved there from Maine. As soon as he corrected some minor technical problems, he would fly the ship over the city so that everyone there could get a good look at it.

The *Examiner* sent a reporter from San Francisco to Oroville, but the man could find no one in the town who knew of the inventor, or a wealthy man who had recently moved there from Maine, or of the airship itself. He could find no place where a 150-foot-long airship could be hidden. Without any sort of corroboration for the story, he concluded that it was nothing more than a hoax. That was supposed to signal the end of the airship.

To make matters worse, if possible, lawyer Collins approached still another California newspaper to tell them that the *Examiner* had misquoted him. The quotes about the airship had come from a friend of Collins' that the *Examiner* had interviewed and which they had failed to verify with him. Collins said that everything his friend had told the reporter was a lie.

Confusion reigned as suspicion then fell on a dentist as the real airship inventor. He had come from Carmel, Maine, and spent time tinkering with his

Drawing of the airship that appeared in the *Chicago Times-Herald*, April 12, 1897.

many inventions. He seemed to fit the profile of the mysterious airship inventor as described by others. It was allegedly confirmed by the inventor that his attorney was Collins, but he claimed that all his inventions had to do with dentistry and not with huge, mysterious airships. The dentist, sick of all the unwanted attention, hid out somewhere other than his home, and reporters, searching for a story, rifled his personal possessions, finding nothing other than copper dental fillings.

Once it was believed that the identity of the inventor and the location of his invention had been discovered, the story began to fade, only to be revitalized almost immediately. On November 24, 1896, the *Oakland Tribune* reported that George Carleton knew the inventor, or at the least knew his name. Of course, Carleton was sworn to secrecy and wouldn't reveal the name of the inventor to reporters. All he would do was confirm that the craft was being tested in the Oroville area, which fit nicely with all the other stories that had been reported, but offered nothing in the way of evidence.

W.H.H. Hart, one-time attorney general of California, announced that the inventor, irritated with Collins for talking too much, had fired him and hired Hart. According to Hart, there were *two* airships, and his job was to consolidate the interests of those who owned them. Hart seemed to believe that one of the airships would be used for war, and there was talk of dropping dynamite on Havana, Cuba, where the Spanish were causing a great deal of trouble at the time, according to the newspapers. Less than two years later, the United States would be at war with Spain after newspaper reports blamed the Spanish for an attack on the *USS Maine* in Havana Harbor (which of course, is a whole other matter and is, of course, parallel with events of the world today … that is, blame for an attack on U.S. interests and then the inevitable war on foreign soil).

Hart's confirmation of the airship, and a "secret informer's" new information that the ship had been flown from Oroville to a barn in Sacramento, seemed to prove, to some at least, the existence of the airship. It had been flown every night, according to various sources, and that was exactly what people had been reporting. The voices heard by some on the ground were identified as engine noise rather than human speech. No one bothered to explain why the ship was only flown at night or over populated areas where it could be seen and then reported in the press.

Hart, however, began to retract a number of his earlier statements, suggesting that he had never actually seen the airship himself. He had talked to a man who had claimed to be the inventor but had no proof that such was the case. He had been convinced of the reality of the airship by the unidentified inventor and by those reports that were coming in every night. That seems to be a sort of circle … the airship must exist because it is reported every night, but no one has seen it on the ground or during the day.

That didn't end the sightings, however. They continued to be made all along the California coast. While some of the sightings were little more than nocturnal lights, that is, strange lights seen in the distance late at night, other sightings were more detailed.

On November 26, 1896, for example, Case Gilson said that he had seen an unlighted airship in the sky above Oakland. Gilson said that it "looked like a great black cigar with a fishlike tail … the body was at least 100 feet long and attached to it was a triangular tail … the surface of the airship looked as if it were made of aluminum.…"

The First Contactees?

Then others reported they had seen the airship on the ground. John A. Horen told the San Francisco *Examiner* that he had met a stranger who took him to a remote location where the two of them boarded the airship. Horen was then treated to a trip to Hawaii and back, made in a single night. Horen's wife, however, found the tale ridiculous, saying that he had been sound asleep at home, next to her, when the flight had allegedly taken place.

What is interesting here, and the reason to take a momentary pause, is that Horen's story of a trip on the craft would be mirrored about fifty years later when other men, such as George van Tassel, would claim extraordinary trips on flying saucers. Like Horen, they would have nothing more than an incredible tale with no proof, but there were thousands who believed them. And unlike Horen, they didn't go to Hawaii, but took trips to the planets in the solar system.

To take this a step further, his tale also mirrors some of the abduction accounts being made from the 1960s on. While some of the earlier stories are of people abducted while outside, they did evolve into reports of aliens in the house, taking one spouse while the other slept, unaware of the home invasion. Horen's tale seems to predict those that would come more than a half-century later.

And then in another report that would mirror those of the late 1940s, fishermen near Pacific Grove, California, supposedly saw an airship land on the water and then float slowly to shore on December 2. It was occupied by three men, one of whom was addressed as "captain" by the other two. The fishermen were told that the ship required some repairs and that the captain was not yet ready to announce his invention to the rest of the world. That would come later.

More people came forward with tales of meeting with the crews of those piloting the airship. In most cases, the airship had some kind of mechanical problems requiring it to land for a short period for repairs. George Jennings told reporters that a traveler had entered his business, a man Jennings claimed to have recognized but whom he would not identify, who was one of the airship inventors. Jennings said he knew the man well, and there had been no reason for him to lie about his invention. No one seemed to wonder if Jennings might not be the one lying since he had no proof that anyone he knew had invented the airship.

Alien Abduction?

What might be the first recorded claim of an attempted alien abduction, and associated with the airship stories, came during the early evening of November 25, 1896. Colonel H.G. Shaw said he, with a companion, Camille Spooner, left Lodi, California, "when the horse stopped suddenly and gave a snort of terror."

Shaw claimed that he saw three figures who stood nearly seven feet tall and were very thin. They looked like humans and didn't seem to be hostile so Shaw tried to communicate with them. According to Shaw, they didn't seem to understand what he was saying and responded with a "warbling" in a type of monotone chant.

Abduction reports dating back to the late nineteenth century bear similarities to more modern stories.

Shaw continued his description, reported in the newspapers of the day in great detail, saying, "They were without any sort of clothing, but were covered with a natural growth as soft as silk to the touch and their skin was like velvet. Their faces and heads were without hair, the ears were very small, and the nose had the appearance of polished ivory, while the eyes were large and lustrous. The mouth, however, was small and it seemed … they were without teeth."

Shaw also said they had small, nail-less hands and long, narrow feet. By touching one of the creatures, he discovered that they were nearly weightless, though he didn't explain how touching them produced that deduction. Shaw said he believed they weighed something less than an ounce. Again, he didn't explain how he had come to that conclusion.

With Shaw close to them, they tried to lift him with the intention of carrying him away. When they couldn't budge either Shaw or his companion, they gave up and flashed lights at a nearby bridge where a large "airship" was hovering. They walked toward the craft using a swaying motion and only touching the ground every fifteen feet or so. Then, according to Shaw, "With a little spring they rose to the machine, opened a door in the side, and disappeared.…"

A week or so later, in early December 1896, two fishermen, Giuseppe Valinziano and Luigi Valdivia, said they had been held captive for a number of hours while the airship crew made repairs. The "captain" of the craft would only provide vague clues about the origin of the ship, but did say the invention would be announced to the world within a few weeks. When the repairs were completed, the men were allowed to leave the ship unharmed. No announcement was ever made.

Once again, it is necessary to note that these tales mirror those told today about flying saucers. The descriptions of the aliens are exotic, but still based on the human design. For those who accept the modern flying saucer reports, these similarities should be quite troubling. If there is nothing but imagination behind the airship reports, then why can't the same conclusion be drawn about modern flying saucers?

By the middle of December 1896, the airship stories began to fade once again from the California newspapers. On January 16, 1897, for example, former attorney general Hart reappeared to say that the airship inventor had left California and was on his way to Cuba where war between the United States and Spain was brewing. Apparently, the airship inventor, a patriotic American, thought his invention could be of some use against the Spanish.

The Great Airship of 1897

In February, however, the airship craze began to spread from California. The *Omaha Daily Bee* reported on airship sightings in the south-central part of Nebraska that had begun in the fall of 1896. The airship had been seen about five hundred feet above the ground as it hovered for nearly thirty minutes giving witnesses a good view of it, according to those early reports.

Shaw also said they had small, nail-less hands and long, narrow feet. By touching one of the creatures, he discovered that they were nearly weightless

Near Big Springs, Nebraska, on February 17, three men reported a "barrel-sized light" rising into the air and saw it descend rapidly as it shot out sparks. On February 18, the *Kearney Hub* reported that the "now famous California airship inventor is now in our vicinity."

Late in the month, February 26, a group of people at a railroad depot in Falls City, Nebraska saw a "big searchlight, moving in a westerly direction, apparently at a speed of about sixty miles an hour, and in the same portion of the sky a red light, much like a [railroad] switch lamp, was plainly seen."

The light seemed to be moving toward Stella, Nebraska, and railroad dispatcher Ike Chidsey wired the agent there. Within minutes the light was seen over Stella. Other reports were made from Beatrice, Wymore, Hastings, Kenesaw, and Hartwell, all in Nebraska. Some of the witnesses said that they had seen the light for several nights but had been reluctant to report anything for fear of ridicule, though there is no indication that other witnesses had been subjected to any teasing. (Another example of the airship stories matching those of the modern flying saucers.) Those reports, coming from railroad dispatchers and telegraphers, would foreshadow a much larger and more complex wave of sightings that would begin in a few weeks and that would be reported throughout the entire Midwest.

The wave seemed to explode on March 29, 1897, when the airship was again reported over Omaha, Nebraska. At the same time it, or rather another airship, was chasing a farmer near Sioux City, Iowa. Robert Hubbert said that he was riding his bicycle and hoping to see the airship "that the whole country is talking about." An anchor was being dragged along the ground by the airship and it grabbed Hubbert, hauling him from his bike. Suddenly, and "none too soon," according to the newspaper account, his pants ripped and Hubbert fell back to the ground. Although he was physically unhurt, he was angry. He told a reporter that it was criminal "for the skipper of the ship to let a grapnel drag on the ground."

Not all UFOs are saucer-shaped, of course. There have been several sightings of cigar-shaped craft, for instance, such as this one based on what a DC-3 pilot and copilot saw over Alabama.

The very next night, March 30, the people of Denver, Colorado reported the airship overhead, and on April 1, it was seen above Kansas City, Kansas. Hundreds reported it as it paused from time to time to play with its searchlight among the clouds. About half an hour after it disappeared from Kansas City, it was reported over Everest, Kansas, not all that far away. Witnesses there said that it resembled a cigar with wings and that it glowed brightly while hovering.

On April 2, it was seen near Decatur, Michigan. According to the story, the first evidence of the airship was a bright light and then behind it, a dark shape. The witnesses said that they could hear a sharp crackling sound and voices.

On April 10, the airship was over Illinois. From Chicago, thousands of people watched an airship displaying its lights. Later the same evening the airship made at least one landing. As it descended near Calinville, Illinois, a crowd began to gather. The airship settled into a pasture and the curious started forward. Apparently, the crew thought the townspeople were too close or were afraid they might be hostile. Before they got close, the ship took off.

Also on April 10, the airship was seen over several Iowa towns. Clinton, just across the Mississippi River from Illinois, reported it first, then Ottumwa farther to the west, and later Albia. That was the third time that the residents of Albia had seen the ship. They also claimed the first report from Iowa.

On April 12, the airship was reported to have landed once again. According to the eyewitnesses, the object was large, cigar-shaped, with wings on the sides and a canopy over the top. A man climbed out and walked around as if looking for damage. After fifteen minutes, the airship "rose to a great height" and disappeared to the north.

On that same evening, an engineer on a train near Chicago said he watched the airship for several minutes but "was forced to turn my attention back to my duties." When he looked up again, the airship was far ahead of the train and near Lisle, Illinois, he lost sight of it.

Trouble for the Airship

The middle of April brought the reports of a series of landings in Iowa. The *Cedar Rapids Evening Gazette* noted the airship had landed on the Union Station in the "wee morning" hours and that several local citizens were taken on board. Charley Jordan quickly made his story known and even signed an affidavit attesting to the truthfulness of his tale of his flight. He was described as "never telling but a few lies and then only about things of importance." Also on board for the flight was W.R. Boyd, who said his whole purpose in going was to "get as high as possible so that he could learn about the condition of the post office." The members of the strange crew were reported to be tired from their long journey but promised to lecture about their trip quite soon. The topics to be discussed included the unlikely subject of Hell.

The night after the Cedar Rapids tale, the airship was captured in Waterloo, Iowa. The *Waterloo Courier* reported that the unusual craft "came to rest on the fairground" and one of the pilots went to the police station to ask that they guard his ship. Arriving at the fairgrounds, the police found a large, twin-cigar-shaped object. All during the day people came to see the ship, the first tangible object to be found that didn't disappear into the night or vanish like the morning mist. That made the story a little more plausible than those being told in so many other locations, including the original sightings in California.

A heavily accented "professor," who claimed to come from San Francisco, told of the dangerous flight across the country that ended in tragedy when the leader of the expedition fell into the Cedar River. Attempts to rescue the man failed, and they landed nearby to attempt to retrieve the body.

By late afternoon, interest was waning, and then ended abruptly. The professor was recognized as a local man, E. A. Feather. He dropped his accent and the ship, such as it was, was finally removed from the fairgrounds, but not before hundreds had seen it and more than one newspaper article had been written about it.

The airship was also making the rounds in Texas during April. A man from Denton, north of Dallas, said that he had seen the object and it was definitely

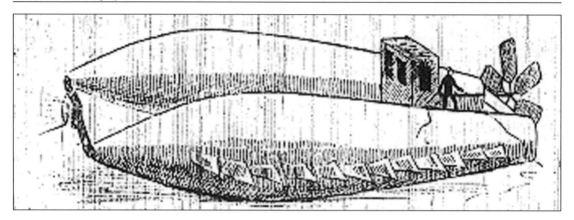

Drawing of the Waterloo airship.

some "kind of manufactured craft." From Hillsboro, Texas, came the report of a "brilliant light, as if coming from an arc light...." and then it was seen gliding over a field nearby.

It seems necessary to point out here that many of these descriptions sound suspiciously like Venus. A brilliant light, like that of an arc light that is bluish white, describes Venus at the height of its brilliance. This, too, is another aspect of the modern UFO phenomenon. Venus can take on a brilliance, and when it is close to the horizon seems to have a shape behind it. Without a search of the astronomical records, and some idea of the direction from the sighter to the object, I can only speculate, but this is a point that needs to be made.

Early on the morning of April 17, two men from Rhome, Texas, said that they saw the airship heading west at 150 miles per hour. The same day, the *Fort Worth Register*, which "hardly cares to repeat it," reported that a man traveling near Cisco, Texas saw the airship landed in a field. Several men were standing around and Patrick Barnes went over to talk to them. At the ship he was told they had some kind of engine trouble but would be leaving soon to go to Cuba to "bomb the Spanish." By one o'clock they had repaired the craft and they took off for the Ozarks to train for their mission.

In Paris, Texas, a night watchman said that he saw a cigar-shaped craft, two hundred feet long, with large wings. Later, in Farmersville, several people said they heard the crew of an airship singing.

The Aurora, Texas, Crash

The Aurora airship crash story, as it was told just days later, suggests the airship appeared about dawn on April 17, 1897, came in low, buzzed the town square and then continued north, toward the farm owned at the time by Judge Proctor. There it hit a windmill and exploded into a shower of debris, damaging the

Judge's flower garden and house, not to mention his windmill. The townspeople rushed to the scene and found the badly disfigured body of the alien pilot. T. J. Weems, a Signal Corps officer (think of an 1897 intelligence officer here), thought the pilot was probably from Mars (because in 1897 they didn't think beyond the solar system).

Being good Christians, and apparently because no one had anything else to do, they buried the pilot after a short memorial service that afternoon. They also gathered several documents covered with a strange writing found in the wreckage and picked up tons of material including silver and aluminum that came from the wrecked airship. Not surprisingly, all that evidence has long since disappeared.

And that's it. No follow-up stories as tourists flocked to Aurora to see the wreckage or visit the grave (and remember here that in Waterloo people arrived all day to look at the ship). No mysterious scientists arriving to inspect the wreckage and add their voices to the speculation. No Army response, though one of their own was on hand to report what he had seen and apparently confirmed the authenticity of the crash. And finally, most importantly, no one ever produced those documents or bits and pieces of the wreckage, though there had been tons of it, at least according to the newspaper reports. Somehow it all disappeared in the years after the event.

The story died at that point, and then was resurrected in the 1960s by UFO researchers after Frank Masqquelette, a reporter of the *Houston Post*, wrote about the crash after the tale had been dormant for six decades. Suddenly the story of the tragedy reappeared and Aurora was finally on the map with those very scientists, researchers, and tourists making the trek to north Texas.

Dr. J. Allen Hynek asked William H. Driskill of Dallas to find out what he could about the story. Driskill found Oscar Lowry, who was a boy in 1897 and who had lived in the area for all his life. But Lowry said the story was a hoax and blamed a stringer for the *Dallas Morning News*, S. E. Haydon, for inventing the tale. Lowry said that Weems had been a blacksmith and Proctor didn't have a windmill.

A large number of people, including Hayden Hewes of the now defunct International UFO Bureau (and remember, coauthor with Brad Steiger on a UFO book), Jim Marrs, who suggested the story was real, and even Walt Andrus, the former International Director of the Mutual UFO Network (MUFON), at various times journeyed to Aurora in search of the truth. They all reported they found a strange grave marker in the Aurora cemetery, they found strange metal with metal detectors, and they gathered reports from longtime Aurora residents or their descendants who remembered the story, remembered seeing the airship, or remembered parents talking about the crash. And, as to be expected today, there was also discussion of government attempts to suppress the data. To them, that made the story of the crash real.

The problem here is that I beat most of these people to Aurora by several months and even years to conduct my own investigation. I talked to some of those same longtime residents who told me in the early 1970s that nothing had happened there. I talked to the historians at the Wise County Historical Society (Aurora is in Wise County) who told me that it hadn't happened, though they wish it had (now probably thinking of Roswell and the tourist dollars pouring into that New Mexico town). Etta Pegues, one of those historians, confirmed that the story was a hoax.

> (N)o one ever produced those documents or bits and pieces of the wreckage, though there had been tons of it....

As had Driskill, I learned then that T. J. Weems, the famed Signal Corps officer was, in fact, the local blacksmith. I learned that Judge Proctor didn't have a windmill, or rather that was what was said then. Now they suggest that he had two windmills. I wandered the graveyard, which isn't all that large (something just over 800 graves), and found no marker with strange symbols carved on it, though there are those who suggest a crude headstone with a rough airship on it had been there at the time. I found nothing to support the tale and went away believing, based on my own research and interviews conducted on the scene, this to be another of the airship hoaxes. A crash story like those today that have little in facts but that are long on speculation.

Metal collected by all those other, later researchers, when analyzed here, in the United States, turned out to be nothing strange or unusual. Some of it was later analyzed in a Canadian lab and their results mirrored those of American labs. So much for the idea that the government, in the guise of the CIA, the Air Force, or the mythical MJ-12, conspired to suppress evidence of the Aurora UFO crash. I mention this only because, once again, we have the foreshadowing of the modern flying saucer age by the Great Airship.

And isn't it interesting that none of the metal supposedly gathered by the town's residents has ever surfaced? The metal analyzed was always recovered by researchers with metal detectors. Isn't it also interesting that the strange grave marker has since disappeared and there is no real photographic record of it? There should be pictures for all the research that has been done and the single picture that has turned up showed not an airship but a coarse triangle with circles in the center. And isn't it interesting that there were never any follow-up reports from Aurora? First the big splash with the crash and then nothing for more than sixty years.

Even worse, a book, *Pioneer History of Wise County* by Cliff D. Cates, published in 1907, only ten years after the crash, mentioned nothing about it. He wrote about fifty years of history but in the 470-plus pages of his book, mentioned nothing about the crash.

In fact, in 1897, there were ten newspapers in Wise County but none of them carried a word about the airship crash. The only newspaper to report on it was Hayden's. Other airship stories that seemed to have more basis in fact were carried in several newspapers.

The Aurora crash wasn't the only report of the destruction of the airship. In the early 1970s a longtime resident of San Angelo, Texas, claimed he had seen the airship fly into a flock of birds and explode in late April of 1897. He didn't try to gather any of the wreckage, he didn't take friends or family out to see the ruined airship, and he apparently did nothing to report it back in 1897. It wasn't until the early 1970s that he made his first mention of the airship crash and then to a reporter for a newspaper rather than to some local official or UFO researcher. He had nothing to validate his claim except that he was old enough to have seen something in 1897.

The LeRoy, Kansas, Calfnapping

On the other hand, the airship, or rather, other airships, were still intact and still flying. According to the reports, including that in the *Yate's Center Farmer's Advocate*, Alexander Hamilton, a Kansas farmer, heard a disturbance among his cattle on Monday, April 19, 1897, and got out of bed to check. Hovering over his cow lot was the airship. It was, according to Hamilton, cigar-shaped, about three hundred feet long with some kind of a glass-encased carriage under it. Inside were six strange-looking beings, but who were human enough that Hamilton identified two men, a woman, and three children.

His affidavit, which has been published more than once, and which had, according to some researchers, made the story more real, said:

> Last Monday night [April 19] about half past ten we were awakened by a noise among the cattle. I arose thinking perhaps my bulldog was performing some pranks, but upon going to the door, saw to my utter amazement, an airship slowly descending over my cow lot about 40 rods from the house.

> Calling Gid Heslip, my tenant, and my son, Wall, we seized some axes and ran to the corral. Meanwhile the ship had been gently descending until it was not more than 30 feet about the ground and we came up to within 50 yards of it…. It was occupied by six of the strangest beings I ever saw. There were two men, a woman, and three children. They were jabbering together but we could not understand….

> When about 30 feet above us, it seemed to pause, and hover directly over a three-year-old heifer which was bawling and jumping, apparently fast in the fence. Going to her, we found a cable about half an inch in thickness … fastened in a slipknot around her neck, one end passing up to the vessel…. We tried to get it off but could not, so we

cut the wire loose, and stood in amazement to see the ship, cow and all, rise slowly and sail off....

Link Thomas, who lives in Coffey County about three or four miles west of LeRoy, had found the hide, legs, and head in his field that day. He, thinking someone had butchered a stolen beast and thrown the hide away, had brought it to town for identification but was greatly mystified in not being able to find a track of any kind on the soft ground....

And to bolster the authenticity of the story, the local newspaper, as well as other men in town, attested to the honesty of Hamilton, suggesting they all believed his, well, unbelievable tale. They claimed they had known Hamilton for years and "that for truth and veracity we have never heard his word questioned and that we do verily believe his statement to be true and correct." These men included an attorney, a doctor, a Justice of the Peace, a banker, and even the postmaster. If no other report from 1897 was to be believed, this one certainly had all the credibility that those others lacked.

Jerry Clark reported that Hamilton had been a lawyer, had served in the Kansas legislature, and was a very successful stock dealer. Those who knew him suggested that he was an honest man. In 1897, they had little reason to doubt his tale.

UFOs have been blamed for livestock-napping and mutilation in rural America.

In the early 1970s, Clark managed to track down the relatives of Hamilton and interviewed an elderly woman who remembered Hamilton returning from town, chuckling about the story he'd invented because it would be published in the newspaper. While that evidence might not convince a true believer, an article that appeared in the *Atchison County Mail* on May 7, 1897, should do it. Hamilton told the reporter, "I lied about it." Those who signed the affidavit about Hamilton's veracity were members of the local liars club. In other words, they all were in on the joke.

Even worse was a letter found by Dr. Thomas "Eddie" Bullard of the J. Allen Hynek Center for UFO Studies. In the May 7, 1897, edition of the *Atchison County Mail*, Hamilton wrote that he had fabricated the tale. There simply is no reason for it to continue to circulate as true. The evidence that it was invented has been uncovered and reported.

But the sad thing here is that many of the UFO books written in the 1960s and the 1970s, before we all began trying to get to the bottom of these stories, report this case straight. They suggest it is true but they didn't have the benefit of the research done by Jerry Clark and Eddie Bullard. We now know that this story of a cattle mutilation, complete with the carcass found in an empty field with no footprints near it, is a hoax.

The Alien Connection

Hamilton's tale, one of the most widely reported and accepted by some of the most skeptical of the UFO researchers, was also one of the few that suggested an outer space connection rather than an Earthly tradition. Most of those who reported seeing or communicating with the pilots and crews suggested they were fellow Americans, some just trying out their new invention, and others suggested they were on a mission to Cuba to attack the Spanish.

One such tale of extraterrestrial visitation came from Reynolds, Michigan, on April 14. According to the witnesses, a flying machine, as opposed to the airship, came down half a mile from town. A dozen farmers who had watched it maneuvering overhead rushed to the landing site. Inside was a giant, manlike creature whose speech was described as musical. Although there were what looked to be polar bear hides inside the cabin, the alien creature didn't use them and seemed to be suffering greatly from the oppressive heat.

One of the farmers tried to approach the ship but was kicked by the giant, resulting in a broken hip. Although the crew was unfriendly, the ship apparently didn't take off and people from surrounding towns hurried to the scene. The creature tried to talk to the people but eventually gave up.

On April 15, near Linn Grove, Iowa, the airship appeared overhead. Five local men followed it for four miles where it landed in the country. When the men got close to the ship, it spread four massive wings and lifted off. The occupants threw out two boulders of an unknown material. The occupants were reported as "queer-looking beings with extraordinarily long beards." The boulders, of unknown material, have long since disappeared so that no analysis was ever attempted.

In another report that would foreshadow much in the modern era, W. H. Hopkins claimed that he had seen one of the airships sitting on the ground in a clearing. Next to it, according to him, was the "most beautiful being I ever beheld." She was naked, of course, with hair that hung to her waist. She was picking flowers and had a lovely, musical voice. Lying in the shadow of the ship was a naked man, with a long beard and long hair, who was fanning himself as if warm.

As Hopkins approached, the woman screamed and ran to the man. Hopkins attempted to tell them that he meant them no harm and eventually communication was established. He asked where they came from and they pointed at the sky, "pronouncing a word which, to my imagination, sounded like Mars."

George Adamski stands before an artwork depicting a beautiful alien woman.

Hopkins was given a tour of the ship. The two beings seemed interested in his clothes and his gray hair. They also examined his watch "with the greatest wonder." Finally he exited the ship and they flew away, "laughing and waving."

Fifty years later, contactees such as George Adamski and George van Tassel would tell similar tales of beautiful people in strange flying machines and sometimes in as little clothing, meaning, of course, none at all. Some would claim the aliens were from Mars, others Venus, but all suggested an interplanetary, as opposed to interstellar, origin for the craft. This is simply another example of the airship stories mimicking those that have been reported during the modern era.

In Merkel, Texas, not all that far from Aurora (given the size of Texas), dozens of people returning from church saw the ship, its anchor snagged in a barbed wire fence. Climbing down a rope in a blue sailor suit was a small man. When he spotted the people, he scurried back up into the airship. The people cut the anchor free and kept it on display for several weeks. It has, quite naturally, disappeared.

There were additional sightings in May. As a single example is the report from near Cassville, Indiana, on May 3. Edwin Shaffer, while passing a gravel pit, noticed a cigar-shaped, forty-foot-long airship sitting in it. He claimed that it was "handsomely furnished on the inside and the aerial craft was inhabited by a crew of midgets who spoke no English."

But the intense interest in the airship was dying out and by the summer of 1897, there were almost no new reports. By the time the modern era of flying saucers began to be reported, fifty years later, almost no one remembered the airships. UFO researchers did not begin to dig for the reports until the 1960s, though there had been a few discussions about them earlier. Captain Edward Ruppelt, at one time the chief of Project Blue Book, the official Air Force investigation, mentioned the wave briefly in his book, *The Report on Unidentified Flying Objects*. Others, such as Charles Fort, devoted a little space to the stories, commenting on their unusual nature but not examining them with anything close to a critical eye.

The Stories Resurface

It wasn't until the 1960s that the airship reports began to enter the UFO literature with any regularity. Jacques Vallee discovered the Alexander Hamilton calfnapping and reported it in his *Anatomy of a Phenomenon* without any critical remarks about it. Vallee took the report at face value. It was then quoted in a large number of books arguing for the reality of UFOs, in general, without anyone bothering to search further, until Jerry Clark made the effort.

Vallee's discovery, the notations made by Charles Fort and others, inspired many to search old newspaper records. Hundreds of accounts were discovered. I spent a lot of time in newspaper morgues and later with microfilm, looking for stories of the airship. Those early sightings were sometimes reported as straight news, while other sightings had a tongue-in-cheek quality that is often missing in modern newspapers.

The problem was that those doing the research in the 1960s made an invalid assumption. They believed that what had been printed in the newspapers in 1897 was the truth, the whole truth, and nothing but the truth. The reality was that many of the airship accounts, just as some of the "straight" news accounts of wars, disease, and other disasters in those days, were invented to sell newspapers. The public was interested in the airship, so reporters and editors gave them what they wanted to read. They reported tales of the airship overhead and speculations about its origins with little regard to the facts unavailable to them. We see the same thing today as the twenty-four-hour cable news channels fill hours with speculation by reporters who have little expertise but who, for the most part, look good delivering their opinions. And when that runs out of steam, they invite two, three, or four other reporters to argue about the reality of the latest news crisis for the benefit of their audience.

All this is borne out in a sad tale from Burlington, Iowa, that was described at the time as one of the "meanest and most discouraging stories of the entire lot." Members of the Burlington newspaper staff sent up a common tissue paper hot-air balloon so that it would carry over the city. The newspaper began to get reports of the airship which they then dutifully published. One of the most distinguished men in the town came forward to say that he had not only seen the airship but had heard voices from it, and that he would sign an affidavit about it. That convinced the Burlington reporters that the entire airship episode was a fake. I will note here that tissue paper hot-air balloons were quite prevalent during the height of the 1960s UFO wave as well, and caused a number of interesting reports.

Some newspapers from 1897 published letters from outraged citizens who claimed they had been identified as witnesses to the airship and who wrote that they had never seen it. Jerome Clark reported that J.H. Tibbles of Rochelle, Illinois "wrote the *Chicago Record* that a report in a Chicago paper notwithstanding, no one in Rochelle had seen an airship on April 3; 'I took it upon myself to hunt down the report, and for several days I have been busy doing so.… I have not found a person who had seen another person who claimed to have seen it.'"

Eddie Bullard noted "how seldom airship reports turned up in the columns devoted to news from outlying communities. The content of this correspondence includes sicknesses, births, deaths, marriages, crop news, and mention of anything new or changing in these areas where newness or change was rare. A crime was a major event, and an airship sighting would surely rate a mention. After reading about a lot of Sunday picnics, weekend visits, and fine hunting dogs, I can say with safety that those mentions are lacking."

In other cases it's clear that the reporters and editors didn't believe the stories, though they were willing to report them. The airship story that originated in Cedar Rapids, Iowa, was reported as straight news but it is apparent that the reporters and the editors didn't take it seriously. They did, however, report the story right up to the point that the Cedar Rapids tale had been trumped by the Waterloo story. Remember, in Waterloo, they had the ship. And that story was reported as straight news during the first day, until the "professor" was recognized and the hoax was revealed.

Bullard's research corroborates this theory. He was suggesting that those reporters and stringers in the outlying areas were more reliable than those in the city. He was suggesting that the newspapers of the day were making it up as they went along. The story from Burlington, Iowa, certainly suggests this is true and even shows the lengths to which they would go.

Clark, who has studied the wave in great detail, noted that by the mid-to-late 1970s "it was becoming increasingly evident that hoaxes played a far more prominent role than anyone had imagined." He was suggesting that unlike the modern era in which the hoaxes are believed to be a relatively minor fraction of

The "airship" used in the Iowa hoax as seen in a photograph printed in the *Waterloo Daily Courier* in 1897.

the whole, in 1897, a great number of the reports, including those that had seemed to be the most reliable and most interesting, were later proven to be hoaxes.

As mentioned, Alexander Hamilton had invented the tale of the calfnapping and his friends who signed the affidavit were fellow members of a liar's club. The Linn Grove landing had never happened, according to a man who lived there in 1897 and remembered nothing about it. The Aurora, Texas, crash was more fantasy, written by a man who wanted his town back on the map. In fact, in histories of the area published just years after the crash, there is no mention of it. And finally, the Merkel, Texas anchor-dragging airship was just another of the hoaxes that filled the newspapers and is strangely reminiscent of a similar report from the Middle Ages.

But there were others who failed to jump on the bandwagon in 1897. The *Des Moines Register* in 1897 put forth another theory about the reliability and the genesis of the airship, at least in Iowa. The reporters noted that the airship was mentioned in Cedar Rapids on April 14 and on the next night it was seen near Fairfield. It was also seen near Evanston, Illinois, "worrying the Chicago papers greatly." The most remarkable account of the airship came on April 15 near Pella, Iowa. According to the newspaper, "many people, among them the Western Union operator, had seen the machine ... if it was true, the Pella airship looked like a sea serpent, a balloon, a winged cigar, and a pair of balloons hitched together with a car swung between them, a car with an aeroplane and three sails, and 19 or 20 other things."

The *Register* article continued by reporting that the telephone in the *Leader* (another Iowa newspaper office) rang and the town of Stuart was "found to be clamoring for fame." They had seen the airship. The story went out over the wire and the Western Union operator said that he could produce dozens of witnesses if anyone cared. He said that the airship had come from the southeast, was traveling about fifteen miles per hour, and had a red light in front and a green one in the rear. The operator's feelings were hurt when he was asked if it was an April Fool's joke.

While the conversation between the newspaper reporters and the telegrapher was evolving into a heated argument, a report came in that the airship was now over Panora, Iowa. The Western Union operator there said that they had seen the airship over their own town coming from the direction of Stuart. It was now moving faster, but had the same appearance as it did in Stuart which the *Register* labeled as a "neat attempt at getting around the description."

As the argument increased in intensity, the number of telegrams about the airship also increased. From Clinton, Iowa, came a telegram saying the airship had flown over the town on April 10. Although the airship was reported to have been seen by several prominent and reputable citizens, the telegram was almost apologetic in its tone.

Immediately came a telegram from Ottumwa reporting they had seen the airship more than once. "An Eldon (Iowa) operator discovered the airship at 7:25 P.M. Ottumwa was prepared for its appearance. It was seen here by half the population. All agreed that it appeared as a red light moving up and down and traveling northwest. Albia caught sight of it at 8:10 and at 9 o'clock it was still visible…. This was the third time that it has been seen in Albia."

The *Register* reported, "The fact seems to be that the airship has been exploited beautifully by telegraphers along certain lines of the railroad. They managed it beautifully for a while and never allowed it to travel too far too fast." The reports were always well done, showing a certain amount of genius. But the rest of the public began to take a hand and the airship reports got too numerous. Some would conflict and it became evident that someone would have to have a whole fleet of airships for all the sightings to be true.

What all this suggests is that the vast majority of the airship stories were hoaxes. Some originated by individuals such as Alexander Hamilton or the people in Cedar Rapids, others were initiated by the newspapers looking for something spectacular to report, and the last bunch were created by the telegraphers along the railroads who were bored late in the evening.

It is now clear that there was no Great Airship invention just before the turn of the last century. Heavier-than-air flight would become a reality in six years. Airplanes would soon begin flying across the country, then across the oceans, and finally around the world. Great Airships would be built by the military to search for enemy subs, or to hover above battlefields so that generals could gather intelligence about enemy movements. Eventually there would even be airship flights across the Atlantic. These would end when the Hindenburg exploded in New Jersey in 1939.

But there is no evidence that a human inventor had flown a Great Airship in 1896 or 1897 anywhere in the country. Although some stories suggested the announcement of the airships was about to be made to the world, it never was.

Or, those on their way to Cuba to bomb the Spanish never made it to drop those bombs.

A few modern investigators have suggested that there was a solid core of airship sightings. Something had to trigger the tales in 1896. They have suggested that we examine, more closely, those stories told in the Sacramento area in November 1896. Those might provide a clue as to where and why these stories began to circulate. It might be that some kind of airship was seen in northern California but then newspapers in other parts of the country climbed on the bandwagon.

But even if that is true, and even if we could identify the core of solid sightings, there isn't much for us to learn from them today. There are no witnesses left to tell us what they really saw in 1896 and 1897 and we have no real records or photographs to examine. Few have interviewed anyone who was around in 1897 and who claimed to have seen the Great Airship. Ed Ruppelt, while chief of the Air Force's Project Blue Book, wrote that he had had a long conversation with a man who had been a copy boy at the *San Francisco Chronicle* at the time of the airship. He remembered almost nothing about those long-ago events except to tell Ruppelt that the editors and a few others at the newspaper had seen the airship themselves.

> What we know today is that the vast majority of the airship cases can be explained as hoaxes but they shouldn't be completely ignored.

There were so many tales invented by newspaper editors and reporters that a single fading memory of a copy boy means very little today. Maybe something unusual was seen near San Francisco and Sacramento. Maybe there had been some kind of cigar-shaped object flying over California so long ago. Those seeing it did the best they could in describing it, using the terminology available to them at that time. Maybe there was a sighting or two of something that was not invention, imagination, delusion, misidentification, or outright fabrication in the fall of 1896.

What we know today is that the vast majority of the airship cases can be explained as hoaxes but they shouldn't be completely ignored. They provide us with an insight that will help us better understand the UFO situation as it stands today.

And that is why the airship stories are so frightening for UFO researchers today. How many of those stories mirror the reports made at present? Everything we find in the modern UFO era was predicted by the airship stories in 1897. That means that if we can write off the airship stories as hoaxes and misidentifications, why can't we do the same thing today? The evidence we find is just as nebulous and nearly unobtainable.

Airships Other Than Those of 1897

Clark has said to me, on many occasions, that the airship transcends 1897. There were stories of an airship seen much earlier, and, of course, stories of it long after 1897.

Clark, in his massive *The UFO Encyclopedia,* reported that on March 29, 1880, over the tiny town now known as Lamy, New Mexico, three men on a late evening walk heard voices coming from above. They described the balloon or airship for *The New Mexican* this way:

> The construction of the balloon was entirely different to anything of the kind ever seen by any of the party, being in the shape of a fish, and at one time was so low that fanciful characters on the outside of the car, which appeared to be very elegant, were plainly seen. The air machine appeared to be entirely under the control of the occupants, and appeared to be guided by a large fanlike apparatus…. The balloon was monstrous in size, and the car, as near as could be judged, contained eight to ten persons.

The men reported that an object had been thrown overboard and they were able to recover it. This was a flower with a silklike paper that seemed to resemble the markings on Japanese tea chests.

The next day the tale got stranger. They found a cup of "strange workmanship" and the flower with the silk paper, which were displayed at the local railroad depot. These were bought by an archaeologist who was working at a nearby site.

On April 5, it was reported that a group of tourists were allowed to see the objects. One of them, a wealthy man from China, recognized the lettering as Chinese, but more astonishing was that he said it was a note from his fiancee. The tourist said that the airship was obviously from China.

According to the newspaper, the man knew that his fiancee was a passenger on the airship, on her way to visit her sister in New York, and knew he would be passing through the small New Mexican town. She'd tossed over the items overboard, sure that he would find them, as a surprise for him.

This tale, told some seventeen years before the Great Airship began its journey, is certainly reminiscent of them and suggests a human inventor, a human crew, and a terrestrial explanation. As Clark wrote, "… the New Mexican report is absurd on its face. Vehicles of the sort described in the newspaper account were not flying or even could fly, in the America of the nineteenth century…."

In a somewhat similar vein, which means simply that the identity of the airship was terrestrial, in March 1892, there were many newspaper accounts of "mysterious" balloons over Europe. They were seen along the border of Polish Russia and Germany, and the speculation was that they were a way of sending German spies into the region. The observers said, according to Clark, "the vehicles appeared fully maneuverable … not subject to the vagaries of the wind … and even able to hover for as long as forty minutes."

What is important here is that at the time, there was talk of flight, balloons had been around for more than a century, and a parachute had been demonstrated in Paris in 1797 by Andre-Jacques Garnerin. He leaped from about 6,500 feet using a parachute that was twenty-three feet in diameter.

In 1872 there was a flight of a gas-powered dirigible. That came some twenty years after a coal-fed, steam power airship was flown. And in 1897 the first all-metal dirigible was flown in Europe.

When Clark suggests there is a core of solid sightings of an airship in the late nineteenth century, there is documentation to back up his claim. During the stories in the United States about all the airships and the talk of training to bomb the Spanish in Cuba, there were experiments going on in Europe to produce the kind of craft that was claimed to be seen over the United States. In fact, in 1873, the *New York Daily Telegraph* sponsored an attempt to fly across the Atlantic in a huge, 400,000-cubic-foot balloon that carried a lift boat. As they were attempting to inflate it, a tear appeared and the balloon collapsed. That was the end of that attempt.

> When Clark suggests there is a core of solid sightings of an airship in the late nineteenth century, there is documentation to back up his claim.

Clark reported in his *UFO Encyclopedia* that the media, magazines, and newspapers of the day were filled with stories of airships. Designs for airships were being published and many of them called for powered flight. By 1897, many had already been flown in Europe with more and more talk of traveling by airship over long distances.

In 1903, the Wright Brothers changed all that with their first powered flight in an airplane and, by 1905, had managed to demonstrate complete turns in the aircraft, which had kept them aloft for more than half an hour. Within eleven years, the first aerial combat would take place as pilots and observers on both sides began shooting at each other with pistols and rifles during the First World War.

All this tells us about the inspiration for the Great Airship stories. Given what was happening, it was not outside the realm of possibility that some of the tales were true, especially when we remember that airships had been flown in Europe. Here, in 1897, there were no airships, at least none that were reliably reported in the press, but that doesn't mean there wasn't something flying about American skies.

There might have been an inventor in a faraway corner of the United States that successfully created an airship. It wouldn't be long after the March and April wave of sightings that a true airship would be flown in the United States. In the end, we are left with a large number of fakes and frauds, and a host of interesting stories but proof of nothing. Besides, if there was a solid core of sightings whether here, Asia, or Europe, the culprits were humans and not alien creatures.

The Modern Era Begins, June 1947

What is considered the modern era of UFO sightings began on June 24, 1947, when Kenneth Arnold, a Boise, Idaho, businessman, saw nine objects flash across the sky near Mt. Rainier, Washington. To that point, no one had actually talked about UFOs or flying saucers and the realm of alien life was solely that of science fiction. True, earlier in the century scientists had been talking of life on both Mars and Venus, and respected astronomers actually drew diagrams of what they believed to be the canal system on Mars. Some scientists thought of ways to communicate across interplanetary space, nearly all of them visual. One man suggested digging gigantic trenches in the Sahara Desert, filling those trenches with oil, and setting them on fire. His plan, which covered dozens of square miles, was to create a beacon in geometric form that Martian astronomers could see.

It is also true that the Great Airship stories included reports of what could only be alien creatures. Those stories, when a location of the aliens was mentioned, was usually somewhere inside the solar system with Mars and Venus as the two most likely candidates.

War of the Worlds

In 1938 Orson Welles broadcast his *War of the Worlds* radio drama and sent thousands into the streets frightened by the thought of an alien invasion. Given the timing, just before the beginning of the Second World War when tensions were at the highest, it might not be so surprising that so many reacted with so much fear. Within hours the country knew that the invasion from Mars was little more than the imaginative rambling of Welles and his radio theater company. Of course, it could be said that Welles had put the idea of Martian invaders into the heads of millions of people, even if no one acted on that notion for another nine years.

Depiction of a UFO sighting by Boise, Idaho, surveyor E. G. Hall.

After the Second World War people were ready for something more, something exciting. The horrors of the war, culminating in the destruction of Hiroshima and Nagasaki in flashes of atomic heat and light, had unleashed a new scientific age. Life, it was thought, was not confined to the earth and there was speculation about who, or what, lived on other planets. Not that any of this was in the overall consciousness of the country. It was there, in the background, sort of hiding from everyone and popping up in science fiction movies and in some science books that speculated on the possibility of alien life.

Then Arnold made his sighting of the strange objects, flying one behind the other, at about 9,500 feet at a speed he estimated to be more than 1,500 miles per hour while he was flying over Washington. This was something that clearly wasn't made in secret projects hidden in the mountains of New Mexico, and it wasn't something that was made by the Soviet Union as they began to press for world domination. This was something strange that had no ready explanation, other than it was strange and almost impossible to believe.

When Arnold landed later in the afternoon on June 24, in Yakima, Washington, he told the assembled reporters what he had seen. In the course of describing the objects, he said they moved with a motion like that of saucers skipping across the water. The shape, however, according to drawings that

Arnold completed for the Army within days of his sighting, showed objects that were heel-shaped with a blunt nose and no noticeable tail assembly. In later drawings, Arnold elaborated, showing objects that were crescent-shaped with a scalloped trailing edge and even a clear canopy over the cockpit.

Hearing Arnold's description of the motion of the objects, reporter Bill Bequette coined the term "flying saucer," though in the next few days, most reporters, and then scientists and Army officers, would call the objects flying discs. The term, then, according to most investigators, didn't originally refer to the shape of the objects, but to the style of their movement through the air.

Ronald Story, a UFO researcher and editor of *The Encyclopedia of Extraterrestrial Encounters*, reported that in early 1992 he was in southeastern Washington, not all that far from Pendleton, Oregon, when he happened to see an editorial written by William C. Bequette. Story called Bequette and asked him about his interview with Arnold back in 1947, and about the invention of the term "flying

Orson Welles famously played a hoax on the entire United States with his 1938 broadcast of an adaptation of *War of the Worlds* by Edgar Rice Burroughs. Many listeners to the radio program thought Martians were actually invading Earth.

saucer." Bequette said that Arnold had described the objects as saucer-shaped. So the world might owe the origin of the flying saucer to Arnold after all.

But then nothing is ever very easy in the world of UFOs. Story said that he had read somewhere else that Bequette had said something different about it. Story wrote, "I can only repeat what he confirmed to me: that he was indeed the man who coined the term 'flying saucer' which was based on Arnold's description...."

Arnold Briefs the Military

Later Arnold would provide the military with a written description of the events. In a document that was originally classified as secret, but that has long since been released, Arnold wrote:

> On June 24th ... I had finished my work ... and about two o'clock I took off for Chehalis, Washington, airport with the intention of going to Yakima, Washington, ... I flew directly toward Mt. Rainier after reaching an altitude of about 9,500 feet, which is the approxi-

mate elevation of the high plateau from with Mt. Rainier rises.... There was a DC-4 to the left and to the rear of me approximately fifteen miles distance, and I should judge, a 14,000 foot elevation.... I hadn't flown more than two or three minutes on my course when a bright flash reflected on my airplane. It startled me as I thought I was too close to some other aircraft. I looked every place in the sky and couldn't find where the reflection had come from until I looked to the left and the north of Mt. Rainier where I observed a chain of nine peculiar looking aircraft flying from north to the south at approximately 9,500 foot elevation and going, seemingly, in a definite direction of about 170 degrees.

They [the objects] were approaching Mt. Rainier very rapidly, and I merely assumed they were jet planes. Anyhow, I discovered that this was where the reflection had come from, as two or three of them every few seconds would dip or change their course slightly, just enough for the sun to strike them at an angle that reflected brightly on my plane.... I thought it was very peculiar that I couldn't see their tails but assumed they were some type of jet plane. I was determined to clock their speed, as I had two definite points I could clock them by.... I watched these objects with great interest as I had never before observed airplanes flying so close to the mountain tops.... I would estimate their elevation could have varied a thousand feet one way or another up or down....

They flew like many times I have observed geese to fly in a rather diagonal chain-like line as if they were linked together.... Their speed at the time did not impress me particularly, because I knew that our army and air forces had planes that went very fast.

A number of news men and experts suggested that I might have been seeing reflections of even a mirage. This I know to be absolutely false, as I observed these objects not only through the glass of my airplane but turned my airplane sideways where I could open my window and observe them with a completely unobstructed view.... When these objects were flying approximately straight and level, there were just a black thin line and when they flipped was the only time I could get a judgment as to their size.

Arnold's sighting didn't gain front-page status immediately. Stories about it appeared in newspapers a day or two later usually on page eight or nine or even farther back, and then with a comment about strange objects in fast flight. It was, at that time, the story of an oddity that caught the attention of various city editors at various newspapers. Arnold claimed later that he thought he had seen some sort of the new jet aircraft and he was a little concerned about breaking the security around it.

Corroboration for Arnold?

Arnold wasn't the only person to see strange objects in the sky that day. Fred Johnson, listed as a prospector, reported watching five or six disc-shaped craft as they flew over the Cascade Mountains about the time Arnold had lost sight of his. He said they were round with a slight tail and about thirty feet in diameter. They were not flying in any sort of formation and as they banked in a turn, the sunlight flashed off them. As they approached, Johnson noticed that his compass began to spin wildly. When the objects finally vanished in the distance, the compass returned to normal.

After learning of the Arnold sighting, Johnson wrote to the Air Force on August 20, 1947, saying:

"Saw in the portland [sic] paper a short time ago in regards to an article in regards to the so called flying disc having any basis in fact. I can say am a prospector and was in the Mt Adams district on June 24th the day Kenneth Arnold of Boise Idaho claims he saw a formation of flying disc [sic]. And i saw the same flying objects at about the same time. Having a telescope with me at the time i can asure you there are real and noting like them I ever saw before they did not pass verry high over where I was standing at the time. plolby 1000 ft. they were Round about 30 foot in diameter tapering sharply to a point in the head and in an oval shape. with a bright top surface. I did not hear any noise as you would from a plane. But there was an object in the tail end looked like a big hand of a clock shifting from side to side like a big magnet. There speed was far as I know seemed to be greater than anything I ever saw. Last view I got of the objects they were standing on edge Banking in a cloud."

Yours Respectfully,
Fred Johnson.

In July 1947, the Army Air Forces had asked the FBI to interview some of those seeing flying discs and Johnson was one of first interviewed. The FBI report contained, essentially, the same information as the letter that Johnson had sent to the Army. The FBI ended their report, saying, "Informant appeared to be a very reliable individual who advised that he had been a prospector in the states of Montana, Washington, and Oregon for the past forty years."

Dr. Bruce Maccabee, a one-time physicist with the Navy, now retired, and who has a private interest in UFOs, wrote in the *International UFO Reporter* that the Johnson sighting is important, not because it takes place near where Arnold saw the nine objects, but because it seems to be an extension of the Arnold sighting. It provides independent corroboration for the Arnold sighting, strengthening that case, and reducing, to ridiculous, some of the explanations

Artist's reconstruction of Arnold's UFO encounter.

that have been offered to explain it by those who believe that there is absolutely no alien visitation.

Importantly, Johnson also made one claim that Arnold had not. He said that his compass was spinning wildly when the objects were near, suggesting some kind of magnetic interference. If that is accurate, we have not only another witness to what Arnold saw but we have the objects interacting with the environment and providing us with a clue about them. This interaction would be an important part of some of the other major UFO cases that would later be reported to the Air Force.

Dr. Donald H. Menzel, the late Harvard scientist, decided that Johnson was being honest in his report, that is, Johnson was not lying about it. Johnson, according to Menzel, was merely mistaken in his analysis of the sighting. Menzel wrote that Johnson had probably seen bright reflections from patches of clouds. It didn't seem to matter to Menzel that Johnson saw the objects only about a thousand feet over his head, watched them through a telescope, and had them in sight for almost a minute before they vanished, disappearing into a cloud. It didn't matter that he said nothing about clouds.

In the Project Blue Book files is a note about the Arnold case, which was labeled as "Incident No. 37." The Air Force officer who reviewed the case wrote, "The report cannot bear even superficial examination, therefore, must be disregarded. There are strong indications that this report and its attendant publicity is largely responsible for subsequent reports."

Not content with a negative note in the file, the unidentified officer also wrote, "It is to be noted that the observer has profited from this story by selling it to *Fate* magazine."

Here, for the first time were two accusations that would be made about many UFO cases, that is, the witnesses were in it for the money, and a suggestion that UFO reports were the result of the "snowball effect." It seems to suggest that Arnold invented his tale with an eye to writing a story about it for *Fate*. There is no evidence to support this, and Arnold had not written any articles for any magazines prior to his sighting nor did he seem to be interested in writing articles for anyone. The editors at *Fate*, and Ray Palmer specifically, who would become one of the first and most vocal proponents of the flying saucers, induced Arnold into writing about what he had seen. Arnold sent him a copy of the report that had been created for the Army.

> He said that his compass was spinning wildly when the objects were near, suggesting some kind of magnetic interference.

The point, then, becomes irrelevant. The article doesn't seem to have been a motive for Arnold, but more of a serendipitous reward for seeing and reporting the objects in the first place. It was Palmer who thought up the idea for the article and not Arnold.

As a sort of ancillary thought, what would have induced Arnold to invent this tale in the first place? It wasn't as if there had been many sightings, or that Arnold would have heard about them even if there were. The initial motivation for money doesn't seem to be there. After the first of the reports in the newspapers, it became clear that some of the others jumped on the bandwagon and began inventing tales about their UFO encounters. But with Arnold, he was the first to have his story reported nationally, and we have to ask, where he would have gotten the idea to do it in the first place? And the evidence for the hoax, at least in this case, is somewhat thin.

Second, though it has been studied by many, and suggested by more, that a single UFO report will generate additional reports, that doesn't seem to be the case. When studying these things in statistical detail, it seems that the news media (or in 1947, the press) learns about them after many sightings have already been made. Often the first of the articles comes about the time the peak of the wave of sightings has been reached and the number of sightings is actually dropping off.

Once the first of the sightings enters into the public arena, then there are those who come forward with their tales, many of which are hoaxes. After Arnold's sighting got national attention in late June, and after the July 4 weekend when there were a number of interesting and credible sightings, the number of stories in the newspapers and the number of hoaxes then skyrocketed.

But the initial point remains the same. The number of sightings reported can be correlated to the number of newspaper articles, but that is a side effect. The number of legitimate reports doesn't seem to be geared to the reporting in the newspapers.

This is, of course, splitting a fine hair. The sightings are not tied to the newspapers and publicity but the number of reports are. In other words, people who have made sightings now know where to report them. These stories suggest, if nothing else, that the newspaper or radio stations are interested in the reports. People then report the sightings that they have made over the last several days and weeks.

More Sightings

So, after the Arnold report, we learn that on June 25, nine objects flying in a loose formation were spotted over Kansas City, Missouri. Two oval-shaped objects, one chasing the other, were reported by Lloyd Lowery near Pueblo, Colorado. In Utah a lone man reported a lone object. Other reports came from Oklahoma, where C.E. Holman saw two light discs, and near Glens Falls, New York, where Louis Stebbins saw a single, reddish object.

On June 26th, reports were made in Utah, Arizona, Oklahoma, Texas, and New Mexico. Glenn Bunting in Logan, Utah, saw a single object flying at high speed. Two hunters made an independent report of the same object.

There was a series of sightings in and around Cedar City, Utah. Royce R. Knight, the airport manager, saw a lone object in fast flight heading to the east. Although in sight for only a few seconds, Royce saw it long enough to give a description and then report that it disintegrated into a ball of blue flame. I suppose that could mean it turned so that the tail flame was toward him and that would suggest chemical propulsion rather than an interstellar drive.

Charles Moore (who isn't related to the Charles Moore who would figure in the Roswell case or Project Mogul, and who would have his own UFO sighting some two years later), driving near the airport in Cedar City, saw a lone object flying to the east. He saw no exhaust or flame near it but did say that it looked like a bright meteor, which, of course, could explain the sighting. Daylight meteors are rare and if a witness is thinking more in terms of flying saucers than natural phenomena he might think of a meteor as a spacecraft. If it is the same one that Knight saw, then the final breakup of the meteor might explain the sighting better than anything else.

On June 27, in the area around White Sands, New Mexico, Captain E. B. Detchmendy saw a high-flying object that seemed flamelike. At about the same

The government denied the existence of the objects and said they were not some kind of secret project. Scientists suggested everything from spots in front of the eyes to a form of war mass hysteria.

time, 9:50 A.M., W. C. Dobbs, who worked at White Sands, reported that he too had seen a high-flying, flamelike object.

In Capitan, New Mexico, not all that far from White Sands and fairly close to the ranch that would figure in the Roswell crash, a Mrs. Cummins and her neighbor, Erv Dill, saw a single shining object descend. They thought it landed in the nearby hills. They said there was a yellow flame and a whistling sound.

It probably should be noted here that White Sands isn't all that far from many of the New Mexico sighting locations and some kind of rocket or missile testing could explain some of the sightings. Except there had been a rocket that had crashed near a town in Mexico in May and all firings had been suspended while the scientists tried to figure out what was happening. On July 3, they attempted another launch, but the rocket never made it off the pad, although it did injure some of those working on the experiment. This moratorium on launches eliminates rockets or missiles, at least during the end of June and early July.

On June 27, the sightings became more widespread and took on an international flavor with reports coming from Canada, Australia, and New Zealand. The flying saucers, at this point, began to enter the public conscious. The newspaper reports and discussions about them had been scattered and light in the days preceding. Now they were beginning to get play everywhere and they were moving to the front page.

Speculation about the flying discs ran from some kind of secret military craft to spacecraft, though the theories suggested Mars and Venus as the home of the visitors, if they proved to be interplanetary. The government denied the existence of the objects and said they were not some kind of secret project. Scientists suggested everything from spots in front of the eyes to a form of war mass hysteria. Newspapers were publishing everything about the flying saucers now, including the wildest speculations. In today's world the talking heads on cable TV, even those without expertise or an original thought, would be telling us what was really happening. It wouldn't matter that whatever they said, today would be overtaken by events of tomorrow. They would change their positions, and continue to pretend they understood, and continue to issue nonsense, just as those experts did in 1947.

In the United States, on June 28, the flying saucers moved east with reports in Mississippi and Alabama. In Montgomery, four military officers reported a high-flying object that moved with sudden bursts of speed and was in sight for about twenty-five minutes.

Military Searches and Reactions

The sightings throughout the United States continued and the speculation about them didn't change. The military was taking an interest in them, and on the west coast, during the July 4 weekend, squadrons as far south as Muroc (now Edwards Air Force Base) in California and as far north as Seattle in Washington were alerted about the possibility of these things being seen close at hand. In Oregon, one squadron was not only equipped with gun cameras, but were involved in an airborne search.

It was also during the July 4 weekend that several sightings were made that were better than normal. First, Captain E. J. Smith of United Airlines said that five objects, smooth on the bottom, had sort of joined formation with him. He and his crew clearly saw the objects and watched them for forty-five minutes. He said that he was sure they weren't clouds, other aircraft, smoke, or weather balloons.

A long series of sightings involving multiple witnesses, police officers, and several formations of objects began during the July 4 weekend in and around Portland, Oregon. C.J. Bogne started it when he and a carload of friends watched four disc-shaped objects streak past Mount Jefferson. The objects made no noise and performed no maneuvers.

Don Metcalfe, an Oaks Park employee, watched a lone object at about one o'clock. Five minutes later police officer Kenneth A. McDowell near the Portland Police Station noticed that the pigeons around him were acting as if frightened.

Overhead he saw five objects, three heading east and two flying south. Although moving at high speed, he thought they might be oscillating as they flew along.

Once again, I point out that this will become an effect reported many times, that is, animal reaction to the presence of the strange craft. It suggests something that is unusual and it suggests something that is real.

Walter A. Lissy and Robert Ellis, patrolmen in Car 82, reported they watched three objects overhead. They might have been the same three that McDowell reported.

Across the Columbia River in Vancouver, Washington, Sergeant John Sullivan, Clarence McKay, and Fred Krives, all sheriff's deputies, reported that twenty to thirty disc-shaped objects flew overhead.

Next three harbor patrolmen on the river near Portland reported six discs flying at high speed. All said the objects were shiny, like chrome hubcaps, and all oscillated as they flew, which sort of confirmed some of the earlier reports.

At four o'clock came more civilian reports. Typical of them was a woman who said that she saw an object, shiny as a new dime, flipping around. It finally flipped out of sight.

These sorts of sightings continued throughout the weekend in the northwest. People wanted to know what the flying saucers were and to that end, some began to post rewards for the "capture" of a flying saucer. By Sunday evening, there would be three thousand dollars available to anyone who could provide pieces of a flying saucer or a solution about their identity. Within days, however, the offers began to expire.

Maury Island and Kenneth Arnold

Kenneth Arnold was not about to disappear from the flying saucer landscape. Ray Palmer, a former editor of *Amazing Stories* and later of *Fate* magazine, grew excited at the continuing reports of flying saucers. Palmer had taken a science fiction magazine on the verge of folding and turned it into one with wide circulation in a matter of months. One of the stories, or more accurately, a series of stories, that created the increased circulation were the tales of Richard Shaver. Palmer had hinted that these were actually true probably as a way to stir up even more interest in them. Shaver, in his rambling style, told of an underworld accessed through deep caves, of a war between the deros and teros, two "robot" societies, one good and one evil, and of their impact on the human race. Almost all that was bad in the world could be traced to the evil robots. By coincidence, the June 1947 issue of *Amazing Stories* was filled with more of Shaver's wild tales.

Palmer had suggested as he published the stories that these underground entities, good and bad, did leave their caves occasionally, and when the flying saucers first appeared over Washington state in June 1947, Palmer was con-

Magazine editor Ray Palmer published stories of UFO and alien encounters in his *Fate* magazine.

vinced that this was the proof of the reality of Shaver's tales. In fact, in an editorial published in October 1947, Palmer excitedly wrote, "A part of the now world-famous Shaver Mystery has now been proved!"

When the Arnold story broke in the national press, Palmer saw the opportunity to publicize his case and by doing that, validate the Shaver mystery. Palmer, as did so many others, wrote to Arnold, asking him to prepare a report for the magazine. Arnold didn't want to do that, but he did send Palmer a copy of the report that he had prepared for the Army Air Forces.

In a few days, Palmer wrote again, this time telling Arnold that he had a letter from a harbor patrol officer telling of a flying saucer sighting that had occurred three days before Arnold had seen anything. Palmer asked if Arnold would investigate and offered to pay Palmer two hundred dollars which, in 1947, was quite a bit of money. Today it is quite a bit of money to pay someone who had no particular expertise and whose only qualifications seemed to be that he had also seen something strange and he lived in the area.

The story, as it was told by Palmer and later by the harbor patrolmen, was that Harold Dahl, his teenage son, and two other harbor patrolmen sighted six doughnut-shaped objects in the sky near them. Five of the craft seemed to be circling the sixth which was in some kind of trouble. As the lone object passed overhead, no more than 500 feet above them, it started "spewing a white type of very lightweight metal" and some kind of "dark-type metal which looked similar to lava rock." The falling debris injured Dahl's son and killed their dog. When the object stopped dropping the metal, it took off, but not before Dahl managed to take a series of pictures.

In another, slightly different version of the story, reported in other sources, the sixth object landed, or crashed, on Maury Island in Puget Sound and then disintegrated, leaving behind some strange metallic-like debris. Dahl collected some of this material and then returned to Tacoma, Washington.

Now the case becomes a little confusing. According to what Dahl told Arnold, and what Arnold reported later, he hadn't said a word to anyone about the damaged object, the photographs, or the metallic debris, but the next day a dark-suited stranger who seemed to know everything about the sighting appeared to warn Dahl not to talk about it. Dahl ignored this warning and told his "supervisor" Fred Crisman about it. Crisman then went out to the beach and found some of the metallic debris, or so he said.

This aspect of the case becomes important to UFO history because this is the first report of a stranger who seems to know all and who dressed in dark clothing. Later, others would report that "Men in Black" had visited them after their UFO sightings. It was just one more first in a long list that can be attributed to Arnold or Palmer or the guys from Maury Island.

Having interviewed Dahl, or rather having talked to him, Arnold and Dahl then headed to Crisman's home to interview him. Crisman showed Arnold the debris that he had recovered, but Arnold was unimpressed. He recognized it as lava and had begun to suspect the story was a hoax.

Arnold wasn't sure what he should do now. He called Captain E. J. Smith, the United Airlines pilot who had seen several disc-shaped objects during a flight on July 4. Arnold, as a private pilot, had respect for Smith, an airline pilot, and Smith eventually joined Arnold in Tacoma. For those interested in such things, Arnold had Room 502 in the Winthrop Hotel, or so it has been reported in a variety of sources.

The next day Crisman and Dahl visited Arnold at the hotel. Crisman now added a new detail. He told Arnold that when he had gone to the beach, he'd seen one of the doughnut-shaped flying saucers that seemed to be searching the bay for something. Crisman, who hadn't been on the boat when the six objects had been seen, now dominated the conversation, as if he knew everything about it.

Arnold was less than impressed with all this and ordered breakfast in his hotel room. There wasn't much talk as they all ate and Arnold read some of the newspaper clippings he had brought with him, almost ignoring the other men. Later Arnold would say that one thing caught his attention. Flying saucers seen over Mountain Home, Idaho, had dropped or expelled cinder or lavalike ash. Here, suddenly, was another, independent report about a craft, or several craft, dropping the same kind of material that Dahl and then Crisman had talked about finding out on Maury Island.

Sometime that night, Arnold received a telephone call from Ted Morello, a reporter for the United Press, who also seemed to know everything that had happened in Arnold's room during his discussions with Dahl and Crisman. Arnold had been about to hang up when Morello made his claim. Arnold gave the phone to Smith and he was told the entirety of what had been going on in apparently private conversations. Fearing the room was bugged, Arnold and Smith began looking for hidden microphones, or as George Earley reported later, they "spent the next hour tearing that room apart, from the mattresses to the transoms." They found nothing.

The next morning, at the hotel, Dahl and Crisman arrived with some of the debris and as Arnold and Smith were studying it, Crisman said they were to have breakfast with two of his crewmen. Dahl and Crisman introduced Arnold and Smith to a couple of tough-looking men who were supposed to be the other crew members who had seen the object. Arnold didn't question them apparently assuming, according to Earley, that the crewmen would repeat the story as told by Dahl and Crisman.

> There was physical evidence from the objects, there were photographs of them, but the story told by the men had some holes in it.

Dahl, or Crisman, also said that they had photographs of the objects. Crisman had the film, he said, which Dahl had given him. Once they saw the film, meaning Arnold and Smith and later Palmer, they all would know the truth. Pictures wouldn't lie.

Arnold was still confused and unsure of what he needed to do. There was physical evidence from the objects, there were photographs of them, but the story told by the men had some holes in it. During the Army Air Forces investigation of his sighting, Arnold had been interviewed by an officer from the Fourth Air Force, Lieutenant Frank Brown. Arnold decided to call him and let him take a turn at trying to figure all this out. Besides, he was trained for that sort of thing.

Ed Ruppelt, one-time chief of Project Blue Book, put it this way:

"For the Air Force the story started on July 31, 1947, when Lieutenant Frank Brown, an intelligence agent at Hamilton AFB, California, received a long-distance phone call. The caller was a man whom I'll call Simpson [which, of course, was Arnold, Ruppelt changed the name because of privacy considerations and the fact that the Air Force files were still classified when he wrote his book] who had met Brown when Brown investigated an earlier UFO sighting.... He [Arnold] had just talked to two Tacoma Harbor patrolmen. One of them had seen six UFOs hover over his patrol boat and spew out chunks of odd metal."

Brown said that he would check with his superiors. If Arnold heard nothing from him in the next hour, he could assume that he, Brown, was on his way. Brown would be flying up from Hamilton Air Field in California. Arnold and Smith waited around the hotel room, but didn't know if Brown was coming until he arrived.

Brown had left the base with another officer, Captain William Davidson, sometime in the afternoon. They flew a B-25 north and then met with Arnold at his hotel in Tacoma just before five that evening. Arnold showed the two officers the fragments and both apparently recognized it as worthless slag. They immediately lost interest. Neither told Arnold this, apparently not wanting to embarrass him. Ruppelt later wrote, "Simpson [Arnold] and his airline pilot friend [Smith] weren't told about the hoax for one reason. As soon as it was discovered that they had been 'taken,' thoroughly, and were not a party to the hoax, no one wanted to embarrass them."

But, of course, it's not clear that either Arnold or Smith had been taken. They were doing what they had been asked to do by Palmer, and they were consulting the experts to determine what exactly had happened. Arnold had been suspicious from the first, though he seemed to run hot and cold. One minute he would think it was a hoax and the next he wouldn't be sure. He simply didn't have the expertise to make an investigation, though he could ask a few questions. The Army Air Forces officers probably should have said something to Arnold about their suspicions, but they were anxious to return to their home field.

There is one other interesting aspect to this. According to George Earley in *UFO* (Issue 157, page 42), Arnold wanted to know what Army intelligence had learned about the flying objects. "Davidson drew a picture on a piece of paper, saying, 'This is a drawing of one of several photographs we consider to be authentic.'"

While that is interesting, it doesn't improve our knowledge. But, according to what Earley wrote, Brown confirmed it saying, "It came from Phoenix, Arizona the other day. We have prints [taken by William Rhodes in July 1947] at Hamilton Field, but the original negatives were flown to Washington, D.C."

Davidson and Brown then left sometime around midnight, claiming they had to return their aircraft to California because of the upcoming Air Force Day celebration; they drove to McChord airfield where their B-25 was parked. They spoke, briefly, with the intelligence officer there, Major George Sander, telling him that they believed Dahl and Crisman had made up the tale and that they knew the story was a hoax. Sander would enter the story later.

At the airfield, they got ready to leave but picked up two "hitchhikers." Not long after takeoff, the engine on the left wing caught fire. Brown left the cockpit to assist the two passengers, the crew chief Woodrow D. Matthews and Sergeant Elmer L. Taff, with their parachutes. With them bailed out safely, Brown returned to the cockpit. George Earley suggested that the pilots probably believed they could save the aircraft. B-25s could be flown with one engine working, though this one was not only stalled, it was on fire.

Taff later said that he saw the left wing burn off and smash into the tail. The aircraft spun out of control and neither of the pilots, Brown nor Davidson, got out. Tragically, they were killed in the crash.

The story had suddenly turned deadly. The Army Air Forces, or maybe more appropriately, the FBI, was brought in to investigate and learned that contrary to published reports at the time, there was no sabotage of the aircraft and no one, or nothing, had shot it down. It was a tragic accident that focused more attention on the UFO sighting than it warranted, given the caliber of they witnesses.

Ruppelt in his book, *The Report on Unidentified Flying Objects*, reported, "Both—(the two harbor patrolmen) [Dahl and Crisman] admitted that the rock fragments had nothing to do with flying saucers. The whole thing was a hoax. They had sent in the rock fragments to [Ray Palmer] stating that they could have

Author Jerry Clark has researched and published extensively on UFO phenomena.

been part of a flying saucer. He had said the rock came from a flying saucer because that's what [Palmer] wanted him to say."

The Army Air Forces then found a solution to the case, and although two men had been killed investigating it, that had nothing to do with the UFO sighting. In fact, there had been no UFO sighting. The men were not prosecuted for inventing the story, though Ruppelt said that it had been considered by the military.

According to Jerry Clark, Arnold apparently never learned the whole truth about Maury Island. As late as 1977, Arnold was still talking about the case when he appeared at UFO conferences. He also used it in an article he did write for the first issue of *Fate* and in his book, written with Palmer, called *The Coming of the Saucers.* Of course, it might have been Palmer's influence that kept the story alive.

Arnold, however, wrote in his *Fate* article, as quoted by George Earley, that Major Sander, when he looked at the fragments, said, "That's nothing but smelter slag. I'll tell you what it is. It's just some kind of a hoax. That's true.'"

But there was another problem with the case, as laid out in the Project Blue Book files and in the FBI documents that are a part of that file. Who was the mystery caller? Who was the man in black that seemed to know everything about the case and was feeding that information to the news media? Who had been telling reporters everything that went on in Arnold's room? Did he have any credibility?

The first wire stories of the crash didn't mention the names of the officers killed, but the mystery caller knew them anyway and used that knowledge to suggest that he was on the inside of the investigation. He was the one who originally suggested that the aircraft had been shot down saying that a 20mm cannon had been used. He claimed it was because the officers carried some of the fragments picked up in the Maury Island area. He asked the reporter why, if he had the names of the officers killed, he couldn't believe that the rest of his information was also correct?

It turned out that the mystery caller did have the right names and the *Tacoma Times,* and a few other newspapers including one in Chicago, carried the story that the B-25 had been shot down. Ted Lantz was one of the reporters, and because the mystery caller had the names right, he believed him. When he learned a day or two later that both men had been intelligence officers, he was convinced that the tale of the shoot-down was true.

But then the story takes another turn. The mystery caller, it turned out, was one of the two harbor patrolmen, though it is never clear which one. Of course, he knew what had gone on in Arnold's room because he had been there, knew the names of the pilots killed because he had met them before they had taken off for California, and, of course, with that information verified, the newspapers printed the rest of his information believing it to be true.

Then, as so often happens in the world of the UFO, there was another twist. Fred Crisman, it seems, according to John Keel, had written a letter to the editor of *Amazing Stories*, Ray Palmer, in 1946. He warned Palmer about continuing the story of deros and teros (you knew we had to get back to them eventually) because he knew it was all true. He had seen them in the caves of Asia while he had been assigned to the Second Air Commando, an aviation unit designed to use special tactics against the Japanese in the China-Burma-India Theater during the Second World War. Crisman wrote:

> Sirs:
>
> I flew my last combat mission on May 26 [1945] when I was shot up over Bassein and ditched my ship in Ramaree roads off Chedubs Island. I was missing five days. I requested leave at Kashmere [sic]. I and Capt. (deleted by request) left Srinagar and went to Rudok then through the Khese pass to the northern foothills of the Karakoram. We found what we were looking for. We knew what we were searching for.
>
> For heaven's sake, drop the whole thing! You are playing with dynamite. My companion and I fought our way out of a cave with submachine guns. I have two 9" scars on my left arm that came from wounds given me in the cave when I was 50 feet from a moving object of any kind and in perfect silence. The muscles were nearly ripped out. How? I don't know. My friend has a hole the size of a dime in his right bicep. It was seared inside. How we don't know. But we both believe we know more about the Shaver Mystery than any other pair. You can imagine my fright when I picked up my first copy of *Amazing Stories* and see you splashing words about the subject.

What is interesting here is that Crisman knew about the Second Air Commando, which did serve in CBI Theater, and the place names all have the ring of authenticity to them. Of course for a con to work, there must be some elements of truth in it, and these little nuggets put Crisman into the right place at the right time to tell his otherwise-outrageous story. Besides, Palmer now had another man telling "eyewitness" stories of the deros and the teros and he wasn't about to challenge what the man said, especially with the circulation of the magazine soaring.

Palmer kept the Maury Island mystery alive as long as he could, but the Army was more than annoyed about the deaths of two officers for what seemed to be nothing more important than a magazine article and some science fiction stories. The investigation, that included the FBI, resulted in both Crisman and Dahl verifying that it had all been a hoax that just had gotten out of hand. They had never meant it to be taken nearly as seriously as it was.

> The investigation, that included the FBI, resulted in both Crisman and Dahl verifying that it had all been a hoax....

In fact, Crisman tried to blame Palmer, saying he only told Palmer what Palmer wanted to hear. But it was Crisman who contacted Palmer with his story of debris from a flying saucer and while it might be suggested that Palmer ignored the shaky nature of the information and evidence, it was Crisman who was there pushing his own agenda. Palmer knew Crisman from his earlier letter, which was published without a name attached. Palmer would later admit that Crisman was the author.

The military investigation, or rather the documents in the Project Blue Book files about the event, suggest that neither Dahl nor Crisman were harbor patrolmen, but owned a salvage boat which they used to patrol Puget Sound searching for anything of value they could find. Ruppelt suggested they had a couple of beat-up old boats they used in their salvage work.

Others who investigated privately later said that the characterization of the boats was unfair. They didn't have a couple of boats, they had a single boat known as the *North Queen* which was only five years old and had been renovated not long before the sighting.

But George Earley, in Issue 155, Vol. 24, No. 2, of *UFO*, explained this more fully. He reported that in the U.S. Treasury Department's *Merchant Vessels of the United States: 1947*, there is a listing that said, "Dahl, Haldor, 1801 N. Union Avenue, Tacoma, Washington. 249586 North Queen."

Some researchers, seeing that name, Haldor Dahl, assumed that this was Harold Dahl and the entry was a misprint. But it turns out there was a Haldor Dahl in Tacoma and he, with a partner, started Strom and Dahl Boat Builders which evolved into the Tacoma Boat Building Company which had built a number of boats for the Navy during the Second World War. One of those was the *USS Affray*, and when the war ended, they bought the boat back from the Navy. They refitted it as a fishing boat and renamed it *North Queen*. Harold Dahl had never owned it, had nothing to do with it, and his boat, as described by Arnold, was much smaller and in a state of disrepair.

Palmer, of course, was not going to allow Arnold, Ruppelt, or the Army Air Forces to destroy a good story. He claimed that Crisman wanted investigators to believe the story was a hoax. Crisman suggested that the Maury Island case could not be separated from the Shaver mystery and that flying saucers didn't come from outer space, but from the inner Earth. Maury Island proved that, at least in

Crisman's mind, and if Palmer didn't believe it, he sure wanted to promote it. The Shaver mystery had boosted the sales of his magazine by tens of thousands.

The metallic debris that everyone had been so concerned about was identified as slag and suggested that it bore a resemblance to similar material from a smelter near Tacoma. Although some suggested the slag had been radioactive, there is nothing in the FBI report to confirm this.

But to show that some things just can't be simple, Crisman pops up on the radar in the late 1960s as New Orleans district attorney Jim Garrison began to investigate Clay Shaw and his relation to the Kennedy assassination. Crisman became one of the minor players when it was claimed that he was one of the three hobos seen in the railroad yards not long after the fatal shots had been fired. Crisman was in the photograph of the hobos that has become part of the assassination legend.

So now we have moved from the possible crash of a spacecraft, to the possible crash of a craft from the inner Earth, to a story of a disabled craft that dumped metallic debris and maybe disintegrated, to the Kennedy assassination. But in all that, we have seen no evidence of anything extraordinary. There are only the tales told by Dahl and Crisman, and even those are undercut by retractions of the two men. They both told investigators that the story had started as a joke and that it had gotten out of hand.

Dahl's son, Charles, who had supposedly been injured by the saucer, was located years after the event and said that it had never happened. Of Crisman, Charles Dahl said he was a smooth-talking con man and that the Maury Island incident was a hoax.

Earley wrote in *UFO* magazine (Issue 157, Vol. 24, No. 4) that no one seemed to have searched for the medical records for Charles Dahl. Earley thought it would be a natural thing to do. If such records could be found, it would confirm part of the story, and while it was suggested by Palmer that he had photostats of those records, no one else ever saw them.

It should also be noted that no material with anything unusual about it has ever surfaced, though Crisman had suggested in the 1960s he still had some of it. The photographs were supposedly taken by the military, through no one ever saw them. In the 1960s, Crisman suggested that he had made duplicate negatives so that the military had not gotten them all, but, of course, the pictures never surfaced.

Finally, in Crisman's obituary, he mentioned his military service and suggested that he had received the Distinguished Service Cross. No record to support this has been found, though there are many databases that have the names of all those who have been awarded the Distinguished Service Cross. Of course, Crisman probably didn't write the obituary, though he certainly must have said something about the award to someone.

The First Crashes

It was on the July 4 weekend that the stories of objects that slipped from the sky and fell to Earth first appeared. In Circleville, Ohio, Jean Campbell, the daughter of a local farmer, was photographed holding up what her father had claimed might be one of the flying saucers. Sherman Campbell had found the remains of a radar target device that was attached to weather balloons so that they could be more accurately tracked. Made of aluminum foil in a complicated box shape, the device would always have a flat face aimed at the radar antenna. The aluminum foil would reflect light just as well so they could be tracked visually. If the target was spinning, it could look like a disc. Campbell, of course, did not know this was called a rawin radar target, nor did he know that rawin targets would enter the news prominently in the next few days, but he did know it was a weather balloon and radar target.

Next came the story of Vernon Baird, a civilian pilot who was flying a P-38 above thirty thousand feet when he spotted a formation of yo-yo-shaped objects behind him. As he watched, one broke formation, then got caught in the prop wash behind his plane and came apart. The wreckage spiraled down, crashing in Montana's Tobacco Root Mountains.

The next day, on July 8, the story was revealed as a hoax. Baird's boss, J.J. Archer, said that they had been sitting around the hangar after listening to stories of the flying saucers and invented the tale.

In Tacoma, Washington, Gene Gamachi and I.W. Martenson said they had watched a number of discs, some of which landed on the neighbor's roof. Of course by the time the reporters arrived the little men from inside and the objects were gone.

An elderly woman in Massachusetts said that she had seen a moon-sized object, meaning, I suppose, something that looked to be the same size as the moon seen in the distance. Inside the craft was a slender male figure that she thought was wearing a Navy uniform.

Speculation continued to run high in the newspapers. There was some talk of interplanetary craft, but most scientists, military officers, or government officials who cared to comment suggested that there were more mundane explanations. The real point is that the flying saucer stories had moved from the inside of the newspapers to the front pages. For several days the headlines had been about flying saucers.

The End of the Reports

Then, suddenly, on July 8, there was an announcement that ended much of the speculation. According to a press release issued by the 509th Bomb Group in Roswell, New Mexico, they had captured a flying saucer. Major Jesse A. Marcel,

Ranchers discover debris near Roswell, New Mexico, in this artist depiction.

the air intelligence, had taken the remains of the crashed craft to Fort Worth Army Air Field for further inspection.

There weren't many details given, but the story, for about three hours, caused a national sensation. Then Brigadier General Roger Ramey, who eventually reached three-star rank (lieutenant general), told reporters that the saucer was nothing more than a weather balloon. In fact, the debris displayed in his office, and shown in photographs published the next day on the front page of many newspapers, wasn't much different than what Sherman Campbell had found and identified a couple of days earlier. The difference was that Campbell, a farmer, had been able to identify the material as parts of some kind of balloon array, and that Marcel, an intelligence officer with the only nuclear strike force in the world, could not. The explanation was that the officers in Roswell had been swept up in the excitement and the hysteria of the time and that was why they failed to correctly identify the rather mundane debris.

About this same time, however, the number of reports was beginning to decline. Or it might be more accurate to say the number of sightings reported in the newspapers began to decline. There had been excitement, especially when there was talk of a flying saucer crash. But all those stories seemed to be hoaxes, wishful thinking, invention, or misidentification. Like the Great Airship of 1897, there were no follow-up stories.

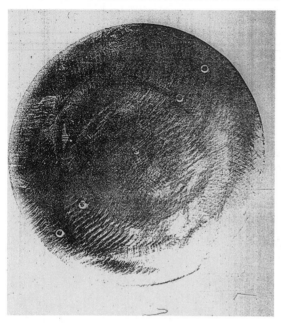

Photograph of the Shreveport disc.

That might have been one of the reasons for the lack of interest in new reports. They were basically the same as those carried in earlier days and those that were different were quickly exposed as hoaxes.

A report from Shreveport, Louisiana, told of a disc that had been recovered by the Army. Photographs of it show an object about two or three feet in diameter that has some wires attached to it and looks to have a slight dome on top. It was, of course, a hoax, but one that would reach to J. Edgar Hoover before all was said and done. Hoover would scribble a note on a request for FBI investigative assistance for interviews of witnesses that came back to haunt UFO researchers. Today, we know that Hoover was referring to the Shreveport case, though for years, this note was used as proof that the government knew more about flying saucers than they were telling.

But this lack of interest did not infect the Pentagon. According to Ed Ruppelt in his 1956 book, *The Report on Unidentified Flying Objects,* "By the end of July 1947 the security lid was down tight. The few members of the press who did inquire about what the Air Force was doing got the same treatment that you would get today if you inquired about the number of thermonuclear weapons stockpiled in the U.S.'s atomic arsenal...."

There was further confirmation of this change of attitude. Where once the military would be happy to speculate, and there was no trouble finding additional information, suddenly those sources were all gone. According to an Associated Press story that was reported in dozens of newspapers on July 9 and discussed later in more detail, the reports of flying saucers "whizzing" through the sky fell off sharply as the Army and Navy began a concentrated effort to stop the rumors.

The question that no one asked was why suddenly, on July 9, did the Army and Navy care what was in the newspapers regarding the flying saucers. It would seem that, suddenly, they had a reason to begin a campaign of suppression. And the only thing that had happened that could cause such a campaign was that they suddenly had an answer about the flying saucers that they didn't wish to share. Suddenly they knew the truth behind the flying saucers and they didn't want some smartass reporter getting too nosy and learning the truth.

And contrary to what they had told reporters, that answer had been found in Roswell.

The Cover-Up Begins

The cover-up began on July 9, 1947, when newspapers across the country carried the United Press story that said, "Reports of flying saucers whizzing through the sky fell off sharply today as the Army and the Navy began a concentrated campaign to stop the rumors."

While a number of explanations can be given for the sudden change in the military attitude about UFOs, the simplest is that they wanted the discussions and speculations to end. Up to that point the newspapers had been filled with stories about the flying saucers. There were theories about what they were, who had built them, what they could do, and what it all meant. No one seemed to care, thinking of this as just another manifestation of what the press had termed the "silly season."

But then, on July 9, it all changed.

Roswell

This seems to be a direct response to the Roswell UFO crash. On July 8, 1947, Lieutenant Walter Haut, then the Public Information Officer (PIO) of the 509th Bomb Group stationed at the Roswell Army Air Field, announced that officers of the group had found a flying saucer on a ranch somewhere in the area.

The Roswell story, as it is usually told, began in early July when ranch manager Mack Brazel found a field filled with metallic debris near Corona, New Mexico. Brazel showed a bit of the material to his closest neighbors, Floyd and Loretta Proctor, and wondered what he should do because he had a pasture filled with it.

Loretta Proctor would later say that the piece he showed her was small, about the size of a pencil, and extremely tough. She said that Floyd had at-

Jesse Marcel

tempted to whittle on it but couldn't mark it. Brazel held a match to it but there was no sign of burning or scorching. She said that she didn't know what it might be.

Floyd thought that Brazel should take the material into Roswell because the base there dealt with things in the sky. Others made a similar suggestion, and a ranch hand, Tommy Tyree, said that there was so much of the debris in one of the pastures that the sheep refused to cross it, meaning they had to be herded around the perimeter of this debris field to get them to water.

Brazel, apparently, on Sunday drove into Roswell and went to the sheriff's office. The sheriff, George Wilcox, suggested that he call out to the base and let them know what he had found. Major Jesse Marcel, Sr., the Air Intelligence Officer, met Brazel at the sheriff's office. After examining the debris Marcel said that he didn't know what had been found.

Brazel led Marcel and the counterintelligence officer, Captain Sheridan Cavitt, out to the ranch. The drive, over the semi-plowed roads that sometimes seemed to disappear into the high desert, took over three hours. They arrived sometime after dark.

The next morning, Brazel saddled two horses. He rode one and Cavitt, who was described as a "good ole West Texas boy," rode the other. Marcel drove a military vehicle and followed along. The terrain was the rolling hills of the high desert, but the ground was solid and his car made the drive easily.

Marcel would later say that the debris field was three-quarters of a mile long and a couple of hundred feet wide. It was filled with metallic debris that stirred in the wind. The fragments were lightweight, having the density of balsa wood, but incredibly tough. Marcel said that he found some parchment-like paper, and in keeping with what was becoming a tradition, used a match to test it. The paper-like material would not burn.

They quickly filled up one vehicle and Cavitt drove it back to the base. Marcel, driving his car now, filled it with more of the debris and then headed back to Roswell. He arrived sometime around midnight and stopped off at his house to show his wife and son what he had discovered. Jesse Marcel, Jr., eleven at the time, found what he now describes as embossed symbols along a short, thin structure that he referred to as an I-beam.

Once at the base, Marcel and Cavitt reported what they had found to the base commander, Colonel William C. "Butch" Blanchard. Blanchard, according to Haut, ordered him to write a press release that said they had found a flying saucer. Haut told UFO investigators in the 1990s that he didn't remember if Blanchard had dictated the release or had just given him the facts so that he could write it.

Haut said that he took the release to the four media outlets in Roswell, the two radio stations, and the two newspapers, and then he went home for lunch. Within a couple of hours, the world was interested in the flying saucer. Haut said that he received telephone calls from all over the world and that he received letters with all sorts of exotic stamps.

Marcel was ordered to take wreckage to Fort Worth, Eighth Air Force Headquarters, so that Brigadier Roger Ramey, the commanding officer, could examine it. Ramey, according to the newspaper accounts, identified the wreckage as part of a weather balloon. He called in Warrant Officer Irving Newton, who confirmed that the material on display in the office was part of a balloon.

And the story died at that point for several decades.

A higher headquarters had overruled the opinion of a lower echelon organization. Pieces said to have been brought forward were shown and it was obvious they were from a balloon. The rancher who found it lived on a ranch with no telephone, but he was in Roswell, on the military base. The Intelligence Officer was not in Roswell and couldn't be interviewed. The sheriff told all who called him to talk to those out at the base. There was simply nowhere for a reporter to go to get any additional information.

Although it was mentioned in a few books and articles, the facts were lost. Frank Edwards, in his *Flying Saucers—Serious Business*, talked about a pie plate and a kite. He did say that it happened near Roswell—which is about the only fact he managed to get right.

An Army Air Forces Opinion

On July 7, 1947, Captain Tom Brown, described as a member of the Army Air Forces Public Affairs Office, said that the AAF had decided there was "something to" all the flying saucer reports. Brown's opinion, which must be considered the Army Air Forces opinion because of who he was and the position he held, was expanded in other stories. He told a reporter that the "tales of flat round objects zipping thru [sic] the sky are too widespread to be groundless." He said that a number of competent airmen, as well as others, had reported them.

He said that the AAF had been checking on these stories for ten days and "still haven't the slightest idea what these things can be."

Brown said, "We don't believe anyone in this country or outside this country has developed a guided missile that will go 1,200 miles an hour, as some reports have indicated."

This is telling us that while the Army Air Forces was interested in the flying saucer reports, and they were attempting to find out what was behind the reports, they didn't know. The speculation was running the gambit from something from another world to spots in front of the eyes. Nearly all opinions were printed somewhere.

The Rhodes Photograph

William A. Rhodes, in July 1947, was a self-employed scientist living in Phoenix who claimed he had taken what might be considered the first good photographs of one of the flying saucers. Rhodes would tell reporters and various government investigators, including those from the FBI and the Army's Counterintelligence Corps, that he had been on his way to his workshop at the rear of his house when he heard a distinctive "whoosh" that he believed to be from a P-80 "Shooting Star" fighter jet (which was the fastest airplane of that particular moment). He grabbed his camera from the workshop bench and hurried to a small mound in his backyard. He estimated that the object was circling in the east about a thousand feet in the air.

Rhodes sighted along the side of his camera, according to what he would later tell a newspaper reporter, Robert C. Hanika, and took his first photograph. He advanced the film and then hesitated, thinking that he would wait for the object to get closer. Then, worried that it would disappear without coming closer, snapped the second picture, finishing the roll and his ability to record the event.

Rhodes' story, along with the pictures, appeared in the Phoenix newspaper *The Arizona Republic* on July 9. In that article Hanika wrote, "Men long experienced in aircraft recognition studied both the print and the negative from which they were made and declined to make a guess on what the flying object might be."

He also wrote, "The marked interest Rhodes has for all aircraft has led most persons who have been in contact with other observers of the 'flying discs' to believe the photographs are the first authentic photographs of the missiles, since Rhodes easily can identify practically any aircraft."

Rhodes said that the object appeared to be elliptical in shape and to have a diameter of twenty to thirty feet. It appeared to be at five thousand feet when first seen and was traveling, according to Rhodes, at four hundred to six hundred miles per hour. It was gray, which tended to blend with the gray overcast background of the sky.

The object had, according to Rhodes and a confidential report from the Project Blue Book files, "what appeared to be a cockpit canopy in the center which extended toward the back and beneath the object. The cockpit did not protrude from the surface but was clearly visible with the naked eye."

There were no propellers or landing gear, but there did seem to be trails of turbulent air behind the trailing points of the object. Speculation was that there were jet engines of some kind located there. The craft moved silently, although Rhodes had said that a jetlike roar was what called his attention to it.

The news stories apparently alerted the military to Rhodes' sighting. Various investigations were launched. On July 14, 1947, Lynn C. Aldrich, a special agent for the Army's counterintelligence corps (CIC) in a memo for the record available in the Project Blue Book files wrote, "On 8 July 1947, this Agent obtained pictures of unidentifiable objects ... from the managing editor of the *Arizona Republic* newspaper. The pictures were taken by Mr. William A. Rhodes ... [of] Phoenix, Arizona, at sunset, on 7 July 1947."

Then, on August 29, according to a "Memorandum for the Officer in Charge," George Fugate, Jr., a special agent of the CIC and stationed at Fourth Air Force Headquarters, interviewed Rhodes in person. Fugate was

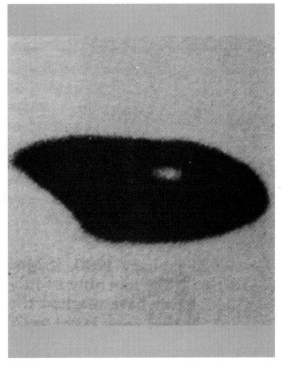

The overall shape of the UFO can be clearly seen in this photo by William Rhodes, though details are unclear.

accompanied by Special Agent Brower of the Phoenix FBI Office. This interview is important because of some of the confusion about location of the negatives and prints of the photographs that would develop later.

During the interview, Rhodes again told the story, suggesting that he thought, at first, it might have been the Navy's "Flying Flapjack" which had been featured on the May 1947 cover of *Mechanix Illustrated*. He rejected the idea because he saw no propellers or landing gear. Later research by various investigators, both military and civilian, shows that the Navy built a single "Flapjack" and that it never flew outside the Bridgeport, Connecticut, area.

At the end of Fugate's report, he wrote, "Mr. Rhodes stated that he developed the negatives himself. He still had the negative of the first photograph ... but he could not find the negative for the second photograph."

On February 19, 1948, Lewis C. Gust, the chief Technical Project Officer, Intelligence Department (though the Project Blue Book files fail to identify the man or his organization beyond that), wrote what might be considered a preliminary report on the analysis of the photographs. "It is concluded that the image is of true photographic nature, and is not due to imperfections in the emulsion, or lack of development in the section in question. The image exhibits

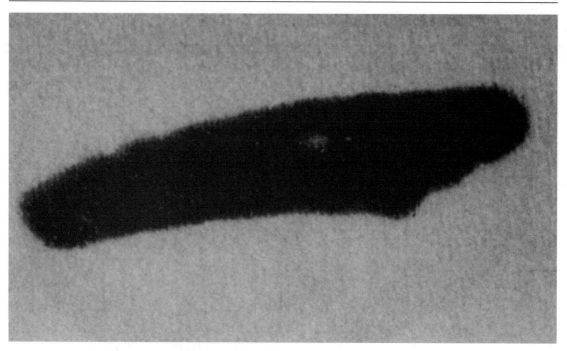

In this photo by Rhodes, the profile of the mysterious craft is apparent.

a 'tail' indicating the proper type of distortion due to the type of shutter used, the speed of the object and the fixed speed of the shutter. This trailing off conforms to the general information given in the report."

On May 11, 1948, Rhodes was again interviewed, but this time by high-ranking people. Lieutenant Colonel James C. Beam, who worked with the chief of intelligence at Wright Field, Colonel Howard McCoy, and Alfred C. Loedding, who was a civilian employee at AMC and part of Project Sign, traveled to Phoenix. They wrote, "Although Mr. Rhodes is currently employed as a piano player in a nightclub, his primary interest is in a small but quite complete laboratory behind his home. According to his business card, this laboratory is called 'Panoramic Research Laboratory' and Mr. Rhodes is referred to as the 'Chief of Staff.' Mr. Rhodes appeared to be completely sincere and apparently is quite interested in scientific experiments."

In fact, that same Grudge Report noted, "In subsequent correspondence to the reporter of this incident, the observer refers to himself as Chief of Staff of Panoramic Research Laboratory, the letterhead of which lists photography among its specialties. Yet, the negative was carelessly cut and faultily developed. It is covered with streaks and over a period of six months has faded very noticeably."

The AMC opinion in the Project Grudge report, which followed Langmuir's statement about the possibility of windblown debris, was, "In view of the apparent character of the witness, the conclusion of Dr. Langmuir [that the photographs be discounted as paper swept up by the wind] seems entirely probably [sic]."

On June 5, 1952, now nearly five years after the pictures were taken, and before the massive publicity about UFOs was about to burst on the public consciousness, Colonel Arno H. Luehman, Deputy Director of Public Information, wrote about "Declassifying Photographs of Unidentified Flying Objects." In the first paragraph of his letter, he wrote, "This office understands that two photographs were taken by Mr. William A. Rhodes of Phoenix, Arizona, and that these photographs were turned over to Fourth Air Force Intelligence in July of 1947. This office has been contacted by Mr. Rhodes who is requesting return of his original negatives."

The letter continued, "The two photographs were copied by the Photographic Records and Services Division of the Air Adjutant General's Office at this headquarters and are in a confidential file of Unidentified Missiles as A-34921AC and 34921AC."

But the important part of the document comes at the end. Aldrich wrote, "On the morning of August 30, 1947, when Mr. Rhodes called at the Phoenix office [of the FBI] to deliver the negatives, they were accepted only after he was advised that they were being given to Mr. FUGATE, a representative of the Army Air Force Intelligence, United States Army, and that there was little, if any, chance of his getting the negatives back. Mr. Rhodes turned them over to this office with the full understanding that they were being given to the Army and that he would not get them back."

On July 14, 1952, in still another letter, we learn that the pictures and negatives were turned over to Air Force intelligence representatives at Hamilton Field on August 30, 1947. In that document, they are attempting to trace the course of the pictures from Rhodes to the FBI to Army intelligence. What this suggests is that the Air Force wasn't sure of where the pictures and negatives were. They were attempting to shift the blame to others for the apparent loss of those pictures, including Rhodes himself.

That same July 14 document, written by Gilbert R. Levy, noted, "A background investigation was run on Rhodes, by OSI, for the benefit of AMC, which reflected Rhodes had created the name PANORAMIC RESEARCH LABORATORY, to impress people with his importance. He was reported to be a musician by trade, but had no steady job. Neighbors considered him to be an excellent neighbor, who caused no trouble, but judged him to be emotionally high-strung, egotistical, and a genius in fundamentals of radio. He conducts no business through his 'Laboratory,' but reportedly devotes all his time to research."

This means, simply, Rhodes had surrendered his photographs and negatives to the government and although they hint that Rhodes knew where they were, that simply isn't borne out in the documents. Even the Air Force officers didn't know where the photographs were. That was why there were letters written from one office to another.

There was never a clear conclusion to the identity of the object photographed by Rhodes. The Air Force, apparently unnerved by the self-employed Rhodes and his lack of visible means of support, at least to them, concluded the case as a hoax. They simply didn't like Rhodes and were apparently unaware that he had held several patents for his inventions and was apparently receiving some sort of compensation for them.

The Secrecy Begins

After the story of the crash at Roswell, after the reports from the airline crew, after the series of sightings in Oregon, and after the Rhodes photographs, the government had had enough. That seems to be the motivation behind the sudden attempts to suppress the stories of flying saucers that was reported on July 9. The question becomes, just what was happening at the highest levels of the government?

According to Dr. Michael Swords, who has attempted to answer this question, those at "topside," meaning those higher in the military chain of command, were confused. Edward Ruppelt, who was one-time chief of Project Blue Book, said they were more than confused, they were scared. They didn't seem to have a handle on what was happening around them and they had no answers for the questions the politicians were asking them.

Even as the number of sighting reports was reaching a peak, the government was attempting to learn more. An FBI document from the time states, "In passing, General Schulgen [Brigadier General George F. Schulgen, Chief of the Requirements Intelligence Branch of Army Air Force Intelligence] stated that an Air Force pilot who believed that he saw one of these objects was thoroughly interrogated by General Schulgen and scientists, as well as a psychologist, and the pilot was adamant in his claim that he saw a flying disc."

On July 9, the day the Army and Navy began a "campaign to stop the rumors," General Schulgen requested that FBI special agent S.W. Reynolds ask for FBI assistance in solving the problem of flying discs. Colonel L. R. Forney, of what would later become the Defense Intelligence Agency, told Reynolds that the discs were not Army or Navy vehicles. That meant they could be Soviet, or from another country that had the hidden technical capability to create them but who were not hostile, or alien craft from another world.

Confusion inside the military continued. Panic, according to Ruppelt, had swept through the halls of the Pentagon and the buildings at Wright Field. The theory that the flying discs might be some sort of new Soviet weapon, developed from captured German documents and by captured German scientists and engineers, dominated the thinking.

The Roswell UFO Museum in New Mexico.

It also became clear to those investigating flying saucers in late July that there was a strange silence from the men at the very top of the government, both military officers and civilian leaders. At the beginning of July, again according to Ruppelt and others, there was a state of near panic. But, by the end of the month, there was still nothing from the topside. Those inside the intelligence community not privy to all the information circulating at the very highest levels could draw but a single conclusion, at least to the thinking of those reviewing the records years later. If those at the top were no longer interested in the flying discs, then they must know all about them, including where they came from, and that they posed no security risk to the United States. Further investigation would be a waste of time because the answers were all known, given that line of reasoning.

Swords, writing *The Summer of 1947: UFOs and the U.S. Government at the Beginning*, noted, "The evidence for this can be found in documents released through Freedom of Information Act (FOIA) requests to the FBI. In a page probably attached to, and certainly related to, an FBI copy of an Air Force document dated July 30, 1947, a ranking USAF intelligence officer states unambiguously: 'Lack of topside inquiries, when compared to the prompt and demanding inquiries that have originated topside upon former events [such as the Swedish ghost rockets of 1946], give more than ordinary weight to the possibility that this is a domestic project, about which the president, etc. know."

At the same time, General Schulgen, trying to find out what was happening, was unhappy with the lack of information in his office and the results of his inquiries. He decided to make a direct request to the Air Materiel Command where the labs and resources to identify the saucers were housed. Accompanying the request was the first "Estimate of the Situation." Although the study contained the specifics of sixteen cases, the body of the report mentions eighteen different reports of flying saucers. These were the best sightings that had been reported as early as May 17, 1947, and as late as July 12. Five of the cases involved military pilots, including a Maxwell Field sighting by four pilots on

> Confusion inside the military continued. Panic ... had swept through the halls of the Pentagon and the buildings at Wright Field.

June 28. Six of them involved civilian pilots, including the July 4 sighting near Emmett, Idaho, made by a Captain E. J. Smith and his United Airlines crew and most of the passengers.

The estimate contained the conclusions based on the information used to prepare it. It seemed that the officers did not think the flying saucers were much of a mystery. They believed they were mechanical aerial objects. They just didn't know whose, but based on the apparent lack of concern from the top, they believed that the discs had to be a highly classified U.S. project. No other conclusion made sense to them.

The response from Twining's AMC staff probably surprised those at those lower levels, including Schulgen. Those below believed that the AMC would know all about the flying discs, yet in his response, Twining was telling them that the phenomenon was something "real and not visionary or fictitious." Not only that, Twining was telling them that his command didn't know what the flying discs were and that they should be investigated.

That had to be confusing. If the flying discs were a U.S. project, then the last thing anyone would have wanted would be an official investigation into them. Any investigation would be a threat to the security of the project and since very few, apparently, were privy to that information, it was clearly highly classified. To end such an investigation one of those on the inside of the secret would have to drop a hint to someone on the outside. If, for example, it was such a secret project that General Twining and the AMC were outside the loop, then another general, on the inside, could call Twining to tell him to drop the investigation. He wouldn't have to spill any details of the project, only tell Twining that it was something he didn't need to worry about because it was being covered by someone else. Twining would then end his inquiries, secure in the knowledge that the solution to the mystery was already known to someone else.

That, however, didn't happen. Instead, Twining suggested that a priority project, with a rating of 2A, be created to investigate the flying saucers. He wanted information found and reported to his office. The priority level of the new project also suggested that Twining wanted his answers quickly.

At that point it seems that the gathering of intelligence data by the Army Air Forces as conducted by the military in 1947 was disorganized, inefficient, and confused. A review of the documents showed that interviews conducted with key witnesses, such as Kenneth Arnold, were not completed until weeks after their sightings, and then not all the important questions were asked. To make it worse, the critical corroboration of the Arnold sighting by Fred Johnson was overlooked. In the "Estimate" sent up by General Schulgen, the dates of some reports are wrong, suggesting that only a superficial investigation had been conducted. It was clear that a coordinated effort to gather data had not been attempted, and the "not stated" entries in many of the cases showed that no one cared enough to re-interview witnesses to get proper answers.

Swords, commenting on this first estimate, wrote, "What explains this confident display of mediocrity? Although we are apparently not dealing with genius here, neither should we assume complete stupidity. This report was not put together with any greater intensity because the authors did not feel that it was necessary. They did not think that UFOs were any great mystery. It was obvious to them that UFOs were mechanical, aerial devices. Whose devices was still up in the air (so to speak), but the indications were fairly clear: despite assurances to the contrary, they must be our own. 'Lack of topside inquiries' made this the only reasonable conclusion in their eyes."

These men, who hadn't exactly shined during their investigation, had no burning passion to find the answers because they were convinced the answers already existed at the very top. Their estimate, according to Swords, was little more than a plea asking, "Can we please quit this nonsense."

Swords said that he believes the report was not forwarded to Twining until late August or early September of that year. Twining's response came on September 24, 1947. According to the documentation reviewed by Swords, the people at Wright Field and the Aircraft Laboratory Engineering Division (Wright Field's secret aeronautical engineering facility) added nothing to the discussion "except a sales pitch for a new project." That is a key point. They merely reviewed what Schulgen had sent to them and nothing more.

The original study had concluded that the UFOs were probably our own and we should quit chasing them. Logic dictated that Twining and the others would say exactly that. Quit chasing them. Instead, they are told that the UFOs aren't ours and, not only to keep the investigation going, but there would be a new project under a new banner with a high priority attached to it. That was not an expected result.

This, then, was the beginning of Project Sign. According to Ed Ruppelt, the 2A priority was the second highest possible. Only the top people at ATIC

[Air Technical Intelligence Center] were assigned to the new project. This was a serious project designed to obtain specific answers to specific questions.

The mission of Project Sign, then, was to determine the nature of the flying saucers. According to Ruppelt, there were two schools of thought. One believed that the Soviets, using their captured German scientists, had developed the flying discs. ATIC technical analysts searched for data on the German projects in captured documents in the United States, and intelligence officers in Germany were doing the same there.

> The original study had concluded that the UFOs were probably our own and we should quit chasing them.

It became clear, however, that the second school of thought, that is, that the UFOs were not manufactured on Earth, began to take hold. No evidence was found that the Soviets had made some sort of technological breakthrough. Even if they had, it seemed unlikely that they would be flying their new craft over the United States. If one crashed, they would have just handed the technological breakthrough to our government.

The initial panic that had bubbled through the Pentagon during the summer of 1947 began to subside. Twining's suggestion for a project was accepted and implemented. That proved that the objects, whatever they were, did not belong to the United States. According to Ruppelt, by the end of 1947, the situation at ATIC had slipped back into routine.

There were, however, some interesting documents prepared. In a Draft of Collection Memorandum, General Schgulen outlined what those working on Project Sign would be doing. It was a listing of intelligence data that would be valuable not only in determining what the flying discs were, but also in discovering how they operated. The "Collection Memorandum" outlined the "essential elements of intelligence" or "the current intelligence requirements in the field of flying saucer-type aircraft." That is, it was telling the field offices what information was desired by those at the top. It was a way of coordinating the collection of the information to ensure that everyone was operating in the same fashion. It really didn't matter here if the objects were manufactured on Earth or made elsewhere.

Project Sign was beginning to work in a coordinated fashion, collecting information to be forwarded to ATIC. The era of panic and confusion was ending by the late summer of 1947. The reason for that is probably no more complex than the passing of time. The pressure from the top for immediate answers had passed. The generals and their top civilian advisors still needed the answers, but as the days mounted, it became clear that nothing new was going to happen. There wasn't going to be an invasion from anywhere. They could relax slightly.

Alien Bodies

From the moment that there were reports of strange craft in the sky, there were reports of the creatures who piloted them and stories of the bodies of aliens killed in crashes. Some of these cases are little more than modern attempts to force ancient myths into an alien framework. Others are simply hoaxes told to amuse fellows or see a name in the newspaper. But a few are of real events that have been concealed behind a layer of government secrecy that is nearly impossible to penetrate.

Killed by Humans

As noted earlier, a tale from France, as described by Brad Steiger and others, suggests alien communication, and while not all versions of the story claim there were bodies, all versions do suggest there had been creatures. In other words, in a few of the stories the aliens were killed by humans, after some sort of confrontation.

The stories from the 1897 Great Airship sightings also suggest alien, meaning unearthly, creatures. The body of the Martian alleged to have been killed when his craft crashed in Aurora, Texas, never existed. As noted earlier, researchers beginning in the 1970s attempted to verify the story, attempted to find the grave, and attempted to find the wreckage. To this point, they have not been successful and if there is a conspiracy involved here, it is to keep the story alive. Some might suggest it is to keep it alive because it diverts attention from the real cases that have been found since 1897.

In the late 1930s, at least according to more modern sources, Cordell Hull, who was Secretary of State under Franklin Roosevelt, saw the bodies of alien creatures kept in glass specimen jars. According to the Center for UFO Studies, in early December 1999 they received a letter dated November 29, 1999, from the daughter of the Reverend Turner Hamilton Holt. In it she wrote:

> Today I want to share some knowledge that has been, by request, kept secret in our family since sometime in World War II. This concerns something my father was shown by his cousin Cordell Hull, the Secretary of State under Franklin Roosevelt. Sumner Wells was his Under-Secretary of State. Hull was a cousin to my father. My father was on some kind of advising committee, and made several trips to Washington, D.C., in that capacity.

> My father, who was young, brilliant, and sound of mind, tells this story to us because he didn't want the information to be lost. One day when my father was in D.C., with Cordell, Cordell swore him to secrecy and took him to a sub-basement in the U.S. Capitol building, and showed him an amazing sight: (1) Four large glass jars holding 4 creatures unknown to my father or Cordell [and], (2) A wrecked round craft of some kind nearby.

> My father wanted my sister and I to make this information known long after he and Cordell were dead, because he felt it was a *very important* bit of information. We have researched your group and feel it is the most reliable group in the country. We hope that you will research and search this information.

> Please don't disregard this because what I have written is true. The jars with creatures in formaldehyde and the wrecked craft are *somewhere*!

> Cordell said they were afraid they would start a panic if the public found out about it.

> Sincerely,
> Lucile Andrew

Mark Rodeghier, the scientific director of CUFOS, passed the letter along to William E. Jones and Eloise G. Watkins, two UFO researchers who live in Ohio. Watkins made several telephone calls to the woman who had signed the letter and a couple of trips to Ashland, Ohio, where she lived.

According to the article that appeared in the winter 2001–2002 issue of the *International UFO Reporter* published by CUFOS, Jones and Watkins wrote that they had interviewed Andrew on February 12, 2000, at her home. She said that she had been told the story when she was much younger and added that Holt had told another of his daughters. In what is one of those bizarre coincidences that dot the UFO landscape, it turned out that the daughter, Allene, is the mother of Watkins. Watkins, of course, knew it was her aunt; she just had never heard the UFO story from her.

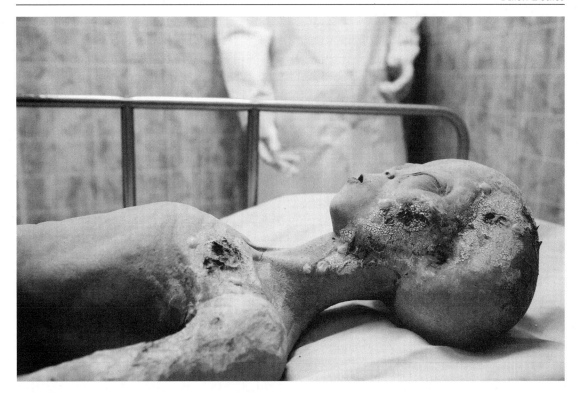

This is a mock-up of an alien body based upon reports that government scientists have autopsied aliens in the past.

On April 3, 2000, Jones and Watkins met both sisters, Lucile and Allene, for a combined interview. They remembered the story independently, but Allene was able to add little detail to the report.

Jones and Watkins attempted to verify as much of the story as they could. Hull left a huge written record of his life, but in the searches of his personal papers, as well as his official documents, they were unable to verify the account. They did learn that at one time there had been a sub-basement to the capitol building, but all that did was confirm that there had been a sub-basement to the building.

They also learned that Hull and Holt were from the same small area of Kentucky and that they had known each other. In fact, it seemed that they were related, though they were little more than distant cousins. As for the story of the bodies in glass tubes in the basement, they were unable to corroborate that part of the story.

The Cape Girardeau Recovery

Charlette Mann wrote to Ray Fowler, a longtime and well-trusted UFO researcher, about an event that seemed to be about a UFO crash. Fowler, who knew of the work of Len Stringfield and his interest in what he would later call crash/retrievals, sent a copy on to him.

"After grandfather returned that night, he explained what he had seen to grandmother, my father, Guy, and Uncle Wayne, but that they were never to speak of it again...."

In that letter Mann claimed her grandfather, a minister, received a late-night telephone call asking him to go to the scene of an aircraft accident. There were hints of something extraordinary, but the letter from Mann was somewhat confusing. There was, however, enough detail in that original letter that Stringfield called her to ask for more detail. He convinced her to rewrite her letter into a more structured report, which he published in his *UFO Crash/Retrievals: The Inner Sanctum* in July 1991.

According to Mann, her grandfather, Reverend William Huffman, was "born in August 1888 and he grew up in Missouri. He attended college in Bolivar and after graduation, he went to a seminary. He was an ordained Baptist minister ... he was a quiet man who was well respected."

He was also a well-educated man for the times and he was a minister, which suggests he was also an honest man. He died before telling Mann about the case, so the information came to her from her grandmother, known by everyone as Floy.

In her May 6, 1991 letter to Stringfield, she provided details that she had heard from her grandmother. She wrote:

It happened in the Spring of 1941. About 9 to 9:30 one evening, granddad got a telephone call from the police department, saying they had received reports that a plane had crashed outside of town and would he go in case someone needed him. Of course he said yes. A car was sent to get him, but my grandmother said it wasn't a police car.

After grandfather returned that night, he explained what he had seen to grandmother, my father, Guy, and Uncle Wayne, but that they were never to speak of it again....

He said they drove out of town 13–15 miles or so, then parked the cars on the side of the road and had to walk 1/4 of a mile or so into a field where he could see fire burning.

Grandfather said it wasn't an airplane or like any craft he'd ever seen. It was broken and scattered all around, but one large piece was still together and it appeared to have a rounded shape with no edges or seams. It had a very shiny metallic finish. You could see inside one section and see what looked like a metal chair with a panel with many dials and gauges—none familiar looking to him. He said that when he got there, men were already sifting through things. There were some police officers, plain clothes people and military men. There were three bodies not human, that had been taken from the wreckage and laid on the ground. Grandfather said prayers over them so he got a close look but didn't touch them. He didn't know what had killed them because they didn't appear to have any injuries and they weren't burnt. It was hard for him to tell if they had on suits or if it was their skin but they were covered head to foot in what looked like wrinkled aluminum foil. He could see no hair on the bodies and they had no ears. They were small framed like a child about 4 feet tall, but had larger heads and longer arms. They had very large oval shaped eyes, no noses just holes and no lips just small slits for mouths. There were several people with cameras taking pictures of everything. Two of the plain clothes men picked up one of the little men, held it under its arms. A picture was taken. That was the picture I later saw. Then, one of the military officers talked to granddad and told him he was not to talk about or repeat anything that had taken place for security reasons and so as not to alarm people. Granddad returned home, told his family. That was all. About two weeks after it happened, he came home with a picture of the two men holding the little man.

After my grandfather died, my Dad kept the picture and was very interested in UFO info. Then when I was 10 or 11, a close friend of my Dad's asked if he could borrow it to show to his folks so Dad let him have it and never got it back.

Stringfield wondered about the picture. This would be a wonderful piece of evidence but, as has happened in all similar stories, the picture has disappeared. It was loaned to another who failed to return it.

Stringfield knew of a similar picture that had been published in various UFO magazines. In this photograph, two military-looking men are holding the long arms of an alleged alien creature. It is clearly a monkey and the picture an obvious and well-known hoax.

Mann, in her May 6, 1991, letter, provided a lengthy description of the photograph she had seen. She wrote:

My recollection from what I saw in the picture was a small man about 4 feet tall with a large head and long arms. He was thin and no bone structure was apparent; kind of soft looking. He had no hair on his head or body with large, oval, slightly slanted eyes but not like oriental from left to right, more up and down. He had no ears at all and nose like ours. His mouth was as if you had just cut a small straight line where it should have been. His skin or suit looked like crinkled-up tin foil and it covered all of him.... I believe he had three fingers, all quite long, but I can't be sure on this.

Stringfield was able to find a copy of the picture he remembered and sent it on to Mann. She replied, "It is nothing like what I saw. Your picture showed men in overcoats while in my picture, the man had no coats [sic].... Your picture shows two women; mine none. The alien in yours looks like a tiny doll, much smaller and shorter than mine."

Mann has given interviews to several other researchers and some of the details of her story have expanded. For example, in a 2008 interview she said that when her grandfather arrived at the scene of the wreck, two of the alien creatures were dead, but the third was still alive. She said that it, or he, or possibly even she, died while her grandfather was praying over it. He then moved on to the other two to offer prayers for them.

> "He had no hair on his head or body with large, oval, slightly slanted eyes but not like oriental from left to right, more up and down."

She also said that the symbols he had seen inside the craft "looked similar to hieroglyphics."

There is some corroboration. In what might be considered a not very persuasive bit of evidence, Clarance R. Schade, who is the brother of the sheriff in the Cape Girardeau area in the 1940s, said that he remembered hearing of a strange crash and he remembers talk of little people associated with it.

Ryan Wood, in *Majic Eyes Only*, reported that Mann's sister provided a sworn affidavit that confirmed the story. In other words, other members of the family are aware of the family history and report they too have seen the photograph and heard the tale.

In February 2008, Tyler, Texas, television reporter Gillian Sheridan interviewed Charlette Mann. According to that report, Mann said, "We got validation by going to the archives in Washington D.C. and to see a top-secret declassified document that stated that there was in fact a crash retrieval in 1941 in Cape Girardeau, Missouri, for me, I have not forgotten holding that paper in my hand and realizing that my families [sic] story was real, was solid, and for me was just an answer to a longtime question."

One of the documents said, "Based on all available evidence collected from recovered exhibits currently under study by AMC, AFSWP, NEPA, AEC, ONR, NACA, JRDB, RAND, USAAF, SAG and MIT, are deemed extraterrestrial in nature. This conclusion was reached as a result of comparison of artifacts (small part redacted) discovered in 1941. The technology is outside the scope of U.S. science, even that of German rocket and aircraft development."

The problem here is that this is part of a leaked MJ-12 document and is dated 24 Sep 47. The MJ-12 documents themselves are wrapped in controversy as noted in another chapter.

The major witness, and the one with the most robust tale, is Charlette Mann. Her sister has corroborated hearing the family talk of the night their grandfather was called out to pray over the bodies recovered from the wrecked craft. The brother of the local sheriff in 1941 also seems to remember something about this.

The problem is simply this. If there had been this crash in 1941, or for that matter some kind of retrieval as seen by Cordell Hull, then the military would have been aware of the possibility of alien space travel and they would have been on the lookout for other examples. They would have expected other examples to be found. That means they wouldn't have been caught by surprise with the flying saucers that were first reported in June 1947 and would have been better prepared for the Roswell UFO crash.

The Roswell Bodies

Robert Hastings, in his book *UFOs and Nukes,* reports on an interview he conducted with Chester Lytle concerning the Roswell crash. Lytle was an extraordinary man who ran his own engineering firm in Albuquerque, New Mexico, and who had worked on the first atomic bomb implosion trigger that was tested in Alamogordo in 1945. When the war ended, Lytle continued to manufacture parts for atomic weapons, worked with the Atomic Energy Commission which is now the Department of Energy, and was involved with many classified military projects. He was a well-known and well-respected man who had a number of UFO sightings and a longtime interest in them.

According to Hastings, he was interviewing Lytle about his involvement with atomic energy and what he might know about UFO sightings near nuclear plants or facilities. Hastings said that with no prompting from him, Lytle moved on to the Roswell crash and told Hastings that William Blanchard, who had command of the 509th Bomb Group in Roswell in 1947, confirmed the alien nature of the event.

Lytle told Hastings that in February 1953, with Blanchard now a general officer, they were in Alaska while Lytle's wife was in Chicago about to give birth. Lytle was desperate to get home and Blanchard said that they could take an Air Force aircraft to Illinois, land at one of the bases close to Chicago, and Lytle could easily get home from there.

While on the flight, somehow the subject of UFOs came up, maybe because of a couple of sightings at Elmendorf Air Force Base near Anchorage sometime earlier. Blanchard then told Lytle that an alien craft had crashed near Roswell. According to Hastings, Blanchard told Lytle that four bodies had been recovered.

Surprised by this, Hastings asked Lytle, "Blanchard actually told you that the Roswell object was an alien spacecraft."

Lytle said, "Oh, absolutely."

A digital re-creation of the crash in Roswell.

In break with the traditional story, Blanchard said that some of the bodies had gone originally to Muroc Army Air Field (now Edwards Air Force Base), but that they all eventually wound up at Wright Field.

Now, granted, this is secondhand testimony about what Blanchard said, but there is no reason for Lytle to invent it, and it is quite clear that Lytle held many clearances and had been trusted with the secrets of the Manhattan Project. He was a credible man.

This testimony fails on one point and that is that we can't verify it with either Lytle or Blanchard. Both men are dead. The documentation that exists is quite limited and subject to various interpretations. At this point, this is an anecdote that provides a bit of insight into the crash … and it is the first time that Blanchard, through Lytle, gave us a number of bodies. Blanchard, according to Lytle, said, "Four."

If this was the only testimony about alien bodies recovered with the Roswell crash, then we might be justified in dismissing it, though there is no reason for Lytle to have invented it. Pappy Henderson was a member of the 1st

Air Transport, part of the 509th Bomb Group at Roswell in 1947. He was a trusted member of Colonel Blanchard's staff and, according to his widow, Sappho Henderson, was called on by Blanchard for special missions. He mentioned nothing to his wife about UFOs, crashed ships, or alien bodies until 1980 when a tabloid newspaper article reported on the Roswell crash. Finally he felt that he could tell her what he knew.

The creatures were, according to what Rowe remembered and what she had been told, about the size of a ten year old....

He told her that he had flown wreckage to Wright Field. At a reunion of his old World War II flight crew, he told them the same thing. He also told them that he had seen the bodies of the alien flight crew in a hangar on the base. Henderson died in 1986 before any of the Roswell investigators had a chance to interview him, so the information about the alien nature of the creatures is all secondhand.

Frankie Rowe, who in 1947 was twelve years old told investigators that her father, Roswell firefighter Dan Dwyer, had seen the bodies of the alien flight crew. He had driven out to the crash site. She said that her father had come home after his shift at the fire station (which lasted about twenty-four hours) and had something important to say. He then told them, according to Rowe, that he had gone about thirty miles outside of Roswell and then a few miles back to the west. He said there had been some kind of a crash and that he had called it a spaceship or a flying saucer or something.

Then Rowe said one of the most important things she would say. According to her, "I remember him saying that some of them helped pick up some pieces of the wreckage. He said he saw two bodies in bags and one that was walking around."

She said, "[H]e said he was sure that there were bodies because the third one would go over to them … he talked about this third one would go back and forth between different parts of the wreckage and was walking around dazed. He didn't say if anyone tried to talk to this person."

The creatures were, according to what Rowe remembered and what she had been told, about the size of a ten-year-old, meaning that they were smaller than a human adult. The color was like that of an insect called Child of the Earth (more commonly called the Jerusalem Cricket), which is sort of copper color or maybe a sort of dark brown.

Rowe also saw a bit of metallic debris that a state trooper claimed to have picked up in the field. Rowe said that she thought it was about a week later. She'd had some dental work done and had gone over to the firehouse to wait so that her father could drive her home. The state policeman was there and he walked up to a table and said to the firemen, "You guys aren't going to believe what I've got." He pulled out his hand and had a piece of metal.

Rowe said, "I think I got to pick it up and crumple it one time. I can only remember doing it one time.… It just didn't feel like anything … it was kind of a pewter color.... Everybody got out their knives or whatever and tried to cut and they tried to burn it."

Unfortunately, as has happened so often in this case, no researcher had a chance to talk with Rowe's father. He died long before the investigation began. But I did have the opportunity to talk with her sister, Helen Cahill. She was married in 1947 and living in California at the time of the Roswell crash, but had heard some discussion about the events during a visit to New Mexico in 1960. Although her information wasn't as complete as that of Rowe, it confirmed, for what it's worth, that Rowe did not invent the tale of the crash. Of course, it does little to validate it, except to suggest that Rowe's father was talking about a UFO crash long before the reports of the Roswell events came to light and at a time when few people thought of UFOs as being from other worlds. Other explanations seemed to make people happier.

There is one problem with all this, however. According to Rowe, she'd had some oral surgery which had begun to bleed, which was why she had been in Roswell in the middle of July 1947. That was why she had been at the firehouse when the state policeman had brought in the metallic debris. Although records are not complete, there are none to show that Rowe's oral surgery was done in July 1947 or that there were later complications.

Skeptics, however, have suggested that her story isn't true and cited both a city councilman who told them that the Roswell Fire Department didn't make runs outside the city limits and that a number of men who had been with the department in 1947 remembered nothing about it.

Records kept at the fire station show that the department did make runs outside the city limits. On June 21, 1947, according to the fire log, Pumper No. 4 made a run "out side city limit." The problem is that there is no listing for a run that would correspond to the date of the UFO crash in early July.

Karl Pflock, in his book *Roswell: Inconvenient Facts and the Will to Believe*, rejected Rowe's story because he'd talked to three former firefighters who claimed no knowledge of the events and who, it was implied, refuted what Frankie Rowe said. To him, this was the "smoking gun." He could find no corroboration for Rowe's story.

But Pflock wasn't quite right in his assertion. According to one of those same firefighters, Pflock didn't tell the whole story, or he didn't get all the facts. One of the men interviewed by Pflock confirmed that the Roswell Fire Department hadn't made a run outside the city to the crash site.

The man confirmed, in two interviews conducted by two different researchers in 2010, the fire department didn't make a run to the crash site, though that says nothing about runs outside the city. But then this long-retired firefighter said something else. When asked if he knew Dan Dwyer, Frankie Rowe's father, he said that a colonel had come out from the base and told them not to go out there to the crash site. That they, the military, would handle it. He added that Dwyer, in his personal car, did drive out to the crash site. Dwyer and not the fire department had gone out, which explains why there is no record of it in the firehouse records and why other firefighters didn't remember it. They were not involved.

The retired firefighter was quite clear about these points. They had been visited by an officer from the base, they had been told not to go out there, but Dwyer, in his personal car, did.

The Walter Haut Affidavit

Walter Haut was an officer with the 509th Bomb Group in 1947. While a member of a flight crew, he had an additional duty as the public information officer for the base. He was the man who wrote the press release that said they had "captured" a flying saucer on a ranch in the Roswell region. For more than twenty years he maintained that the only thing he had done was write and deliver the press release. He didn't see the craft and he didn't see the bodies. He told every researcher and investigator that he had a very limited role in the Roswell case. Colonel Blanchard had dictated his role to him.

But then, in about 2000, Haut's story began to change. Wendy Connors and Dennis Balthaser interviewed Haut after a French film crew had been to

New Mexico to interview him about the UFO crash. He said that he had seen the bodies … or body, depending on which statement by Haut you wish to accept. He later expanded these statements in his interviews with Connors and Balthaser. He even consented to having a video recording made of that interview.

But the water is a still more muddied. Gildas Bourdais, a French UFO researcher who has written his own book on the Roswell crash, said he had talked to the French crew director and that Haut said nothing about bodies on camera. On UFO UpDates, Bourais wrote, "He [Vincent Gielly] told me that, when he did his filmed interview of Walter Haut with Wendy Connors, Haut looked like someone who wished to say more, but could not. This lasted a long time, and he finally decided, a little disappointed, to end the interview. But then, he found Wendy, alone in another room, extremely disappointed because, she told him, she felt Haut was just

Walter Haut

about to talk when he ended the interview. That's what Gielly told me. He did not tell me that Haut had talked about seeing the craft and bodies. If he did, he may have promised not to repeat it, I don't know."

So, there is now a question of just what Haut did say to the French crew and what he said on camera as opposed to what he said in private. Connors and Balthaser said that Haut said something to the French which inspired the two of them to seek an audience with Haut to explain his earlier years in the military and, according to them, ask a few questions to clarify the situation Haut found himself in back in 1947.

For those who have seen the Connors/Balthaser interview, there are some very disturbing statements by Haut. He is either badly confused, or he is deeply conflicted about revealing secrets he had kept for more than sixty years, or he just couldn't keep his new story straight, probably because of his advanced age. He left a somewhat rambling mishmash of contradictory information.

Here is just a short portion of part of that rather confused statement: "That's a rough one [about the appearance of the craft] I haven't even thought about it low these many years and I honestly can't even visualize it, whether still in it's shape, but a lot of dings in it.... I do not remember.... I would venture a guess that probably a diameter of, uh, somewhere around 25ft.... To the best of my remembrance there was one body ... it was relatively a small body comparable to uh, oh maybe a 11 year old, 10 or 11 year old child. It was pretty well beat up. I cannot come and give you, to be honest, anything other than that. I remember something about the arms and I am trying to visualize that and all of a sudden it starts going through my little head that that they show some of those long arms in the cartoons.... I thought there was several bodies ... for some reason I feel there were several bodies ... the more I think about it the more I start to get an idea it was single body."

And then to thoroughly confuse the issue, Haut retreated to the line he had been using from the very beginning in the late 1970s and early 1980s as he talked with various UFO investigators. He said, "I didn't even see one. I just wrote a press release."

Connors then said, "I am talking about when you saw a body in the hangar partly covered by the tarp. You only saw the one."

Walter said, "Yes."

But to really complicate the issue, Walter also said in that same interview:

"I don't really know. I ... it hurts me to try and give an answer because I am not certain of the whole thing. I feel there has been information released that uh maybe shouldn't have been released, maybe the information that we got in the operation of releases maybe something you can put out to anybody. I just ... I don't know, I don't want to talk about a lot of the detail number one because I don't have a lot of knowledge about the detail, everybody thinks that I saw them, I didn't, I put out a press release that Colonel Blanchard told me what he wanted in the press release and I ran it into town and gave it to the news media and went home and ate lunch."

The affidavit, however, is a very clear and concise statement about all this. Haut said (or rather signed the statement that said … and that is probably a distinction we should make at this point because of some of the controversy):

… Before leaving the base, Col. Blanchard took me personally to Building 84, a B-29 hangar located on the east side of the tarmac. Upon first approaching the building, I observed that it was under heavy guard both outside and inside. Once inside, I was permitted from a safe distance to first observe the object just recovered north of town. It was approx. 12 to 15 feet in length, not quite as wide, about 6 feet high, and more of an egg shape. Lighting was poor, but its surface did appear metallic. No windows, portholes, wings, tail section, or landing gear were visible.…

Also from a distance, I was able to see a couple of bodies under a canvas tarpaulin. Only the heads extended beyond the covering, and I was not able to make out any features. The heads did appear larger than normal and the contour of the canvas suggested the size of a 10-year-old child. At a later date in Blanchard's office, he would extend his arm about 4 feet above the floor to indicate the height.

There are other statements that Haut made over the years, including ones that I recorded. Everyone knows that he said, for decades, all he had done was write the press release. Now there is a new statement in which he is in the middle of this with all the inside knowledge that anyone could hope for.

> "I thought there was several bodies … for some reason I feel there were several bodies …"

The problem is not that his earlier statements contradict his later statements, but that his later statements were highly confused, and highly contradictory even inside one interview, and inside one statement in that interview. Haut is on the record in too many places saying that all he did was write the press release. He is seen in the Connors/Balthaser interview giving that same story but wrapping it around tales of bodies and craft.

There are those who suggest that Haut was conflicted about all this, maybe by his age, or maybe it is that he wanted to honor the oath he had taken so long ago. He wanted to honor the promise he had made to Colonel Blanchard so long ago. But he also believed that the information was too important to be withheld and that it belonged, not just to the Army, the Air Force, or the government, but to everyone. Even as he provided hints about what he had seen and what he knew, he wasn't able to tolerate talking about it directly. He had to come at it from the side.

Had Haut's later statements been consistent inside the context of the interview and had they been consistent throughout that interview and other, later ones, then we could say that he was providing us with information that he'd had all these years. But that's not what we have here. We have contradictory statements.

Enter Richard C. Harris

There is some confirmation from another source that does provide relevant information. Richard C. Harris, who was an assistant finance officer of the 509th, lived in Albuquerque. During my interview with him, I saw a frail man who needed live-in help. He was, naturally, quite interested in the Roswell UFO case, having served at the base in 1947. He is in the Yearbook, so there is confirmation that he was there at the right time.

But in his living room was a small bookcase that held a stack of books dealing with UFOs, the Roswell case, and MJ-12. Harris was a firm believer in MJ-12 and alien visitation.

This simply means that he was familiar with the case as it had been written about in the various books. He had seen many of the documentaries of the case so he could have been badly contaminated as a source. Having seen the documentaries and read the books and magazine articles doesn't mean that what he said was based on what he had read and seen and not wholly on his memories, but we must be aware that it all could be colored by those other sources.

Richard Harris

Anyone who has served in a command position or a position of responsibility in the military knows that everything must be paid for. There are all sorts of funds that are designated for all sorts of purposes and it is considered illegal to take funds appropriated for one purpose and use them for another. This means that funds meant to pay for a unit's flight training, for example, can't be used to transport alien bodies and craft from one location to another. Funds must be designated for that purpose. (Unless, of course, it's a cross-country navigation problem and therefore training, and if some of the wreckage, or an alien body or two, are on the aircraft, hey, that's just a bonus.)

No, it doesn't have to say moving an alien body from Roswell to Wright Field, but the funds will have to be appropriated for moving equipment from Roswell to Wright Field. The money must be juggled.

Harris said that they worked hard to find the money from legal sources, that they worked hard to cover the real purpose because there would be audits, and there would be examinations that had nothing to do with the crash but everything to do with looking for fraud. So the money spent to house those brought in, for the aircraft flights to and from various locations, for the special equipment, and to pay the soldiers were all juggled around so that it was properly annotated and properly spent. Harris was proud of the job they had done covering the paper trail (not unlike comments that Colonel Patrick Saunders, the Roswell base adjutant in 1947, had made to family members about hiding the trail).

The key point of Harris' story was this little anecdote. He said that he had been out near one of the hangars and ran into Walter Haut. Haut told him what was on the other side of the door, meaning one of the dead aliens, and told Harris he could take a quick look. Harris said that he put his hand on the doorknob, but didn't turn it. For some reason his curiosity failed him at that point. He didn't take the look that Haut had told him to.

This, of course, suggests that Haut had deeper knowledge and Harris told me this more than a decade before the Haut affidavit was published. It is some corroboration for Haut's new story. It's not a very good corroboration, but it is some.

Another Firsthand Account from Roswell

Thomas Gonzales was stationed in Roswell in July 1947, and told Don Ecker and John Price that he had seen the alien creatures. At the time he was a sergeant in the Transportation section, but apparently he was used for part of the recovery operation.

He said that the craft itself looked more like an airfoil than it did like one of the flying saucers. He didn't say much about the craft, but concentrated on what he called the bodies of the "little men." He said that they were not like those little gray men who were responsible for alien abductions.

In his interview with me, Gonzales was not very articulate, but was able to communicate his observations. He did one other thing. He carved a number of wooden figures that he said resembled the alien beings he had seen. These show a range of beings, all with fairly large, black eyes. Their arms are crossed on their chests and one or two of them suggest large hips, but that might be little more than poor carving technique.

Gonzales said that after he participated in the recovery of the aliens, he was transferred off the base quickly. He said that it happened so fast that he lost some of his personal property and the transfer caused some trouble for his family.

These wooden aliens were carved by eyewitness Thomas Gonzales.

The Tomato Man Pictures

In what is one of the worst cases of a misidentified picture, UFO researchers announced they had received photographs of an alien body taken at the scene of a 1948 UFO crash in Mexico.

A year after the Roswell UFO crash, another object reportedly fell about thirty miles southwest of Laredo, Texas, across the Rio Grande River in Mexico. Then-Secretary of State General George C. Marshall, who figured prominently in the Aztec just months before, coordinated the retrieval with the Mexican government so that American military forces could take charge of the wreckage. Marshall, according to the story, claimed it was an experimental craft from White Sands Proving Grounds that had gone out of control and crashed just over the border.

This part of the story wasn't all that far-fetched given the history of missile tests in the area. A rocket launched from White Sands had gone out of control and crashed near Juarez, Mexico, across the border from El Paso, Texas, in 1947. Fortunately no one was injured and the damage was minimal but launches at White Sands were suspended for several weeks until new safety procedures could be designed.

Colonel John W. Bowen, who was the provost marshal at Fort Worth, according to this story, was detailed to take charge of the operation in Mexico, though there were military bases closer including Fort Bliss in El Paso and Fort Hood near San Antonio. The crash area was quickly cordoned off and men were sent in to secure it and clean up the wreckage. It was hauled from Mexico to a location in San Antonio for processing, investigation, and eventual shipping to other Air Force facilities that could exploit the find.

However, before that was done, a special photographer was sent in, at least according to a man who claimed to be that photographer. He said that he was a Navy photographer and his job was to photograph everything as it was found as a way of documenting the case. This source surfaced in December 1978 and told researchers at the Mutual Anomaly Research Center and Evaluation Network (MARCEN) that as a young man, he had been detailed to take photographs of a flying saucer wreck.

To prove it, he included an eight-by-ten glossy print showing the body of one of the aliens killed in the crash. When the MARCEN members questioned him, suggesting that to them this looked more like a human pilot killed in a light plane crash, they received a three-page reply with much more detail.

According to the story told by this man, at about 1322 hours (1:22 P.M.) on July 7, the Distance Early Warning (DEW) line detected an object traveling at speeds of more than two thousand miles per hour as it flew over Washington state, headed to the southeast. As it entered the airspace over Texas, two fighters were scrambled to intercept and identify the object.

As the two F-94 fighters approached, the UFO made a 90-degree turn without decreasing its speed. At 2:10 P.M., other fighters, which had joined the pursuit, radioed that the object was slowing and now wobbling. At 2:29 P.M., it disappeared from the radar, but by using triangulation, the military realized that the object was down, in Mexico, but not all that far from Laredo. That is, unless it had flown for any distance under the radar coverage. Then it could be anywhere.

At about 6:30 P.M., an American detachment, apparently sent from Carswell Air Force Base, was on the scene of the crash, which had been located by others. The detachment commander was notified that a special photographic unit was going to be dispatched to preserve the scene in pictures. This included the anonymous source who had somehow retained copies of some of the photographs he'd taken of this "top secret plane crash."

Alleged Alien Body Photo
Crash of 7/48

This purported photo of an alien was taken by Col. John W. Bowen and given to researchers at the Mutual Anomaly Research Center and Evaluation Network (MARCEN).

According to this guy, the photographic team was picked up in an L-19 at 9:30 P.M. He said it was uncomfortable in the small airplane with the five team members and all their equipment on board.

He said that they arrived at 2:10 A.M. and circled the area so they got an overview of the crash site. They saw a disc-shaped object that was still burning on a heavily vegetated hill. Apparently, there were no Mexicans, either civilians or military, near the site, and it was in a remote area.

According to the source, although the craft and the debris were unusual, some of it looked as if it had come from Earth. There was, however, an absence of wiring, glass, wood, rubber, or paper. The whole thing looked to be held together by bolts, but they couldn't remove them and finally just used brute force to chisel them off. They used diamond drills and saws, and on the lighter metals used cutting torches so they could disassemble the craft and take it in pieces to the various Air Force facilities for study.

A metallurgist who was unidentified by the photographer, and therefore remains anonymous, apparently told the photographer that the structure was a honey-combed crystalline that was not like anything he had ever seen on Earth. He thought it might be silicon-based.

The body found in the wreckage, and photographed by the source, was about four feet, six inches tall with a large head. There were no eyes, destroyed by either the crash or the fire, but there were eye sockets. There were no visible ears, nose, or lips, and there was just a slit for a mouth without either teeth or a tongue. The arms were longer than a human's would be on that short of a frame and ended in a four-digit claw. The legs were of normal proportions with short feet but no toes. Both the arms and legs seemed to have joints in about the same place as humans.

These details were provided by the source who heard the doctors talking as they conducted their preliminary autopsy on the site while he took pictures. Because he had official business, his movements were not restricted while he was on the site.

The next day, at about 1:00 P.M., a C-47 arrived and the body was then shipped out of Mexico. The man didn't know where it might have gone. What was left of the wreckage was then loaded into trucks to be transported into the United States. He didn't know their destination either.

The photographer wrote that he then returned to White Sands and began to develop the film and make the prints. He worked with a team of other photographic experts and they all were watched by Marines. The team was disbanded when their task was completed and the commander of that detachment, whoever he was, returned to Washington, never to be seen or heard from again.

A few years later, the photographer said he removed forty negatives from the Top Secret file, made duplicates, and then put the original pictures back. That was why he had the pictures of the burned alien creature … or so he said.

William Steinman reported in his book, *UFO Crash at Aztec*, that, according to members of MARCEN, including Willard McIntyre and Dennis Pilichis of The UFO Information Network (UFOIN), and a booklet they wrote, McIntyre and Pilichis were able to secure an original negative. That is, one of the copy negatives that the Navy man had made in the late 1940s or early 1950s. They sent it off to Kodak for analysis. According to Kodak, at least as reported by McIntyre and Pilichis, Kodak found the negative to be at least thirty years old and they could detect no evidence of photographic trickery. Saying nothing about the image contained on the negative, they concluded that the negative showed no obvious signs of tampering.

Ron Schaffner of the old Ohio UFO Investigators League (OUFOIL) put together a report on the photographs, based on research that he had conducted. He said that he, along with colleagues, wrote to Kodak, asking them about the tests they had conducted on the negatives. He wrote about the Kodak response, saying, "We were not surprised when the response came back that Kodak was not aware of any photo work done on the pictures enclosed. Furthermore, their representative said that Kodak would not perform any type of testing that we desired for authenticity."

There were other problems with this story. The L-19 that the photographer rode in could not carry five passengers. It was a modified civilian aircraft that would originally carry four, but the L-19 had been reduced to a two-seat aircraft. That is, it carried a pilot and one passenger.

There is a problem with claiming that the UFO was spotted by radars on the DEW Line. While distance early warning (DEW) was probably discussed in 1948, and military planners realized that a Soviet missile attack would probably come over the North Pole, the line itself hadn't been built yet. It wasn't until February 15, 1954, that the United States and Canada agreed to build the DEW Line, so those radars were not in place in 1948.

The troubling aspect of this case is that the photographer supplied, eventually, two photographs of two bodies he claimed to be aliens. Both are very

A recent photograph of the crash site at Aztec.

gruesome. Both show what was once a living creature that has been badly burned. According to some, those creatures are aliens. To others, they are not.

Although the photographer had claimed there were no wires in the craft, in one of the pictures, you can see the burned remains of those wires. There seems to be other, terrestrially made debris around the body as well, including a six-sided bolt.

The clincher, however, for most UFO researchers, for the skeptics, and nearly anyone else, are the wire frames of a pair of standard-issue aviator glasses without lenses. These can be seen near the left shoulder of the body.

It is quite clear that this photograph, claimed to be an alien, is of a human being killed in an aircraft accident. The burns, and the swelling of the head, are consistent with exposure to high temperatures. Damage done to other areas of the body visible in the picture, and damage done to the wreckage, are consistent with a fire. The man who provided the pictures must have known what they showed, but invented the story of the dead and burned alien to make it sound better.

This is the picture of a human killed in an aircraft accident. It seems wrong that this unidentified source should be able to exploit it in this way. Family and friends of the pilot would be quite distressed to learn what has happened here, but in today's hardened society, no one seems worried about that.

This report should be removed from the ufological records because it has a clear explanation. It should be relegated to a footnote, only because there is published information, both in book form and on the Internet, that claims this might have been extraterrestrial. No matter what a few confirmed believers might think, this has nothing to do with alien visitation.

The Alien Autopsy

It might be said that the story of the alien autopsy doesn't begin in 1995 when the rumors began to circulate, but in 1993 when Ray Santilli met with British UFO researcher Philip Mantle. Santilli, the man who ended up with the film, was or is a British music promoter who had been in the United States searching for footage of some of the early stars of rock and roll. He learned that an elderly man held some key footage that might have been from an early performance of Elvis Presley made in Cleveland, Ohio. Santilli certainly wanted that footage.

Based on information published by Mantle in his *Roswell Alien Autopsy* book and published by Noe Torre of Roswellbooks.com, British rock musician Reg Presley, who had been the lead singer for The Troggs, was told by his manager that Santilli had some film that he, Presley, might find interesting. Presley talked to Santilli and Santilli sent him a copy of what would become known as "The Tent Footage."

This dark and rather unspectacular film showed what was claimed to be the autopsy of an alien creature inside a tent in New Mexico, apparently taken in 1947. Presley said that he contacted two UFO researchers, and all three were convinced the footage had been shot originally on videotape and not photographic film. They were not impressed.

This wasn't the only footage that was rumored to exist. Santilli had suggested there was other footage available but that it was going to cost a great deal of money to buy that film from the owner. Santilli gave Presley more details on the other footage that would eventually be seen by millions in dozens of documentaries about UFOs and UFO crashes aired around the world.

Presley, because of his work on crop circles, had been invited to participate on a live talk show that aired in England on January 9, 1995, though Mantle suggested it was on January 14. Presley called Santilli and asked permission to mention the autopsy footage. Presley would say later that Santilli hesitated, but then gave permission.

At that point Presley had been told that there was other, better footage available and he hoped that claim was true. He might have suspected that he was about to unleash a firestorm and, according to what he told Mantle later, by the time he got home from the live show, his telephone was ringing. There were calls from around the world inquiring about the claims of film of an alien creature.

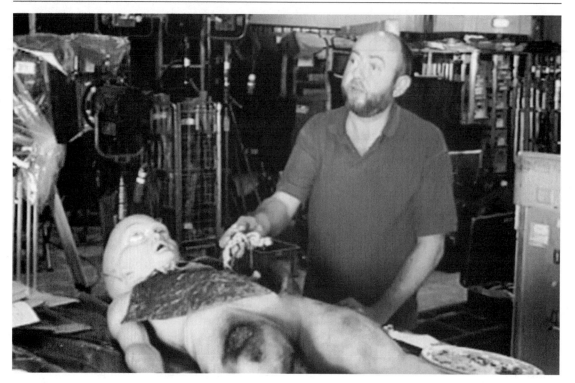

John Humphreys works on the model alien he created.

It was months before Presley, along with crop circle investigator Colin Andrews and another fellow, also interested in UFOs, saw the other rumored footage. This showed an autopsy conducted in what seemed to be a hospital morgue with the doctors dressed in some sort of contamination or chemical protective suits complete with helmets and separate air, and another doctor observing behind some sort of glass wall, wearing a surgical-type mask. This would be the film that would intrigue the rest of the world.

The whole story then, as told by Santilli, suggested that an American Army cameraman who had filmed the autopsy had somehow managed to keep some of that film. These were originally suggested to be "out-takes" or reels that needed special processing, according to the cameraman, but somehow were never returned to Army control. He would later claim that he had been caught in the rift when the Air Force broke off from the Army and that somehow all this highly classified material had gotten lost in the process. It seemed to be a fairly cavalier way to handle material that should have been highly classified, but that was what the man allegedly told Santilli.

Among those searching for answers about the autopsy was an American, Kent Jeffrey, an airline pilot who had an interest in UFOs in general and the Roswell UFO crash in particular. According to Jeffrey's information, Santilli had paid about a hundred thousand dollars for the film but Santilli would later not provide any sort of monetary figure.

The story circulated by Santilli at that time was that the cameraman had made a duplicate of the original film so that the Army wouldn't know that some of it was missing. That was, of course, a different story than the film being "out-takes," which was the original claim. Or an even later claim that somehow, as the Air Force broke off from the Army, no one had ever arrived to claim the film.

There were other reports from other researchers as well. First word was that there were fifteen rolls of film of about ten minutes each. That meant two hours and thirty minutes of footage. There was a preliminary autopsy in a tent, more of an autopsy in a hospital operating room, film of the debris field with President Truman walking across it, and pictures of the craft as it was lifted onto a flatbed truck to be taken out of the area. All of the descriptions sounded as if the film was spectacular and authentic because, if nothing else, it would be nearly impossible to produce the footage of President Truman on the crash site, let alone the film of a huge truck and saucer being lifted onto it by a crane.

More information about this appeared when, in the spring of 1995, Mantle sent a letter to various UFO researchers identifying the cameraman as Jack Barnett. Apparently, according to some sources, Santilli had slipped up and inadvertently revealed the man's real name. Searches began trying to locate any Barnett who had a connection to motion picture photography, whether through the military, old newsreel services, which had been one suggestion, or Hollywood.

Years later, Santilli would say that he had invented the name as a red herring. It took researchers in different directions as they tried to find a Jack Barnett who fit the description that had been developed about the cameraman. None of those searches bore fruit, though it convinced some that the autopsy was a fake.

And it shifted the inquiry from the footage itself to the search for a man. If Barnett could be found, it would go a long way to establish the authenticity of the film.

With interest in the film mounting, Santilli decided that something more had to be done. You might say that he saw an opportunity that was slipping away. An opportunity that he had spent two years creating. He arranged for members of the media, representatives from television networks around the world, UFO researchers, and a few others who could get to London, to screen the film on May 5, 1995.

Kent Jeffrey, because of his airline job and his seniority in his position at the airline, could attend the screening without incurring the costs of an airline ticket to London. After seeing it himself, he would write a lengthy report on his impressions during that screening. In a special bulletin issued by the International Roswell Initiative (an organization Jeffrey had created in an attempt to

Ray Santilli in 1995

uncover more information about the Roswell UFO crash), dated May 25, 1995, Jeffrey outlined his whole experience at the showing of the film. He wrote:

> The film in question is presently in the possession of a company in London, Merlin Productions, owned by a Mr. Ray Santilli. On Friday, May 5, 1995, there was a special showing at the Museum of London. There were approximately one hundred people present.... Despite the fact that the film is totally unauthenticated, it has received extensive publicity in Europe....
>
> The actual showing of the film took place just after 1:00 P.M. in a small auditorium that is part of the Museum of London complex. A handout was distributed at the sign-in table consisting of a copy of the alleged MJ-12 briefing papers and a yellow cover sheet referencing the 1947 Roswell crash and the 509th Bomb Group (at Roswell Army Air Field). Merlin Productions was apparently very concerned about pictures being taken because everyone was physically searched (frisked) for cameras upon entering the auditorium. There was no speaker or announcement to formally welcome those present or to introduce the film. This seems somewhat bizarre and discourteous, as people had come from all over the world for this showing. Also

conspicuously absent was a person on stage afterward to publicly answer questions pertaining to the film....

At about 1:05 P.M., the lights dimmed and the film started rolling. Before the actual pictures began, a few short statements scrolled by on the screen with reference to the film having been "acquired from the cameraman who originally shot the footage" and to the copyright being "exclusively owned by Merlin Communications." Interestingly, one would think that if the film were genuine, the copyright would be "exclusively owned" by the United States government.

Also, contrary to what had been said previously about "10-minute reels," there was now a statement on the screen that the film was recorded on "three-minute" reels....

The film opened abruptly with its single scene of a small operating or autopsy room with plain white walls and a table in the middle containing an unclad body lying face up. Two individuals in white anti-contamination suits, complete with hoods and narrow, rectangular glass face plates, were the only figures visible in the room. A third person, dressed in white hospital-type garb, was visible through a large glass partition, or window. Although he was outside the sealed room standing behind solid glass, he was wearing a surgical mask that covered his entire face....

Jeffrey described the procedures that were followed in the autopsy room as the two doctors circled the body, cutting into it in what seemed to be a rather cavalier fashion. It is clear from the footage that the cameraman was also in the room, circulating and trying to stay out of the way of the doctors, and there was no sign of a mounted camera in that footage. The film was black and white and the focus, at times, was inadequate. It also seemed odd, at least to some, that the cameraman never seemed to get in the way of the doctors, and the doctors never looked at the camera or the cameraman. To some, this suggested footage created with professional actors rather than doctors and an Army cameraman. After all, amateurs always look into the camera at some point, but these guys didn't.

The film was black and white and the focus, at times, was inadequate.

Jeffrey, in his report, wrote, "I would like to state up front and unequivocally that there is no (zero!!!) doubt in my mind that this film is a fraud."

Although there was a claim of many canisters and a suggestion of more than two hours of film, all that was released by Santilli for broadcast by various television networks around the world lasted just over twenty minutes. In addition, there were then scenes of the metallic debris collected and displayed on tables in a single room. A lone figure is seen, moving among it, lifting some of it, but he is photographed from the rear so that his identity, like that of those in the autopsy footage, is masked. There is nothing in any of the scenes that allow for independent verification or for identification of any of those participating at any level.

Before any of the specials could be aired around the world, the *Sunday Times* in London published an article with the headline, "Film that 'proves' aliens visited earth is a hoax." The article, written by Maurice Chittenden, reported that "experts called in by Channel 4 [a British television network], which is due to screen the film as part of a documentary on August 28 [1995], have declared it bogus. A source close to the documentary said: 'We have had special effects guys look at it and they say it's a fake.'"

Chittenden continued in the article, writing, "Among the flaws found by *The Sunday Times* are: 'Security coding' on one film disappeared when its accuracy was challenged. A 'letter of authentication' from Kodak was signed by a salesman. President Truman, supposedly visible on the film, was not in New Mexico at the time [and Mantle said much later that this was not a claim made by Santilli]. Symbols seen on particles of wreckage are totally different to those remembered by an eyewitness. 'Doctors'—performing a supposedly unique autopsy on an alien—remove black lenses from his eyes in a matter of seconds, as if they knew what to expect."

These points were, for the most part, the same that had been raised by UFO researchers during their attempts to verify the authenticity of the film. What was most troubling was not that there were problems, but that the revelation of those problems resulted in an alteration of the story. When evidence was presented that suggested the security markings, for example, were more appropriate to Hollywood than they were to the American military, those markings disappeared. That, in and of itself, suggested the film was a hoax.

Santilli, however, maintained that the film was authentic. To prove it, he was going to allow some of the documentary producers an opportunity to meet with the cameraman. If they could sit and talk with him, then one of the major problems, the lack of provenance, would be eliminated. But the meeting never materialized. John Purdie, the producer of the Channel 4 documentary in Great Britain, did receive a phone call from a man who claimed to be the cameraman. They spoke for two minutes and almost no questions raised by Purdie were answered. It proved nothing.

The Film Analysis

Kodak came up again. In its September 1996 issue, *Fortean Times* reported, "The hint of conspiracy is underlined by Ray Santilli.... Asked whether he still plans to accept Kodak's offer to analyze the film, he answers: 'With all due respect to Kodak, I simply do not trust an American corporation with lucrative defense contracts.' Way to go, Ray."

Small pieces of the film began to circulate in the spring of 1995 as the story began to leak. A short segment of leader, the opaque strip at the beginning of a movie, was provided for analysis. Kodak confirmed that a coding on it, a square and a triangle, suggested the film might be from 1947. The problem was Kodak recycled the codes, so the film could have been manufactured in 1927 or 1967. Besides, there were no images on the leader, so it could have been a piece of film from anything or anywhere, not necessarily from the autopsy footage, and therefore proved nothing other than Santilli had a piece of film with the proper coding on it. It was why Kodak wanted a piece of film with the alien image on it.

Santilli did provide a few people with small sections of film with some kind of image on them. Philip Mantle had three or four frames that contained a brightly lighted doorway, or what might have been a doorway, that might have been part of the autopsy footage, but then again, it might not. Mantle told others that he had no footage with the alien or the interior of the autopsy room visible which would prove that it was part of the film. Just that brightly lighted door that might have been part of the original autopsy footage, or might just have been a few frames of another film used because the film was from the right era.

Bob Kiviat, producer of *Alien Autopsy: Fact or Fiction*, broadcast on Fox Television in the United States in 1995, was also given a small section of film. Again nothing that would identify it as having come from the actual autopsy footage could be seen. His original section of film was even shorter than that provided to Mantle.

Kodak insisted that they could provide fairly accurate dating, but they required several feet of film. They suggested that, over the years, film would shrink, and by measuring the distance between the sprockets, they could estimate the age. Chemical analysis, especially since the basic composition of film had changed after 1947, could provide additional clues. Kodak insisted they receive, at a minimum, one frame with the alien visible on it. That way they would know that their analysis was not being wasted on something that came from another film. That didn't happen and it appears it never will.

But the argument about film testing didn't end there. According to Neil Morris, a UFO researcher living in England, "A piece of film has been tested. Bob Shell's [Shell was one-

Santilli holding a film can containing the movie of an alien autopsy. The film later disappeared.

time editor of *Shutterbug* magazine] fragment was submitted to an Italian University for chemical analysis. The tests concluded the film stock was Kodak Cinepac Triacitate stock but as kodak [sic] had only published details of vers 1 and 2 out of 4 types produced, it wasn't possible to make an exact identification though a very close match was found for type 2. Kodak Triacitate film was phased out in the mid 1950s in favour of the tougher Polyester film base still in use today...."

Which, of course, makes you wonder why it was necessary to go to Italy for the analysis and why it wasn't completed by Kodak. That is not to say that the Italian analysis is of no value, only that since the film was Kodak stock it would have been better to get an answer from Kodak.

Morris also wrote, "Bob Shell allowed his fragment to be tested as he believed at the time it was no use in verifying the films [sic] age, but as I have shown [in other arguments] his fragment matches exactly those seen on Ray's "Footage" VHS tape and when combined with those fragments shows a sheet covered table in what could be the autopsy room with bowls, clipboard, and table. Some clips in the AA [alien autopsy] show a doorway in wall 4 which collates with the doorway seen in Bob's fragment, a doorway and a wall Spyros [Melaris, who was involved in the creation of the film] maintains he did not build in his 'set'...."

But the problem here is that the argument is centered around some speculations and not on concrete evidence. It would seem that if the autopsy was real, then those holding the film would not be playing games with the authentication. They would be providing everything they could to aid in this, unless there was a reason to keep people guessing.

The Cameraman and Authentication

After the British and American specials were aired, there was renewed interest, and Santilli's company began selling raw videotapes of the autopsy footage for about fifty dollars each. It was claimed that additional footage, not seen in the specials, was on the video, but that was of the tent autopsy which was so dark as to be nearly useless as evidence, more of the debris footage, and little else.

Other problems with the film began to surface as well. For example, it had been suggested early on that the film showed the autopsy of the body of a being recovered after the Roswell crash. Other information, including the alleged date of the autopsy and the date of the crash, did not follow the conventional wisdom of the Roswell case. Santilli and his friends, and the cameraman communicating through Santilli, were now suggesting the crash and recovery had taken place more than a month earlier, that is, in late May 1947, and while still in New Mexico, not all that close to Roswell.

Almost universally, UFO researchers, television producers and reporters, and anyone else interested in the film were demanding the cameraman come forward. Without him, to complete the chain of custody, the film was useless. Couple this to the fact that Santilli, to that point, had refused to provide anything that would be of value in authenticating the film, the only conclusion available was that the film was just an interesting aberration and probably a hoax.

Santilli, through his various contacts including Bob Shell, finally offered the cameraman's alleged audiotaped statement. Shell, appearing on Cable Radio Network's September 2, 1995 edition of *UFOs Tonight!* hosted by Don Ecker, said that the transcript being circulated by him and Santilli was an exact transcript of the cameraman's statement given at an earlier date. Under close questioning by Ecker, Shell said that he had heard the original tape and read or typed the transcript himself, so that he could verify the authenticity of the transcript. At any rate, the transcript was an exact copy of what the cameraman had said. This discussion, recorded as a matter of course by Ecker, as he did with all his radio programs, would become important to understanding more about the case.

> Almost universally, UFO researchers, television producers and reporters, and anyone else interested in the film were demanding the cameraman come forward.

During the conversation, Ecker said, "Somebody in the United Kingdom sent me allegedly the cameraman's statement, along with some facsimiles that were allegedly the film labels. Now, a number of weeks ago I read this entire statement verbatim on the air. And I think this is somewhat telling in itself. Now, this is purportedly this gentleman's actual statement. And I think it's very safe to say in this statement may be information he originally gave Ray Santilli, this is not the way an American former serviceman would ever describe himself. Have you...."

Shell interrupted at that point and said, "What you have is probably the first version of that."

"Yeah," said Ecker, ignoring what Shell had said. "And what I'm saying [is] this was passed off as his actual statement by Santilli, originally. And I think it's very safe to say that just ain't so, okay? It was passed off deceptively."

Shell responded by saying, "Well, yeah, but I think you have to understand what exactly happened. The cameraman made a taped statement. The tape was mailed to Santilli ... Santilli had one of his secretaries transcribe it. The secretary is British."

"Okay."

Shell continued. "So quite a bit of British [terminology] got into the transcript.... I have gone over and retranscribed it and posted it this week on CompuServe's library."

Ecker asked, " From the actual tape?"

"Yes."

"You have a copy of the tape?"

"Yes."

Later, Shell would deny that he had heard the actual tape or that he ever spoke to the cameraman. In other words, Shell, if he repaired the "transcript," did so without having heard the tape himself. It would mean that he was altering the transcript for no reason, other than to remove the incriminating British colloquialisms from it.

Santilli, when questioned about the transcript, said, using the same excuse as that given by Shell, that the tape had been transcribed by a British secretary and she had changed the wording. It was a clumsy attempt to explain why common British terms were sprinkled through a statement allegedly made by an American. There would be no reason for a secretary to change the wording, even if some of the American slang made no sense to her. It would also mean that Shell's claims of an exact transcript were false. To put it kindly, he had been mistaken when he said otherwise.

> From Roswell, he was driven overland to the crash site, which, again, makes no sense logistically.

From this "documentation," we learned that the cameraman claimed he remembered very clearly that he had received a call to go to White Sands. On the statement, parenthetically, it says Roswell. But Roswell is not the same as White Sands. The missile range at White Sands was, and is, an Army facility, and it is nearly 150 miles from Roswell. If the cameraman was going to White Sands, why not fly him to the Alamogordo Army Air Field, now Holloman Air Force Base, less than twenty miles away? That part of the statement made no sense, unless it was an attempt to keep Roswell attached to the story for the commercial value of the Roswell name.

The cameraman, apparently casually, made a change in the scenario that is quite significant. He said, "I was ordered to a crash site just southwest of Socorro."

But Socorro isn't to the northeast of White Sands, so the directions are wrong. And flying into Roswell still makes no sense if the destination is Socorro. Either Alamogordo or Albuquerque would make more sense and there were military facilities in both locations.

According to the cameraman, he returned to Washington, D.C., from one assignment. He was then given his orders and flew out of Andrews Army Air Field, onto Wright Field, and then on to the Roswell Army Air Field. From Roswell, he was driven overland to the crash site, which, again, makes no sense logistically.

To anyone who has studied a map of the United States or the Roswell case, there is no reason to do this. Why fly a cameraman from Washington to Dayton, Ohio, and then on to Roswell? Even if they felt the need to land first in Ohio, the trip into Roswell still makes no sense. Why not fly into Kirkland Air Force Base in Albuquerque or directly into Alamogordo? In 1947 there was no interstate highway system, but there was U.S. Highway 85. A trip from either base to Socorro was easy and quick. Today a trip from Roswell to Socorro is still long and difficult and even today it involves a long segment of two-lane highway that is barely wide enough for two cars to pass.

Where Did Santilli Get the Footage?

Under pressure to explain how he found the footage because there seemed to be some holes in his story, to put it kindly, Santilli provided a new scenario for the discovery of the film. Kent Jeffrey, still interested in the case, and still trying to get to the bottom of the story, wrote in the *MUFON Journal*, "… the person from whom he [Santilli] had purchased the Elvis footage was not really a military cameraman after all. He now claimed that he had met the real cameraman after he purchased the rights to the Elvis film from Bill Randle in Cleveland during the summer of 1992 (previously Santilli had given the year as 1993)."

In the August 28, 1995, Channel 4 documentary, Santilli referred to a collector of some sort who had put up the money for the autopsy footage. He had said, repeatedly, that he, Santilli, did not have access to the film itself because the collector had it in a vault. It would be up to the collector to offer samples of the film for analysis. Santilli could do nothing to help researchers, which, of course, was another dodge and a new and different story about the footage.

Michael Hesemann, who was working with, if not for, Santilli, has told many that the alien autopsy footage is from a crash site near Socorro, New Mexico. Hesemann has claimed that he has located the "real" crash site and is the only researcher to have done so (though now, others say they have located it as well, including American Ed Gehrman, who is absolutely convinced he has been to the "real" crash site). Hesemann has also claimed that the real date of this crash is May 31, 1947. Because this is not the Roswell case, Hesemann believes it explains the discrepancies between what researchers have learned about Roswell and the facts that have surfaced around the Santilli autopsy film.

The Tent Autopsy

The whole story turned again in July 1998. Philip Mantle, working with Tim Matthews, alerted their colleagues in the UFO field that the tent footage was faked. They had found and interviewed one man who claimed to have worked on that segment of the autopsy footage. He had explained the situation to Mantle and Matthews.

According to Mantle, Matthews learned that the tent footage had been created by a firm in Milton Keynes called A.R.K. Music Ltd. Those who put the tent footage together had experience with video and computer equipment. Mantle and Matthews named the names of those men involved.

In December 1998 the situation became even more complicated, if possible. Santilli, learning that Bob Kiviat, who had produced the original autopsy

Philip Mantle (left) with Spyros Melaris.

special in the United States for FOX, was now producing a second in which he would show the tent footage was a fake. The spin began again.

According to Santilli, the tent footage was not part of the original alien autopsy film. According to what Santilli was now saying, he had maintained this position all along and had warned Kiviat in 1995 the tent footage was flawed. Santilli claimed that Kiviat was going to run a disclaimer about the tent footage, but in the end, Santilli claims he won and the tent footage was pulled from the broadcast. Of course, it is possible it wasn't used because the footage was of such poor quality, dark to the point of being obscured, that it made no sense to broadcast it although such footage, even in that rough shape, would be of significant historical value. That is, if it could be validated, it would be a valuable historical document even in its poor shape, but that just didn't happen.

According to one version of how the tent footage came to be, it was originally part of the material that Santilli had received from the cameraman but because it was so bad, he had asked a studio in Milton Keynes to do what they could to enhance the image. Sometime after he had received the enhanced image, he returned to the United States to show it to the cameraman. At that point the cameraman said that he didn't remember photographing the tent footage or the style in which it had been filmed.

This, of course, makes no sense because if the cameraman hadn't photographed it, where did it originate? Even if the "re-created" footage was just that, a re-creation, then the cameraman might have wondered about the authenticity, but he would have remembered photographing it.

When Santilli returned to England, he learned that his friend and the owner of the studio had played a joke on him. They had been unable to retrieve anything from the film so he, the studio owner, had staged it as a joke. Santilli, then, not to compromise the importance of the "real" autopsy film, told all that the tent footage should not be used as part of any documentary that included the other autopsy film.

But Santilli went on to say some things that are extremely important. He said that Andy and Keith (one of the men who worked at the studio owned by Andy) were good friends of his. They didn't act out of malice, but just to play a joke on their friend. This statement, however, shows that Santilli did know people who could fake the film, and in fact, had faked some of it.

The "Real" Autopsy Footage

Mantle, having revealed that the tent footage of the autopsy had been "re-created" as a joke, now learned more disturbing things about the rest of the film. What would be the final nail in the alien autopsy coffin had been found. Mantle sent out an Internet alert to various UFO researchers that said:

> The show starts off with Santilli claiming that he saw the real film of aliens and that he purchased it from a former U.S. military cameraman. However, there is now a change in the story. Santilli & his colleague Gary Shoefield claim that it took 2 years to buy the film & that when it finally arrived in London 95% of it had "oxidised" and the remaining 5% was in very poor condition.

> They therefore decided to "reconstruct" it based on Santilli's recollection and a few frames that were left. To do this they hired UK sculptor John Humphreys. Humphreys tells of how he used sheep's brain for the brain and lamb's leg for the leg joint.

> The cameraman's interview film is also a fake. The man in the film is someone they literally brought in off the street and gave him a prepared script to read from.

> Santilli and Shoefield continually try to insist that the AA film as we know it is a restoration, but in fact it was made by John Humphreys.

> To try and justify they claim that some of the surviving original frames are seen mixed in with the reconstruction/restoration. Inter-

Humphreys' model alien, showing the head in detail.

estingly neither Santilli, Shoefield, or Humphreys could point out where and which are these frames when viewing the AA film.

Santilli admitted that the six-fingered panels in the debris film were the result of "artistic license" and he even produced one of the I-beams from the boot of his car. The debris film was also made by John Humphreys.

In fact, Humphreys is the surgeon in the film, and a former employee of Shoefield's in behind the window. He's Gareth Watson, a man I met several times in Ray's office.

Nick Pope and myself appear briefly in this show and I dare say Nick will have his own comments to make.

For anyone interested in the AA film I do recommend watching this if you can. I've taken part in another show for Channel Five in the UK the content of which I am not permitted to disclose.

After watching this tonight I can honestly say that I do not believe one word of either Santilli or Shoefield and I have no doubt that the film is nothing more than a complete fake.

There is and never was any original film and there is and never was any US military cameraman. Santilli & Shoefield had little credibility as it was but now they have none.

The alien autopsy film is dead and I hope to put it to rest, once and for all, soon. Watch this space.

But the truth here seems to be something other than a joke. While Santilli was talking about the joke, another new voice, that of Spyros Melaris, was heard. Melaris had been involved from nearly the beginning, and he had seen the tent footage before almost anyone else. Mantle, in his book *Roswell Alien Autopsy*, laid it out in an interview that he conducted with Melaris.

Spyros Melaris and the Alien Autopsy

According to that interview, Melaris was an aspiring filmmaker in the mid-1990s, and as part of that plan, that is, to find work as a filmmaker, he FAXed to a number of music producers and publishers his plan to be at the MIDEM music industry event in Cannes, France. One of those he FAXed was Merlin Group owned by Santilli and it was one of the few that responded. Santilli planned to meet with Melaris in Cannes to discuss the possibility of making a documentary about that event or other music-related events.

By accident, Melaris ran into Santilli in a restaurant and at that first meeting, Santilli mentioned the tent footage of that autopsy. Although Melaris didn't think much of the tale, he was intrigued enough to agree to meet Santilli in London to see the footage. When he saw it, Melaris' first reaction was that it hadn't been shot on film but on videotape.

Santilli seemed surprised that Melaris pointed that out so quickly, but then, remember, Reg Presley's reaction was that it wasn't film but videotape. Santilli realized that if Melaris spotted the flaw that quickly, then everyone would be able to spot it just as quickly. The tent footage would have to be abandoned.

Even this meeting is now wrapped in controversy, with those insisting that the alien autopsy is real, claiming that Melaris didn't meet Santilli until April 1995. Philip Mantle, as of May 9, 2012, said, "Spyros [Melaris] met him [Santilli] in February 1995 at a TV conference in France. Santilli, who has changed his story many times, says otherwise. The alien autopsy story was in existence long before this. I was contacted by Santilli in 1993. The tent footage was made in 1993."

With that the February 1995 meeting ended, but Melaris wasn't through with either Santilli or the alien autopsy. The idea intrigued him and he talked to a friend, John Humphreys, who was a sculptor who had done some TV and movie special effects. Together they discussed how to do the film right and with that Melaris went back to Santilli, and the idea of the autopsy moved from the tent to a hospital in Fort Worth.

Gary Shoefield (left) and Ray Santilli—Philip Mantle

In his book, Mantle goes into detail about making the creatures. According to what Melaris said:

> John Humphreys of course made the alien's bodies. The mould [sic] was actually based on John's ten-year-old son who was quite tall. As a trained sculptor Humphreys had also studied anatomy so he was the man who played the surgeon in the film in one of the contamination suits and he also played the soldier in the Debris Footage. Gareth Simmons, a colleague of Santilli's and Shoefield's was the man in the surgical mask behind the glass....
>
> According to Spyros the first "Alien Autopsy" film went pretty much as planned. However, upon completion Geraldine [Melaris' girlfriend at the time and not her real name] noticed that a few of the medical procedures were not correct. They therefore had to make another creature and film another one [autopsy].... The foam latex used to fill the dummy had not worked right and an air bubble had left a hollow space in the creature's leg. Humphreys was dispatched to the local

butchers by Spyros to get a leg joint of a sheep. This was inserted into the hollow part in the alien's right leg, a few other things were added, the outside of the leg was gently burnt with a blowtorch and hey presto, the leg wound.

Melaris also told Mantle, as outlined in his book, about the research that went into creating other aspects of the film. Melaris' girlfriend, Geraldine, did the research to ensure that the props were from the proper time frame (even so far as communications with Kodak, in which they learned about the coding system that was recycled every twenty years), and to the way the doctors moved around the alien creature. She made sure that the instruments used, and the "set decoration" such as the autopsy table, were all consistent with the proper period.

Even with the research that had been conducted, even with the attention to detail, there were other clues that this was a hoax. Some of it had nothing to do with the autopsy but can be seen as a sort of "signature." Some-

Spyros Melaris

thing that I noticed when I saw the footage of the debris that was picked up on the crash site. There was an English word visible on one of the I-beams.

In the interview published in *IUR* is a short segment called "The Wreckage and I-Beams." Mantle explained:

> Melaris created the "alien writing" from Greek lettering, ancient Egyptian stylizing, and his own artistic license. (Humphreys then manufactured the wreckage.) The writing on the main large beam, if translated correctly, reads "Freedom." He thought this a fitting name for an alien spacecraft. While designing the letters that spell Freedom, Melaris noticed that if the word is turned upside down, the word "Video" could be discerned. He adjusted some of the letters to better facilitate this reading, so the piece would throw a little red herring into the mix.

It would seem to me that the appearance of an English word, one referring to the medium that would tell the world of the find, is too big a coincidence. Would anything in an alien language and using alien writing show an English word, especially one that suggested video?

Those who believe that the alien autopsy is real reject this clue. In an email dated May 5, 2012, one of those wrote that "there isn't a 'VIDEO' although it

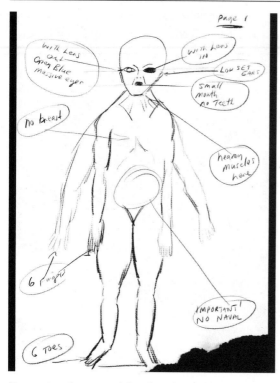

Front view drawing of the alien drawn by Spyros Melaris.

may seem like that at first and there is a resemblance."

Of course it is more than just a resemblance. The word is embedded on one of the I-beams, and although the characters are quite stylized, it does say, "Video."

There were plenty of other clues to suggest the whole thing was a hoax. The classification markings on the film canisters disappeared after they were criticized as belonging to Hollywood rather than the American military. The cameraman, who was crucial to film, was never identified, and years later Santilli would say that he had invented the name that had been "leaked" to UFO researchers.

But the biggest problem is that Santilli would never submit the film for proper scientific analysis. Kodak had said they would be happy to date the film if they were given a segment with the alien on it. Santilli was understandably reluctant, given the nature of the film, but if Kodak could verify the age of the film, it would become that much more valuable. Of course, if they found it to be much younger than the 1947 date, then the value would evaporate.

This controversy should have ended years ago after British television exposed more of the hoax. Philip Mantle then sent a letter to his colleagues in the UFO community. That letter said:

> Tonight showed the SKY ONE TV show "Eamon Investigates— Alien Autopsy."
>
> Philip Mantle

The Arguments Continue

But it doesn't put anything to rest because there are those who continue to believe there is something real hidden in the autopsy footage. The sort of documentary that was done, with the objective goal of learning precisely what is known about the alien autopsy and who did what to bring it into the public arena, should have ended this.

To learn what some of those diehard advocates thought about all this, I sent off a couple of inquiries. I had expected to see a tempering of the attitudes about the film and maybe a little disappointment in what had been released, including the statements made by Santilli and Humphreys, but instead, I learned that they had rejected all that material and were again suggesting that a frame-by-frame analysis would prove that there was something credible about the alien autopsy story.

I emailed Ed Gehrman about these new details, including the admissions by Santilli about the "re-creations" of the hospital autopsy and that Santilli had never revealed who the cameraman was, and without that, there was no provenance for the film.

In responding to these questions, Gehrman wrote:

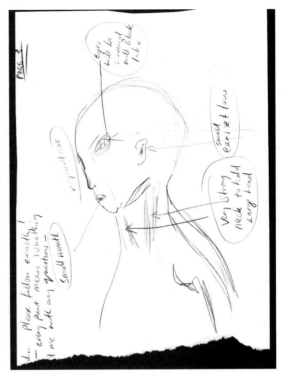

Side view of the alien as drawn by Melaris.

> Why is it up to me to prove the provenance of the footage. It isn't possible until Ray decides to give out some film for testing. But the testing will only give the date the film was produced, not when it was shot so there still would be unanswered questions. Fox did all the research they thought was necessary on the film. They talked to the cameraman, and were willing to accept his story.

> They showed the footage to many special effects persons and pathologists and a host of other experts and all gave the footage their collective OK. Philip Mantle was working side by side with Ray from 1994 on, and defended Ray all the way because he had seen another autopsy. I talked with Bob Kiviat the other day and he told me that there were layers of approval. Fox and others have never sued Ray for fraud. Ray has never changed his story about the cameraman. He has never admitted that he hoaxed anything.

> He stated that some of the footage was destroyed so he "restored" some of the autopsy material. I believe he and crew probably tried to duplicate the footage but never succeeded.

When asked about the faked footage that now not only included that taken in the tent of the alleged original autopsy, but now most of the autopsy in the hospital morgue, Gehrman wrote:

> This is all explainable. The cameraman gave Ray some fragments of film and he took these fragments to some friends who he thought might be capable of connecting them together. These friends could-

n't deal with the fragments but they didn't tell Ray. They decided to make an alien autopsy of their own, which they did and the result was the "tent footage." Have you ever seen this faked footage, beginning to end?

It is nothing like the AA and is obviously a fake and it doesn't contain any information. One of the makers showed the model for the head of the alien which does indeed look like the creature's face.

How did they know what the creature looked like if they didn't have original footage to go by?

Ray's friends gave him the faked tent material, and told him it was the real thing, as a huge joke on Ray.

But they never told Ray the punch line. He thought it was real and began showing it to selected folks and Fox. He then showed it to the cameraman and the cameraman told him it was fake and that Ray should not include it in the package. After that Ray stopped showing it, but some tapes had already been printed so some of the first tapes, which I have, show the tent hoax footage but most don't. It shouldn't be included as criticism of the AA. It's a red herring and eventual dead end. The main joker has admitted, in a letter to Ray that he was totally responsible, and Ray was simply the butt of a bad and misleading joke.

Now, those supporting the film as authentic have added a new twist, which is that some real autopsy footage is mixed in with the faked. They have found, according to them, six places they believe a jump or change in the film can be detected and these lead to identification of the real autopsy footage.

Overlooking the fact that it would be nearly criminal to contaminate the real footage with faked because it would destroy the credibility of all the film, why not just release what is good. There are, according to Santilli and others, about four minutes of the real footage left. There is no need to mix in anything, no reason to create new footage to expand the running time to twenty minutes, no reason to fake anything. Those four minutes, if authenticated, would be nearly priceless. Now, if they truly exist, they are worthless.

But there is another aspect to this. Melaris said that his girlfriend, as they reviewed the film, noticed that some of the medical procedures were not quite right. Melaris decided to reshoot some of the footage and to do that, he needed to create a second creature. When the supporters of the autopsy suggest that there are hints of more film, possibly a second creature, and of some slight changes from the faked footage to the "real," we now know why.

There are two films that were shot. It was necessary to reshoot some of it for "accuracy's" sake. Not real footage of an autopsy of an alien creature, but two separate faked films put together to extend the length of the footage. This explains the subtle changes that some of the autopsy researchers have noticed.

The Last Hurrah of the True Believer

And as noted, the real problem is the lack of a provenance, and that provenance would be the cameraman. I suggested there was no cameraman, and Gehrman wrote:

I believe I know the name of the cameraman. We contacted his second wife before she died but she didn't confirm anything, except he was a cameraman during the war. I have his death certificate and an application for SS. He was active in the US Army until 1945 and then worked for the US armed forces as a private contractor for ten years from 1945–1955. I have small samples of his hand writing and printing and his numbers and they seem to match the writing on the film canisters.

I'm not giving out his name just now. He died in August of 95 right after Ray sealed the Fox contract, but before the TV showing. Ray is protecting his family and I've decided to do the same.

In the end, we are left right where we had begun. Gehrman cannot supply the cameraman's name, though he believed he knows it. He didn't talk to the cameraman, but to his widow, who denied knowing anything about it. There might be a son to give us information, but we don't know that, so we are left with the word of Ray Santilli that the cameraman exists.

The case comes down to this. There is no provenance for the film because Ray Santilli has effectively blocked all attempts to provide it. The film itself has not been independently tested with the results verified by another lab. Kodak demanded, and rightly so, footage with the alien on it. They could have dated the film if allowed to test it.

Santilli said that the tent footage was faked. He said that most of the hospital morgue footage was faked, the men who created the films and the creatures, Humphreys and Melaris, have explained how they did it and why. The debris footage contains an English word, and again we're told how that happened.

Yet we are supposed to believe that there is some "real" footage sandwiched in with all that which is faked. But why even consider that now that nearly everyone involved in the promotion of the alien autopsy has come out to explain it was faked. There is no reason to consider this real and many UFO researchers are surprised that anyone still thinks there is anything of value on the film.

But the stories told by Ray Santilli do have one advantage, at least for him. People still believe and people are still willing to part with their cash to see the film or buy copies of it, and while it is still producing money, Santilli will continue to spin the story.

Aztec, New Mexico

Beginning in the late 1940s, there were many other tales of alien bodies recovered at the site of spacecraft crashes. The first of these to gain widespread recognition, at least in the minds of some, is associated with an alleged crash near Aztec, New Mexico, on March 25, 1948. The basic information was provided publicly by Frank Scully who was a columnist for *Weekly Variety*, a tabloid devoted to Hollywood news and not known for its hard-hitting journalism.

In his first article, published on October 12, 1949, Scully wrote about a crashed saucer in the Mojave Desert with information of a second, smashed disc found in the Sahara. Neither of these two crashes would be explored in detail and the locations of the crashes would be changed in later accounts. Or it might be said that the number of crashes was expanded from there.

According to Scully's article, "The one that landed in Africa was more cracked than a psychiatrist." Scully claimed there had been sixteen men inside the saucer and no women, all small, "about the size of Singer Midgets. They weren't Singer Midgets because all these have been accounted for. Neither were they pigmies [sic] from the African jungle."

Scully reported that the interior of the saucer was loaded with pushbuttons and control instruments but that no one, after they entered the craft, had wanted to push anything for fear of blowing themselves up. He also said they had bombarded the ship with cosmic rays and Geiger devices to make sure there was nothing lethal hidden inside, though, of course, the Geiger counter measures radiation but doesn't produce it, which suggests something about Scully's scientific knowledge.

About a year later, Scully would publish *Behind the Flying Saucers* which greatly expanded on this story and a couple of other columns he had written

Welcome sign outside of Aztec, New Mexico.

about UFOs. His focus in the book was the flying saucer crash near tiny Aztec, New Mexico, in March 1948. He also mentioned two other crashes that had taken place in Arizona including one in Paradise Valley. There was little or nothing about the Mojave Desert or the Sahara crash.

According to Scully's sources, one of which was later identified as Silas Newton, and according to Newton's sources, one of which was a man later identified only as "Dr. Gee," three radar stations, including an experimental site situated on a mountaintop, spotted one of the saucers traveling at eighteen thousand miles per hour at about ninety thousand feet. The experimental radars were equipped with a high-power beam that, according to these sources, interfered with the power generation of the craft, knocking it down.

Because there were three radars involved in the sighting, they could triangulate the position of the crash and the military was quickly dispatched for the retrieval. According to Scully and his sources, they spent two days observing the craft before they ventured close to it. Inside they could see the bodies of the flight crew. Probing with a long stick through a small hole in a porthole, they hit a button or knob or a switch that activated a hatch, opening the craft.

The bodies, all sixteen of them as Scully had noted in his October 1949 column, were laid out on the ground. They were between three and three and

Abandoned radar site in New Mexico.

a half feet tall (thirty-six to forty-two inches), had dark brown skin, were perfectly normal, meaning they were well-proportioned humans except for their small size, and were wearing old-fashioned clothes made of some strange cloth that was nearly indestructible.

The craft and the bodies were taken to Wright-Patterson Air Force Base. The bodies, or at least some of them, were dissected and were found to be human in every way, except they all had perfect teeth. When the study was completed, some sources suggested that the bodies were buried, but it is unlikely that they would dispose of what could be thought of as unique biological specimens in such a cavalier fashion. That means they would be stored for further research.

Scully said that he had been able to examine some of the material recovered, which suggests in the world today that he might have been in on the hoax from the beginning. He said he had seen a "tubeless" radio and some small gears that belonged to either Newton or Dr. Gee. Scully said that the metal had been extensively tested by undisclosed laboratories, but no one had been able to identify the material, or rather that was what Scully had been told by his source or sources.

Scully was sure of his information and produced his book *Behind the Flying Saucers*, which was published in September 1950. Scully may have been reluctant to name names in the beginning, but in 1950, Silas Newton gave a lecture at the University of Denver in which he discussed, to some extent, the Aztec UFO crash. This lecture, according to the story, was Scully's attempt to learn the truth about UFOs and the crashes and the bodies, and to learn what the general public might believe about flying saucers. Because of the positive reaction there, he decided to go ahead with his book.

The FBI and Aztec

An outgrowth of that lecture, because of the publicity generated by it, was an internal FBI document dated March 22, 1950 from SAC Guy Hottel in Washington. He was sending the report on to the director of the FBI and this concerned the flying saucers. Clearly, in 1950, there was still an interest in the subject at the highest levels of the FBI and the March date means it was sent in prior to the publication of *Behind the Flying Saucers* but after the Denver lecture.

Hottel wrote, "An investigator for the Air Forces stated that three so-called flying saucers had been recovered in New Mexico. They were described as being circular in shape with raised centers, approximately 50 feet in diameter. Each one was occupied by three bodies of human shape but only 3 feet tall, dressed in metallic cloth of a very fine texture. Each body was bandaged in a manner similar to the blackout suits used by speed flyers and test pilots."

In the second paragraph, he wrote, "According to Mr. ... information, the saucers were found in New Mexico due to the fact that the Government has a very high-powered radar set-up in that area and it is believed the radar interferes with the controlling mechanism."

He ended the report by writing, "No further evaluation was attempted by [redacted] concerning the above."

It does seem odd that here is a report of three UFO crashes in which bodies were recovered, Hottel has the name of the man reporting this, and a suggestion that the Air Force is involved, but he is going to do nothing more with it. This suggests that he knew that the information wasn't very good but was passing along what he had heard anyway, which in this case was little more than rumor, and then he considered the matter closed.

The story of the memo, at least as discovered by Karl Pflock as he investigated the Aztec crash, was that story originated in the *Wyandotte Echo*, a newspaper in Kansas City, Kansas. That information was provided by Rudy Fick, who said he learned of it from I. J. Van Horn and Jack Murphy, who mentioned Coulter, who was in reality George Koehler. Koehler got his information from Silas Newton, and the circle is now complete.

In fact, Koehler's name surfaced early in the original investigations of the Denver lecture. J.P. Cahn wrote, in a 1952 exposé about the Aztec UFO crash and Silas Newton in *True*, that "To test public receptivity to the saucer revelation, the oil man-geophysicist appeared as an anonymous guest lecturer before a University of Denver elementary-science class on March 8, 1950, escorted by George T. Koehler, who is a salesman for Denver radio station KMYR. The lecturer told in detail of Dr. Gee's findings and drew some blackboard diagrams. News of the lecture leaked, of course, beyond the cloistered walls, and the how-come of university sponsorship raised a local tempest that blew off the lecturer's cloak of anonymity. His name was Silas M. Newton...."

It does seem odd that here is a report of three UFO crashes in which bodies were recovered, Hottel has the name of the man reporting this, and a suggestion that the Air Force is involved, but he is going to do nothing more with it.

In 1991, William E. Jones and Rebecca D. Minshall from the MidOhio Research Associates published a preliminary study on their investigation into the Aztec crash in general and the Denver lecture in particular. They acknowledged William Steinman and his claims about Newton's Denver lecture that appeared in Steinman's book *UFO Crash at Aztec*. Jones and Minshall thought it would be a good idea to talk with Francis F. Broman who, according to the legend of this story, had been a science teacher at the University of Denver in 1950. It was to his class that this mysterious lecturer, Silas Newton, told of his involvement in the Aztec retrieval. In June 1991, they located Broman. They wrote, "Mr. Broman essentially verified what Steinman had written about the incident. For the record, the class was entitled 'Science and Man.'"

They went on to say that Broman was contacted by some sort of government official after the class. He was never sure if it was the FBI or Army intelligence, he just didn't remember. He said the telephone interview took place within a couple of hours of the lecture and the caller wanted to know what he and his colleagues thought of the information presented. Broman said that he had found the presentation unconvincing, as did many of those who attended it.

With Scully now convinced that the book would be taken seriously and that people would be interested, he went ahead and finished it. It was published in September and was a hit, climbing the bestseller list. With that sort of interest, several newspapers and magazines were interested in verifying the information contained in it. After all, if it could be proven that a flying saucer had crashed, it would be the biggest story of the last one thousand years. Dr. Gee believed that the doomed flight had originated on Venus. In 1950 no one knew that Venus had a surface temperature that could melt lead, which effectively ruled it out as a point of origin. Most thought of it as a planet covered with tropical oceans and islands, which accounted for the impenetrable cloud cover.

J. P. Cahn and the Aztec Crash

J. P. Cahn was commissioned by *True*, though some suggest he was on a freelance assignment without a formal promise of publication, to learn the whole story of Newton, Dr. Gee, and the Aztec crash. When the *San Francisco Chronicle* passed on the story, afraid of lawsuits, Cahn approached the editors of *True*. This magazine had published much of what Major Donald Keyhoe had to say about flying saucers, and now, according to Cahn, he was assigned to learn what he could about Scully's claims, the flying saucer crash landing, and the mystery men Scully cited as his sources. Cahn lost no time in beginning his investigation into Scully, Newton, Dr. Gee, and the flying saucer crash outside Aztec.

The first thing that came out was that Newton's background was not as pristine as he had suggested. He had boasted that he had rediscovered the Rangely Oil Fields in Colorado, but others said that simply wasn't true. Colorado oilmen said that there was no evidence for this claim. Both Newton and the mysterious Dr. Gee, in the guise of Leo GeBauer, would eventually be convicted of fraud in some kind of scam that involved a device to locate oil and the rediscovery of the fields. All of this came about after Scully's book and Cahn's exposé were published and might be irrelevant here except as a testament to the character of the men involved.

But to be fair, it seems that Newton's background wasn't entirely disreputable. Newton apparently held an undergraduate degree in geology and he attended both Baylor and Yale. It seems that he held some sort of two-year degree from Baylor and he was a graduate of Yale. In the early twentieth century, having any degree was important and Newton apparently not only had a degree but one from an Ivy League school.

He also was apparently an accomplished golfer. According to Frank Warren, and according to several period newspapers, Newton won a number of tournaments, including the 1918 Virginia State Amateur Golf Championship. Later he seemed to have won a number of championships in Colorado.

There are suggestions that Newton was a multimillionaire before he got caught up in the Aztec story. Again, according to Frank Warren and to an article published by the Associated Press on October 31, 1930, Newton's net worth was something like forty million dollars. There is no confirmation of the wealth other than Newton's claim and the newspaper article.

Newton, in a letter to Frank Scully on July 2, 1951, wrote that "I've made and lost millions in the oil business and I've been in it most of my life…. I've been broke, but I can go back and to any place I've ever been and I think I'm welcome…."

But not all the references for Newton were as good. In 1955, Newton was in court for selling fifteen thousand dollars of worthless securities in Utah. In 1958, he was again in court that involved one hundred thousand dollars and two others. In fact, some information suggested that Newton was in legal trouble as early as 1928 and when he died in 1972 had an estate of just sixteen thousand dollars, though others suggest it was no more than twelve thousand. He had debts that totaled more than $1.3 million, according to probate records.

Frank Scully

Cahn, trying to find the truth of the story, eventually arranged a meeting with the seemingly reluctant Newton and told him that he, Cahn, was authorized to pay up to thirty-five thousand dollars for the story of the UFO crash and all its ancillary components, providing that Newton could prove his claims. Newton then showed Cahn some photographs and several small discs or gears that Newton claimed were of some mystery metal that came from the recovered flying saucer.

Cahn, of course, wanted one of the discs for independent analysis but Newton was reluctant to let any of them go. If this was truly metal from an alien spaceship, then Newton might have trouble getting more, so his reluctance is understandable. He said he would provide documentation to prove they were pure but he wouldn't allow Cahn to have one for independent testing. This is usually a sign that there is something wrong.

Cahn had several small discs made, based on his memory of what those held by Newton looked like. Cahn figured that at some point he might have the opportunity to switch one of his discs with one of those belonging to Newton. To age them properly, he carried them around in his pocket so that when, during one of their meetings Newton displayed the discs again, Cahn was ready. However, he was horrified to see that none of his fakes looked much like those Newton had. His were thinner and lighter and smaller. He used the heaviest, the one that resembled Newton's discs the most, to make a switch. Newton noticed nothing and wrapped up Cahn's fake with the others and put them back in his pocket.

Cahn took the disc to Stanford laboratories for analysis. They found it to be rather poor grade aluminum that contained no traces of anything they couldn't identify and instead of withstanding temperatures up to 10,000 degrees as Newton claimed, it melted at 650 (F) degrees. Lead melts around 800 (F) degrees so if the object came from Venus, it would have been molten just sitting on the surface of the planet.

But now, in a new book, *The Aztec Incident* by Scott and Suzanne Ramsey, this switch of tiny discs is retold. According to them, Newton suspected that something like that might happen and that he didn't trust everything Cahn had been saying. Newton created some fake discs of poor-quality metal so that when Cahn made the switch—stole in both the words of Cahn and the Ramseys—Cahn was taking a fake. The point was to cost Cahn some money by having him test a fake sample.

> GeBauer admitted to Cahn that he was the mysterious Dr. Gee, though Scully would suggest that Dr. Gee was a composite of eight men.

Cahn was also able to learn the identity of Dr. Gee to his satisfaction (and apparently by accident). He was checking the telephone calls made by Newton and noticed that many went to Leo GeBauer in Arizona. Dr. Gee, according to the tale, had been a chief research scientist during the Second World War and had studyied magnetism with an eye to defeating some of the enemy's detection capabilities. It was also thought that by masking the magnetic signature of ships, some mines that used magnetism as a fusing device would be rendered useless.

More research found that GeBauer had a degree in electrical engineering from Louis Institute of Technology in Chicago, but he had never been in charge of 1,700 scientists as claimed by Scully in his book. In fact, while GeBauer was supposed to be running these highly classified projects for the U.S. government, he was actually working in AiResearch where he was responsible for keeping the lab machinery working. It other words, he wasn't much more than a glorified maintenance man who happened to have a degree in electrical engineering.

GeBauer admitted to Cahn that he was the mysterious Dr. Gee, though Scully would suggest that Dr. Gee was a composite of eight men. Other investigators would repeat that claim. There was no single person who was Dr. Gee. He was a composite. Not that it matters. GeBauer later tried to retract his statement about being Dr. Gee.

The Ramseys also suggest that GeBauer never admitted to this. They publish a letter by GeBauer in which he denies the claim. In a "To Whom It May Concern" letter that is undated, GeBauer wrote, "I have been asked by J. P. Cahn of the San Francisco Chronicle if I were the Dr. Gee in Scullys [sic] book. I am making this statement to all concern: I am not the Dr. Gee mentioned in the book...."

Ignoring the letter and the subsequent denials, Cahn was satisfied that the story was a hoax, concocted by Newton and GeBauer and using the idea of alien technology to lend a note of science to their machinery. Cahn didn't believe that Scully was directly involved in the hoax, but he must have had some suspicion, especially when the truth about Newton began to surface. Reportedly, Scully was annoyed when he learned that the story was a lie … at least some suggested this later.

Scully, however, published a piece just prior to the publication of the Cahn exposé and after he had received many negative reviews of his book. Not that the negativity mattered much because the book was a national bestseller and Scully claimed he was offered seventy-five thousand dollars for the film rights. Scully told the movie studio they'd need a lot more money because Dr. Gee had said he would not talk even if offered twenty million.

Which seems to contradict the claim that Dr. Gee is a composite of eight scientists. There were, in fact, many such contradictions in the various stories told by Newton and GeBauer, not that it mattered all that much. The killer blow was their convictions for fraud. If nothing else could stop the Aztec story, this could do it. Two of the principals were convicted of fraud in a federal court.

With that, nearly all reports of flying saucer crashes were rejected by UFO researchers as well as nearly everyone else. This one tale, that had given so much hope to researchers early on, had been jerked away and it affected UFO research for decades. No one was interested in tales of flying saucer crashes regardless of the source, regardless of the credibility, number of witnesses, or the quality of the evidence.

Robert Spencer Carr and the Aztec Crash

But this tale was not dead yet. At a press conference in 1974, a retired university professor, Robert Spencer Carr, claimed that he had talked to five people who had inside knowledge of a flying saucer crash and he believed it to be the Aztec case. Carr refused to reveal his sources, but he did manage to intrigue the national press for a couple of weeks with his story.

As he told it, the facts matched those which Scully had reported two and a half decades earlier. He did talk about the radar stations and the triangulation. He suggested the landing was a soft one, on a triangular gear. Carr said law enforcement got there with guns drawn and approached the thirty-foot-in-diameter ship. Through a thumb-sized hole in the dome of the disc, they could see twelve little men slumped near their instruments.

Carr said the military and the scientists, who had arrived after the sheriff managed to open the door, removed the bodies. They were muscular and solid with light hair and blue eyes. They all wore the same clothes, which were some kind of blue uniform.

Len Stringfield.

These bodies were taken to Edwards Air Force Base rather than to Wright-Patterson, but were later moved, along with their craft, to Wright-Patterson. One of the bodies was dissected with surgeons flown in from Washington, D.C. Their blood type was "O." Carr claimed to have received the information from a nurse who was involved with the dissection and she said that she could think of no reason to take this story to her grave. She apparently did not explain the blood type.

Under pressure from the press and UFO researchers, Carr still refused to name any names. He underscored that he had five sources, but he was going to hold those names in confidence because he had promised to do so. At that point, for me and for many others, Carr's tale moved into the realm of fantasy. There was no way to verify anything that Carr said, and he was repeating, to some extent, the Scully tale which we all believed to have been discredited and without the names of the sources or some other clues, there was nothing more to be done.

Len Stringfield, who reopened the research into what he termed Crash/Retrievals, talked to Carr privately. According to what Stringfield would later say, Carr did reveal the names and Stringfield said he knew the names too. Stringfield would not reveal the names either, but Stringfield's comments carried a great deal of weight with those inside the UFO community. Where Carr would be dismissed because of the confidentiality and his lack of standing inside UFO research, Stringfield would be believed because of his credibility.

In 1975 Mike McClelland wrote an article for *Official UFO* claiming that "The UFO Crash of 1948 is a Hoax." He provided a look at both Carr's new story and Scully's old and found they were generally similar but had some sharp disagreements.

McClelland also wrote that he had interviewed several "highly reliable 'old-timers' from Aztec, including Deputy Sheriff Bruce Sullivan, who would have been in high school at the time of the UFO crash. According to McClelland, "He has lived in Aztec all his life and 'never knew or heard anything about it.'"

Coral Lorenzen, who had founded APRO, talked to Sullivan after the Carr story broke in the newspapers in 1975. Sullivan told her that he had deputies out combing the area for any information that would prove or disprove Carr's claims. Sullivan told Lorenzen, "Nothing has been found."

McClelland also interviewed Lyle McWilliams, who had been in business in Aztec his whole life and was thirty-two in 1948. According to McClelland, "He recalls nothing of the incident except for the original claim and has always treated it as a joke."

That testimony is interesting because McWilliams does remember the first story to appear in Scully's book, and that was only about a year or two after the crash. Surely, had something happened, McWilliams would have known about it at the time.

McClelland interviewed Marguerite Knowlton who lived near Hart Canyon since 1946. Hart Canyon is where the UFO came down, but according to her, nothing happened near the canyon, and that would include heavy equipment brought in to create the roads and remove the crashed craft. She did suggest that McClelland talk to George Bowra, who owned the Aztec newspaper in 1948.

McClelland interviewed Bowra, who said that he had not carried anything in the newspaper about the event in 1948. He had, however, done an article that suggested he had been abducted by aliens. It was done tongue-in-cheek and wasn't meant to be believed.

McClelland concluded—based on the work he had done, the people he had interviewed, and the reactions of most to his questions—that nothing had happened. They were aware of Aztec's brush with UFO crashes, but they believed it had all come from the book by Scully rather than any firsthand knowledge. It was something stuck in the folklore of the town, but it wasn't something that had happened.

William Steinman, Wendelle Stevens, and Aztec

And while this seemed to end the questions for a while, it certainly wasn't the end of the Aztec story. In 1986, William Steinman along with Wendelle Stevens published *UFO Crash at Aztec*. The Aztec story was revitalized once again, with the claims of new witnesses, new information, and better corroboration. But it was nothing more than a rehash of the information published by Scully with injections of Steinman's personal investigation and escapades in Aztec.

Steinman's tale followed that given by Scully in which the craft had been tracked by three radars and the downed craft was located outside of Aztec, New Mexico. The scientific team, backed up by members of the military, checked the craft, but could find no seams or rivets or cracks. It looked as if it was something that had been cast in one solid piece.

Unable to find any sign of a door or hatch, they used a hammer to break through the glass of a porthole and then used a long pole to push buttons on a control panel. This opened a door and allowed the scientists entry into the craft.

Eventually all the bodies were removed and taken away for study elsewhere. The craft was also removed for study. Steinman, enamored with the mythical MJ-12 committee, put the names of these men into the story, explaining what their roles were, or rather, might have been back in 1948. Unfortunately, before Steinman begin his research, all those identified as members of MJ-12 had died.

Steinman did travel to Aztec to conduct a search. After he made a stop at the newspaper and searched through the back issues from February to June 1948, which yielded nothing, he drove around the town. He found a sign advertising a garage sale and being something of a "garage sale fanatic" according to him, he stopped by. Here was his first break because when he mentioned the UFO crash to Vivian Melton, she told him that she knew about it and she knew where it had happened.

While this was an interesting lead, and with Harvey Melton, Vivian's husband, helping, Steinman was able to find the crash site. The problem here is that the Meltons didn't arrive in Aztec until 1972, so they had seen nothing themselves. They were, at best, secondhand witnesses to the crash.

Through the Meltons, Steinman also interviewed a man Steinman identifies only as W. M. Although Steinman in the mid-1980s wrote that W.M. had died, Jones and Minshall, in the early 1990s, were able to identify W. M. as Wright G. McEwen, who was still alive. Steinman suggested that McEwen had been a deputy sheriff in 1948 and had left town shortly after the crash, apparently afraid for his life and of what he had seen.

Jones and Minshall learned that McEwen had in 1948 been a deputy, but he knew nothing of the UFO crash. His wife, who also lived in Aztec at the time, knew nothing about it and said that the town was small and had something like that happened, they all would have known about it quickly.

Jones and Minshall interviewed Pat Melton, the daughter of Vivian and Harvey. She said that Steinman had upset a lot of the people in Aztec with his aggressive style of interview. You might say it was more like an interrogation. And he put words into people's mouths about the events. He made a "lot of speculative assumptions," according to Pat Melton. She said that many in Aztec did not like his approach to the investigation or his conclusions drawn from it.

Another of those who had been around Aztec in 1948 was Henry Knowlton, and he believed he had once owned the land where the crash is said to have happened. He bought it in the 1950s from Harold Dunning and later sold it to Rowland Chaffee. When Jones and Minshall asked him about the UFO crash, he said the story had been around for a long time, he didn't know how it started, but it wasn't true.

What this tells us is that Steinman's view of the Aztec crash is badly skewed by his enthusiasm for the tale, his inability to separate fact from fantasy, and his hearing one thing from the locals and turning it into something else.

Aztec slab and concrete slab that was allegedly poured to support the crane to remove the saucer. They are important only because they are there, and Ramsey has attempted to test them so he can date them … so far the tests have not been completed.

Using Steinman's own words, this can be demonstrated. On page 256 of his book, he wrote, "I went and confronted Mr. W. M. at his farm on 8 July 1982. There, I introduced myself and immediately asked the question: 'What can you tell me concerning the crash and recovery of a flying disc by the U.S. Military out in Hart Canyon in 1948?'"

According to Steinman, "W.M. got down off his tractor and straightening himself up, stated, very belligerantly [sic], 'Nothing happened out in Hart Canyon in 1948!! Why do you people from so far away keep asking about that flying saucer crash?'"

On that same day, which would be July 8, Steinman "confronted" Mr. H. D. who was Harold Dunning, and who owned the land back in 1948. When he asked about the UFO crash, Dunning apparently snapped, "I don't know anything about what you are talking about—now leave me alone!!"

Steinman wrote, "I Sensed [sic] a tenseness and nervousness in his voice, almost as if he were at one time coerced and coached into answering in that way."

Of course another way to look at it is that Dunning, an eighty-three-year-old man when Steinman was there, was tired of repeated inquiries into something that had not happened. He was tired of being asked the same things and snapped, not because he had been coached, as Steinman speculated, but because he didn't like being interrupted for nonsense.

Steinman added nothing of consequence to the Aztec tale, other than his wild speculations and relatively poorly researched conclusions. Some of what he wrote is obviously in error and the rest is not based on solid ground. All he did was keep the Aztec story alive a little longer until others had a chance to review his work and his conclusions.

And once again the Aztec case went dormant. If it was mentioned at all, it was as a hoax perpetrated by Newton and GeBauer and aided by Scully, though he was often characterized as the innocent dupe of the two con men.

Scott and Suzanne Ramsey and the New Investigation

But rumors began to circulate that another investigation, one that had lasted more than twenty years, had uncovered spectacular new information and that Aztec was not a hoax. This new information would convince many of the reality of the crash and we all just had to wait until the information was properly organized and then published.

It was Scott and Suzanne Ramsey who had conducted the lion's share of the research, but they were aided by Frank Warren and Dr. Frank Thayer, and all four are mentioned on the cover of the book. This would break the case wide open with better evidence. And, at first, it looked as if it might.

In the very first chapter there is a discussion of Doug Noland, a longtime resident of Aztec who made a name for himself in other arenas but eventually moved to Arizona. Noland was quoted heavily, but the taped interview was conducted by someone named Randy and Scott Ramsey didn't know who this Randy was.

Ramsey said the tape came to him from John Lear, but Lear didn't remember who Randy was, though Lear was also at the interview, now characterized as more of a conversation than an interview. Although he didn't tape it, Ramsey did interview Noland before Noland died, and he did take notes.

Noland talked about how he and Bill Ferguson had ended up in Hart Canyon on March 25, 1948. They arrived after a number of the locals and some police, but before the military could get there to take over. Noland said that they crawled all over the object until they found a small hole in one of the portholes. According to Noland, as reported by Ramsey, "Bill, who was ignoring the orders to stay away from the craft, was trying to poke around the craft with a fire-

Scott Ramsey

pole or something he pulled off one of the trucks. Soon he hit some damn thing, and a door or walkway appeared. Some of us had to look inside and see what the hell else was in there...."

But Scully, whose authority was the mysterious Dr. Gee, wrote, "When we arrived on the ground they decided the best thing to do was not to touch it or try to get into it. They studied the ship from a distance for a matter of two days...."

Continuing with this tale, Scully wrote that Dr. Gee said, "... we decided that it was probably safe.... Apparently, there was no door to what was unquestionably the cabin. The outside surface showed no marking of any sort, except for a broken porthole.... Finally we took a large pole and rammed a hole through this defect in the ship.... We assumed that there must have been a door of some kind ... so we prodded around with the pole ... on the opposite side from the broken porthole, we hit a knob, or a double knob ... to our amazement and surprise, a door flew open."

This statement from Scully and attributed to Dr. Gee seems to contradict the statement made by Doug Noland that his friend, on the scene for only a short period, used a pole to open the door. There is no way to reconcile these differences other than to say that when Noland was interviewed in the mid-1990s, the story told by Scully and the Aztec case had been well publicized. There had been two books and any number of newspaper and magazine articles about it. Noland's testimony, such as it was, could have been contaminated.

Other witnesses offered are not much in the way of witnesses. There is Virgil Riggs who lived in the Aztec area and had seen the "armada" of UFOs over Farmington, New Mexico, in 1950. He had heard about the Aztec crash, but he had seen nothing himself. In fact, his father, who sometimes participated in discussions of the crash in an Aztec café, didn't believe that it had happened.

Riggs, however, as an Air Force-enlisted man stationed in England, met another low-ranking enlisted man, Donald Bass, nicknamed "Sam," who claimed to have participated in part of the retrieval operation.

According to what Riggs told to Ramsey, Bass had been part of a guard detail at the Aztec site. He'd seen the bodies as they were loaded onto trucks and believed they had been taken to Ohio, apparently meaning Wright-Patterson Air Force Base.

In an interesting little tidbit, Bass had said there had been a late snowstorm in the area. He was surprised to see the snow accumulate on the military vehicles, but it apparently didn't stick to the alien craft. This is the first and only mention of snow at that time.

Ramsey, of course, wanted to talk to Bass. He was the guy who had seen everything, but he had some difficulty tracing him. He eventually had some luck in finding the family, only to learn that Bass had been killed in Vietnam by a hit-and-run driver.

A check of the Vietnam Veterans Memorial website was unable to confirm this. No one named Donald Bass was killed in Vietnam. No one named Bass had been killed while serving with the Air Force in Vietnam, and no one named Bass had been killed by a hit-and-run driver while in Vietnam.

Of course that only means that the information that Ramsey obtained from another source about the fate of the man is inaccurate, but says nothing about the overall story. It was second-hand, at best, and without corroboration from Bass it adds little to the overall case.

Solon Lemley Brown

According to Ramsey, Walter Sayre was the son of a deacon in a Baptist church. Solon Lemley Brown was the pastor. Brown was making the rounds of various congregations in the Four Corners area (meaning Colorado, New Mexico, Arizona, and Utah) and on one of his trips, in the early morning, came across the activities out near Hart Canyon. He was either asked to help, or followed the cars out to the canyon to see if he could help.

When he got to the top of the mesa, he saw the disc-shaped craft and was approached by a police officer who told him there were bodies inside. He was told that the military was coming and about all he could do was look inside. He saw two or three bodies slumped over their control panels or in their seats.

Before he could do much, or see much, the military arrived to take control. Brown didn't know if they were Air Force or Army. They separated everyone into groups but Brown stood off to the side with the police officers. He watched as the military men brought out some of the bodies.

In minutes, the man in charge of the military came over and told Brown that what he had seen was of the highest military secret and he could never tell anyone what he had seen. Brown asked questions that were ignored. Eventually he left the mesa.

He returned to his church, but felt he had to confide in someone even though he'd been told only hours earlier to say nothing. He selected one of the deacons of his church to confide in. That evening he told Bruce Sayre and his son Walter what he had seen. Brown was so overcome with emotion as he related the story that tears streamed down his face. Walter Sayre remembered this because he'd never seen a man cry before.

Once again, the testimony is not from the witness, but from someone who heard the story from a witness. According to Ramsey, Sayre was sincere in what he described, and the scene seemed to have been emotional enough that it stuck in his mind.

The problem is that Ramsey was able to locate Brown's son, Dr. Autrey Brown, also a man of the cloth. Autrey Brown told Ramsey that he had never heard the story from his father but did confirm that if his father had been sworn to secrecy, he would not have told his son about it. This seems to contradict the fact that Brown told his deacon about the crash.

Brown did say that his father had been pastor in a church not all that far from Roswell and he believed that members of that congregation had mentioned something about the Roswell crash to him. Autrey Brown wondered if it wasn't possible that Walter Sayre had misunderstood what had been said about the location of the crash and the time frame in which it occurred.

The End of Aztec?

This is a case that simply will not die. Those who advocate it today suggest that we remove Scully, Newton, and GeBauer from the equation and begin looking at the new evidence that has been found. Ignore the fact that the reports originated in Scully's *Variety* column and that the first column was anything but serious … and ignore the fact that some of the crash locations shifted as the story evolved.

With all the research that has been carried out, it would seem that the evidence would be a little more convincing than it is. Realizing that the events took place more than a half-century ago and that many of the primary witnesses, if there were any, are long gone, it still seems as if there is more to suggest hoax than reality.

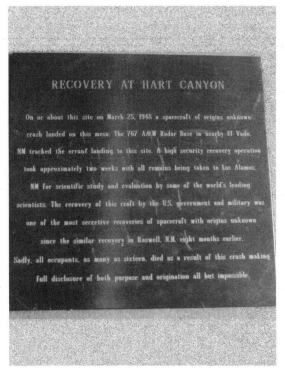

RECOVERY AT HART CANYON

On or about this site on March 25, 1948 a spacecraft of origins unknown crash landed on this mesa. The 767 A&W Radar Base in nearby El Vado, NM tracked the errant landing to this site. A high security recovery operation took approximately two weeks with all remains being taken to Los Alamos, NM for scientific study and evaluation by some of the world's leading scientists. The recovery of this craft by the U.S. government and military was one of the most secretive recoveries of spacecraft with origins unknown since the similar recovery in Roswell, N.M. eight months earlier. Sadly, all occupants, as many as sixteen, died as a result of this crash making full disclosure of both purpose and origination all but impossible.

A sign commemorating the Aztec incident.

There is one other aspect to this story. Karl Pflock, who had been around UFO research since the 1960s and who had been a member of the NICAP Washington, D.C., committee, looked into the Aztec case.

According to Pflock, he had located a copy of a personal diary that had been kept by Silas Newton. He wasn't allowed to keep the original, wasn't allowed to make copies or even take the photographs, and he was a little bit leery of the source. But the lead was just too good to ignore.

Pflock learned that Nick Redfern, a researcher who had been living in Great Britain but who eventually moved to the United States, had obtained a copy of Newton's FBI file and asked if he might get a copy. Pflock had hoped there would be some samples of Newton's handwriting in the file that he could use to compare with the diary. Redfern said that Pflock offered to pay the costs of copying and postage, so he had no reason to refuse. He sent Pflock the copy.

There were no samples of Newton's handwriting in the file, but Pflock wrote later, "In November 1998, I obtained from William L. Moore a copy of Newton's holographic will, which I took with me to what turned out to be my last meeting with my source. The will unquestionably is in Newton's hand, and while I'm certainly not a handwriting expert, the comparison left no doubt in my mind that he wrote the journal, too."

Ramsey, of course, had heard about this as well and wanted to explore this avenue. According to him, "Karl admitted during his videotaped lecture to the UFO Symposium in 2002 that he never knew who this secret person was, how to contact him, or whether or not the diary was real. The diary, Karl claimed, exposed Aztec as nothing more than Silas Newton pulling off a hoax, and the only mystery was why the military showed up at Newton's residence, telling him that they knew the Aztec story was 'bunk' but to keep up the good work."

According to Nick Redfern, in his book, *Body Snatchers in the Desert*, Pflock, in a self-published paper, wrote about all this, saying:

In 1998, under curious circumstances, I was made privy to a fascinating document about one of the most controversial cases of the Golden Age of Flying Saucers, the so-called Aztec crash of 1948. I

An artist's reconstruction of what the Aztec crash site based on Frank Scully's acocunt.

had little more than a passing interest in the case until 1998, when a source, who insists on complete anonymity, showed me a handwritten testament, set down by the key player in this amazing, often amusing, truth-is-stranger-than-fiction episode.

It seems that what I was shown was … something penned by sly old Silas Newton, but what can we say about the veracity of its content? After the Denver Post revealed he was Scientist X, Newton received two visitors at his Newton Oil Company office in Denver. These men claimed to be with a highly secret U.S. Government entity, which they refused to name…. Newton writes, "They grilled me, tried to poke holes in my story. Had no trouble doing it and laughed in my face about the scientific mistakes I made. They never said so, but I could tell they were trying to find out if I really knew anything about flying saucers that had landed. Did not take those fellows long to decide I did not. But I sure knew they did." …

Newton's visitors told him they knew he was pulling a scam and then gave him what may have been the surprise of his life. "Those fellows said they wanted me to keep it up, keep telling the flying saucer story and that they and the people they worked for would look out for me and for Leo. I could just go on doing what I always did and not worry about it.

Ramsey then explains that he questioned Pflock on the "secret" source and whether Pflock had ever compared any of Newton's handwriting to the diary. According to Ramsey, Pflock said that he had been unable to find any samples of Newton's handwriting. Pflock, under questioning, said that the source was Newton's nephew, which, of course, doesn't exactly protect the man's identity since Newton didn't have all that many nephews. In fact, according to Ramsey, Newton had none.

Based on this exchange, Ramsey believes the tale of the diary to be a hoax, either concocted by Pflock for unspecified reasons, or by someone else lying to Pflock. Either way, this alleged diary does nothing to undermine the importance of the Aztec tale.

But all this doesn't quite track with other information. As noted, by 1998, Pflock did have samples of Newton's handwriting. Nick Redfern added, "By 2001, Karl had several other extensive samples of Newton's writing, and collectively this material—he told me—matched the journal."

Although Ramsey's book discusses this episode briefly, and he notes that although Pflock had lived close to the Aztec area for many years and had attended many of the symposiums, he thought it strange that Pflock had never been to the crash site. He thinks it strange, but if Pflock believed the story to be a hoax, then he would believe there is no crash site to visit. Pflock apparently had no desire to walk around in the desert.

The story of Aztec is certainly the story of conspiracy, but it seems that it was a conspiracy to invent a crash rather than to hide one. The evidence is weak, the eyewitness testimony is shaky, and if Pflock is to be believed, and there is no reason to doubt him, Newton admitted as much. It would seem that there is little left to question … until the next researcher comes along and begins to turn over the soil one more time.

The Robertson Panel

The Robertson Panel, which might be considered the first attempt to convince the public that there was nothing to the UFO phenomenon, had its beginnings in 1953 and was the result of a series of sightings over Washington, D.C., in July 1952. On two consecutive weekends, UFOs had been seen over the capital by airline and military pilots, by people on the ground, and they had been picked up by multiple radar sets at both the civilian airports and the military bases. These sightings, known as the Washington Nationals because of the radar images seen by operators at the Washington National Airport, caught the attention of the president, who wanted to know what was going on. They also resulted in one of the greatest newspaper headlines ever. The *Cedar Rapids Gazette* reported across the front page, "Saucers Swarm over Capital."

One of the results of all the UFO sightings that summer was the creation of a panel of experts to examine the UFO phenomenon. These were men at the top of their fields, whose names were recognized around the world, and who could be counted on to do a job. The official name was The Scientific Advisory Panel on Unidentified Flying Objects. It was better known as the Robertson Panel, named for its chairman Dr. Howard Robertson.

The CIA, aware of the potential intelligence problem that was developing because of UFO sightings, began a series of what they thought of as informal discussions about them. These were chaired by H. Marshall Chadwell, at the time the CIA's Assistant Director of Scientific Intelligence. Chadwell did go to Wright-Patterson Air Force Base with Frederick Durant (who surfaces later on the Robertson Panel) for a series of briefings on UFOs by those investigating them.

In September 1952, Chadwell wrote to the Director, Central Intelligence (DCI) telling him, "Recently an inquiry was conducted by the Office of Scien-

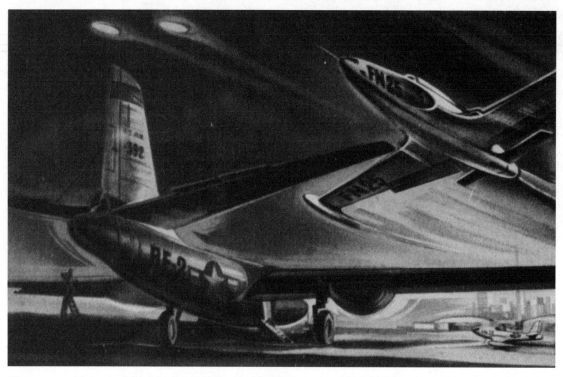

Planes scramble at Andrews Air Force Base after UFOs are seen over Washington, D.C.

tific Intelligence to determine whether there are national security implications in the problem of 'unidentified flying objects,' i.e., flying saucers; whether adequate study and research is currently directed to this problem in its relation to such national security implications; and what further investigation and research should be instituted, by whom, and under what aegis."

What this tells us is that at the highest levels of the intelligence community, meaning here, the CIA, the director was being told about UFOs and a problem they could pose. Chadwell was suggesting that they needed to determine what should be done about this problem.

Chadwell, then, seems to answer the questions that he has posed. He wrote, "[P]ublic concern with the phenomena indicates that a fair portion of our population is mentally conditioned to the acceptance of the incredible. In this fact lies the potential for the touching-off of mass hysteria.... In order to minimize the risk of panic, a national policy should be established as to what should be told to the public regarding the phenomena."

In other words, the public can't be trusted to think for themselves, they are easily led, and that the men and women of the CIA should determine how much of the truth they should be told. In fact, these are the same conclusions that would be reached by the Robertson Panel some five months later.

But we really need to understand this. Those at the highest levels of the government, especially those inside the intelligence community, determined that the public was not smart enough to be told the truth. They could be easily led, and it was up to the CIA to decide just what they "needed" to know, as opposed to what the whole truth might be.

Major Dewey Fournet, who was the Pentagon officer charged with the UFO responsibility, said that he had received a call from Frederick Durant. According to Fournet, "[H]e asked me to make a presentation to the CIA which I gave them a few of my own opinions based on what I had observed … from that the idea of the Robertson Panel spawned. And Fred, through his superiors, convened it."

Well, not exactly, according to the documented history. It can be argued that the idea of the panel already existed by the time Fournet made his presentation to the CIA and he was asked to make the presentation so that they could decide the direction to take. In December 1952, just weeks before the group actually met, Chadwell decided to form the scientific advisory panel. Dr. Michael Swords, who reviewed all this history carefully, said that Robertson had apparently accompanied Chadwell and Durant to Wright-Patterson. According to Swords, Robertson accepted the assignment against his better judgment, but Chadwell insisted. Robertson said that he had to "strong-arm" four other scientists to join him in this alleged scientific evaluation, which, of course, suggests a certain bias had already set in.

Swords, who reconstructed the history of this panel using documents from a variety of sources, including those housed at the J. Allen Hynek Center for UFO Studies (CUFOS), the declassified Project Blue Book files now available online, and the files of the National Investigations Committee on Aerial Phenomena also housed at CUFOS, said, "The first guy who gets to do this [meaning serve on the committee] is Thornton Page because Page is handy. Page turns out to be the junior member … but he doesn't know anything about UFOs. Robertson sent him an article to read.…"

Swords said, "I think Alverez [Dr. Luis Alverez] is the next guy … and Alverez comes in hostile.… Robertson has to get two more people.… I think Goudsmit [Dr. Samuel Goudsmit] is probably the last guy … and I'm not sure when they talk Lloyd Berkner into [it]. Goudsmit is just incredibly hostile [to the idea that UFOs are anything other than hallucination and hoax]."

From this it seems that the panel is not receptive to the idea of UFOs being alien craft, but then it isn't necessary for them to enter the investigation as believers, as long as they are willing to look at the evidence. But that doesn't seem to be the case. They came into it with preconceived notions and they weren't going to be convinced of anything else.

Dr. J. Allen Hynek, who was there (but as the Air Force consultant to Project Blue Book and not a member of the panel) would later tell Swords that the members of the panel entered the committee room with the idea UFOs were going to be debunked from the absolute beginning. According to what Hynek told Swords, Alverez and Goudsmit were saying "nothing but hostile things and Goudsmit is saying wiseass things…. Page is more open-minded and Berkner is not there."

Captain Edward Ruppelt, who was the chief of Project Blue Book in 1952 and into 1953, described the Panel. In his book, *The Report on Unidentified Flying Objects*, he wrote, "When this high court was convened … one of three verdicts would be acceptable. 1. All UFO reports are explainable as known objects or natural phenomena; therefore the investigations should be permanently discontinued. 2. The UFO reports do not contain enough data upon which to base a final conclusion. Project Blue Book should be continued in the hopes of obtaining better data. 3. The UFOs are interplanetary spacecraft."

But the sad fact here is that the panel was a *fait accompli* before the first meeting. According to the research carried out by Swords, not everyone was in on it. The panel had been salted, not by skeptics, but by men who were hostile to the idea of alien visitation. They weren't interested in determining if some UFOs might be alien, they only wanted to end the discussion about them in the public arena. To them, there was nothing more real to flying saucers than there was to the Easter Bunny and everyone should agree with their assessment.

Under the auspices of the CIA, the panel met for the first time on January 14, 1953. According to Ruppelt, the first two days were made up of his review of the work done by and the findings of the various Air Force projects, that is, Sign, Grudge, and finally Blue Book. Ruppelt reported that his team, and those who preceded him, had analyzed 1,593 reports and found explanations for all but 429. Confidence in those explanations ranged from known to possible, which meant they thought they knew what had caused a sighting but couldn't prove it. This also meant that nearly a third of the sightings had no explanation.

Swords had learned a little more about the exact chronology of events in the meetings during his discussions with Hynek. During the first half-day, no one was allowed into the meeting room except for a couple of CIA men that included Chadwell and Philip G. Strong. Hynek and Ruppelt cooled their heels outside for their chance to enter and present their information.

Ruppelt made it clear during his presentation that most of the data they had gathered was observational. That is, they had relied on the abilities of the witnesses to accurately estimate size, distance, and speed. Ruppelt wrote, "We could say only that some of the UFOs had been traveling pretty fast."

Ruppelt pointed out that radar cases were available, but open to the interpretation of the operators, which put them into the category of observational. They had to rely on the abilities of the radar technicians and operators for their

J. Allen Hynek.

interpretation of what was seen on the scope and no one had any idea of how reliable those observations might be.

Ruppelt also said there were no good physical evidence cases. He was unaware of the Roswell UFO case, and in a search of the Project Blue Book files over the years, only a single mention of Roswell has been found. It is in another case and is in the second paragraph of a three-paragraph story. The article only suggests that the officers at Roswell have been issued a "blistering rebuke" for their claim of "capturing" a flying saucer.

Ruppelt also said that most of the photographs they had seen were fakes, some crude, others more sophisticated. He also suggested that photographs, no matter how good, would not prove the case. In the world of today even videotape of flying saucers in motion are easy to fake, making photographic evidence even more problematic.

The difference was movies, and Project Blue Book had two that were good. One of them, taken in Montana in 1950, showed two brightly lighted objects crossing the sky, passing behind a tower and over a rooftop. It was a short segment, but it was fascinating.

There were two witnesses in this case Nick Mariana, who took the film, and Virginia Raunig, who was with Mariana and saw the objects in the sky. While she watched them, Mariana ran to his car to get his 16mm movie camera so that he could film them. He ran back to where he could see the objects clearly and exposed the short film.

According to Mariana, the two objects crossed the sky in a straight line. On the film, the objects seem to flash brightly once and then move away from the camera. In less than twenty seconds, according to Mariana's estimate, the UFOs disappeared. Raunig watched the objects as Mariana filmed them but said she had only seen them for five or ten seconds.

The Montana Movie

This case becomes important because it involves indirect evidence and the question of the Air Force integrity in the investigation of UFOs. While some of the evidence of the flying saucers seen on the film has been lost, the evidence that the Air Force tampered with the film can be proven.

The testimony of the witnesses, Nick Mariana and Virginia Raunig, tell us the accepted answer, Air Force fighters, is incorrect. Both witnesses said they had seen the fighters in another part of the sky before they saw the UFOs and that the objects they saw had a specific non-aircraft-like shape to them. The witness testimony, then, does not lead to the aircraft explanation and if there is a fault with that testimony, it is the lack of numbers. We have two people on the record and it would be much better if there had been a dozen scattered around the city but no one else came forward. Or rather, those who might have seen something were ignored by Air Force investigators.

Quite naturally, Mariana was excited by the film and once it had been processed and returned, he showed it to various civic groups. At one of these meetings, someone suggested that the Air Force might find the film interesting. In October 1950, an officer from Maelstrom Air Force Base, which formerly had been named Great Falls AFB, arrived to interview Mariana about what he had seen and what he had filmed.

Early analysis of the film proved nothing. Mariana said that the objects had been in sight for about twenty seconds, but later measurements based on the time it took to retrieve the camera suggested they were in sight for closer to a minute. The Air Force suggested that two jet fighters were in the area at the time and bright sunlight reflecting from the fuselages might account for the bright glow and the disc shape, and they didn't seem overly interested in taking the investigation further.

There are notes in various case files, including those at Project Blue Book, suggesting others did see the something in the sky that day, but since these leads surfaced as a result of the publicity about the movie and it was several weeks after the fact, none of them were pursued. Had someone done that in 1950, we might be having a different discussion today. This witness testimony was rejected simply because it was considered to be contaminated, a fact that was not in evidence. And, to the Air Force's way of thinking, if they didn't interview the witness, then he or she simply didn't exist. This attitude would be in evidence in other multiple witness cases.

The real prize in this case was the film of the objects. Here was something that could be taken into the lab and measured. To study this aspect of the case, the witness testimony was unnecessary. No interpretation of what they saw was needed. There were images on the film and that should be sufficient.

Interestingly, in 1950, when first contacted about the film, the Air Force didn't particularly care about it. They learned that two fighters might have been in the area at the time and that was all they needed to know. The solution was built out of this.

Scientific investigation came about in the mid-1950s when, Dr. M. L. Baker, Jr., then with Douglas Aircraft Company, began a detailed analysis. Using the evidence available on the film, Baker was able to make a number of calculations. Using the foreground detail, as well as the speed of the objects as evidenced by their motion, he concluded that if the objects were about a quarter mile from the camera, they were at 320 feet of altitude and moving at eighteen miles an hour. If they were ten miles away, they were at 12,800 feet and traveling at 690 miles an hour.

> There are notes in various case files, including those at Project Blue Book, suggesting others did see the something in the sky that day

Baker ran a series of tests using both actual aircraft and scale models. Filming with a camera similar to the one used by Mariana, he photographed aircraft at varying distances and altitudes. At twelve miles, a DC-3 seemed to duplicate a portion of the Montana movie.

Studying the film carefully, Baker determined that the objects were two miles from the camera. According to his work, at that range, the F-94s the Air Force offered as the solution to the case would have been easily identifiable as aircraft. As the distance from the camera increased, so did the speed until at twelve miles—the range at which the DC-3 momentarily duplicated the film with reflections off the fuselage—the estimated speed was about two times that possible for the airplane. The details of the aircraft were only masked for a few seconds, meaning that Mariana would have been able to identify them had they been DC-3s. Besides, there was no evidence of two DC-3s in the area flying in formation at the time he shot the film.

Based on his examination of the film, Baker decided that it didn't show birds or balloons and he was fairly certain that had it been aircraft that at some point the reflections hiding the detail would have disappeared because of the length of the film and the time it had taken Mariana to get to his car to get out the movie camera. In other words, the length of the film did not translate into the absolute length of the sighting.

And here is where they ran into another problem. Mariana claimed that his film had been altered by the Air Force. He said that about thirty frames had been cut from the beginning of the movie in which the oval shape of the objects was clearly visible. The Air Force denied that they had altered the film but there was a letter in the Project Blue Book files in which the Air Force did admit to taking out a frame because the sprockets had been damaged. This is where the evidence of a cover-up begins, and it suggests something more about the nature of the Robertson Panel.

Claiming a cover-up is a serious allegation and the question becomes, can we prove it? And this is where we can conduct a little more science, if we allow our definition to expand a bit. Barry Greenwood leads the way on this and offers just such proof, and in doing so provides an illustration on scientific investigation.

The Greenwood Investigation of the Film's Length

In a September 2000 article, "On the Question of Tampering with the 1950 Great Falls UFO Film" published in the *UFO Historical Revue*, Barry Greenwood wrote:

> First was John Wuertner, Mariana's attorney.... When interviewed about the film … Wuertner said that the Air Force kept the film for a long period [and] "… I know doggone well that that tape when it was returned, was little or nothing to it." Wuertner said that he recalled better views of the film in the original cut. " … when I saw it compared to what came back, it wasn't complete. The main part that I recall that didn't come back was when it was right overhead. Now it started in the east and as it arose on the horizon then there was a part cut out and all we have left was the part disappearing over the west." He added that there was the appearance of spinning. " … if it were uniform, you'd get the same reflection on the same spot. But as it turned, you could get the definite reaction of spinning." Moreover, he continued, "If I had to make an estimate of what I thought had been cut off, I would say that it was, oh gosh, maybe one-fourth to one-fifth—it would be hard to say. But it would seem that they cut off the most obvious part. In other words, the part to me that seemed to bare out his contentions more than anything else."

> Another testament came from E. P. Furlong, managing editor of the *Great Falls Tribune*. He saw the film originally, then later on TV, feeling that the TV version was considerably shorter. He was likely referring to a broadcast of the film *UFO* (1956) which included the entire film available after Mariana received his edited copy.

> Tony Dalick ran a sporting goods store where the film had been run before being sent to the Air Force. He testified that there was "a lot

Wright-Patterson Air Force Base, where about fifteen feet of the film was sent, but seven feet of that film disappeared.

missing, perhaps 2-3 feet." He remembered two objects, definitely spinning, shaped like a wafer of peppermint candy. The objects were closer and clearer on the unreturned part of the film.

Craig [of the Condon Committee, which was investigating the Montana movie as part of their Air Force-financed work] interviewed Nicholas Mariana seventeen years after the event. He clarified some aspect of the sighting detail.

On the alleged spinning motion: "You could see the spinning action of the center portion in the middle of the film."

On the "notch" allegedly seen as a reference point for the spinning motion: "... there was a little break between the actual rest of the body of the machine and this portion of it. You could see there was action. You couldn't see it with your eye but you could see it after I got the telephoto film back."

On the diagonal cut at the beginning of the film: "The reason I know it was cut, too, was that they came back with the original and they had spliced it diagonally. Well, I never used the diagonal splice. I used horizontal splice...."

Barry Greenwood wrote:

Let's look more at the film strip itself. As mentioned earlier, I had obtained a 16mm print of the Air Force's copy years ago from the National Archives.

The length of the actual Great Falls footage is 6 feet, 3/4 inch, with a 42-inch blank lead and a 52-inch blank end. The total length of the filmstrip is about 14 feet. There is no telling when the blanks were added on but they were not part of the original film and they were certainly added by the Air Force.

According to Captain Byrnildsen's [original Air Force investigator of the movie] transmittal letter of October 6, 1950, approximately 15 feet of film was sent to Wright-Patterson AFB. But in a clipping cited in Jerome Clark's *The UFO Encyclopedia* (2nd ed. 1998) from the *Great Falls Tribune* (October 6, 1950), Byrnildsen is said to have told the reporter that he picked up 8 feet of film from Mariana. Unless someone made errors in quoting the footage, it seems like Byrnildsen picked up eight feet of film from Mariana, added on the blank footage and sent the finished product to Wright-Patterson. My copy of the film, with blank filler, is 14 feet, in close agreement with what was sent to Wright-Patterson.

If you've been reading carefully, you can see a problem. The supposedly complete copy of the edited Air Force print, that which Mariana received after having had his film "reduced," is nearly two feet shorter than the lowest estimate of what the Air Force had said they had received at Wright-Patterson in 1950! Since on a viewing of the existing print there are no major jump cuts in the sequence, which flows rather smoothly, and since the film ends about where the witness has testified (the objects moving into the distance and disappearing), one must conclude that about two feet of film is missing from the beginning of the sequence.

This is exactly what Mariana claims. It is also in good agreement with the testimony of Tony Dalick, the sporting goods store owner who had seen the footage before and after the claimed editing by the Air Force, saying that he felt "two to three feet" were missing from the beginning.

In 1956, Dr. Robert M. L. Baker produced an analysis of the Montana film, a treatment that was later updated and printed in *The Journal of the Astronautical Sciences* for January-February 1968, under the title "Observational Evidence of Anomalistic Phenomena." He concluded that nearby jet aircraft should have been resolvable on the film, but at greater distances the brightness and speed of the images were too great to have been aircraft. In other words, the objects were unidentified. Of relevance to this article are remarks in Baker's article about the filmstrip itself. He said that his analysis focused upon just 225 frames of the film because of the presence of foreground objects, by which precise measurements could have been made. 65 frames at the beginning of the film were not used except for brightness measurements. This gives us 290 frames total that Baker had available of the UFOs (290 frames? Ed.). The film was given to Baker for study by Greene-Rouse Productions, the makers of the documentary *UFO* mentioned earlier. The clip was the end product supplied to Mariana after the 1952 Air Force analysis, and supplied to Greene-Rouse Productions when a deal was struck to use the footage in the documentary. Greene-Rouse arranged an independent analysis, presumably to be sure that the film showed truly anomalous images.

Now the problem with this is that my copy of the Air Force Montana print is only 243 frames long. 47 more frames had disappeared between 1952 and the time I had obtained the film from the National Archives! Could it have been that the Air Force clipped the footage again, knowing that the film was to be released publicly sometime after the mid-1970s upon the transfer of Blue Book records to

A photo of what appears to be two UFOs over Great Falls.

the National Archives. We might want to title the remaining sequence of the Montana footage "The Incredible Shrinking Film"!

The Air Force had already decided that the film had shown two F-94s (see Project Blue Book's conclusion). This was in spite of the 1952 reinvestigation by the then head of the Air Force's Project Blue Book, Captain Edward Ruppelt, at the direction of the Pentagon. Ruppelt had said that in 1950 there was no interest on the part of the Air Force in UFOs. Their pre-Blue Book program, Project Grudge, had written off the Montana film as jets after a quick viewing.... Upon examining the data anew, the new study narrowed down the possible explanations to the F-94s in the area. But as Ruppelt explained, "First we studied the flight paths of the two F-94s. We knew the landing pattern being used on the day of the sighting, and we knew when the two F-94s landed. The two jets just weren't anywhere close to where the two UFOs had been. Next we studied each individual light and both appeared to be too steady to be reflections. We drew a blank on the Montana movie—it was an unknown."

If the head of Project Blue Book decided that the UFOs were unexplained after a lengthy investigation in 1952, who decided that the conclusion in the Blue Book files should remain "aircraft"? There were no further investigations of the Montana film. Perhaps it was the same decision making process that performed the film alterations?

Probably the greatest debunking of UFOs came in the form of the Condon Committee, which functioned from 1966 to the publication of its report "The Scientific Study of Unidentified Flying Objects." The project was created ostensibly to relieve the Air Force of having anything further to do with UFO investigations. UFOs had become a nuisance problem for the Air Force, stuck in a no-win situation of chasing down mostly ordinary reports, 90% of which were identifiable as mundane stimuli. The Condon Report dismissed any notion that UFOs were worthy of scientific attention, or that they posed a threat to national security.

Yet their discussion of the Montana film is curiously less critical than one had become used to in dealing with the typical Air Force public relations machine at the time.

The Committee's investigator of the Montana film, Dr. William Hartmann, said in the report, "Both individuals (Mariana and Raunig) have recently affirmed the observation, and there is little reason to question its validity. The case remains unexplained. Analysis indicates that the images on the film are difficult to reconcile with aircraft or other known phenomena, although aircraft cannot entirely be ruled out."

After summarizing the case, Hartmann, attempting to explain a discrepancy in the witnesses' estimates of the duration of the sighting, said the discrepancy "probably refers to the fact that Witness 1 (Mariana) made about 20 seconds of film." That's 5 seconds, or 80 frames of film, more than the current Air Force print; or 2 seconds, or 32 frames, more than the Baker copy obtained from Greene-Rouse Productions. The 2-second difference is in close agreement with Mariana's claim that at least an estimated 35 frames were shaved from the original.

Hartmann concludes by summarizing arguments for and against aircraft reflections being responsible for the images. He states, "While such a hypothesis (the F-94 explanation) is tenable, it conflicts with some of the soft data. It is judged reasonable only to regard this object as unidentified."

This illustrates the point of cover-up and conspiracy so well. Greenwood has taken a look at the Montana movie, at the physical dimensions of the movie, something that is outside the realm of subjective opinion, and provided an answer to the question of Air Force manipulation. What he proves, and what could be duplicated, are the measurements of the film. We can determine either by a frame count or by actual measurement of the film that it has been reduced significantly.

While this much detail about the movie doesn't say much about the Robertson Panel techniques, or the Air Force investigation for that matter, it does prove the point. At the end of their research, they decided that the movie showed the two jet fighters that might, or might not, have been in the area, ignoring the witness testimony. With the movie shortened to remove the frames on which Mariana said the disc shape could be seen, what had been some important proof became just a short film of two bright spots that could be almost anything.

The examination of the film, with those frames removed, doesn't allow for a conclusion of alien spacecraft. The hard data on the film, based on the various studies, show that the aircraft explanation doesn't work. It should leave the film as "unidentified."

According to Ruppelt, the last day of Robertson Panel meetings was reserved for a review of the films. Ruppelt believed these were the best evidence held by Blue Book. No one believed they had been faked, which meant that no one considered them to be hoaxes. There were other mundane explanations available, at least in the minds of those on the panel.

It was on that last afternoon, a Friday, with Hynek invited to stay inside the meeting room, that Robertson was given the task of writing the final report. Swords wrote about this, based on his review of the documents and his discussions with Hynek about it.

"Both individuals (Mariana and Raunig) have recently affirmed the observation, and there is little reason to question its validity. The case remains unexplained."

"I can't imagine that H. P. Robertson, a guy like him, is going to sit down and late into the evening and bang out a draft of the report on his own that somehow, mysteriously, the next morning is already read by Lloyd Berkner and has already been taken by Marshall Chadwell to the Air Force Directorate of Intelligence and been approved," Swords wrote. "So when they show up on Saturday, Robertson presents this draft to the rest of the committee and the rest of the committee does minor revisions.... There are some remarks that are out of line that they decided are not going to be included."

Swords noted that this seems a little unreal. According to him, "It seems an amazingly cut-and-dried deal that by the time Saturday shows up, here's this mildly to be revised draft that has already been seen by one of the other committee members who wasn't even there for the first two and a half days. It's already been seen by Chadwell and the U.S. Air Force."

Dewey Fournet, who had the chance to review the data, who had been present for some of the sessions, and now had a forty-year perspective, said that the scientists had no choice in their conclusions. For him and for them, the evidence simply wasn't persuasive. There was little more than the testimonies of the witnesses, none of whom had appeared in front of the committee so that their observations could be examined. Others, later, would simply refer to such testimony as "anecdotal gossip," which much later would become the rallying cry of the debunking community.

But to understand the Robertson Panel it is necessary to understand what was happening at the time. UFO sightings, including radar confirmation and fighter interception of the objects, had just happened over Washington, D.C. UFOs were flying around over the capital and it appeared that the Air Force was unable to stop them. This appeared to be a threat to national security, if nothing else, with the emphasis on appeared.

> Although hindsight shows that such an attack was impossible in 1952, those in intelligence at the time didn't know the sorry state of Soviet missile and bomber development.

But if the UFOs were nothing more than hoaxes, mirages, misidentifications, and limited sightings, meaning that the witnesses had not gotten a good look at objects, then national security wasn't an issue at all. If the UFOs were all basically imaginary, regardless of the stimulation, then the Air Force was doing its job because there was nothing to intercept, there was nothing to challenge, and nothing to fear.

They did suggest, however, that there was one area of concern. Fournet mentioned, as did Ed Ruppelt, that too many UFO reports at the wrong time could mask a Soviet attack. Although hindsight shows that such an attack was impossible in 1952, those in intelligence at the time didn't know the sorry state of Soviet missile and bomber development. They thought that a sudden flood of UFO reports, as had just happened in July 1952, could create havoc in message centers; as the classified message traffic increased, critical messages might be lost in the overflow. A possible Soviet attack might be lost in that overflow.

With this as a concern, the Robertson Panel decided to address the issue. The report said that "although evidence of any direct threat from these sightings was wholly lacking, related dangers might well exist from: a. Misidentification of actual enemy artifacts by defense personnel. b. Overloading of emergency channels with 'false' information … c. Subjectivity of public to mass hysteria and greater vulnerability to possible enemy psychological warfare."

The report continued, creating what they thought was a need to reduce or suppress UFO reports. "Although not the concern of the CIA, the first two of these problems may seriously affect the Air Defense intelligence system, and should be studied by experts, possibly under the ADC. If UFOs become discredited in a reaction to the 'flying saucer' scare, or if reporting channels are saturated with false and poorly documented reports, our capability of detecting hostile activity will be reduced. Dr. Page noted that more competent screening or filtering of reported sightings at or near the source is required, and that this can be accomplished by an educational program."

This, at first, seems that this is a reasonable idea. But in the event of a Soviet attack, the communications would not come solely through the communications centers at various levels of command. Those on the front line of the attack, meaning those who were manning the various radar fences, who were at the various forward Air Force bases, would communicate more directly with their superiors.

In other words, no one would rely on a classified message that needed to be encrypted, decrypted, and carried from the message center to the headquarters, wherever that headquarters might be. In 1952, those at the forward bases would have picked up the telephone, one of the many dedicated lines, and spoken directly to their superiors, probably telling them that a coded message would be coming, if it was needed.

But the idea of an educational program to teach people to spot the natural and astronomical phenomena did make some sense. If the public was more familiar with the phenomena that appeared in the sky including meteors, Venus, and weather events, then the number of UFO reports might be significantly reduced because those who once might have been fooled would not be able to tell the difference between Venus and something flying in the atmosphere.

The problem arises when the whole of the educational program is examined. Under that banner, the panel recommended, "The Panel's concept of a broad educational program integrating efforts of all concerned agencies was that it should have two major aims: training and 'debunking.'"

Some of the ideas offered weren't all that bad. The training, according to the Panel, would result in witnesses being able to identify those "unusually illuminated objects.... This training should result in a marked reduction in reports caused by misidentified cases and resultant confusion."

The problem with the Panel's report came in the next paragraph where they used the word "debunking." While almost all agree that to debunk myths, legends, and fantasies is a good idea, here the suggestion seemed to be a propaganda campaign aimed not at explaining those cases that were misidentifications, misinterpretations, hoaxes, or mistaken identity, but in simply convincing people there was nothing to the UFO reports. In other words, debunk the whole of the UFO phenomena with little regard to the accuracy of the information.

Robertson wrote, "The 'debunking' aim would result in reduction in public interest in 'flying saucers' which today evokes a strong psychological reaction. This education could be accomplished by mass media such as television, motion pictures, and popular articles. Basis of such education would be actual case histories which had been puzzling at first but later explained. As in the case of conjuring tricks, there is much less stimulation if the 'secret' is known. Such a program should tend to reduce the current gullibility of the public and consequently their susceptibility to clever hostile propaganda. The Panel noted that the general absence of Russian propaganda based on a subject with so many obvious possibilities for exploitation might indicate a possible Russian official policy."

The Panel discussed what they had meant by an educational program. Many in the UFO community have seen it as more of a "disinformation" program, designed to explain all UFO sightings with the mundane so that interest in UFOs would disappear. It was to convince people that UFOs were nothing more than misidentifications, hallucinations, and hoaxes, and therefore not worth investigating.

To take this even further, it was suggested by some who were at many of the Panel's meetings that the information presented to the members had been "managed" to lead to several predetermined conclusions. The Panel had a limited life, they were unable to examine some of the sightings and questions in detail, and when there was a stumble, Robertson had a quick answer. For example, while some of the members were intrigued by the "Utah" movie, Robertson thought it merely showed birds and was quite vocal in his explanation of it.

The Utah Movie

The Utah movie was a film taken in 1952 near Tremonton, Utah, by Navy Warrant Officer Delbert C. Newhouse. He was traveling to a new duty station when he and his wife spotted a loose formation of objects in the clear, blue sky. He thought enough of them to stop the car and retrieve his 16mm movie camera from the trunk. He then made a short film of the objects as they swarmed high in the sky. When of one of them broke away from the formation he followed it, allowing it to cross the frame to provide some reference for later analysis.

> Examination of the film by experts ... suggested ... the objects were internally lighted, and that they weren't balloons or birds.

These were bright white objects seeming to wheel in the late morning sun. Examination of the film by experts, in the same depth that the Montana movie had been studied, suggested, at least to the Navy analysts, the objects were internally lighted, and that they weren't balloons or birds. They were unable to identify them as anything conventional. In other words, they were stumped.

But Robertson presented a film of seagulls soaring above the ground and suggested this was what Newhouse had seen. He thought that the birds were at the extreme range of vision and therefore no flapping of the wings could be detected. They were just bright white blobs reflecting the bright sunlight in the late morning sky.

This, of course, ignored two important points. One was that Newhouse was a Navy officer and had seen seagulls many times in the past both over land

and out to sea. It wasn't as if he was experiencing something new that should have confounded him.

But, more importantly, when Newhouse was interviewed by Air Force investigators, he told them that he had seen the objects at a much closer range. They were disc-shaped objects but by the time he stopped the car, retrieved his camera, and began to film, they had moved off, into the distance, so the shape was not readily visible.

So, Robertson and his allies had dismissed two of the best pieces of evidence, the movie footage taken in Montana and Utah. With that out of the way, a careful presentation of the data allowed for a biased picture to be drawn. It could be argued, based on what is now known, that the Panel was designed specifically so that time would not allow embarrassing questions to be asked. It can also be suggested that the Panel was loaded with scientists who had already formed their conclusions before they looked at a single bit of the evidence or read a single word of testimony. It can be suggested that some of the truly extraordinary cases that had been submitted had been overlooked, especially those by scientists. And it can be argued, based on the timing, that the final report was written before a single minute of testimony or data review had been accomplished.

If the Panel was designed not to actually review the status of the UFO investigations—but rather to reduce public interest and suggest that UFO study was a waste of resources—could the designer have had enough confidence in his own abilities to micromanage the results so that they would come to his conclusion? How could he be sure that some wild card wouldn't jerk his plans off the rails and lead the Panel in another direction?

This seems to have been a big risk to take. It also implies that those managing the information at the top were not afraid that too much would be learned by the Panel members. If the plan had been to convince the Panel members that there was little to the UFO sightings so that this impression could be conveyed to the general public, it seemed to have worked. According to Swords, Robertson, Chadwell, and the others at the CIA, they were just the sort of heavy thinkers who could design such a plan and pull it off. When all is said and done, the only member of the Panel who was even mildly unbiased was Thornton Page, and he was overwhelmed by the prestige of the other, high-powered members and the personality of Robertson.

The Panel's ultimate purpose, it might be said, was to determine if UFOs posed a threat to national security. The cases they reviewed contained little more than sighting information and nothing to suggest UFOs might be hostile or threaten national security. Such a conclusion would come later, in the form of the Brookings Institute study that would examine the results of two societies learning about the other. That is to say that when a technological superior society meets with a technological inferior one, the inferior society ceases to exist. That doesn't mean it was conquered. It means that the introduction of the technology will radically alter the society so that it begins to need that technology to survive, and by doing that, is changed, many times for the worse.

The odd thing about the Robertson Panel was its suggestion that UFO investigations through Project Blue Book should be expanded and that the project should lose its classified status. Robertson believed that the best way to debunk the UFOs and to educate the public was to make everything transparent. Besides, he knew that the really good UFO reports were not part of the Blue Book system.

The Bolender Memo

J. Allen Hynek, who was a scientific consultant to Project Blue Book for many years, often said that the really good cases didn't make it into the Blue Book files. He knew, from his experience, that some of the reports that should have gone to Blue Book by regulation simply didn't show up there. He suspected another reporting system, but he couldn't prove that there was one. And had his suppositions been correct, then he was talking about a conspiracy to hide UFO information.

Brigadier General Arthur Exon had been the base commander at Wright-Patterson Air Force Base in the mid-1960s. The base commander is similar to the mayor of a city. He is responsible for the facilities and support of the various base operations such as military police, repair, and upkeep. In fact, in today's Army, each facility has a unit known as the "mayor's cell."

Exon said that while he was base commander he would periodically receive a telephone call to prepare an aircraft for a mission outside the local area. That meant he was to supply an aircraft from those assigned to Wright-Patterson and that aircraft could be sent almost anywhere in the world given the capabilities of military aircraft.

Exon himself described this on May 19, 1991. He said, "I know that while I was there … I had charge of all of the administrative airplanes and had to sign priority airplanes to the members who would go out and investigate reported sightings…. I remember several out in Wyoming and Montana and that area in the '60s, '64 and '65…. I knew there were certain teams of people, they're representing headquarters USAF as well as the organizations there at Wright-Pat, FTD and so on…. When a crew came back it was their own business. Nobody asked any questions…."

He expanded on this, saying, "The way this happened to me is that I would get a call and say that the crew or team was leaving … there was such and such a time and they wanted an airplane and pilots to take X number of people to wherever…. They might be gone two or three days or might be gone a week. They would come back and that would be the end of it."

Asked about the overall control of these teams, Exon said, "I always thought they were part of that unholy crew in Washington that started keeping the lid on this thing."

Everything said to this point suggested that the operation was run through FTD, the parent organization to Blue Book at Wright-Patterson. But in an interview conducted about a month later, on June 18, 1991, Exon clarified what he had meant.

Asked if these teams of eight to fifteen people were stationed at Wright-Patterson, he said, "They were, they would come from Washington, D.C. They'd ask for an airplane tomorrow morning and that would give the guys a chance to get there [Wright-Patterson] by commercial airline…. Sometimes they'd be gone for three days and sometimes they would be gone for a week. I know they went to Montana and Wyoming and the northwest states a number of times in a year and a half…. They went to Arizona once or twice."

> "I always thought they were part of that unholy crew in Washington that started keeping the lid on this thing."

He also said, "Our contact was a man, a telephone number. He'd call and he'd set the airplane up. I just knew there was an investigative team."

What all this boils down to is an attempt to cover the activity. The team, whoever they were, would fly into Dayton, Ohio, on commercial air and then drive out to the base. If a reporter attempted to trace the movements of the team after it had been deployed, the trail led back to Wright-Patterson. After that it just disappeared.

This outside team, or outside teams, were made up of eight to fifteen individuals at a time when Project Blue Book had three military men and a single secretary assigned. They were stationed at Wright-Patterson, but the other teams were assigned somewhere else, and there is no reason to assume that all members of a team were assigned to the same base. They would come together as needed.

This all suggests, strongly, that there were other people involved in the investigation of UFOs and they were not members of the Project Blue Book team. Hynek hints that the good reports went somewhere else and Exon suggested that an investigative team was stationed elsewhere and called when needed. They don't appear to be part of Blue Book.

Brigadier General C. H. Bolender provided the documentation to prove the point. On October 20, 1969, some seventeen years after the Robertson Panel ended its truncated investigation of UFOs, Bolender wrote about Project Blue Book and the investigation of UFOs. Part of his memo is a response to questions about what the University of Colorado was doing and how that might affect national security.

In paragraph four of his memo, Bolender wrote, "As early as 1953, the Robertson Panel concluded 'that the evidence presented on Unidentified Flying Objects shows no indication that these phenomena constitute a direct physical threat to national security.' … In spite of this finding, the Air Force continued to maintain a special reporting system. There is still, however, no evidence that Project Blue Book reports have served any intelligence function. Moreover, reports of unidentified flying objects which could affect national security are made in accordance with JANAP 146 [Joint Army, Navy, Air Force Publication] or Air Force Manual 55-11, and are not part of the Blue Book system."

In other words, the suspicions of Hynek and Exon were confirmed by this document. There was, and still is, a system for reporting of UFO incidents. The Air Force, by its very nature, is charged with the protection of the United States, and UFOs flying through our airspace threatens that security. What they have done is take civilian reporting, and a responsibility to report back to civilians, out of the loop. Now all the data collected, all the information derived, can remain safely hidden inside the military bureaucracy.

The Final Truth

As for the Robertson Panel, Dewey Fournet (who was in attendance for some of the sessions), years later, believed that the Panel members were honest in their evaluations of the UFO sightings. Remember, he believed that the evidence presented was weak and the only conclusions that could be drawn were those that were drawn. But Fournet had not been there for everything and he did not know that the final report existed, at least in rough draft form prior to the final sessions, and might have existed before any evidence was heard.

What the evidence shows us today is that the Robertson Panel wasn't a group of highly credentialed and highly placed scientists taking a dispassionate look at UFOs. It was a Panel designed with specific conclusions formed prior to any work of the Panel, and according to Mike Swords, with the report written before the last testimony was given. It was clearly approved prior to the last day of the Panel, and was designed to end interest in UFOs by explaining everything even if those explanations were less than solid.

In other words, which would be repeated in later documents, possible solutions should be treated as if they were the actual solutions. Cases that were labeled with a probable or possible, suddenly had the qualifications removed. UFOs were to be explained. Period.

The MJ-12 Conspiracy

On May 31, 1987, the *London Observer* announced that a British UFO researcher, Timothy Good, had in his possession documents that claimed the United States had not only recovered the wreck of an alien craft, but they also had found the bodies of the alien flight crew inside it. With the story picked up by Reuters and put on the international wire, William Moore, Jaime Shandera, and Richard Doty in the United States came forward saying that they had copies of these documents as well.

The whole story, however, as it is told by the proponents, is that in 1984 Shandera, a Hollywood film producer, received a roll of undeveloped 35mm film, in the standard brown paper wrapper, postmarked in Albuquerque, New Mexico. The film, when developed, contained what is now called the Eisenhower Briefing Document (EBD) and the single-page letter that became known as the Truman Memo. According to the documents, the briefing was prepared by Rear Admiral Roscoe Hillenkoetter (or so it is often alleged) for the President-elect Dwight Eisenhower and was delivered to him, Eisenhower, on November 18, 1952, as he was being briefed before his inauguration as President.

The EBD suggested that there had been a crash of an alien ship, and that the ship and the dead crew had been recovered by members of the Army Air Forces, and all the material and bodies had been flown to Wright Field outside of Dayton, Ohio. The document said, specifically:

> On 07 July, 1947, a secret operation was begun to assure recovery of the wreckage of this object for scientific study. During the course of this operation, aerial reconnaissance discovered that four small human-like beings had apparently ejected from the craft at some point before it exploded. These had fallen to earth about two miles east of

the wreckage site. All four were dead and badly decomposed due to action by predators and exposure to the elements during the approximately one week time period which had elapsed before their discovery.

There was also mention of another crash of "a second object, probably of similar origin" near the small Texas town of Del Rio on December 6, 1950, or more specifically the El Indio–Guerrero area of Mexico. Although the crash was in Mexico, American authorities were able to secure the site and remove the craft and bodies. These too were taken to Wright Field.

According to the portions of the document leaked to Shandera, who shared them with Moore, there were other, more interesting sections of the Eisenhower Briefing Document, but those had not been included on the film. Attachment "H," for example, supposedly contained maps and photographs. While the maps would have been easy to fake, photographs, especially of the alien bodies either in the field or being autopsied, would have been nearly impossible to forge. Had Attachment "H" been included, it would have gone a long way in providing some corroboration for the parts of the document now held by Moore and Shandera and would have supplied some very powerful information about UFOs.

> (N)early everyone inside the UFO community was talking about the Majestic-Twelve, but the conclusions about it varied wildly.

Analysis of the object, material from it and the bodies, allegedly completed at Wright Field, seemed to confirm that the craft was of extraterrestrial origin. Further study was authorized by a presidential executive order on September 24, 1947, signed by then-president Harry Truman. This document, referred to by some as a special, classified executive order, said, "As per our recent conversation on this matter, you are hereby authorized to proceed with all due speed and caution upon your undertaking. Hereafter this matter shall be referred to as Operation Majestic-Twelve."

Moore and Shandera sat on these documents until the spring of 1987. At that time, British writer and researcher Tim Good, who claimed to have received a copy from a source in the CIA, showed the EBD to the press. This forced Moore's hand, and Moore released a copy (censored by Moore) to the American media. It was not long before articles about the briefing had appeared in the *New York Times* and the *Washington Post,* and it also became the subject of a segment of ABC-TV's late-night news program *Nightline*.

After this publicity, nearly everyone inside the UFO community was talking about the Majestic-Twelve, but the conclusions about it varied wildly. Some believed the documents to be a classified report about alien spaceship crashes, others thought it was disinformation created to draw attention away from the investigation into the Roswell UFO crash or some sort of operation directed at the Soviet Union, and others thought of it as misinformation. In other words, they believed the briefing to be a hoax created not by the government, but by someone inside the UFO community who had a working knowledge of how briefings were created at the highest levels. They were motivated by their desire to keep the media spotlight focused on them.

In June 1989, the *MUFON UFO Journal* carried a story about the documents that included an illustration on the front that was a page of the Eisenhower Briefing Document. At that time, much of MUFON's leadership believed that the document was authentic. It proved not only that some UFOs were alien, but that the U.S. government had learned the truth shortly after Kenneth Arnold had made his sighting of nine objects in June 1947.

The discovery, or the leaking of the EBD, seemed to be the ultimate outcome of something that had begun forty-two years earlier when UFOs first burst into the headlines. It was suggested that the very first of the official UFO investigations had begun in the early days after the Arnold sighting. It had been laid out in the files of the UFO projects and it was revealed by former Air Force Captain Edward Ruppelt.

Ruppelt, who had been the chief of Project Blue Book in the early 1950s, wrote a book, *The Report on Unidentified Flying Objects*, that seemed to support the idea of a super-secret committee. In the book he explained, "By the end of July 1947, the security lid was down tight. The few members of the press who did inquire about what the Air Force was doing got the same treatment that you would get today [that is, 1956, when the book was published] if you inquired about the number of thermonuclear weapons stockpiled in the U.S.'s atomic arsenal. No one outside of a few high-ranking officers in the Pentagon knew what the people in the Quonset huts that housed the Air Technical Intelligence Center were thinking or doing."

And then he added, "The memos and correspondence that Project Blue Book inherited from the old UFO projects told the story of the early flying saucer era. These Memos and pieces of correspondence show that the UFO situation was considered to be serious; in fact, very serious. The paperwork of that period also indicated the confusion that surrounded the investigation; confusion almost to the point of panic. The brass wanted an answer quickly, and people were taking off in all directions."

As noted earlier, this activity led, indirectly, to the letter signed by Nathan Twining and dated September 23, 1947. The date is important because the Truman memo that accompanied the EBD carries the same date. That suggests one of two things. Either the person who created the memo was aware of the UFO history, or those at the top levels of the U.S. government were coordinating their activities in their attempt to learn what was happening in 1947.

While Twining was advocating the creation of a classified project to be run by the military, Truman, in the memo, seemed to be directing the creation of a committee of mixed military officers and civilian scientists to exploit the

ALIEN MYSTERIES, CONSPIRACIES AND COVER-UPS   [177]

find from Roswell. While one, directed by the military, would have a classification level of secret, the other, the committee created by Truman, would be classified top secret, code word. It meant that unless someone possessed both a top-secret clearance and code word clearance, he or she would be denied access to the information. It was a much more highly classified project than the one run by the military.

And, if what had been found outside of Roswell had been an alien spacecraft, the technology that built it would be in the hands of the United States. It was a secret worth protecting. Only the brightest of the people in the government and military would be privy to the information. For all others, existence of the committee and its mandate would be denied for decades.

But someone with this alleged inside knowledge was not happy with the security situation and had photographed the beginning of the Eisenhower Briefing Document and the Truman Memo creating the committee. Now all that needed to be done was to verify the authenticity of the documents and the case for alien visitation would be proved, the case of government cover-up would be proved, and the conspiracy to keep all this quiet would be proved. This would be the smoking gun.

> All these documents suffered from one major problem and that was the anonymous nature of their source.

The first problem encountered for UFO researchers was that there was no provenance for the documents. They arrived anonymously in the mail and on undeveloped film. Bill Moore, after repeated requests from those inside the UFO community, and a few from the outside, finally presented the envelope the film had come in, showing that the package had allegedly been mailed from Albuquerque. There was no return address and that meant the chain of custody, or the chain of evidence, stopped right there. That is, it could be followed no further than Bill Moore and Jaime Shandera, and that was the first of the problems encountered when attempting to verify the authenticity of the documents.

Additional corroboration of the existence of MJ-12 was offered by Moore. A telex, known as the Aquarius Telex, from the Air Force Office of Special Investigation (AFOSI) that mentioned, in a single line, the MJ-12, seemed to prove that not only had MJ-12 existed, but that its life had extended over a number of years. This was clearly proof that there was a provenance for this document, one that could be followed, or so it was claimed.

All these documents suffered from one major problem and that was the anonymous nature of their source. Moore and Shandera seemed to answer that question with the discovery (in the National Archives in Washington, D.C.) of a memo from Robert Cutler, a special assistant to the President, to General Nathan F. Twining. This memo suggested that the "NSC/MJ-12 Special Studies Project" should "take place during the already scheduled White House meeting of July 16 [1954]...."

Moore, who claimed that he had received a number of cryptic postcards that referred to specific numbers that seemed to align with files held at the National Archives known as Record Groups, said that he had found the Cutler-Twining memo in a box of NSC documents that had only recently been declassified. The copy that Moore produced was authenticated as a "true copy" of a document held by the National Archives. This seemed to answer the question of provenance.

With all that, it seemed that MJ-12 had moved into the arena of having been authenticated, at least in the minds of many in the UFO community. Here was a document with a provenance, which had been found in the National Archives, and if that was true, then it suggested that the other, original MJ-12 documents could be authentic. For a moment, it seemed that MJ-12 had broken open the UFO field. The evidence for a cover-up was in hand, and the existence of alien visitors was proved.

The Skeptics Object

Quite naturally, those at the other end of the ufological spectrum believed that the documents were a hoax. Almost from the beginning they were offering evidence that something was wrong. American journalist and UFO researcher Phil Klass voiced his opinion quickly and then began a search to prove that he was correct. One of the first things that he discovered was that the signature on the Truman Memo matched exactly to that on another document. This suggested to some that the memo was a hoax and if the memo was a hoax, then the EBD that accompanied it was probably a hoax as well.

A questioned-document expert, originally identified only as P. T. by Klass, said that it was clear to him that the signature had been copied from an authentic document dated October 1, 1947, had been pasted onto the Truman Memo, and then photocopied to remove the telltale cutlines.

It later became clear that P. T. was Peter Tytell and his expertise as a questioned-document expert was sound. Stan Friedman attempted to lessen the importance of Tytell's opinions by suggesting Tytell had worked for the CIA at one point. Ironically, it was Friedman who had sent copies of the original MJ-12 documents to Tytell for his analysis. Tytell, then, is an accepted expert by both sides in the debate over authenticity, but one who is quoted only by the debunkers and ignored by the proponents. Later the smear of Tytell would continue to remove his testimony from the discussion.

Tytell, after his analysis of both the EBD and the Truman Memo, said that the typeface used on the Truman Memo was most consistent with a Smith-Corona P102, which was used on typewriters after 1966. If true, this, by itself, meant the Truman Memo is a fake since it was supposedly created in 1947. Even if we accept the idea that the document dates no earlier than 1952, the date of

Phil Klass.

the Eisenhower Briefing, the date is too early for the typewriter used. Tytell said, "This is the slam dunk." To Tytell, the typewriter problem proved the memo a fake.

Friedman wasn't convinced by Tytell's argument. Friedman, in his book, writes about the typeface controversy: "Other examiners disagree with Klass's CIA source about the typewriter used for the rest of the memo." This is clearly an attempt to discredit Tytell's objection to MJ-12 by associating him with Klass and the CIA but again, it was a source originally approached by Friedman himself.

One of the sources that Friedman preferred and who he cited as a questioned-document examiner was a "man who worked for the USPO [United States Post Office, which is, of course, the United States Postal Service] who disagreed with Tytell." Friedman didn't offer the name of this man, how he had conducted his research, or what his expertise in questioned-document examination might be.

Another source that Friedman has used to support his case was Moore and Shandera's *The MJ-12 Documents: An Analytical Report*. Friedman wondered why other researchers and interested parties have not used it or referenced it in their work and why they haven't found it persuasive. The reasons others might have avoided it may be as simple as the twenty-five dollar price tag and the fact that it was self-published more than a decade ago. Few people outside of the UFO community even know that it exists.

But the real point comes up in the conclusions which Friedman apparently didn't read as carefully as he should have. Moore and Shandera have looked at all the documents that they consider somehow related to the MJ-12 controversy and that were available to them when they prepared their report.

Of the Eisenhower Briefing Document, they write, "[W]e give a value of 75% to the likelihood that the document is authentic, and 25% to the possibility that it is a fabrication."

Of the Truman Memo, they write, "As the document as a whole, it is either authentic or a well-done and very probably official fabrication. We give a value of 35-40% for the former possibility, and 60-65% for the latter." Or in other words, they believe the greater possibility is that the document is fraudulent. They don't mention that if the Truman Memo is a fake, then the EBD is probably a fake as well.

Friedman, when challenged about the identities of his questioned-document examiners, admitted that he didn't have the names of the experts. If he was relying on information provided by Moore and Shandera and believing them competent to make any sort of authoritative analysis, then he was relying on the opinion of two amateurs who produced the results that Friedman wanted to see, or rather seemed to produce the results he wanted to see. In such a case Tytell wins the argument based on his expertise and training and the only logical conclusion is these original documents are faked.

More importantly, Tytell pointed out that he wanted to see their (the unidentified questioned-document experts') report so that he could understand exactly what their expertise was. According to Tytell, unless they have a complete A-to-Z strike up of both the uppercase and lowercase letters, as well as all the symbols and numbers for the typeface of the Underwood UP3A, their argument is without merit. Tytell said repeatedly that he had all the drawings from the Underwood factory for the type style Friedman and the others claim it is. He said, "I have samples from typewriters with that type style on them that I used to type the text of the memo." In other words, he could make a letter-by-letter examination of the type styles and draw an expert's conclusion that the type style on the Truman Memo is from a typewriter that didn't exist until after 1960.

In fact, on February 13, 2001, Friedman added to his objections of Tytell's comments. He wrote, "I am aware of Peter Tytell's offhand, informal, unwritten comments about the typewriters. However, he has, to the best of my knowledge, never provided a formal, official, written, paid-for analysis."

The objection to Tytell's comments, then, circle his reluctance to prepare a written report. There is a good reason for that. According to Tytell, he wants to be paid for his analysis and until someone comes up with his fee, he isn't going to provide the written document. Friedman simply rejects what Tytell said because Tytell did not supply the written report or, more likely, because Tytell didn't come to the conclusion that Friedman wanted. Tytell is convinced the documents he examined are fakes.

The Truman Signature

The second major problem on the Truman Memo, again according to Tytell, is Truman's signature. The signature on the executive order matches, exactly, another Truman signature, this one from a letter dated October 1, 1947. The positioning of the signature on the memo also makes it suspect. Truman habitually placed his signature so that the stroke on the "T" touched the bottom of the text. On the disputed Truman Memo that is not the case.

Moore and Shandera, in their *The MJ-12 Documents: An Analytical Report* write, after measuring the Truman signature, that it isn't an exact match. They suggest it is close, and, according to various handwriting experts, this makes the signature more consistent with authenticity.

The controversy over that memo wasn't ended there. Joe Nickell and John Fischer, two skeptics who were interested in MJ-12, received a copy of *The MJ-12 Documents: An Analytical Report* in 1991. Nickell and Fischer believed, according to an unpublished paper, *Further Deception: Moore and Shandera's MJ-12 Report*, "[The Moore and Shandera report] provides lessons in how not to investigate a ufologically related questioned document case.... Not only is neither a trained investigator, let alone a document specialist, but both are crashed-saucer zealots and one (Moore) has actually been suspected of having forged the documents."

Then, to make their case, Nickell and Fischer again examine the status of the investigation of the Truman Memo. They reinforce their conclusion that the document is "an incompetent" hybrid, and say that "no genuine memo has yet been discovered with such an erroneous mixture of elements." Moore and Shandera dismiss this criticism, according to Nickell and Fischer, "with the cavalier observation that there was 'a wide variety of styles and formats in acceptable use at the time.'"

The important point here is that there is a mixture of errors on the Truman Memo. It could be suggested, if there was but a single mistake, it could have been a one-time occurrence. Unfortunately, as noted, there are other errors on the document as well and that suggests to many that it is fraudulent.

Nickell and Fischer had also pointed out that the Truman signature had been "placed uncharacteristically low." Moore and Shandera countered by saying, "The problem with this assertion is that those who make it used only letters signed by Truman as the basis for their study." Nickell and Fischer responded, writing, "We did no such thing ... here Moore and Shandera are guilty of outright misrepresentation ... we studied typed letters and memos, handwritten notes, engraved thank-you cards, inscriptions and photographs.... In every instance where Truman had personally signed the text ... our observation of close placement applied."

Friedman, however, rejects this argument, pointing out, correctly, that Nickell and Fischer have not reviewed every single document signed by Truman. That means, somewhere, there could be another Truman signature that conforms to that on the MJ-12 memo. Of course, Nickell and Fischer's examination was of a representative sample of sufficient size for them to draw a legitimate conclusion. It is now incumbent on the proponents to produce a legitimate Truman document signed in the same manner but they have failed, to this point, to do that.

The only exceptions to this that have been found are documents that contain Truman's signature but were not signed by him. That is to say, his signature had been printed on the document. As a case on point, many veterans of the

Second World War have a certificate signed by Truman but the signature was printed on the document rather than signed individually by Truman.

In the final argument listed in their response, Nickell and Fischer again examine the evidence that the signature on the questioned memo is an exact duplicate of an authentic Truman signature from a letter dated October 1, 1947. They write that "in forensic comparisons in which distortion can be a possibility—e.g., in attempting to match fingerprints, or to link a paint flake to a chipped surface—the Moore-Shandera (actually Maccabee) approach is not used. Instead, experts establish matching by demonstrating that an array of distinctive features in one item is also represented in the other. Using this approach, competent examiners have determined that the two [Truman] signatures do in fact match."

Friedman does provide one additional argument about the authenticity. He has said, repeatedly, that no one seemed to notice that the Truman Memo was typed with two typewriters. He points specifically to the date, and he suggests that this is a further proof of authenticity.

An example of President Truman's signature appears on this letter recognizing the then-new state of Israel. Note the appearance of the capital T.

But those who work with questioned documents suggest otherwise. According to them, the use of two typewriters is one of the markers of a faked document. Rather than being an indication of authenticity, then, the use of two typewriters is an indication of fraud and becomes just one more reason to reject the MJ-12 documents.

Peter Tytell and His Examination

In a tape-recorded interview with Peter Tytell on August 20, 1996, he was asked specific questions about the Truman signature. To him, this was another "slam dunk." It was a second major problem with the document which shouted fake at him.

Friedman has pointed out that the signature from the memo, when placed over the signature from the October 1 letter, is not an exact match. He then belittles the claim that stretching in the copying process would lead to the differences in the signature. He also notes the careful measuring of the various components in the signature carried out by Moore and Shandera, proving their case. He suggests, because the two signatures are not an exact match, a reversal of an earlier opinion, that the signature must be authentic.

Such things, that is, the measuring of the signature looks good, looks scientific, but is just so much "eyewash," according to questioned-documents experts. In other words, it has no relevance in a discussion of copied signatures, especially since the original document is unavailable and had been originally photographed and then printed from 35mm film rather than copied on a Xerox or Minolta or Panasonic.

In fact, there are appearances on the Truman signature that suggest it had been altered prior to it being applied to the memo. One expert said, "That is a demonstrable, transplanted signature." And if it is a transplanted signature, the memo is a fake. Ironically, one of the experts consulted by Friedman would make a similar determination, as noted later.

Tytell said,

Klass is the one who came up with the prototype signature. And that's an absolute slam dunk. There's no question about it. When you look at the points where it intersects the typing on the original donor memo [that is, the October 1, 1947 letter] for the transplant, you can see that it was retouched on those points on the Majestic-12 memo. So, it's just a perfect fit. The thing was it wasn't photocopied and it wasn't photographed straight on…. The guy who did one of the photographic prints had to tilt the base board to try and get the edges to come out square so whoever did the photography of the pieces of paper was not doing this on a properly set up copy stand. It was done, maybe on a tripod, or it was done hand held. However it was done, the documents were not photographed straight on…. There's a slight distortion of the signature but it is not enough to make the difference here. Nowadays it you could probably get it to fit properly with computer work but it's not that the signature is an overlay but it's that at those discrete points, and their dumb document examiners talked about the thinning of the stroke at this point. At that particular point, at the exact spot where it touches a typewritten letter and it has to be retouched to get rid of the letter.

When the discussion turned to the measurements made by Moore and Shandera, he said, "Oh, give me a break…. It's just eye wash and what they're doing is looking at the distortions that you get from the photocopying process…. We're dealing with photocopies of photocopies of photocopies of the October first donor document signature."

The argument about the signature has moved into a new arena. Dr. Robert Wood and his son Ryan suggest that the Truman Memo signature might be authentic because Truman used an "autopen" to sign some documents. This strange device would sign four documents at once. If true, then the signatures could be exact. To prove their point, they need to find one of the other two, but have been unable to do that.

Of course Tytell's note that the signature on the Truman Memo has been altered would rule out the autopen argument. There would be no reason to alter the signature if Truman had used an autopen, but would be if the signature was lifted, by copying, from one document and then pasted on another.

> In fact, there are appearances on the Truman signature that suggest it had been altered prior to it being applied to the memo.

In fact, a close examination of the signature shows the same dots and spots from the donor document. This would suggest that it wasn't signed with an autopen, but that it was a photocopy of a real signature lifted from another, authentic document.

Tytell went on to enumerate other problems with the whole Eisenhower Briefing. He said:

> And it was just perfect because the whole thing of the twelve pages or however many pages it was. Most of the pages were just blank pages with just five words on them, like Top Secret Memo or Appendix A or something like that. The bulk of the narrative said see this appendix for the metallurgical analysis. See that appendix for the autopsy. Now those particular appendices, in order to make them look credible would require a considerable amount of technical knowledge and vocabulary. There is no question about that. You have to know how to talk the talk to write something about metallurgy or anatomy. And you can just say the metallurgical reports found that this was unlike anything that we've ever seen but then you have to list the most advanced tests that would be available in 1947 but would not be available in 1955 and you have to know too much. And you have to know the lingo of the human anatomy. You have to be a doctor basically to say that this structure is not like that structure. So I can see why nobody would bother to fake those.

He continued by saying, "But a simply bureaucratic memo from somebody who is steeped in bureaucratic lingo from having pored through these archives as I'm sure that all the people involved on both sides of this issue have done. To fake one of those, that's no big deal.... To get the right people on there and throw in one or two anti-UFO people just for fun.... That's not a problem."

Finally, he said, "I want to smoke these people out because, quite frankly, I want to nuke them. These people are going around aiding in the ... why do you want to do this? I'm somewhat annoyed at these people who say they are document examiners who go out there and support a blatantly bad piece of paper. Shame on them. I want to smoke them out ... MJ-12 as a documentary hoax, which is what I take it to be, annoys me. I don't know who the hoaxer is."

Dueling Experts

Tytell, who had been sent the documents by Friedman, concluded that they were faked. He believed them fake because of his expertise, his complete strike-ups for a wide variety of typewriters, and the mistakes that he found in the documents themselves. He communicated these negative results to Friedman, but Friedman ignored them. Instead, Friedman said that four other document examiners said the documents were authentic, but provided no name or credentials for those four experts until he identified one man, James A. Black, who had been hired by Dr. Robert Wood. He was not one of those other four.

In fact, Friedman dismisses Tytell's analysis as an "off-the-cuff opinion." But he also notes that Tytell is a world-class questioned-document examiner that he, Moore, and Shandera had chosen to analyze the MJ-12 documents. According to Friedman, Tytell didn't want his name associated with this and he issued no formal report. According to Tytell, he provided no written report because no one would pay for his services, which is not quite what Friedman was saying. He said that he would issue a final report if someone would pay his fee.

Friedman wrote about another aspect of this, saying, "Fortunately Dr. Robert M. Wood hired an expert, James A. Black, to perform a professional examination," implying here that somehow Tytell's analysis was less than professional.

Black then reported, "My knowledge of typewriter fonts permits me to conclude that the letter was likely to have been typed by an Underwood Standard typewriter. The portions of the letter that can be clearly visualized match those of a typewriter exemplar of an Underwood Standard typed in May 1940."

Tytell would, of course, dispute this saying that a complete workup or strikeup of the font to include the special characters, the numbers, and the symbols is necessary to be certain. There are many typewriter fonts that look quite similar when there is a simple comparison just between the letters. Tytell worried that such would be the case with the MJ-12 documents and there would be positive results if the complete strikeup was not used for comparison. That seems to be the case here.

Interestingly, and reported by Friedman, Black also said that the Truman signature was most likely a reproduction or a copy of a real signature. He wrote, "I reached this opinion because the ink line is homogenous and feathering is absent at the end of the lines."

In other words, Black was confirming Tytell's opinion that the signature had been copied from another source document and then copied to remove the incriminating cut lines. This is indicative of a forgery, but Friedman spins it, suggesting that the EBD might have been typed at the CIA and that the CIA would have been able to lift the signature. Now, suggests Friedman, the CIA was the area where the documents were manufactured, which, of course, doesn't make them authentic. It just provides another suspect in the creation of the forgeries.

The Aquarius Telex

In what might be the initial step in the MJ-12 conspiracy, the first reported mention of MJ-12 was in a teletype message that had been originally classified as "secret" and was dated November 17, 1980. This document was allegedly sent from the AFOSI headquarters at Bolling Air Force Base near Washington, D.C., to the 17th District AFOSI Office at Kirkland Air Force Base in New Mexico. It reports on the analysis of negatives from a UFO film. It was given to Moore by Richard Doty and Moore showed it to other researchers in January 1981, which establishes a timeline of the introduction of MJ-12 into the civilian consciousness.

The teletype message said, in all capital letters:

USAF NO LONGER PUBLICALLY ACTIVE IN UFO RESEARCH, HOWEVER USAF STILL HAS INTEREST IN ALL UFO SIGHTINGS OVER USAF INSTALLATIONS/TEST RANGES, SEVERAL OTHER GOVERNMENT AGENCIES, LED BY NASA, ACTIVELY INVESTIGATES [sic] LEGITIMATE SIGHTINGS THROUGH COVERT COVER ... ONE SUCH COVER IS UFO REPORTING CENTER, US COAST AND GEODETIC SURVEY, ROCKVILLE, MD 20852. NASA FILTERS RESULTS OF SIGHTINGS TO APPROPRIATE MILITARY DEPARTMENTS WITH INTEREST IN THAT PARTICULAR SIGHTING. THE OFFICIAL US GOVERNMENT POLICY AND RESULTS OF PROJECT AQUARIUS IS [sic] OUTSIDE OFFICIAL INTELLIGENCE CHANNELS AND *WITH RESTRICTED ACCESS TO 'MJ TWELVE'* [emphasis added].

By 1981 the U.S. Air Force had announced it was no longer interested in investigating UFO reports, except when they were sighted over air force bases and other installations.

To understand this, it is necessary to understand another alleged conspiracy that developed near Kirkland AFB, which is in Albuquerque, New Mexico. Also in Albuquerque, in the 1970s, was a businessman and physicist, Paul Bennewitz, who began picking up bizarre messages on his radio equipment that he believed were communications from alien creatures. He also believed that he saw UFOs over the Manzano Mountains which housed a nuclear weapons facility and a test area. More importantly, he filmed some of these lights or objects.

Bennewitz told others about what he had seen, filmed, and heard, and while some believed he was deluded, those out at Kirkland worried about what he had discovered. Not aliens communicating with one another or their home world, but the low-frequency nets used in communication with American submarines in far-off areas and far underwater. They were afraid that he might inadvertently tip off the Soviets about the method of communication which would allow the Soviets to develop a technology to receive the messages.

On October 24, 1980, Bennewitz contacted the chief of Kirkland security, Major Ernest Edwards, who directed him to the AFOSI and an NCO named Richard Doty. That meeting resulted in a long report that said Bennewitz had been studying UFOs for about fifteen months and that he had tapes that showed high periods of electrical magnetism being emitted from the Manzano/Coyote Canyon area, and that he had films of the unidentified objects over that same location, taken in the same time period.

The report concluded, saying, "After analyzing the data collected by Dr. BENNEWITZ, Mr. MILLER, a GS-15 [meaning a government service employee and who was the Chief, Scientific Advisor for Air Force Test and Evaluation Center at Kirkland and was a rather high-ranking civilian] related the evidence clearly shows that some type of unidentified aerial objects were caught on film; however, no conclusions could be made whether the objects pose a threat to Manzano/Coyote Canyon areas. Mr. MILLER felt the electronical [sic] recording tapes were inconclusive and could have been gathered from several conventional sources. No sightings, other than these, have been reported in the area."

Bennewitz was then invited out to the base to present his evidence to another small group of officers and scientists. Apparently, it didn't go all that well because Doty told Bennewitz, a week later, that the AFOSI was no longer interested in his sightings and recordings.

Bennewitz, unhappy with these results, communicated with New Mexico senator Harrison Schmitt, who asked the AFOSI what they planned to do about Bennewitz's allegations. Schmitt, learning that no investigation was planned, called Brigadier General William Brooksher, and while Harrison was satisfied with the results of the conversation with the general, Bennewitz was not. He enlisted the aid of New Mexico's other senator, Peter Domenici. Domenici talked first with Doty and then Bennewitz. It was at that point that Domenici lost interest so both of New Mexico's senators were out of the investigation.

It was about this same time that Moore was busy promoting his book about the Roswell UFO crash. According to what he would later claim, he did a radio show in Albuquerque and on his way out of the studio, the receptionist told him that he had a telephone call. The caller identified himself as someone who worked out at Kirkland. Moore arranged to meet the caller in a nearby restaurant. That man turned out to be Richard Doty.

The players for this part of the drama were now all in place. Moore lived in Arizona but had met Doty, who claimed great inside knowledge of the UFOs and the workings of the Air Force investigations. Bennewitz lived in Albuquerque and believed that he was watching UFOs and listening in to their coded communications almost on a daily basis. Doty was stationed at Kirkland in Albuquerque and had interviewed Bennewitz about his UFO discoveries so it could be said that he, Doty, also had an interest in UFOs.

> Not only had alien bodies been recovered near Roswell, but in 1949, an alien creature had been captured and housed at Los Alamos until it died in 1952.

According to what Moore would later claim, he was then recruited to assist AFOSI in their ongoing investigations of Bennewitz and they promised him that he would become privy to the highly classified information about UFOs that would turn the world on its head. Not only had alien bodies been recovered near Roswell, but in 1949, an alien creature had been captured and housed at Los Alamos until it died in 1952.

To be treated to all this inside information, all Moore had to do was spy on Bennewitz for the AFOSI, or so he thought. He would also spy on the Aerial Phenomena Research Organization (APRO) which wouldn't be difficult because Moore was a member of the board of directors. APRO, of course, was interested in UFOs, and it had a more liberal policy about them that included research into alien encounters and alien abduction, which might suggest that the AFOSI had a greater interest in APRO than the other civilian UFO groups.

Moore began to pass disinformation to Bennewitz. One of those documents, according to what Moore told Jerry Clark in a 1990 interview, was something Doty claimed he had gotten right off the teletype, meaning right out of the classified communications center at Kirkland, and was sharing with Moore even though that violated various laws and military regulations. This was the Aquarius Telex. Doty showed it to Moore but didn't let him have a copy of it then.

Later Doty gave it to Moore to give to Bennewitz, but Moore said that he noticed that there had been changes to it. Moore said that NSA had been changed to NASA, and there was that mention of the U.S. Coast and Geodetic Survey. This, Moore speculated, was a retyped version of the real classified message. Moore, worried that the AFOSI would close down his inside information conduit, agreed to slip it to Bennewitz, but then held on to it for several weeks. Finally he handed it over to Bennewitz.

This seemed to be a genesis of the Aquarius Telex, created by the government to fool and to discredit Bennewitz. Moore claimed to have seen the real original so that he knew this version was bogus. But there is another version of this story, or rather a reason for the retyped version of the Aquarius Telex that surfaced sometime later inside the UFO community. And that turns everything else upside down.

After questions about the authenticity of the Aquarius Telex began to circulate in 1989, the late Richard Hall, of the Fund for UFO Research (FUFOR), confronted Moore about the it. Moore admitted, according to Hall, that he, Moore, had retyped the memo and pasted on the headings because the original was too poor to read easily. He said that he had created nothing and had added nothing to the text, but was just trying to improve the document so that it would be useful as an illustration of the reality of MJ-12. Moore never offered the original, with the reference to MJ-12 on it, to prove this version of his story. Even a poor copy would have gone a long way to prove the truth.

Later still, Moore denied that he had retyped the document. That, however, doesn't matter in today's world. Nearly everyone agrees that this document, known universally as the Aquarius Telex, is a fake. When MJ-12 is discussed, few even mention it. And the real point is that the first document to be publicly presented that mentioned MJ-12 is an admitted fake, which should taint the rest of the document pool.

Friedman, in fact, in a February 2001, letter, wrote of the Aquarius Telex, "I am not sure what you mean by the Aquarius Telex and don't even mention in *TOP SECRET/MAJIC* [his book on the Majestic-Twelve] or in 'Final Report on Operation Majestic 12.'" He realized early on that this would not bode well for the reality of MJ-12 and certainly didn't want to take the discussion into the realm of the Aquarius Briefing.

Much later, as I attempted to learn more about the "Aquarius Documents," I queried both Friedman and Robert Wood about them. Both promised to respond to questions about the reality of Aquarius but both failed to supply any additional information about it.

The Fakers

There is another aspect to MJ-12 that demands discussion and that is who created MJ-12. Was it created by President Truman as a way to exploit the find in Roswell? Was it a way to reverse-engineer the alien technology for the benefit of the United States and the contractors that the government decided to help? Was it disinformation created to fool the Soviet Union or divert attention away from the truly mysterious UFOs? Or was it a creation by those inside the UFO community to entice other witnesses into the public arena?

Bill Moore might have inadvertently answered the questions in the early 1980s. He had said, to several of his colleagues, that he was thinking about creating a Roswell-type document that would suggest the crash was real and that the information was now in the public arena. He wanted to use this to convince reluctant witnesses that it was now legal for them to talk about what they had seen and done in 1947. The release of the document would show that the information was already in the public eye, so that anything they had to say was no longer classified and they wouldn't be prosecuted for revealing the formerly classified information.

In the real world, however, such reasoning is in error. Those who have been privy to classified information are not allowed to discuss it with those who do not have the proper security clearances. Even with the information out and printed in newspapers, discussed on television and radio, or talked about inside the UFO community, those who learned it through classified contacts are not allowed to verify the validity of the information, or even suggest that they know anything about it. You might say that the phrase "I can neither confirm nor deny" was created for these circumstances.

A black-and-white photo of a purported UFO hovering over homes in Passaic, New Jersey, in 1952. It later proved to be a fake.

In the real world, however, there are those who do not understand this, even if they have been trained in the handling of classified information. Captain W. O. "Pappy" Henderson, when he saw a story about the Roswell crash in a supermarket tabloid, handed the paper to his wife, Sappho, and said, "I've wanted to tell you about this for years. Now that it's in the paper, I guess I can." But, of course, he wasn't supposed to tell her because he had learned of the crash through classified sources.

And it is that attitude that might have led Moore to the idea that an official-looking document might persuade other, reluctant witnesses to share what they knew. Moore discussed the idea with several people, including Stan Friedman and Brad Sparks.

It came as no surprise to some that Jaime Shandera, a close friend of Moore, received a document that suggested the crash at Roswell was real. In the few pages of the Eisenhower Briefing Document available, it gave away enough to prove there had been a crash and a high-level cover-up of those facts. It had been orchestrated by the White House, or in this case, President Truman, and access to the information was extremely limited.

Although there were always arguments about the authenticity of the documents, a major blow was delivered when Bob Pratt, a writer who had an interest in UFOs, died. His papers, including much of his UFO research and his notes and correspondence on a novel about a UFO crash, were donated to MUFON. Those documents added to the debate about MJ-12 and might have suggested a genesis of the idea.

According to Pratt's papers, he was working with Bill Moore and Richard Doty on a fictional account of a mythical committee formed after the recovery of an alien spacecraft. According to Pratt's notes, he was discussing with Moore the dates and data that appear in the first of the MJ-12 documents and talking about MJ-12 two years before he, or rather Shandera, received the 35mm film with the Eisenhower briefing on it. Moore, according to the notes now available as an example, said to Pratt:

Well, that was '53 ... fully 11 months after the Robertson Panel, and there were all sorts of doings and goings on between the CIA and the NSC where the CIA was attempting to—it's not clear which way it was going, whether the NSC was attempting to get the CIA to take over things or whether it was vice versa. I've never been quite clear, on who was trying to influence whom, but if you read that message it is very confusing. And especially when a lot of those documents make reference to attachments which aren't there. So I have just sort of conjectured that the NSC got control of it at the point in time where Truman was ending his administration and Eisenhower was beginning his. If you stop and think about the point in time of the Robertson Panel, it happened just on that transition phase. See, Truman had not run for reelection in '52, in November. Eisenhower wins and takes office in January, January 20, and you've got the Robertson Panel deliberating in there, and it could well be that somebody was trying to determine how to go on with the change in administrations, which would have presented a problem for that sort of a thing, especially if it had gotten highly developed and the decision had already been made that this has got to be kept locked tighter than a drum. How then to deal with it with an incoming president whose reaction is not certain. And that's a point that nobody's ever brought up that I've heard in discussion. Nobody's ever noticed that that date is very interesting.

The early connection between the main players in this minor conspiracy is the paper Brad Sparks delivered at a recent MUFON conference. In it Sparks traced the history of MJ-12 in its first incarnation as a novel to be written by Moore, Doty, and Pratt. Quite a bit of the MJ-12 stuff surfaced in that novel.

Using the information from Pratt's personal notes (a sample of which was quoted earlier) and interviews with various UFO researchers, Sparks, along with Barry Greenwood, concluded that MJ-12 is a hoax. Sparks believed it was a sanctioned disinformation campaign by the AFOSI with Moore and Shandera as the willing participants, or maybe the unwilling dupes. The evidence, whichever direction taken, leads clearly to hoax, regardless of the spin put on it or the reason for its creation.

Sparks points out that this report is the most heavily footnoted article to ever appear in *The MUFON Symposium Proceedings*. It contains facsimiles of many of the documents and it outlines the evidence clearly and concisely. It should drive the final stake through the heart of MJ-12, but nothing in UFO research ever sinks completely. There are always those who will attempt to resurrect it by claiming that was a disinformation campaign that contains some "real" information. All we have to do is figure what is real and what is fake.

> Although there were always arguments about the authenticity of the documents, a major blow was delivered when Bob Pratt, a writer who had an interest in UFOs, died.

Government Disinformation?

Sparks and Greenwood, in their MUFON Symposium paper, laid out the case that the creation of the MJ-12 documents wasn't by UFO researchers, but was done with the knowledge and the guidance of AFOSI. Specifically, it was Richard Doty. The chronology they created was slightly different than that which had been floating around in UFO circles since the EBD was first released, suggesting that there was something called the Aquarius Project and that it was the first indication of alien contact.

According to Sparks and Greenwood, many in the UFO community, when talking about the Aquarius Documents, think primarily of the Aquarius Telex and remember the only copy available is the "retyped" version that Moore had been showing. But they wrote that the original Aquarius Documents, which included a 1977 briefing to President Carter, might have also been the genesis of the Eisenhower Briefing Document. The Carter briefing, according to them, was an updated version of the EBD.

Sparks and Greenwood reported that in December 1981, Moore met with Doty and at that meeting Doty provided a great deal of information about crash retrievals and the bodies of the flight crews. These were the original Aquarius Documents and they had been prepared for Truman and then modified for Eisenhower and later still for other presidents.

By the time the briefing was updated for Carter, it contained information that suggested that Jesus Christ was an alien and that the extraterrestrial creatures had been manipulating human DNA for thousands of years with the goal of genetically engineering the human race.

Moore was the first to see the Carter Briefing, and according to him, it was early in March 1983 that he received a telephone call inviting him, eventually, to view the documents. Of course, the whole thing was filled with cloak and dagger because UFO research requires a little spy mystery. Moore was given instructions that had to be followed precisely before the early evening meeting in a hotel room. There was a knock on Moore's motel door and a stranger entered carrying a sealed package. He told Moore that he had nineteen minutes to review the material, that he could do anything he wanted with it, and at the end of the time, the stranger would return expecting to receive the material back.

When you think about it, this is an absurd situation. The stranger is supposedly handing Moore top-secret documents but isn't allowing him to keep them. Instead, he leaves the room so that Moore could do whatever he wanted with them. Moore, not being a stupid man, took out a camera and began to photograph them. He used a quarter in each frame for scale. And then, fearing that the pictures would turn out poorly, he began to read each of the documents into a tape recorder, using the word "line" to denote the end of a line, and naming each punctuation mark so that he could, if necessary, reconstruct the documents as they had been typed. It turned out that it was a smart thing to do because the pictures were underexposed and poorly focused so the physical evidence, such as it was, was no longer available.

When the time was up, the stranger returned, took the papers, counted them, stuffed them back into the envelope, and disappeared into the night. Moore was left with only his poor-quality photographs and the sound of his own voice reading the documents on the tape. It seems absurd that if Moore was free to photograph them, why the stranger hadn't just brought him photocopies originally? Why was he, Moore, limited to nineteen minutes to study them? And wasn't this about the craziest leak that had ever filtered material from the government to the private sector? It seems to be filled with "movie" logic, but nothing that could be considered logic in the real world.

Moore, later describing the documents, suggested that they appeared to be notes created to either prepare a classified report or they were notes taken during a classified briefing. Moore also suggested that there was little that could be done to verify the information, which seems to be no surprise in the world today. In 1987, however, Moore and his partner Shandera decided that they would release some small segments of this document to see if other researchers had seen them, or other documents with similar information, and recognized them or had copies of them. No one came forward.

Other Classified Projects

The Carter documents, as Moore described them, named a number of classified projects including Aquarius, Sigma, Snowbird, and Pounce. Little real information was provided and a great deal of it was hidden originally by Moore and Shandera. Of interest, however, is the section dealing with Project Sigma. According to that, contact with aliens had been established nearly two decades after the Roswell crash.

Sigma suggested that the first positive contact was made on April 25, 1964, when an intelligence officer met aliens during a pre-arranged landing at Holloman Air Force Base near Alamogordo, New Mexico. Exchange of information was in the alien's language, and that these sorts of meetings continue until today.

Snowbird, according to the documents, is the Air Force mission to test fly a "recovered" alien craft. This project is continuing in Nevada, which is a veiled reference to Area 51, the tales told by Robert Lazar, and the wild speculations of others. It should be noted here that although Moore suggested he received this information in 1983, the release of the data did not come until after Robert Lazar had suggested to KLAS television reporter George Knapp in Las Vegas that he, Lazar, had seen

William Moore.

nine alien spacecraft at Area 51. Lazar's story is questioned because of a lack of corroboration for it and an inability to verify much of Lazar's claimed education.

What was disturbing about all this was that the source of the material, once again, was Moore and Shandera. There was no place to go, no government agency to be questioned, no FOIA requests to be filed that would provide corroboration, no real provenance for the documents other than Moore's unidentified stranger and his envelope of classified material and Moore's voice on tape. All we had was the integrity of William Moore and the fuzzy, poorly lighted photographs that no one saw.

Linda Howe and the Carter Briefing

But Moore wasn't the only UFO researcher contacted by a government agent who supposedly knew the truth about UFOs, MJ-12, or crashed flying saucers and alien visitation. Linda Howe stumbled into the mix when she was asked by Home Box Office (HBO) executives if she would produce a documentary on UFOs for them. In March 1983, she signed a contract.

While in New York during the negotiations with the HBO executives, she had dinner with Peter Gersten, who would later sue the government in an attempt to shake loose UFO-related files, and Pat Huyghe, a science writer with an interest in UFOs and who, with Dennis Stacy, would publish both *The Anom-*

Dennis Stacy.

alist, a journal about the paranormal, and Anomalist Books, which deal with a wide range of special-interest topics.

Gersten told Howe about an Air Force OSI agent who was currently stationed at Kirkland by the name of Richard Doty. He claimed to know some very interesting things about UFO visitation and influence on human evolution and who might be willing to talk on camera about those things. Gersten would attempt to set up some kind of a meeting between them, if Howe was interested. Of course she wanted to interview him.

Doty agreed to a meeting, and Howe flew to Albuquerque. There was allegedly some sort of mix-up at the airport, with Doty insisting that he had been there all the time but had missed her, and Howe insisting that no one had been there to meet her as promised. Howe knew an officer at Kirkland and called him. He eventually called Doty, and Doty and Howe finally got together.

A new meeting was arranged and it was decided that they would meet at the air base. Once they arrived at Kirkland, Doty took Howe to "his boss' office," and then arranged for her to sit in a specific chair because "eyes can see through windows." Howe believed she had been asked to move so that hidden microphones would be better able to pick up her voice as they discussed UFOs and the documents she was about to see. It is just another example of the strangeness that surrounds MJ-12 and the sort of logic that permeates these tales.

Doty said to her, "My superiors have asked me to show you this." He took an envelope from a drawer, opened it, and handed Howe several sheets of paper. He warned her that she could not copy them, could not make notes about them, and that she could only read them, which, of course, allowed for Doty to then deny he had shown her anything. Moore had been luckier when he was told that he could do anything he wanted as long as it only took him nineteen minutes to do it.

The title of the document, or report, was *A Briefing for the President of the United States on the Subject of Unidentified Flying Vehicles*. Since there was no date on the report, nor was the president named, Howe had no way of knowing for which president the report had been prepared. Later information would suggest the president was Jimmy Carter and this was what became known as the Aquarius Briefing.

The documents that Howe read mentioned the July, 1947, Roswell crash, as well as another one near Roswell in 1949. It also sug-

Peter Gersten.

gested that an alien had survived one of these crashes and that it was taken to a "safe house" at Los Alamos National Laboratory, north of Santa Fe, New Mexico. The aliens, according to this document, were small, gray, and humanoid, which by 1983 and thanks to abduction researchers was becoming the standard description of the alien creatures, at least in the United States. According to Howe, the alien was befriended by an Air Force officer, and the creature had died on June 18, 1952.

The document mentioned other crashes, including Kingman, Arizona, in 1953, the Aztec, New Mexico, crash of 1948, and the Del Rio crash in 1950. The bodies from each of these accidents were removed and sent on to various military and governmental facilities for study and the craft sent for reverse-engineering. The metallic wreckage was transported to Wright-Patterson for testing in the facilities there.

The reason for believing that the document Howe saw was the Carter Briefing was because it, too, mentioned Snowbird, Sigma, and Aquarius, as had the Carter documents seen by Moore earlier. In these new documents there was also a mention of Project Garnet, which was designed to investigate alien influences on human evolution.

According to Howe, these documents, and other unnamed government sources, suggested the "grays" were from a nearby solar system and had manipu-

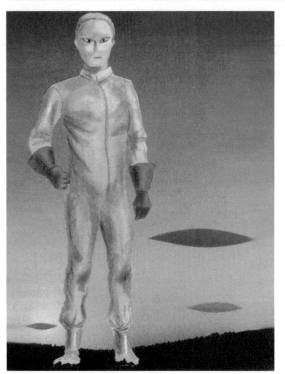

There are several types of aliens that have been described, one of which is the "Nordic" aliens, which are tall and rather handsome beings.

lated the DNA of primates at various time intervals including 25,000, 15,000, 5,000, and 2,500 years ago. It also suggested that the grays created a being about 2,000 years ago to teach humanity about love and nonviolence. In other words, Jesus Christ was created by the aliens, at least according to these documents and Howe's unnamed sources. This, of course, annoyed any number of people when they heard about it.

The document also hinted at another alien race known as the "Talls" or "Blonds" or Nordic types, which have also been reported during abductions. They had been engaged in a three-hundred-year war with the grays and they were responsible for some of the Earth-based violence including the cattle mutilations reported in many parts of the country and some of the human mutilations reported in other parts of the world.

The documents, again according to Howe, suggest that Project Blue Book was a public relations operation that was supposed to divert attention from the real investigative projects. Doty, in his conversations with Howe, mentioned MJ-12 but suggested the MJ stood for "Majority" rather than Majestic. Whatever the real name, it was a committee of twelve high-ranking government officials, scientists, and military officers who set the policy for the cover-up and the dissemination of disinformation about UFOs and government interest in them into the public mainstream.

This could be seen as corroboration for what Moore had suggested about his clandestine meetings with unidentified strangers in motel rooms. If Moore was making up his story, surely Linda Howe would not invent a similar story, or incorporate elements of Moore's report into hers. It is clear from the timing of various events that Howe could not have heard about Moore's activities because he wasn't talking to much of anyone about them in 1983 and it would be much later that he began to talk at all.

But there is a link here and it is an important one. Moore knew Doty. They had been working together for some time and, thanks to Bob Pratt, we know Doty and Moore had even collaborated on a novel together that included the elements of MJ-12. Pratt suggested that he, with Moore and an unidentified third man (Pratt believed it to be Doty) had written a novel in 1980-81 in which MJ-12 figured prominently. And this means that there was a link between Doty and Moore so the information supplied by Moore, of his strange meeting in a hotel room, is not independent of Howe's meeting with Doty. Both Moore and Howe knew Doty and that could tie the information together.

There is a draft of that novel in Pratt's papers which are held by MUFON. But some of that material is marked "Pratt Sensitive" so that it has not been released. Very few people have seen the draft, but it apparently lays out the MJ-12 material and is the first place that it arises.

In fact, according to Greenwood and Sparks, Pratt suggested that they do it as a novel because there was little in the way of verification of the supposedly real material. Pratt, apparently, wanted to check the sources and the facts, but since that wasn't possible given the alleged sources, he hesitated. He didn't want to write a nonfiction book that might blow up in his face when challenged by his fellow journalists. The way to do that was to use fiction as a cover.

Aliens are often described as small, gray humanoids.

Majestic-12 Operations Manual

Another document, sent through the mail and on undeveloped photographic film so that there was no provenance for it, was a document labeled "Extraterrestrial Entities and Technology Recovery and Disposal." This is, according to the front cover, the "Majestic-12 Group Special Operations Manual."

Once again, a document about the alleged MJ-12 committee has come, ultimately, from an unidentified source. It is a document that has been circulating in the UFO community for a number of years and is now part of the Majestic-Twelve Project and the mythology of MJ-12.

A study of the manual reveals that a great deal of work went into its construction. This was no simple, quick, and dirty job. It suggests someone who is familiar with the military-style manuals that have been produced for decades. The cover is impressive, looks authentic, and even includes a "seal" to add to the visual impact. Unfortunately it is the seal of the Department of War, an organization that ceased to exist about seven years before the manual was printed.

The manual itself is short, with the table of contents showing Appendix III beginning on page thirty-one. That appendix, according to the manual, contains the photographs. No copy of the manual in the hands of UFO researchers contains any photographs, and in fact, most copies end on page twenty-three.

Again, as with the other MJ-12 documents, the manual is classified as "Top Secret/Majic Eyes Only." Those inside the government and the military report that an "Eyes Only" classification mark is contradictory here. "Eyes Only" documents are created for a specific person, to brief that person on a highly classified subject. A document might be created for the "Eyes Only" of the president, but it would not be put on an operations manual. Once the "Eyes Only" recipient has read the document, it is usually destroyed. There would be a single copy of it because it was created for the "Eyes Only" of a specific person. It would defeat the purpose of a manual.

> (T)he cover of the document violated the federal regulations in effect in April 1954. If the document is authentic, it should conform to those regulations.

A real mistake seems to be that the manual is classified as "Restricted." According to the Herbert L. Pankratz of the Eisenhower Library, "The classification markings on the alleged MJ-12 document are not consistent with federal regulations for the marking of classified materials as of April 1954 [the date on the manual]. The 'Restricted' classification category was terminated by executive order in November 1953 and would not have been used on a document in April 1954. Federal regulations also require that the cover page reflect the highest level of classification for any material in the document. Since 'Top Secret' is a higher category than 'Restricted,' only 'Top Secret' should have appeared on the cover of the document."

In other words, the cover of the document violated the federal regulations in effect in April 1954. If the document is authentic, it should conform to those regulations. This document, like all the other MJ-12 documents, seems to be at variance with the proper government regulations in force at the time of its creation. Proponents will claim that these regulations weren't ironclad and that variations do exist. However, documents created at this level would be closely monitored and would adhere to the proper regulations, especially since those regulations had just been changed. The classifications on the manual, like those on the other MJ-12 documents, are wrong and there is no reason for them to be wrong. It smacks of hoax.

Pankratz continued in his letter of February 6, 1995, saying, "In addition, we have no evidence in our files that a security classification referred to as 'MAJIC EYES ONLY' ever existed. Executive Order 10501 was signed by President Eisenhower on November 5, 1953. It set up three classification categories: 'Top Secret,' 'Secret,' and 'Confidential.' A fourth category, 'Restricted Data' (not the same as 'Restricted'), was established by the Atomic Energy Act of 1954 and it is used only with regard to nuclear weapons." The manual, then, contains an obsolete classification mark. That is a second major mistake made by the creator of the document.

As with the rest of the Majestic-Twelve Project papers, the manual contains many anachronisms. On page 4, for example, the manual instructs the retrieval units on how to keep the press and the public from learning about the alien craft. They suggest explaining the sightings and crashes as "meteors, downed satellites, weather balloons...." But on the date that the manual was issued, April 1954, there were no artificial satellites in orbit and a suggestion by military officials that one had been recovered would have generated more press interest, not less.

It is clear that someone with a great deal of time, an intimate knowledge of the UFO phenomenon, and a computer with good word processing and graphics programs created the MJ-12 manual. That person, however, had not worked with classified material, nor did he or she understand the system. That explains why the mixed classifications are found on the front cover of the manual. It also explains why an obsolete term "Restricted" was used. That was an attempt to conform to the original documents.

> There is no doubt that the MJ-12 Operations Manual is nothing more than a fake.

The opinion that the manual is a fake is shared by a number of researchers. In March 1999, a coalition of UFO researchers from the Center for UFO Studies, Project 1947, and the Fund for UFO Research issued a joint statement about the Operations Manual. The joint statement said, in part, "We believe this document to be a hoax; a deliberate fake designed to mislead the public and to plant false information in the UFO research community by person or persons whose motives are unknown."

Those who signed the joint statement included Don Berliner, an aviation writer and historian who had been singled out by the perpetrators of the hoax and who was a member of the Fund for UFO Research. Jan L. Aldrich, a retired Army master sergeant who had been an intelligence NCO (sergeant), a classified-document custodian, and a top-secret control officer, also signed the statement. Thomas P. Deuley, a retired naval officer who had been a crytological officer and a Communications Security (COMSEC) custodian, was another of those who signed the statement. They were joined by Dick Hall, former chairman of FUFOR, and Mark Rodeghier, the current director of CUFOS.

Each brought an expertise to the table, and each reviewed the Operations Manual in light of his expertise. All concluded that the document was a fake. This was a cross-section of the UFO community and included Berliner, who had originally received the manual. Their conclusion that the manual was a hoax was not qualified in any fashion.

There is no doubt that the MJ-12 Operations Manual is nothing more than a fake. It does not conform to the regulations, it contains inaccurate and anachronistic information, and it is incomplete. The manual should be rejected as the fake it is.

Majestic-Twelve Project

When it began to seem that the last had been heard of MJ-12, that all the documents that had been published contained some fatal flaw that led to the conclusion that MJ-12 was a hoax, a new round was started. More documents were found, more documents were identified and published, new sources came forward, and new questions were asked.

Although there had been rumors that a new package of documents had surfaced, it wasn't until October 11, 1998, that Dr. Robert Wood and his adult son, Ryan, announced that they had received a large package that contained dozens of such documents.

The new group of about forty documents contained about 125 pages of information about MJ-12 and its alleged operations, but it also contained a few documents that had already made the rounds.

Like all the others, this group of documents surfaced without a provenance. Wood told researchers at the Omega Communications conference hosted by John White that he had received them from a California-based researcher named Timothy Cooper who had become an "expert" on using the Freedom of Information Act to acquire UFO-related material. While that was interesting, it appeared that, according to Cooper, he had received most of the new documents from a third party identified only as Cantwheel. It was not explained exactly who Cantwheel was or how he had acquired so much MJ-12 material. Cantwheel has, of course, since died, and is therefore no longer available to answer questions.

According to the documents, Field Order 862 was issued by President Truman's Office of Assistant Chief of Staff and ordered the Interplanetary Phenomenon Unit (IPU) to head to New Mexico. A seven-page document dated July 9, 1947, subtitled "Extraordinary recovery of fallen objects in New Mexico," provides descriptions of the debris recovered and details where the various pieces of debris were sent.

That same document describes the deaths of some of the men involved in the retrieval operation. Four technicians who were on the site became extremely sick during the recovery and three of them died of heavy bleeding after being taken to the hospital. One of the military policemen on the scene later committed suicide.

Another of the documents suggested that Nathan Twining investigate the crash. In a three-page report, Twining suggested that the craft was powered by "atomic engines" and that it was doughnut-shaped and about thirty-five feet in diameter. This seems to be a reference to the discredited Maury Island case and the object described by the alleged witnesses.

The longest of these documents is the MJ-12 Operations Manual which had originally been sent to Berliner. The Woods' investigation uncovered nothing new about the Operations Manual. They do argue, however, that the

Investigators examine the site of an alien landing in Socorro, New Mexico.

anachronistic use of Area 51 might be appropriate. According to them, Area 51 referred to a map location that could well have been in use prior to 1954 when the manual was allegedly written. They don't explain how the material would be sent to a base that hadn't been built in 1954 even if there was a map reference on it.

One of the most interesting of the documents is dated September 24, 1947, which might be part of the Eisenhower Briefing that was not included in the first leaks of that document. It identifies a new acronym for the UFOs, referring to them as "unidentified lenticular aerodyne technology" or ULAT. Clearly ULAT means alien spacecraft.

According to that document, ULAT-1 had been recovered at a location southeast of Socorro, New Mexico. That seems to imply that part of the Barney Barnett story is accurate, though the crash was not far to the west on the Plains of San Agustin as originally believed, but rather closer to Socorro. This could be seen as a thin corroboration to the now discredited Santilli autopsy film.

Those who believe in the authenticity of MJ-12, and Robert and Ryan Wood are numbered among them, have found what they believe to be proofs of the authenticity of these new documents. They noticed that in some of the documents there was a raised "z," that is, every "z" is slightly above the position of the other letters printed on the same line.

A number of authenticated documents printed by the Government Printing Office (GPO) in that same year seem to exhibit the "flying z." To some, this suggested the documents are authentic.

But many problems, suggesting fraud, have also appeared. First, and foremost, are the claims that no one knows where the documents originated. There is no way to use Freedom of Information to acquire authentic copies of the documents. There is no government agency which will admit that they are the source of the documents, or that copies of the documents are stored at their offices. The trail runs from the Woods to Cooper to the dead Cantwheel, and then no farther.

In a similar circumstance, UFO researchers learned of a project code named Moon Dust. Part of the Moon Dust mission was investigation of foreign UFO sightings. There were documents, but Air Force officers denied that such a project ever existed. The difference, however, is there is a provenance of some of the Moon Dust documents. They came from the Department of State and other researchers, using FOIA requests, were able to obtain them. On many, in the block for the "subject," there were the code words "Moon Dust." It was clear that there had been a secret project with that code name and Air Force denials about it were erroneous. In other words, there was a provenance and others could find the same or different authentic documents that discussed Moon Dust. No one, however, has been able to verify the code name Majestic-Twelve or MJ-12 or any of the various abbreviations of it. The documents keep surfacing, inside the UFO community, with neither the provenance nor the pedigree needed to be convincing.

As with the Operations Manual, there are anachronisms in the new batch of documents. First, in a document entitled "1st Annual Report of the MAJESTIC TWELVE PROJECT," there is a mention of a retro-virus (with a hyphen in it). This term, in a document dated 1952, caught the eyes of a number of researchers. All wondered about when retro virus had entered the language.

UFO researchers began a quick survey of the relevant scientific literature and realized that the term retro virus (a group of viruses that, unlike all other viruses and cellular material, carry their genetic fingerprint in the RNA) didn't exist in 1952. The mechanism of the retro virus was discovered by Howard Temin, who began work on the problem in 1960. Apparently, another scientist, David Baltimore, working at MIT had independently duplicated Temin's work and they published a joint article on June 27, 1970 in *Nature*. It was after this article that the term "retro-virus" entered the lexicon. The question to be asked was the same question that had been asked in the past. How could a paper produced in 1952 make reference to a term that did not exist in 1952?

Those wishing to believe in the MJ-12 documents found what they believed to be a logical explanation for this problem. Wood, in searching for a possible alternative use of the term, including the hyphenated "retro-virus" that might have been used prior to 1970, found a number of scientific articles that mentioned retrograde organisms that predated the 1952 Annual Report. Wood wrote that Robert Green, as early as 1935, had suggested that all viruses were retrograde organisms.

Wood wrote, "One reasonable scenario is that the writer of this section of the 1st Annual Report of the MAJESTIC TWELVE PROJECT, perhaps being obsessed with jargonizing, may have simply shortened the term 'retrograde virus' to retro-virus.'"

Others didn't find the suggestion reasonable. To them, the use of retro virus, with or without the hyphen, suggested a document that had not been created in 1952 but much later, and that was, therefore, fraudulent.

Another of the anachronisms was the position of General Hoyt S. Vandenberg in 1952. The 1st Annual Report, because of what it mentions, had to be written in either late 1951 or in 1952. The cover page lists one of the members, Gen. Hoyt Vandenberg, as the "Vice Chief of Staff, United States Air Force." The problem was that Vandenberg was Vice Chief of Staff in 1947 when MJ-12 was allegedly created, but by the summer of 1948, he had been promoted to the Chief of Staff of the Air Force. There is no way that he would have been listed on any official document created in 1951 or later as a vice chief of staff.

Still another anachronism is found in a document dated "February 1948." In the lower left corner of the memo, there is a list of agencies that are to receive the document. Listed among those is "USAFOSI." The problem is that in February 1948, the Air Force Office of Special Investigation (designated as AFOSI) did not exist. Worse for the creator of the document, it was never called the USAFOSI.

These anachronisms, then, were inserted as a way of limiting the damage done if the documents leaked into the public arena. There are those who have argued that these "poison pills" have been built into the MJ-12 documents to "destroy" them.

What these researchers are suggesting is that some information, hopelessly out of place or inaccurate, was included in each of the MJ-12 documents. When they were leaked into the public arena, these "poison pills" would be found and that would suggest, to skeptics and disbelievers, that the documents were fraudulent. The tactic, according to the researchers, is well known in intelligence circles that routinely create disinformation. It is the purpose of that disinformation to discredit the document or the individual who has it.

> What these researchers are suggesting is that some information, hopelessly out of place or inaccurate, was included in each of the MJ-12 documents.

The problem with the thinking is that this sort of thinking is slightly off-kilter. Most disinformation is not created to self-destruct. It is created to take the enemy, whoever that enemy might be, in the wrong direction for as long as possible. For it to self-destruct would be to defeat its purpose.

However, if a leak is found that does compromise true classified information, then bad information is often pumped into that leak with the hope that all information retrieved from that source will the be discredited. But that is not the same as disinformation or the same as what is seen here. If MJ-12 was disinformation, as some have suggested, the effort would be made to make sure that nothing was found to suggest that it was fraudulent because that would defeat the purpose. Besides, those creating it would have enough intimate knowledge of the situation to keep from making basic mistakes. They would know what the situation was.

The Majestic-Twelve Project, with its huge release of documents, should be taken for what it is. Without a proper provenance, with the anachronisms that dot it, with the information that seems to embrace almost every aspect of the Roswell case, it simply must be considered at best dubious and at worst, another hoax.

Summation

So, the questions become: Who faked the MJ-12 documents and why would they do it?

The answer seems to be two-fold. First culprit is the government, in the guise of the Air Force, but more specifically, Richard Doty, operating with the knowledge of his superiors. According to Greenwood and Sparks, as outlined in their 2007 MUFON Symposium paper, "AF Regulations lay out a vast array of such covert warfare operations that are authorized for AFOSI to carry out, even against law-abiding U.S. citizens and organizations."

Greenwood and Sparks reported, "But the purposes had been previously revealed by Doty to Moore, then to Pratt ... where Moore explained how the disinformation operation against ufology works."

They then quoted from the twenty-five page manuscript that Pratt made from his interview with Moore. Moore told Pratt, "How many people would it take working full time to sow confusion, keep the UFO groups off balance...? It wouldn't take many ... one in each of the three major organizations [which at that time would have been MUFON, CUFOS, and FUFOR, but in the past would have been NICAP, APRO, and MUFON] and one for the smaller organizations that were deemed to be worth the trouble ... they could quite effectively keep everybody off balance by feeding disinformation or feeding little bit[s] of truth to get somebody off on another track...."

The point that Moore was making, or it might be said that Doty was making, was that it wouldn't have to be a big operation with many people involved. It would take a little effort to get those who dealt with the press to maintain an attitude of debunking, meaning Air Force spokesmen and governmental officials saying there wasn't anything to these sightings because in all their investigations they found nothing at all. In fact, a perfect example of that was the 2010 White House response to the petition asking for a release of information about alien visitation. The White House made a statement that there wasn't anything to these ideas of UFOs and aliens, and nothing further was going to be said about it.

As another example, Moore said that when NICAP began to have some success with its call for congressional hearings, and the threat to the Air Force was growing, they simply derailed NICAP at that point.

Moore said, "And now all of a sudden we find out that their board was riddled with CIA people [including Roscoe Hillenkoetter and Karl Pflock who said he had been associated with the CIA and who was a member of the Washington, D.C., NICAP committee] and the guy who replaces Keyhoe as director [Col. Joseph Bryan III, USAFR] has questionable connections...."

Orfeo Angelucci

Moore continued, saying "you encourage an Adamski [George Adamski who claimed to have met Venusians] and a Richard Andolucci [Orfeo Angelucci, another contactee] ... you encourage any number of those people ... they don't take much encouragement.... All they need is a little attention ... and they do the job for you without you having to pay them. The same sense with Phil Klass. They don't have to put him on the payroll. They just need to encourage him to continue what he's doing. So, any time he flags in his effort they dump a little more seemingly bona fide debunking information on him that 'it couldn't be so because'—and he takes it from there. Why pay him?"

You might say that the investigation of Newton and Aztec is an example of this. The Air Force telling him there is nothing to it but to keep doing what he is doing, which is leading people in the wrong direction. That is, if you accept Karl Pflock's information about the Newton diary.

Moore made a similar point in 1989, and did virtually the same thing when he confessed at the MUFON Symposium in Las Vegas that he had been an unpaid agent of the AFOSI. He warned the audience, "Every time one of you repeats an unverified or unsubstantiated bit of information without qualifying it as such, you are contributing to the process...."

At that point everything seemed to have come full circle. Moore said that he had been working with the AFOSI so that he could learn the truth about alien visitation. His contact was Doty. It was Doty who had briefed him on the Aquarius Project, as he, Doty, had briefed Linda Howe. It was Doty, Moore, and Shandera who, with the aid of Pratt, were going to write a novel about MJ-12 because, according to Pratt, they didn't have the evidence to do a nonfiction book. It was Moore and Shandera who received the MJ-12 documents in the mail without a return address, but with a postmark of Albuquerque, and Doty lived in Albuquerque.

So with all this information, the question is still whether MJ-12 was government disinformation or was it a hoax cooked up by someone else for some other reason?

Back a decade or more, I was collecting videotaped testimony from Roswell witnesses for the Fund for UFO Research's oral history project. I was in California with Stan Friedman and we, quite naturally, began to discuss MJ-12. I had heard from a couple of people that Bill Moore, one of those who released the MJ-12 documents into the public arena in 1987, had been talking about creating a "Roswell" document to try to shake things loose.

> The plan was to put out a document that would closely mirror the situation in 1947 and force those involved in the cover-up to reveal part of it....

Moore, I had heard, thought he had taken the investigation as far as he could without some sort of revelation or dramatic discovery. The plan was to put out a document that would closely mirror the situation in 1947 and force those involved in the cover-up to reveal part of it as they attempted to learn who knew what and how much of it they knew.

Friedman confirmed for me that it was true. Bill Moore had told him the same thing. But when the MJ-12 documents surfaced, Friedman thought nothing of that conversation and the fact that the documents had not gone to Moore but to an unknown film producer whose only tie to the UFO community seemed to be Bill Moore.

Barry Greenwood had heard the same thing and reported in his *Just Cause* newsletter of September 1989, on page ten, "After Moore released the first wave of MJ-12 documents in 1987, CAUS [Citizens Against UFO Secrecy], and particularly Larry Fawcett, spoke to Moore about cooperation in researching the story in the form of filing FOIA requests, etc. as an effort to flesh out information. Moore rejected the offer, adding that he wanted to 'put bread on my table.'"

But disinformation implies that it was an official operation of some kind and in this case the overseeing agency is AFOSI, at least to Sparks' way of thinking. I'm not sure it was a sanctioned mission; it might have been more of Doty seeing a gravy train and leaping aboard with his buddy Bill Moore than it was any kind of planned AFOSI operation. At this point, it really doesn't matter because in either case, the conclusion of hoax is the important one. Government disinformation or opportunism by Doty and Moore makes no difference in the end. They both lead to hoax and to more than two-and-a-half decades of chasing the documents.

Those who believe that MJ-12 is authentic often point out that to fake these documents, the forger would have to have a great deal of complex historical knowledge. It wouldn't be something that someone on the outside could do, meaning here, of course, outside the government agencies that deal with the UFOs. This was an argument for the creation being the work of insiders.

In the past I had argued that Stan Friedman had suggested that he, and Bill Moore, did have this knowledge. In *The Roswell Report,* edited by George M. Eberhart for the Center for UFO Studies and published in 1991, Friedman had written, "The simple fact of the matter is that Moore, Shandera, and I had already picked up on all the names on the list prior to the receipt of the film (except for Dr. Donald Menzel) as a result of the many days spent in historical archival research that begun a decade ago because of the Roswell incident.... We had noted who was where in early July 1947 when the Roswell incident occurred...."

But Stan's research, along with that of Moore, was even more in-depth. Karl Pflock, in his column "Pflock Ptalk," published in Jim Moseley's semi-serious and periodically published *Saucer Smear,* wrote, "In 1976, ufologist Brad Sparks discovered Menzel had a UFO sighting near Alamogordo, New Mexico,

when he was in the area in 1949.... Then in 1977, Sparks circulated a paper on Menzel, his presence in New Mexico in the 1940s, and his sighting and his distortions and outright attempts to suppress it."

Pflock noted here that one of Sparks' readers was Friedman, showing that Friedman was aware of Menzel's ufological history. That Friedman knew about this is important.

Pflock continued, "In 1982, Canadian engineer-ufologist Wilbert Smith notes on his 1950 indirect interview of American scientist Robert Sarbacher surfaced. Smith alleged Sarbacher ... had confirmed crashed saucers were being studied by a super-secret U.S. government group...."

Pflock wrote next, "According to my sources, Friedman instantly concluded the group had been established to study the Roswell saucer and bodies and fingered Menzel as the most likely leader of the outfit because he was 'right on the scene' when the

Karl Pflock

crash occurred…. Friedman quickly worked up a list of probable members of the 'Sarbacher-Smith group,' which my sources say included not only Menzel but *all* [emphasis added] on the EBD MJ-12 roster. Over the next couple of years, Friedman quietly but enthusiastically touted his theory about Menzel and the saucer-study panel to ufological colleagues."

Then, of course, Moore and Shandera supposedly received the MJ-12 material anonymously in the mail in 1984. Moore and Shandera were, at the time, working with Friedman on the Roswell case. In fact, Moore wrote *The Roswell Incident,* published in 1980, and Friedman has complained ever since that the promised big acknowledgment for him wasn't in the book.

And finally, in "1987, they [meaning Friedman and Moore] went public with the EBD and MJ-12 at the National UFO Conference. Friedman made much of his 'Who'da thunk it?' surprise on discovering Menzel's involvement, uttering nary a word about his earlier notions."

So, the evidence is there that Moore and Friedman had the knowledge to cook up MJ-12. Friedman bragged about knowing who was where but there is no evidence that he had anything to do with the EBD or any of the MJ-12 documents. He did the research on the various individuals and passed all that along to his then-partner Moore. The evidence does point a finger at Moore, and by extension, Shandera.

Philip Klass noted that Moore employed a bizarre dating system that was a hybrid of the military format and the civilian method but which is also used in Europe. He used a zero as a placeholder in single-digit dates and a comma after the month and before the year as in 06 December, 1947. The true military format has neither the zero nor the comma. This points another finger at Moore as one of those who created MJ-12. And, since he knew Doty, who was in the Air Force at the time and familiar with the handling and marking of classified documents, Moore could have created MJ-12 with Doty's help. This was Klass' theory.

MJ-12 boils down to a conspiracy to either dump disinformation on UFO researchers to force them into research paths away from the truth, or it was a creation of specific UFO researchers in an attempt to persuade witnesses, in this case former military personnel, to share secrets with them about the Roswell case. Either way, MJ-12 was a conspiracy to mislead, and it has been working quite well since the mid-1980s.

The UFO Projects

After the summer of 1947, with flying saucer reports dominating the first few weeks, with stories of alien ships crashing, and with reports from military and civilian pilots, the government and the military took notice. Documentation available in the Project Blue Book files suggests that high-ranking military officers and civilian government leaders were concerned about possible alien missions. If the flying saucers represented an alien race, then invasion of Earth might be the objective. They simply did not know what to expect.

It might be said that there was no real effort, in the beginning, to hide the truth. They were responding to the sudden appearance of physical craft that outperformed anything in the military inventory. But during that summer the War Department was undergoing a reorganization, as were other elements of the federal government, and this added to the confusion. Too much was happening too fast.

Ed Ruppelt, writing in *The Report on Unidentified Flying Objects*, said, "The paperwork of that period also indicated the confusion that surrounded the investigation; confusion almost to the point of panic. The brass wanted an answer quickly, and people were taking off in all directions."

By late summer, the panic had eased slightly as speculation about the nature of UFOs changed into something that had to do with the Soviet Union. It was thought that their German scientists, captured at the end of the war, were doing better than our German scientists. Ruppelt reported that with UFOs being seen near our testing centers at Muroc Air Force Base (later Edwards AFB), the White Sands Proving Ground, and atomic bomb plants, the efforts to identify the objects became more concentrated.

Orders were issued to investigate all UFO sightings and gather as much information as possible. The FBI was asked for help to investigate the backgrounds of witnesses, and J. Edgar Hoover agreed as long as the FBI was given access to all discs recovered.

The Hoover Note

Hoover was referring to a case from Shreveport, Louisiana, dated July 7, 1947. According to a report dated 23 July 1947, the intelligence office at Barksdale Field near Shreveport had received a report that a flying disc had been located, or crashed, in Shreveport. A witness told the Army officers that he (a man named Harston but not further identified) "had heard the disc whirling through the air and had looked up in time to see it when it was approximately two hundred feet in the air and coming over a sign board adjacent to the used car lot where he was standing ... [witness] stated that smoke and fire were coming from the disc and that it was traveling at a high rate of speed and that it fell into the street...."

The following day, the Army investigators talked to another witness who told them in an interview "that he had made the disc [created it] in order to play a joke on his boss and that the starter had been taken from a fluorescent light and two condensers from electric fans."

The witness described how he put it together and then "sailed the disc in front of his boss's car, but that his boss failed to notice the disc and drove away. [The witness] further stated that some man (presumably Harston) saw the disc fall into the street ... he [the witness] was of the opinion that anyone who examined the disc could readily tell that it was not dangerous, and that it was the work of a practical joker."

With that the Army closed their investigation. But the FBI was still interested. The FBI document covers the same information but added a single detail. According to the FBI document, "Harston stated that the disc made a sound when traveling through the air similar to a policeman's whistle and that the smooth side was toward the earth while in flight."

There was a handwritten note that said, "10 July 47—Maj. Carlau (US Br of ID) says FBI advises this was a hoax."

It was about this time, in July 1947, that the Army asked the FBI for assistance in investigating the flying saucers, or rather, and more importantly, for help in investigating the witnesses. J. Edgar Hoover responded to the request which came from the Army Air Forces' Brigadier General George F. Schulgen, at the time Chief of Requirements Intelligence Branch, by writing, "I would do it but before agreeing to it we must insist upon full access to discs recovered. For instance in the La. case the Army grabbed it and would not let us have it for cursory examination."

The question that surfaced was what did the "La. case" mean? Skeptics and debunkers pointed to the Shreveport recovery. That seemed to answer the question.

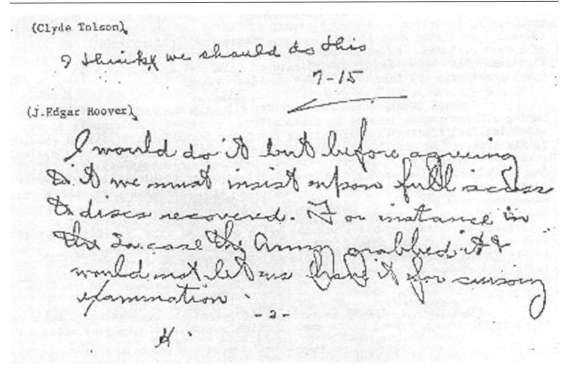

(Clyde Tolson)

I think we should do this

7-15

(J. Edgar Hoover)

I would do it but before agreeing to it we must insist upon full access to discs recovered. For instance in the La. case the Army grabbed it & would not let us have it for cursory examination

The note written by J. Edgar Hoover about helping with the UFO investigation.

The problem was that the case file for the Shreveport crash is readily available in Project Blue Book files. The FBI was not cut out of the case and the Army didn't grab the saucer or refuse to allow the FBI to inspect it. In fact, just the opposite is true. The FBI had seen the file, seen the disc, seen the pictures taken of it, and even pronounced that it was a hoax.

In 1947 the flying saucers appeared in a domestic environment which, to Hoover, suggested that the FBI was the agency responsible for gathering intelligence about them. The Army Air Forces, however, charged with the defense of the skies over the United States, thought otherwise. That would give rise to a "turf war." That is, Hoover believed that the Army was attempting to usurp his authority by investigating the UFO sightings inside the United States. He seemed to believe the FBI had been "cut out of the loop." He wasn't going to have another agency tromping over the ground he believed belonged to the FBI.

The Hoover document, then, is understandable in the context of the times. Hoover was fighting a turf war with the Army Air Forces, trying to pry into what military officers considered their areas of responsibility. Hoover wanted to be on the inside of the discussion. He would require information in response to his assistance in background investigations of those who saw flying saucers. From Hoover's point of view, this was empire building and had nothing to do with the reality of flying saucers.

> It seems odd that Hoover would mention a crashed disc and a recovered disc so casually.

There is another issue here, and that is if the La. note actually referred to Shreveport. Looking at the files, it certainly does seem to point in that direction. It seems odd that Hoover would mention a crashed disc and a recovered disc so casually. It would seem that he knew something else and wanted to make sure that he was involved because if there was a crashed disc and it was not of Soviet origin, and Hoover was probably sure it wasn't American made, it had to be from another planet. Hoover, who might never have suggested something so far out to anyone, might have privately thought it could be possible. He didn't want to miss out on the biggest story of the millennium. The fact that Hoover's note is ambiguous only deepens the mystery rather than solving it.

Brigadier General George F. Schulgen's Other Letter

As he was soliciting the aid of the FBI, Schulgen was also trying to find out what was happening in a physical sense. He wrote to the Air Materiel Command, then at Wright Field in Ohio, asking for their analysis of the situation. That is, he sent along the files of some sixteen UFO sightings, though he mentioned eighteen. These were the best sightings to date; they included one from May 17, 1947, and ended with one on July 12. Five of the cases were made by military pilots, including one from Maxwell Field, Alabama, by four pilots on June 28. Six of the sightings involved civilian pilots, including the July 4 sighting by Captain Smith and his United Airlines crew.

Schulgen's estimate contained conclusions based on the information contained in it. His conclusion was that there wasn't much of a mystery about flying saucers. To them, the objects were mechanical. They just didn't know who was flying them or rather, to which country they belonged. But, since there seemed to be no real investigation giving the number of sightings, their conclusion was that the flying saucers were American and highly classified. Nothing else explained the lack of concern by those at higher levels of the military chain of command.

AMC, commanded by Lieutenant General Nathan Twining, rather than acknowledging that he, and AMC, knew all about the flying saucers, sent a letter that probably surprised those who received it. He said that the phenomenon was something and that it should be investigated. That letter has been in the hands of UFO researchers for decades.

In response to Schulgen, Twining, or rather members of his staff who prepared the document for his signature, wrote:

1. As requested by AC/AS-2 there is presented below the considered opinion of this Command concerning the so-called "Flying Discs". This

opinion is based on interrogation report data furnished by AC/AS-2 and preliminary studies by personnel of T-2 and Aircraft Laboratory, Engineering Division T-3. This opinion was arrived at in a conference between personnel from the Air Institute of Technology, Intelligence T-2, Office, Chief of Engineering Division, and the Aircraft, Power Plant and Propeller Laboratories of Engineering Division T-3.

2. It is the opinion that:

   a. The phenomenon reported is something real and not visionary or fictitious.

   b. There are objects probably approximately the shape of a disc, of such appreciable size as to appear to be as large as manmade aircraft.

   c. There is a possibility that some of the incidents may be caused by natural phenomena, such as meteors.

   d. The reported operating characteristics such as extreme rates of climb, maneuverability (particularly in roll), and action which must be considered evasive when sighted or contacted by friendly aircraft and radar, lend belief to the possibility that some of the objects are controlled either manually, automatically or remotely.

   e. The apparent common description of the objects is as follows:

      (1) Metallic or light reflecting surface.

Page two begins with the following heading: basic Ltr fr CG, AMC WF to CO, AAF, Wash. D.C. subj "AMC Opinion Concerning 'Flying Discs.'"

      (2) Absence of trail, except in a few instances when the object apparently was operating under high performance conditions.

      (3) Circular or elliptical in shape, flat on bottom and domed on top.

      (4) Several reports of well kept formation flights varying from three to nine objects.

      (5) Normally no associated sound, except in three instances a substantial rumbling roar was heard.

      (6) Level flight speeds normally above 300 knots are estimated.

   f. It is possible within the present U.S. knowledge—provided extensive detailed development is undertaken—to construct a piloted aircraft which has the general description of the object in subparagraph (e) above which would be capable of an approximate range of 7000 miles at subsonic speeds.

   g. Any developments in this country along the lines indicated would be extremely expensive, time consuming and at the considerable expense of current projects and therefore, if directed, should be set up independently of existing projects.

h. Due consideration must be given the following:

(1) The possibility that these objects are of domestic origin—the product of some high security project not known to AC/AS-2 or this command.

(2) The lack of physical evidence in the shape of crash recovered exhibits which would undeniably prove the existence of these objects.

(3) The possibility that some foreign nation has a form of propulsion possibly nuclear, which is outside of our domestic knowledge.

3. It is recommended that:

a. Headquarters, Army Air Forces issue a directive assigning a priority, security classification and Code Name for a detailed study of the matter to include the preparation of complete sets of all available and pertinent data which will then be made available to the Army, Navy, Atomic Energy Commission, JRDB, the Air Force Scientific Advisory Board Group, NACA, and the RAND and NEPA projects for comments and recommendations, with a preliminary report to be forwarded within 15 days of receipt of the data and a detailed report thereafter every 30 days as the investigation develops. A complete interchange of data should be effected.

4. Awaiting a specific directive AMC will continue the investigation within its current resources in order to more closely define the nature of the phenomenon. Detailed Essential Elements of Information will be formulated immediately for transmittal thru channels.

N.F. Twining
Lieutenant General, U.S.A.
Commanding

This response must have surprised Schulgen and his subordinates. They had assumed that those higher up would have known what was happening. They had assumed that the flying saucers were some kind of top-secret project and they would be told to ignore it. After all, if it was a top-secret project, the last thing that anyone would want was to have a bunch of lower-ranking officers attempting to investigate.

Yet this is exactly what they were being told to do. Not only that, they were given a priority and a security classification themselves. Ruppelt reported that the project was assigned a 2A classification, which while not the highest, was certainly a project that required special attention.

The mission of Project Sign, at least according to Ed Ruppelt, was to determine what the flying saucers were. There were two schools of thought. One suggested they were Soviet, and intelligence officers began searching the captured records of German project, looking for a clue. Other intelligence officers in Germany were doing the same thing.

Those opposed to this idea thought it would be foolish for the Soviets to be flying over U.S. territories. If one of the saucers crashed, then the Air Force would be able to reverse-engineer the craft. In other words, it would be handing over a huge technological leap to the enemy, and intelligence officers didn't believe the Soviets would do that.

The second school of thought was that the UFOs were not manufactured on Earth. At the time, they were looking at interplanetary craft and not something that was interstellar.

During the summer, there had been a panic percolating through the Pentagon, but as time passed, they began to relax. Although the sightings continued, there had been no effort by the pilots of those craft to land and there were no hints that they were hostile. According to Ruppelt, by the end of 1947, the routine at ATIC began to return to normal. Twining's plan had been implemented, and Sign was set to begin operations.

> The mission of Project Sign, at least according to Ed Ruppelt, was to determine what the flying saucers were.

Ruppelt, in his book written about the end of the summer, "As 1947 drew to a close, the Air Force's Project Sign had outgrown its initial panic and had settled down to a routine operation. Every intelligence report dealing with the Germans' World War II aeronautical research had been studied to find out if the Russians could have developed any of the late German designs into flying saucers."

That line of inquiry went nowhere. If the saucers were Soviet, and there was no evidence that they were, and if they weren't American, and all aspects of the U.S. government from the new Department of Defense to the Department of State were denying they were secret U.S. craft, then just what were they? If the flying saucers were real, meaning solid objects flying through the sky, and if they weren't based on any technology that was created on Earth, then just what were they? The obvious answer was extraterrestrial.

The Air Force continued to investigate flying saucers and assemble data about them, but there was no real drive behind the investigation. They were just going through the motions.

Then, on January 7, 1948, a National Guard pilot, Captain Thomas Mantell, was killed chasing the flying saucer.

The Mantell Incident

Although it seems that a logical answer for the case has been found, it is still wrapped in controversy. Mantell was leading a flight of four F-51 aircraft on a ferry mission to Kentucky.

It was at 1:20 P.M. when the tower crew at Godman Army Air Field at Fort Knox, Kentucky, spotted the large, bright, and apparently disc-shaped object high

Thomas Mantell.

overhead. They alerted the operations officer and he in turn alerted the base commander, Colonel Guy F. Hix. None of them in the tower were immediately able to identify the object.

For nearly an hour and a half they watched the object that seemed to hang motionless in the sky. People in the towns near the base also watched the UFO, some claiming that it was moving slowly to the south. Some said that it hovered and then began its slow flight.

At 2:45 P.M. the situation changed when Mantell's flight requested permission to fly through the area. The UFO was still visible and Mantell was asked if he would check on the object to try to identify it. Mantell replied that his was a ferry flight but he would attempt the intercept. He began a spiraling climb to fifteen thousand feet.

As he reached fifteen thousand feet, more than a thousand feet above the altitude he was authorized to fly at without oxygen on board, he radioed (according to disputed records) saying the object "is above me and appears to be moving half my speed." Later, as he continued his climb, he would say that it was "metallic and it is tremendous in size."

The records are confusing about the altitudes that various pilots reached. Clearly Mantell and two of his wingmen climbed to fifteen thousand feet. Most of the documentation suggests that all three aircraft reached twenty-two thousand feet, where the two wingmen who had stayed with him, Lieutenant A. W. Clements and Lieutenant B.A. Hammond, turned back. The oxygen equipment of one of the fighters had failed, or had not been properly serviced on the ground before the flight, and military regulations required that oxygen be used above fourteen thousand feet. Hammond radioed that they were abandoning the intercept, but Mantell, who according to all available documentation had no oxygen equipment on his aircraft, or at the very least had no working equipment, continued his climb anyway. He did not acknowledge the last message from Hammond.

For thirty minutes, as the flight chased the huge object, each of the wingmen broke off the intercept. Now, at 3:10 P.M., Mantell was the only pilot left chasing the object and he was alone at twenty-three thousand feet. According to the documentation available in the Project Blue Book files, he either told his wingmen that he was going to climb to twenty thousand feet [again giving rise to the dispute over his altitude] and if he could get no closer or observe anything else, he would break off the intercept. Or, being unable to resolve the identity of the object, he said that he said he was going to climb to twenty-five thousand feet for ten minutes.

The last that anyone saw of him, he was still climbing toward the UFO but made no further radio calls to either his wingmen or the control tower at Godman. By 3:15 everyone had lost both radio and visual contact with him.

Fearing the worst, a search was launched and just after 5:00 P.M., on a farm near Franklin, Kentucky, the remains of Mantell's F-51 were found scattered over about a half a mile. Mantell's body was inside the broken cockpit. His watch had stopped at 3:18 P.M. From the evidence it seems that Mantell was killed in the crash of his aircraft.

An investigation began immediately, as was required by military regulations. It was a two-pronged attack. One was to determine what happened to Mantell and why he had crashed. In other words, it was a standard aircraft accident investigation. The second was to identify the object, or objects, that he had chased. This was a UFO investigation.

Re-creation of the UFO encounter experienced by Thomas Mantell.

According to the documentation, the cause of the accident was Mantell's climb to twenty-five thousand feet without proper or working oxygen equipment. Subsequent research by both civilian and Air Force medical personnel have proven that pilots flying above fourteen thousand feet can begin to experience the effects of hypoxia, a lack of oxygen in the blood. The higher the altitude, the faster the onset of the effects. Although mountain climbers and others living at high altitudes can be acclimated to the thin atmosphere, most people are not. In fact, in some, the effects can be seen at altitudes as low as seven or eight thousand feet.

Mantell had told his wingmen that he was going to climb to twenty-five thousand feet and circle for ten minutes. If he couldn't get any closer to the UFO, he would break off the intercept. The problem, however, was that Mantell's "useful consciousness" at that altitude would have been about two minutes, and since he had been flying at twenty thousand feet or more for several minutes, he might not have remained conscious that long.

This was the conclusion of the official accident investigation. In essence, it is pilot error. The report was properly classified in 1947. This was done in accident investigations so that those giving testimony would be honest in what they said and didn't have to worry about retribution.

The UFO Aspect of the Mantell Investigation

Those who saw the UFO were interviewed officially. Boiled down to their essence, these statements provided a glimpse about Mantell and what he had seen. Questioned on several points within days of the sighting, these men reported what they remembered Mantell saying. While the exact wording was lost, and contrary to some published reports, no tower recording was made, the meanings were quite clear. From Mantell, each of these witnesses reported:

> Info taken from reports of radio conversation between Control at Godman and NG 869 essentially as follows:
>
> Col Hix's account. NG 869: "Object traveling at 180 MPH—half my speed."
>
> Lt Orner's account. NG 869: "High and traveling about 1/2 my speed at 12 o'clock position."
>
> Later: "Closing in to take a good look."
>
> No further word heard by Orner.
>
> T/Sgt Quinton A. Blackwell: NG 869: At 1445 [2:45 P.M.]. "Object traveling at 180 MPH directly ahead & above me now and moving at about 1/2 my speed."
>
> Later: "I'm trying to close in for a better look."

At 15,000 ft: "Object directly ahead of and above me now and moving about 1/2 my speed. It appears to be metallic of tremendous size. I'm trying to close in for better look."

No other word heard by Blackwell from NG 869.

Capt Gary W. Carter: NG 869: "Object going up and forward as fast as he was"—approx 360 MPH

"Going to 20,000 feet and if no closer will abandon chase."

No further contact heard by Capt Carter—apparently, last word ever received from NG 869.

These same witnesses, who watched the object for more than an hour, sometimes through binoculars, offered a range of descriptions that, in the end, matched more or less one another. Their words might have been different, and they searched for their own comparisons, but they all described the same basic object. They reported:

Col Guy F. Hix: "It was very white and looked like an umbrella."

"I thought it was a celestial body but I can't account for the fact it didn't move."

"I just don't know what it was."

He said it was about 1/4 size of the full moon and white in color. Through the binoculars it appeared to have a red border at the bottom at times and a red border at the top at times. It remained stationary (seemingly) for 1-1 1/2 hours.

Capt Carter: "Object appeared round and white (whiter than the clouds that passed in front of it) and cold be seen through cirus [sic] clouds."

From interview with Duesler (accompanied by LTC E. G. Wood):

Wood said that the object appeared about 1/10 the size of a full moon, if the thing were a great distance away, as compared to the diminishing size of the P-51s flying toward it, it would seem that it was at least several hundred feet in diameter.

After dark, another or the same object appeared in approx 234 [degrees] from Godman at 6 [degrees] elevation. This body moved to the west (259 [degrees]) and then down. The shape was fluid but generally round with no tail, the color changing from white, to blue, to red, to yellow, and had a black spot in the center at all times.

NOTE: Later, an astronomer was contacted who attempted to account for this phenomena as either Venus or a comet. (?)

PFC Stanley Oliver: "Resembled an ice cream cone topped with red."

Captain Mantell tried unsuccessfully to chase down a UFO with his P-51.

Lt Orner: (Through binoculars) "Could not determine of [sic] object radiated or reflected light. Thru binocs [sic] it appeared partially as parachute with bright sun reflecting from top of the silk, however, there seemed to be some red light around the lower part of it."

What is interesting here is the descriptions all suggest something with a rounded top and then a long and tapering underside. The weather balloons, with which they all would have been familiar in 1948, all would have been about fifteen to twenty feet in diameter and would have been round or ball-like. The color of those balloons would have been tan and they wouldn't have been highly reflective unless carrying a rawin target device made of aluminum foil. Clearly the descriptions provided by the witnesses do not fit with a weather balloon and radar reflector, but do fit with that of a Skyhook balloon, which in 1948 was a classified project.

The problem, however, was that the Air Force couldn't admit that one of their pilots had been killed chasing what might have been an alien spacecraft. They needed to identify the object so that it could be labeled, and little care was given to that explanation. As long as they could label it, even if the label didn't fit, they would be happy with it.

A Skyhook balloon was mistaken to be a UFO, according to one theory explaining Captain Mantell's encounter.

One of the first culprits mentioned in the official files was Venus. Looking at only the direction of the object in the sky, and given the time of day, Air Force investigators noticed that Venus would have been occupying that part of the sky. According to the astronomical charts available, at the time of the initial UFO sighting, Venus could be seen in the daylight sky in the approximate location of the UFO. A few of the investigators thought that Venus, if seen by Mantell, might explain the sighting.

Astronomers consulted acknowledged that Venus would have been visible, but doubted that a random search of the sky would have found it. Although bright enough to be seen in the daylight, it would have blended easily into the surrounding sky. If there was even the lightest of haze, Venus probably wouldn't have been visible to those on the ground. Or, in other words, Venus was not an acceptable explanation, and the cause of the sighting would have to be found elsewhere.

In the official files, one of the reports goes into depth about Venus. "However, under exceptionally good atmospheric conditions and the eye shielded from the direct rays of the sun, Venus might be seen as an exceeding tiny bright point of light. It can be shown that it was definitely brighter than the surrounding sky, for on the date in question, Venus has a semi-diameter of six seconds of arc…. While it is thus physically possible to see Venus at such times, usually its pinpoint character and large expanse of sky makes its casual detection very unlikely." They were, in effect, saying that Venus was visible but they didn't think it was the answer.

The Air Force investigator was not finished with the Venus answer, however. He wrote, "The chances, of course, of looking at just the right spot are very few. Once done, however, it is usually fairly easy to relocate the object and call the attention of others to it. However, atmospheric conditions must be exceptionally good."

Relevant to this theory is, of course, the weather data. The weather at Godman AAF, available in the Project Blue Book files, showed that they started the day overcast, but that gradually the cloud layer broke up so that blue sky could be seen. The visibility at Godman varied between eight and twelve miles. This suggests that there were not the optimum sky conditions necessary for someone to see Venus in the daytime.

When the astronomers said that Venus was not a likely answer, they began to look elsewhere. The official report said, "It had been unofficially reported that the object was a Navy cosmic ray balloon. If this can be established, it is to be the preferred explanation." This is suggestive of an investigation that is not interested in the truth but in labeling the case.

But this section of the Project Blue Book report was anything but consistent. Having said that it was Venus, that it wasn't Venus, and that it was a balloon, the investigator now explained why it wasn't a balloon. "If one accepts the assumption that reports from various locations in the state refer to the same object, any such device must have been a good many miles up … 25 to 50 … in order to have been seen clearly, almost simultaneously, from places 175 miles apart."

Now, having run through all sorts of explanations, the investigator wrote, "It is entirely possible, of course, that the first sightings were of some sort of balloon or aircraft and that when the reports came to Godman Field, a careful scrutiny of the sky revealed Venus, and it could be that Lieutenant [sic] Mantell did actually give chase to Venus."

Finally, the investigator wrote, again, that it was Venus, but for that explanation to work properly, he needed a balloon and one other object as well. Given these three items, though there is no evidence that all three existed, he believed he could explain the case. He wrote, "Such a hypothesis [that is, Mantell chasing Venus] does still necessitate the inclusion of at least two other objects."

All of this suggests something about the investigations as they were being carried out in that era by the military and the personnel at Project Sign. It was a search for labels, but not necessarily a search for solutions. They were willing to accept nearly anything as an answer as long as they could remove a mysterious case from the files. And Mantell's case, because of the sensational aspects as well as the public interest, was certainly one of those to be solved at all costs.

In 1952, a major magazine wanted to print an article about how spectacular UFO sightings had been explained through proper research and investigation. Because the spin of the article was that flying saucers did not exist, the Pentagon cooperated with the writer and the magazine. High-ranking Air Force officers assured the magazine editors that Mantell had chased Venus. In a move that was sure to anger the reporter and the magazine editor, a week after the magazine was published the Air Force released a new answer. Mantell had chased a balloon.

Air Force Responsibility

The solution to this case would have come much sooner had the Air Force not been interested in disproving UFOs but had been interested in finding answers. Clearly Venus has nothing to do with this sighting. The fact that it was in the sky near the right location at the time is irrelevant and has confused people for much too long. The weather data, available to the Air Force investigators, provided sufficient reason to reject Venus as the culprit. Still, the Air Force was insistent, even in the face of evidence to the contrary, that Venus was responsible, if not for all the sightings, at least in part for the Mantell side of the case. Venus, as a culprit, has been eliminated for all but the Air Force.

There is no need to create a number of balloons or other unidentified and unreported aircraft in the area to find a solution. All the talk of another balloon or object is also irrelevant.

Given the descriptions provided, the fact that Skyhook balloons were being launched in the right time frame, and given the size and shape of those balloons, it seems reasonable to believe that Mantell chased a Skyhook. Neither he, nor anyone else at Godman Army Air Field, would have been familiar with the Skyhooks. They were virtually unknown in 1948. They certainly would have been huge, fluid, and would have looked metallic because they were made of polyethylene.

> Given the descriptions provided, the fact that Skyhook balloons were being launched in the right time frame, and given the size and shape of those balloons, it seems reasonable to believe that Mantell chased a Skyhook.

Mantell's suggestion, that the object was moving at half his speed, or later suggestions that it was moving away from him as fast as he was flying toward it, are the result of optical illusion. He was looking up, at a silver, more or less circular object, against a bright background. He had no reliable estimate of the size or the distance. Without those facts, he was fooled into believing that the object was maneuvering away from him. There are no indications in the witness testimony to suggest the object was moving more than ten or fifteen miles an hour. It was moving with the winds aloft as the data indicate.

When the file is carefully studied, when the descriptions are considered, there is but a single conclusion. This was a Skyhook balloon compounded by an enthusiasm for the mission and a tragic mistake.

And it is clear from this information that the Air Force was going to solve the case no matter what it took. They changed their answer several times, coming back to Venus and balloons. They finally settled on a Skyhook balloon, but only after the flaws in other solutions were pointed out.

The Estimate of the Situation

In September 1948, the Air Force, after a year of official and unofficial investigations, produced an "Estimate of the Situation" that has become part of UFO folklore. Originally classified as top secret and then ordered destroyed because it didn't match the opinion of the Air Force Chief of Staff, Ed Ruppelt reported that he had seen the document. According to Ruppelt, the original estimate suggested that the flying saucers were of extraterrestrial origin.

Very few people ever admitted to seeing the document, so the source of the information is Ruppelt. He mentioned it in his book, but then, according to what Mike Swords discovered, much of the material had been edited out. An examination of that material provides an interesting insight into Project Sign and the investigation of UFOs, as it transpired in the late 1940s.

CUFOS and FUFOR obtained Ruppelt's papers so that they had the opportunity to explore what Ruppelt knew about the Estimate. Using that as source material, Swords wrote an article for the *International UFO Reporter*. To show what had been left out of Ruppelt's books, he used italics to show the deleted material. The following is based on Swords' review of Ruppelt's papers.

> In intelligence, if you have something to say about some vital problem you write a report that is known as an "Estimate of the Situation." A few days after the DC-3 was buzzed, the people at ATCI decided that the time had arrived to make an "Estimate of the Situation." The situation was UFOs; and the estimate was they were interplanetary!
>
> It was a rather thick document with a black cover and it was printed on legal-sized paper. Stamped across the front were the words TOP SECRET.
>
> It contained the Air Force's analysis of many of the incidents I have told you about plus many similar ones. All of them had come from scientists, pilots, and other equally credible observers, and each one was an unknown.
>
> It concluded that UFOs were interplanetary. As documented proof, many unexplained sightings were quoted. The original UFO sight-

Edwards Air Force Base (originally the secret Air Force Test Center, Muroc) in southern California is where a number of UFO sightings have been reported by military personnel.

ing was by Kenneth Arnold; the series of sightings from the secret Air Force Test Center, Muroc [later, Edwards Air Force Base]; the F-51 pilot's observations of a formation of spheres near Lake Mead; the report of an F-80 pilot who saw two round objects diving toward the ground near the Grand Canyon; and a report by the pilot of an Idaho National Guard T-6 trainer who saw a violently maneuvering black object.

As further documentation, the report quoted an interview with an Air Force major from Rapid City AFB (now Ellsworth AFB), who saw twelve UFOs flying in a tight diamond formation. When he first saw them there were high but soon they went into a fantastically high-speed dive, leveled out, made a perfect formation turn and climbed at a 30 or 40 degree angle, accelerating all the time. The UFOs were oval-shaped and brilliantly yellowish-white.

Also included was one of the reports from the AEC's Los Alamos Laboratory. The incident occurred at 9:40 A.M. on September 23, 1948. A group of people were waiting for an airplane at the landing strip in Los Alamos when one of them noticed something glint in

ALIEN MYSTERIES, CONSPIRACIES AND COVER-UPS

the sun. It was a flat, circular object, high in the northern sky. The appearance and relative size was the same as a dime held edgewise and slightly tipped, about fifty feet away.

The document pointed out that the reports hadn't actually started with the Arnold incident. Belated reports from a weather observer in Richmond, Virginia, who observed a "silver disc" through his theodolite telescope; F-47 pilot and three pilots in his formation who saw a "silvery flying wing"; and the English "ghost airplanes" that had been picked up on radar early in 1947 proved the point. Although reports on them were not received until after the Arnold sighting, these incidents had all taken place earlier.

When the estimate was completed, typed, and approved, it started up through channels to higher command echelons. It drew considerable comment but no one stopped it on its way up.

Vandenberg at the Pentagon eventually received the "Estimate" but apparently was less than impressed. At that point, according to Ruppelt, "it was batted back down. The general wouldn't buy interplanetary vehicles. The report lacked proof."

Swords reported that a group of military officers and civilian technical intelligence engineers was then called to the Pentagon to defend the "Estimate." They all seemed to believe that the UFOs were interplanetary but their defense of it failed. Not long after that happened, everyone named was reassigned. Swords noted, "So great was the carnage that only the lowest grades in the project, civilian George Towles and Lieutenant H. W. Smith, were left to write the 1949 Project Grudge document about the same cases."

Clearly, after Vandenberg "batted" the report back down, and after the staff was significantly reduced, the fire went out in the investigation. Project Sign limped along. It was clear to everyone in the military establishment that Vandenberg was not a proponent of the interplanetary theory. Those who thought otherwise risked the wrath of the number-one man in the Air Force and the quickest way to find their career in ruins was to support the idea. They'd just had a practical demonstration of that and if an officer couldn't figure that out, then he was on his way out.

The End of Project Sign

A final report called "The Findings of Project Sign" was written. This described the motivation for starting the project, who worked on it, and the results of their investigations. In the summary it noted that the report was based on "243 domestic and thirty (30) foreign incidents. Data from these incidents is being summarized, reproduced, and distributed to agencies and individuals cooperating in the analysis and evaluation.... The data contained in reports received are studied in relation to many factors, such as guided missile research activity, weather and other atmospheric sounding balloon launchings, commercial and military flights, flights of migratory birds, and other considerations, to determine possible explanations for sightings."

They did note, however, "The objects sighted have been grouped into four classifications according to configuration:

1. Flying discs, i.e., very low aspect ratio aircraft.
2. Torpedo or cigar-shaped bodies with no wings or fins visible in flight.
3. Spherical or balloon-shaped objects.
4. Balls of light.

But, they also wrote, "The possibility that some of the incidents may represent technical developments far in advance of knowledge available to engineers and scientists of this country has been considered. No facts are available to personnel at this Command that will permit an objective assessment of this pos-

The British have also categorized types of UFOs seen over their nation, as seen in this diagram available at the National Archives UK.

sibility. All information so far presented on the possible existence of space ships from another planet or aircraft propelled by an advanced type of atomic power plant have been largely conjecture."

Or, in other words, with the Chief of Staff of the Air Force, the number-one man in an Air Force uniform telling his subordinates that he doesn't accept an extraterrestrial answer, no one at Project Sign is going to risk his career by suggesting otherwise. They provided a nod in that direction, but then said it wasn't the correct solution and that it was only guesswork anyway.

The recommendations were a little surprising then. They suggested, "Future activity on this project should be carried on at the minimum level necessary to record, summarize, and evaluate the data received on future reports and to complete the specialized investigations now in progress."

They then wrote, "When and if a sufficient number of incidents are solved to indicate that these sightings do not represent a threat to the security of the nation, the assignment of special project status to the activity should be terminated."

Sign, it seems, was going to be turned into an organization for training. The personnel assigned to it would be interviewing witnesses, gathering data, and would learn how to interrogate people so that the best evidence could be found. Of course, they didn't believe there were alien spaceships, so that training would be applied in other arenas, such as the search for enemy airmen who might have bailed out over friendly territory.

On December 16, 1949, Project Sign ended. The Air Force announced that Project Saucer, the cover name given to the investigation, had been closed. They had found nothing to suggest that the flying saucers posed a threat to national security and they found no evidence that they were either an advance in Earth-based technology or that they were alien in nature. The general public was left with the impression that the Air Force was no longer investigating flying saucers.

This was not true.

Project Grudge

According to the documentation that is now available to researchers, the name, Project Sign, was originally classified. The Air Force had told the public that the name of their UFO investigation was Project Saucer, but that was part of their cover story. Later, according to those Air Force sources, the name, Sign, was compromised. That meant that those not authorized to know it had learned of it. The solution, or course, was to change the name to something else and continue to investigate.

That is what the Air Force did.

But the investigation into the flying saucers never actually ended.

Even with nearly everyone in the Air Force believing that UFO investigations should be reduced, if not ended, that didn't happen. In the Sign report of February 1949, there is a page that notes the title of the project was changed to Grudge, and the authority for it was, "Hq, USAF, Deputy Chief of Staff, Materiel, Washington 25, D.C., dated 30 Dec. 1947."

The project retained its 2A priority and the purpose was "to collect, collate, evaluate and interpret data obtained relative to the sighting of unidentified objects in the atmosphere which may have importance on the national security, and to control and effect distribution of all objective information as requested to interested governmental agencies and contractors."

Ed Ruppelt, who had been given the task of leading the Air Force investigation, wrote, "Everything was being evaluated on the belief that UFOs couldn't exist. No matter what you hear, don't believe it."

In August 1949, there was another study conducted which concluded that the project be reduced in scope. The authors of that report wrote "that Psychological Warfare Division and other governmental agencies interested in psychological warfare be informed of the results of the study."

Just months later, on December 27, 1949, it was announced that Project Grudge was to be closed. The final report, released to the press, was hundreds of pages long and was filled with the type of jargon that the military seemed to favor.

The Grudge report was made up of 237 of the best UFO sightings. J. Allen Hynek and his staff were able to explain some of them as astronomical phenomena. The Air Force Air Weather Service and the Cambridge Research Laboratory were also able to reduce the number of unexplained sightings. Weather balloons and the huge, classified Skyhook research balloons accounted for some sightings, including that made by Thomas Mantell.

But some of the explanations offered seemed to have been offered just to explain the sightings. The Rhodes photographs which had seemed to defy explanation were identified as bits of paper blown aloft by the wind and photographed on a cloudy day against a dark gray background.

The press seemed to be underwhelmed by the report. Ruppelt said that the press grabbed the appendix labeled "Summary of the Evaluation of Remaining Reports" and found it confusing. Few would, of course, wade through the entire document to see what might be hidden in it, if anything.

Ruppelt wrote that the reporters he knew found the results impossible to believe. He said that he talked to one longtime Washington reporter. Ruppelt wrote, "He said the report had been quite impressive, but only in its ambiguousness, illogical reasoning, and very apparent effort to write off all UFO reports at any cost. He, personally, thought it was a poor attempt to put out a 'fake' report, full of misleading information, to cover-up the real story. Others, he told me, just plainly and simply didn't know what to think—they were confused."

Grudge, as did Sign, came with a number of conclusions that didn't necessarily reflect the information. They were:

1. Evaluation of reports of unidentified flying objects constitute no direct threat to the national security of the United States.

2. Reports of unidentified flying objects are the result of:

    a. A mild form of mass hysteria or "war nerves."

    b. Individuals who fabricate such reports to perpetuate a hoax or seek publicity.

    c. Psychpathological persons.

    d. Misidentifications of various conventional objects.

This, of course, confused Ruppelt simply because he had been ordered by those at a much higher level to re-evaluate the UFO program, seek better reporting systems, and continue to search. In the civilian world, it was suggested that Grudge was the end of the line in the world of the UFO. Of course, it was not.

The Levelland, Texas UFO Sightings in 1957

It has been said by skeptics, scientists, governmental leaders, and military officers that there is no evidence that UFOs are anything other than illusions, misidentifications, hallucinations, and hoaxes. They have said, repeatedly, that there is no evidence that UFOs—meaning alien spacecraft—have visited the Earth. They have found nothing in all the cases investigated and all the time spent discussing UFOs that warrant further study. The questions have been answered and the debate, for them, is over.

And if they truly believed all this, they would be wrong.

On November 2, 1957, a series of sightings began around the tiny Texas panhandle town of Levelland that, had they been properly investigated at the time, would have yielded the evidence those skeptics claim doesn't exist. It was a series of sightings made by multiple witnesses in multiple locations that involved interaction with the environment and possible landing traces. Had UFO researchers in 1957 investigated the sightings then and had the Air Force been interested in learning the truth rather than proving UFOs were not spacecraft, the direction of UFO research might have been different. Had everyone not been arguing with everyone else, something concrete might have been learned. Today all we can do is look at the evidence that is now more than a half-century old and try to understand what happened then and why it happened as it did.

Sightings before Levelland

Before the object invaded the Levelland area and exhibited a variety of what are now known as electromagnetic effects, something was seen in the surrounding area. About nineteen hours before the first of the sightings in Levelland, a driver near Canadien, Texas, northeast of Amarillo and near the Oklahoma border, saw a "submarine-shaped" object that was about fifty feet long and red and white. As it landed nearby, his headlights failed. He saw a small humanoid creature near the object, which is the only case from this area and time in which an occupant was observed.

At about eight that evening, the owner of KCLV in Clovis, New Mexico, Odis Echols, reported he had seen a glowing object rapidly flying to the southeast. Clovis is not far from the Texas border and not far from Levelland.

Near Midland, Texas, which is something over a hundred miles from Levelland, the Ground Observers Corps logged a number of reports of a large bluish object. It was flying west at a low altitude.

Just before the reports began in Levelland, at about 11:20 P.M., Calvin Harris and Sandy McKean, tower operators at the Amarillo, Texas, airport, saw a bluish object moving across the sky. McKean said that he had never seen anything so spectacular.

Pedro Saucedo and Joe Salaz

Pedro Saucedo (or Saucido, depending on the source) later said that he was driving toward Levelland along Route 114 (which then was designated as

Pedro Saucedo was driving along Route 114, shown here, when a large, glowing object crossed in front of him.

Site where Pedro Saucedo saw the UFO.

Route 116). Don Burleson said that the actual location is where Route 114 intersects with Five Mile Road, some 5.3 miles west of Levelland) when a large, glowing object crossed the highway in front of him and landed not all that far away. He said that as it touched down, the lights on his truck dimmed and the engine died. When it landed, Saucedo dived out the door and rolled out of the way, frightened by the strange object.

Charles Maney and Richard Hall, in their *The Challenge of Unidentified Flying Objects* published by NICAP in 1961, wrote that Saucedo, a Korean War veteran, said, "When it got near the light of my truck went out and the motor died. I jumped out of the truck and hit the dirt because I was afraid.... The thing passed directly over my truck with a loud sound and a rush of wind. It sounded like thunder and my truck rocked from the blast."

His passenger, Joe (or Jose) Salaz (or Palav, Palaz, Salav or Salvaz, depending on the source), sat petrified with his eyes glued to the blue-green object as the glow faded into a red so bright that he couldn't look directly at it. The object rested on the ground for three or four minutes while Salaz sat still, as if motion would attract attention. Although as frightened as Saucedo he remained where he was and he got a very good look at the UFO.

According to Don Keyhoe in *Flying Saucers Top Secret*, "As Salav [sic] watched from the cab, the strange machine settled close to the road. Whether

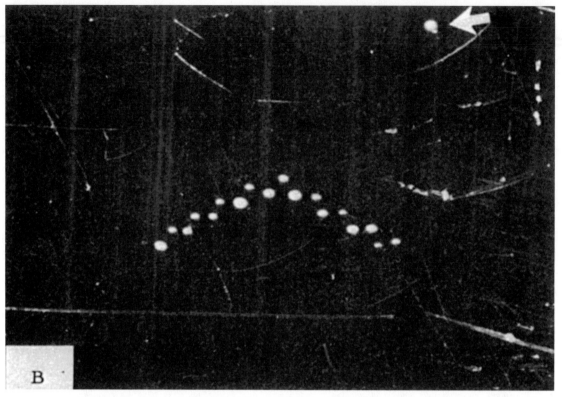

This formation of UFOs was spotted by several witnesses over Lubbock, Texas, and captured in this photo by Carl Hart.

it landed or was hovering just off the ground, Salav could not say—the blue-green light was too bright. For two or three minutes the UFO remained there. Then it quickly lifted, its glow changing to a red as it climbed."

During the time the torpedo-shaped object sat on the ground, both men believed they could hear noise coming from it. Then, as suddenly as it appeared, but now glowing bright red, the UFO shot up into the sky, vanishing in seconds.

As the UFO disappeared and Saucedo crawled from under his truck, both the lights and engine began working again. Afraid that he would run into the object if he continued to Levelland, he drove to another town to call the Levelland police about 10:50 P.M. A deputy sheriff identified by some as A. J. Fowler (and also identified as a police officer rather than a deputy or as a police dispatcher, again depending on the source) listened to his report, but laughed it off as just another flying saucer story, ignoring the obvious distress of the witness. Or, as Fowler believed at first, the caller was drunk and seeing things and that, too, meant he paid no attention to the witness.

But as happens so often with UFO sightings, there are discrepancies in this original tale, many of which mean little. Newspapers report that Saucedo actually talked to the sheriff when he got to Levelland. Clem told reporters that Saucedo "was pretty shook up when he got into town."

Saucedo was also reported to have said that the UFO had streaked right overhead. "It sounded like thunder, and my truck rocked from the blast. I felt a lot of heat."

Or, as reported by the *Chicago Daily Tribune* on November 4, 1957, Siado (in still a different spelling of Saucedo) said that he "heard a roar like a clap of thunder. Then his car lights went out and the motor stopped."

A few days after the sightings, the lone Air Force investigator on the case, Staff Sergeant Norman P. Barth of the 1006th Air Intelligence Service Squadron, made a short trip from Reese Air Force Base in Lubbock into Levelland to interview Saucedo, among the few other witnesses that the Air Force had identified. Barth gave Saucedo a low reliability as a witness. Barth wrote in his report filed with Project Blue Book, "SOURCE [Saucedo] appeared to be [deleted by Air Force officers]. He stated his occupation was a barber; however, Sheriff [Weir] Clem ... stated that SOURCE was a part-time farm laborer, dishwasher, barber, etc. SOURCE had no concept of direction and was conflicting in his answers."

Saucedo provided a written statement to Barth that said, "To whom it may concern, on the date of November 2, 1957, I was traveling north and west on route 116, driving my truck. At about four miles out of Levelland, I saw a blue flame, to my right, front, then I thought it was lightning. But when this object had reach [sic] to my position, it was different, because it put my truck motor out and lights. Then I stop, got out, and took a look, but it was so rapid and quite [sic] some heat, that I had to hit the ground, it also had three colors, yellow, white and it look like a torpedo, about 200 feet long, moving about 600 to 800 miles an hour."

The Air Force, in an attempt to explain this case as quickly as possible, reported, "Investigation proved that a rotor had been changed on the farmers [sic] truck the previous day PD [period]. One piece of the old rotor had not been removed and had wedged in between the points causing the electrical system to be now non operative PD [period]. This statement was obtained from the mechanic who had repaired the truck PD [period]."

In other words, the Air Force was suggesting that the dimming of the headlights and the stopping of the motor were the result of a faulty repair on the truck's rotor made sometime earlier. But this explanation fails to provide a reason the headlights would dim and the engine stop, and then seemingly spark back to life on their own when the UFO disappeared. This was an explanation offered repeatedly for Saucedo's sighting, but it explained nothing at all about it.

On the flip side of that coin, others, such as Maney and Hall, described Saucedo as a combat veteran of the Korean War. Donald Menzel and Lyle Boyd,

Weir Clem was sheriff in Levelland, Texas, when he had to field reports of UFOs in his jurisdiction.

in their *The World of Flying Saucers* also mention that Saucedo was a veteran of the Korean War. Most seem inclined to give the benefit of the doubt to a veteran, especially when most of the negative comments come from the Air Force investigator and might be a prejudice against anyone who claims to have seen a flying saucer. There have also been negative comments made because Saucedo's name is spelled almost like saucer and some saw some sort of conspiracy there, but a witness' name is a witness' name and there is nothing that can be done about that.

There is another point of controversy and that is whether Saucedo called the sheriff's office or drove there in person. Menzel, in his book, wrote, "Crawling out and seeing the object disappear in the direction of Levelland he [Saucedo] restarted the engine and drove back to Levelland to report the incident to the sheriff."

This adds to the confusion of the night by suggesting that Saucedo restarted his truck, but this is the only place that is implied. Then adding that Saucedo drove to the sheriff's office seems to contradict other reports. It seems clear, however, that Saucedo used the telephone and did not drive to Levelland at that time.

More Sightings

About the same time that Saucedo and Salaz were driving to another town, Air Force Technical Sergeant Harold D. Wright and his wife were driving along Texas Farm Road 1073 near Shallowater. According to the statement he gave the Air Force, "… my wife, 2 children and myself departed my father's home … in the vicinity of Anton, Texas, my wife and I noted occasional lightning and at the same time static on our radio…. I turned south (at Shallowater, Texas)…. In just a few minutes later this bolt of lightning occurred to our southwest. At the time, my radio and lights went out for approximately one to three seconds, and then came back on. My wife and I remarked [that] was certainly a strong bolt of lightning to put out our lights and the radio."

Newell Wright (no relation to Harold Wright), a nineteen-year-old college student at Texas Tech in Lubbock, was nearing Levelland when he glanced at his dashboard ammeter. Wright (whose name was redacted from the Air Force report) told the Air Force investigator, Barth, "I was driving home from Lubbock on state highway 116 [which is, of course, the same highway that Saucedo was on and the one that was later redesignated] at approximately 12:00 P.M. when the ammeter on my car jumped to complete discharge, then it returned to normal and my motor started cutting out like it was out of gas. After it had quit running, my lights went out. I got out of my car and tried in vain to find the trouble."

Wright continued, "It was at this time that I saw this object, I got back into my car and tried to start it, but to no avail. After that I did nothing but stare at this object until it disappeared about 5 minutes later. I then resumed trying to start my car and succeeded with no more trouble than under normal circumstances."

Later, in his interview with Barth, Wright would provide some additional details. He said that the object was oval-shaped and that he thought it was about the size of a baseball held at arm's length. He estimated that the object was about seventy-five to a hundred feet long. One of the important facts was that he had the opportunity to get a very good look at the object, which wasn't all that far away and stayed on the ground for several minutes by his estimation. It wasn't a streak of light in the distance.

The site where Jim Wheeler encountered a UFO in Levelland, Texas.

The only problem with this sighting is that Wright didn't make his report until the next day. By that time, the news media was alerted and reports of the sightings in and around Levelland had been published. It could be said that Wright got his idea by what he had read in the newspaper, though there is no evidence that the media influenced him at all and no evidence that he invented the sighting for the publicity. He just reported his experience, which might have some relevance for investigators.

Of course, it could also be pointed out that Wright, learning of other reports, added his to the mix. He might not have thought about calling the sheriff until after he learned others had made their reports to Levelland Sheriff Weir Clem. Or, it might be suggested that he had thought no one would believe him until he learned that others had seen the same thing.

Barth's evaluation of Wright said, "SOURCE seemed to the investigator to be very sincere about his sighting. He was appalled at the amount of publicity given him and was anxious to have the sighting resolved. He was unhesitating in his replies; however, during the course of further questioning, he admitted uncertainty in some of his answers. SOURCE can be considered usually reliable."

About the same time, Jim Wheeler was driving along Route 116 about four miles from Levelland when he spotted an egg-shaped object sitting on the road. He told NICAP investigator James A. Lee that the object cast "a glare over the area."

As he approached, his lights dimmed and his motor stopped. As he started to get out of the car, the UFO rose into the sky. As it disappeared, the car lights came back on and he could restart his car. He called the police in Levelland as soon as he could.

At just after midnight on November 3, Ronald Martin saw the red-glowing, egg-shaped object sitting on the road about four miles east of Levelland. As he approached to within about a quarter mile, his car engine died and his lights went out. While the UFO sat on the ground, Martin said the color was bluish-green. When he started to get out of his car, the UFO lifted off swiftly and silently. As it disappeared, Martin's car engine started again and the lights came on.

But there is a discrepancy with this report. According to NICAP records, Martin didn't say anything about the electromagnetic effects cutting off his engine. According to that report, he saw the object first in the air, but that it landed about three hundred or four hundred feet in front of him. He didn't report this to the Levelland Police until the next afternoon.

This means there is conflicting information about the Martin sighting. It would seem that the Air Force would want to exploit this, especially if Martin said that his engine had not been stopped and his lights not dimmed, but they seemed to have missed it.

Almost as the police in Levelland hung up the telephone from talking with Wheeler, Jose Alvarez (or Alverez, depending on the source) near Whitharral

The site where Frank Williams had his sighting.

called to report that he had seen the egg-shaped object that killed his car's engine. And, a few minutes later, Frank Williams walked into the station to report the same sort of thing.

The reaction of law enforcement in Levelland was that someone was playing some sort of an elaborate joke. No one there believed that a glowing red egg, or a bluish-green oval, was terrorizing the populace. Besides, the weather was poor, with mist and drizzle, and there had been thunderstorms in the vicinity, off and on all evening, at least according to what Barth would later report. The Air Force would claim that these facts were important.

As the police officers discussed it and tried to laugh it off, Jesse (also identified as James) Long called to report that he was driving on a country road northwest of Levelland when he came upon a landed, bright red craft. His truck engine died and his lights went out. Unlike the others, Long got out of his truck and started to walk toward the object. Before he could get too close, the UFO took off in a sudden burst of speed. After it was gone, Long reported that his truck engine started easily.

By this point Levelland Sheriff Weir Clem decided that something truly strange was happening around his town. But he didn't like the idea of chasing lights in the night sky, especially with the weather as bad as it supposedly was. Thunderstorms were still in the area, again according to what has been reported since the sightings, and though they had caused some problems earlier, it was no longer raining in town. There was no excuse for not trying to find the object. Or

rather no reason for Clem to remain in the office when he could be out searching for the object.

Weather Effects

Or maybe the weather wasn't quite as bad as has been reported by the Air Force
in the years since. There seems to be a conflict about that as well. The Air Force
report said, "The night was dark with a 400 foot ceiling, a complete overcast, and
light drizzle. Heavy thunderstorms had just passed through the area."

The Levelland *Sun*, however, reported, "Weathermen said they could not
explain away the sightings. There were no thunderstorms in the area."

James McDonald, a scientist with a deep interest in UFOs, in a prepared statement in Symposium on Unidentified Flying Objects, wrote that he "dug out the
weather maps and rainfall data. A large high pressure area was moving southward
over the Texas Panhandle, completely antithetical to convective activity and lightning of any sort … a check of half a dozen stations in the vicinity revealed that
there was not even any rain falling during this period no had more than a small
amount fallen in the hours earlier that day when a cold front went through."

Skeptics point out that the best interpretation of the weather is that it was
a dark and stormy night, there had been rain, and there was a mist in the air.
These conditions, they believe, might have been conducive to reports of engines stalling and lights failing. What they don't explain is why these manifestations were limited to the area around Levelland, and limited to the night of
November 2 and the morning of November 3 in that area, and why they don't
manifest themselves under similar weather conditions.

The Air Force Search for an Explanation

About an hour after Martin's sighting, Sheriff Clem decided he would have to
investigate. He left the office with Deputy Sheriff Patrick McCullogh and drove
the back roads and the highways in the Levelland area. About 1:30 A.M. they saw
the glowing UFO in the distance. They couldn't seem to get very close to it, or
at least that was what they said publicly in 1957 after having talked to the Air
Force investigator.

According to Barth, he found Clem to be "fairly reliable." He wrote,
"SOURCE impressed the investigator as being of average intelligence.… He
was rather pleased with the sudden importance of the county."

In the interview Clem told Barth that he was out looking for the object
that had been reported and while traveling south on Oklahoma Flat Road, at
about twenty miles an hour, he saw the streak of light. It had a reddish glow and
moved from south to west. Clem thought that it was about 800 feet long and
about four hundred yards away.

Other researchers reported that Clem had said privately he was considerably closer. He described the object as an oval "like a brilliant sunset." He said that it passed over the road about three hundred yards in front of his car.

Donald Burleson, a man living in Roswell, which is not all that far from Levelland, only about three hours over the modern roads, found the daughter of Sheriff Clem when he was doing some research into these sightings nearly fifty years later. Burleson reported in the *Roswell Daily Record* in 2002, "Aided by the Chamber of Commerce, we [meaning Burleson and his wife, Mollie] were able to find one of the late sheriff's daughters and I interviewed her twice."

> Burleson said that the description and the location he received independently from Reno matched that given by the sheriff's daughter.

According to Burleson, "She [Ginger (Clem) Sims] described her father having tried to drive close to an airborne object, and having his engine and lights die."

That, of course, put him much closer to the object than had been reported before or to what the Air Force would claim that he had seen. If he was close enough to the object that it would stall his engine, he was close enough to get a good look at it.

Burleson also reported that "she said that she remembers his being called out to a ranch northeast of town to see a ring-shaped spot burned into the ground. The ranch owners had called the sheriff about the burned area."

Burleson also reported that he interviewed a witness named Carolyn Reno who said that she had been a child living in the area in 1957, and that her father had taken her out to see a burned spot in the prairie grass that was something over twenty feet in diameter. Burleson said that the description and the location he received independently from Reno matched that given by the sheriff's daughter. Unfortunately the information was developed almost fifty years too late to do researchers today any good.

Richard Ray, a reporter for FOX Channel 4 in the Dallas–Fort Worth area, also investigated the case in 2002. He spoke with the widow of Sheriff Clem and she told him, "Well, he just said he'd seen a thing that lit down in that pasture with lights and all. It come down and then it went back up as fast as it come down."

Ray also interviewed a retired college professor, Nathan Tubb, who said, "In my opinion, there's no way he would fabricate or embellish something of this nature. He was an honorable person."

The real question is if Clem was so involved in this in 1957, why didn't he say anything at the time. Again, according to Burleson and to Clem's daughter, "The Air Force visited him after his sighting(s) and advised him to 'drop it' and forget that he had ever seen anything."

There is another reason, and that was given to Ray during his investigation in 2002. According to Ray, "In the meantime, Sheriff Clem was beginning to endure some ridicule."

And his widow said, "He just got so he wouldn't talk about it."

Skeptics will point out that the record in 1957 showed that Clem was only reported to have seen the object, or lights, in the distance, some nine hundred feet away, and they'll reject out of hand this new information. It is, after all, from the sheriff's daughter, a secondhand witness, the sheriff's widow, another secondhand witness, and a friend, a third secondhand witness. All this was added to the case nearly fifty years after the fact. In today's world, it is interesting, but there is no way to verify it. All these reports should be noted, but the weight given to them should be fairly light.

About the same time that Clem was out chasing the light, two highway patrol officers and Constable Lloyd Bollen saw the UFO in the distance. They were unable to get very close to it and reported the same sort of thing as Clem did officially, that is, a red glow in the distance. That meant there were five law enforcement officers who thought they had seen the object, though none reported they got very close to it and none saw much more than a streak of light in the distance. Remember, that was officially. Clem, remember, had gotten closer and saw an oval-shaped object, at least according to what his family said.

Also in that vicinity about that time was Ray Jones, the Levelland Fire Marshal. He was searching for an explanation for the many UFO reports that were being made that night. He saw a streak of light not far from him. His lights dimmed and the engine sputtered until the object was gone, but he didn't report a shape for the object and he didn't report that his engine died completely.

Also part of the Air Force file on Levelland was a report from a man living in Whiteface, Texas. He told Barth, "While driving north about 7 miles north of Sundown, Texas, I saw a light about the size of a basketball about 200 or more feet above the ground traveling from east to west … a bright red light giving off a glow.… An object above it seemed to hold up the light on a cable or hose appearing … between the light and the balloon object above it. It continued swinging north to south 3 or 4 minutes by then at a fast rate of speed it went up into the clouds and disappeared the light went out."

Barth, after only a few hours in the Levelland area, and after interviewing only a few of the witnesses, thought he had solved some of the sightings. As noted earlier, he believed he had come up with an explanation for one of the stalled vehicles, that is, the broken rotor.

Of course, there were more reports of the car engines being stalled, including that of Ronald Martin, which was investigated by the Air Force. And we can't forget that the sheriff who, through his daughter, also said that his engine had stalled. The broken rotor scenario doesn't explain those cases. Nor does it explain why Saucedo's truck began to operate once the UFO was out of sight.

Missing Witnesses

The Air Force investigator did not find, nor did he apparently try to find, some of the witnesses who were in Levelland on November 2, but who had returned to their homes by November 6. It is clear from the Air Force files that Barth didn't speak to Jesse Long, of Waco, Texas, who said the object had killed his engine, which couldn't be explained by the broken rotor in Saucedo's truck. Nor did he find or interview Jim Wheeler, Jose Alvarez, Ray Jones, or Frank Williams, the farmers near Petit, or the man driving from Seminole to Seagraves, all of whom said the proximity of the object had killed their car engines and dimmed their lights.

> "Object observed for only few seconds, not lengthy period as implied by press."

In an unclassified message to the commander of the Air Technical Intelligence Center, it was noted about the Levelland sightings that "contrary to [Donald E.] Keyhoe's [Director of NICAP] and Washington press reports only three, not nine persons witnessed the incident. Object observed for only few seconds, not lengthy period as implied by press. Mist, rain, thunderstorms and lightning discharges in scene of incident, fact not quoted in newspaper releases."

Barth went on to propose a number of possible solutions that were speculative in nature. "The amount of rain in the area, together with the condition of the crops, could have developed a phenomenon similar to St. Elmo's fire.... The possibility of burning excess gas from nearby oil operations reflecting off low clouds existed.... The possibility of lightning stalling a car and extinguishing the lights existed; however, the possibility decreases as the number of such incidents increases.... A check with the oil companies in the area revealed that a limited amount of excess gas from oil operations was being burned.... A check for downed power lines during the period was made with negative results.... The other witnesses reported in newspaper accounts as having observed the object had either disappeared or returned to their homes, leaving no forwarding addresses."

Barth apparently didn't press Clem or his deputies, nor did he interview the other law enforcement officers who saw the red light, nor did he talk to the fire marshal. And, of course, he never learned about the burned area found in the prairie grass on the ranch north of town, or if he did, he didn't mention it in his reports back to Project Blue Book.

Of course, it could be said that Barth did talk to them about what they had seen and that he wrote a second report that was not part of the Project Blue Book system. In fact, the NICAP *UFO Investigator* for January 1958 provides a hint of probability for this scenario. According to a letter to NICAP, Major General Joe Kelly admitted that UFO reports were classified as "For Official Use Only" (FOUO, the lowest level of classification). This was done, according to Kelly, to protect those witnesses who had requested anonymity.

He also retracted a statement in which he had suggested that NICAP had been given all the UFO information that the Air Force had. Apparently, he had told a member of Congress that NICAP had everything that the Air Force had and was forced to admit that this wasn't true.

What we see in Barth's statements to Blue Book is a great deal of irrelevant material. There were thunderstorms, but those had dissipated by the time the sightings began, or so he claimed. Oil-refining operations created gas that was burned and might have been reflected by the clouds, though the residents of the area would be familiar with those operations and would have no motive to suddenly see strange objects in the reflections on the clouds. Besides, the oil companies said that very little of that burning had occurred on the dates in question.

Although the Air Force didn't interview them—and therefore to the Air Force they didn't exist—there were a number of people, all named in various newspaper and other media stories, who did report their car engines and lights affected by the proximity of the UFO. Reporters and others did find them and quote them in the newspapers. And rather than search for these additional witnesses, the Air Force ignored them, suggesting in their responses to Keyhoe and NICAP that such people didn't exist, or if they did, they saw nothing of consequence. The Air Force just attacked Keyhoe for his inaccurate statements, which today can be proven to be true. There were more than three witnesses and in fact more than the nine claimed by Keyhoe.

So contrary to what the Air Force reported internally, and suggested to the press publicly, there were the number of witnesses claimed by Keyhoe. In fact, Keyhoe's number turns out to be too small when the law enforcement officers are counted in the number. And the length of the sightings varied from a few seconds to several minutes. The Air Force was attempting to suggest that the witnesses had seen, and misinterpreted, lightning flashes that somehow caused them to stall their vehicles.

The Air Force did, to their satisfaction, solve the Levelland case. According to the Air Force files, "After very extensive checks and detailed investigations by the Air Force and with complete collaboration with both Air Force and non-governmental scientists it was concluded that the sighting was due to a very rare phenomena [sic], ball lightning. The cause for the witnesses [sic] cars stopping could be attributed to the sudden disposition of moisture on distributor parts, especially if moisture condensation nuclei were enhanced by increased atmospheric ionization. In one instance a faulty distributor was determined as being the cause of the motor stoppage."

The problem with this explanation is that the existence of ball lightning was in dispute in 1957. Ball lightning is extremely rare and there are no cases of it being reported in the same area multiple times. It flashes into existence, can penetrate walls, or roll down the road, and then flashes out of existence. There is no mechanism reported or associated with ball lightning that would let it stall

Donald Keyhoe

a car engine, dim headlights, or cause a radio to fade. It is only recently that science has been able to confirm the existence of ball lightning, so in 1957, the Air Force was reaching for an explanation just to write off the case. By 1957, the attitude in the Air Force investigation was to explain sightings rather than investigate them. Barth and his one-day search for witnesses shows just how important UFO reports were to them.

There is one other fact that seems to have been missed in other studies of this case and might have an impact on it. Scientists, in attempting to replicate the dimming of lights and the suppression of the engines, could not produce a magnetic field of sufficient strength to interrupt the flow of electrons to dim the lights and stop the engines. In their experiments, once the magnetic field was eliminated, the engines failed to restart on their own. This suggested to them that the claims of the witnesses in Levelland were in error and therefore could be ignored.

However, in a number of the cases, the witness said that the engines stalled when the object approached, and they couldn't restart them. Once the object was gone, the engines started easily. Jesse Long and Newell Wright both said that they started their engines. Martin might not have had any engine trouble. The records today are somewhat confusing.

Of these witnesses, Barth only interviewed Newell Wright. Barth believes that the wet weather caused his car to stall because the rotor had been compromised, meaning that it had gotten wet. While this certainly would have caused the car to stall, it would have been an ongoing problem every time it rained or the weather was wet and there is no indication in the Blue Book file that such is the case. And it would have made restarting his car difficult until the rotor dried out.

What is important in this event is the number of independent witnesses who told of the object in the area and added the dimension of dimmed lights, radio failure, and the stalling of car engines. Many of the claims were made to the sheriff or police before there was any media attention for the sightings. Those suggesting some sort of mass hysteria have a major stumbling block, and that is, how did these witnesses tell the same story within an hour or so of one another without hearing or reading the media reports that began the next day?

We should talk about this case in a scientific vein. There is always talk of multiple chains of evidence, meaning that there are things going on besides the witness reports. Yes, this is one chain of evidence, and the fact that we have many who told of their experiences before there was media coverage is important. It is also important that the witnesses were scattered all over that area of Texas, meaning they didn't know one another and didn't know of one another's sightings.

A second chain would be the interaction with the environment. Had the Air Force acted quickly, we don't know what they might have learned from the cars that had been stalled. It wasn't just Saucedo and his truck, but others in various makes of cars and farm equipment. Checking the big combines with dual engines might have yielded some interesting results, but the lone Air Force investigator never thought of that and didn't even know about some of the witnesses. The evidence and witness testimony ended up being ignored.

The third chain of evidence is, of course, the burned area that had been reported to Sheriff Clem. Yes, we learned of it decades after the fact, but Burleson did find two independent witnesses for it. Again, we don't know what sort of information might have been found by a proper scientific investigation of that area because one wasn't made in 1957. In the days following the report, a great deal of information might have been determined by a careful scientific study of the burned area. But, of course, a burned area is physical evidence of the event, and the Air Force was busy attempting to prove that nothing had happened other than a couple of panicked citizens and a college student who reported the glowing UFO that stalled their car engines and put out their headlights.

We had witnesses to a brightly lighted craft that landed. We had interaction with the environment in the form of what is called electromagnetic effects. And we had landing traces in the form of the burned areas. Three different chains of evidence for this case. The only thing that might have made it better would be good-quality photographs or a piece of material from the craft.

Instead the Air Force responded with a single NCO who talked to a few people over the course of a day and then left, concluding that Saucedo's rotor had failed, no one saw much of anything, and that too many people started talking about UFOs too quickly after the fact. The Air Force investigator made much of the fact that within days of the sighting, hundreds of others were telling tales of low-level flying saucers and their electromagnetic effects. Once the story was out in the newspapers, on the radio, and told on television, then a "mass hysteria" could kick in. But that doesn't explain the sightings in Levelland late on the night of November 2 and very early in the morning of November 3.

It could just as easily be suggested that Levelland marked not the beginning of the wave of UFO reports, but marked the middle of it. The increased number of reports to the Air Force after the Levelland sighting might be explained in a simple fashion. People, now realizing that the Air Force was gathering the information about UFOs, now felt an obligation to report what they had seen. The story sparked not a series of sightings but a series of reports, a subtle but real difference.

Disappearing Aircraft and Missing Pilots

It might be said that Thomas Mantell was the first pilot killed chasing a UFO, but he certainly wasn't the last. Throughout the modern history of UFOs, there are many incidents in which pilots have been lost while attempting to intercept UFOs. As with the Mantell case, the government response was less than candid, and in some of those cases, it can be suggested that the cover-up was in place before the security lid was clamped down.

Truax Air Force Base

On November 23, 1953, radar operators at Truax Air Force Base picked up an unidentified return over the Soo Locks area in the Great Lakes region and in what was designated then as restricted air space. Because of that, a fighter was scrambled from Kinross Field to intercept and identify the intruder. Given the date, in the middle of the cold war, such a reaction was not all that unusual.

What was unusual was what happened. The Air Force fighter found the object and flew toward it. The blips merged on the radar screen, which didn't alarm the operators because one object could easily have passed over the other, but the blips never separated.

According to the official Air Force report on this aircraft accident:

F-89C, Serial No. 51-5853A, assigned to the 433rd Fighter-Interceptor Squadron, Truax Field, Wisconsin, was reported missing over Lake Superior at approximately 2000 Eastern Standard Time (EST) on 23 November 1953. The aircraft was scrambled from Kinross Air Force Base, Michigan to participate in an Active Air Defense Mission. The aircraft and crew had not been located as of 1 January 1954.

On 23 November 1953, F-89C, Serial No. 51-5853A, was scrambled by "Naples" [which would be their call sign] GCI [Ground Controlled Intercept] to intercept and identify an unknown aircraft flying over Lake Superior. The interceptor became airborne from Kinross Air Force base, Michigan at 1833 EST. Original radar control of the aircraft was maintained by "Naples" GCI and at 1841 EST control was transferred to "Pillow" GCI. The aircraft was flying at 30,000 feet at this time. At 1847 EST, at the request of "Pillow" the aircraft descended to 7000 feet to begin the interception. Location of the aircraft was then approximately 150 miles northeast from Kinross AFB and over northern Lake Superior. At 1851 EST, the interceptor pilot was requested to turn to a heading of 20 degrees to the cutoff vector. After the turn was completed, the pilot was advised the unidentified aircraft was at 11 o'clock, 10 miles distant. Radar returns from both aircraft were then seen to merge on "Pillow's" radarscope. The radar return from the other aircraft indicated it was continuing on its original flight path, while the return from the F-89 disappeared from the GCI station's radarscope.

The unknown aircraft being intercepted was a Royal Canadian Air Force Dakota C-47), Serial No. VC-912, flying from Winnipeg to Sudbury, Canada. At the time of the interception, it was crossing Northern Lake Superior from west to east at 7,000 feet.

The pilot [First Lieutenant Felix Moncla, Jr.] and radar observer [Second Lieutenant R. R. Wilson] were assigned to the 433rd Fighter-Interceptor Squadron, Truax AFB, Wisconsin. They were on temporary duty at Kinross AFB, Michigan, while the base's regularly assigned personnel were firing gunnery at Yuma, Arizona. The pilot had a total of 811:00 hours of which 121:00 hours were in F-89 type aircraft. He had 101:00 instrument hours and 91:50 hours night time. The radar observer had a total of 206:45 hours of which 11:30 hours were at night.

Search for the missing aircraft was conducted by both USAF and RCAF [Royal Canadian Air Force] aircraft without success. All civilian reports of seeing or hearing the aircraft were investigated with negative results.

The Air Force solution then, as it is now, is that the unidentified target, that is, the UFO, was the Canadian plane, though the Canadian government continues to deny this. The Air Force said that the F-89 was never closer than several miles to the Canadian aircraft and has no explanation why the F-89 disappeared after the blips merged. Although they haven't said it, it would seem that a collision between the two planes would have knocked them both out of the sky rather than just the jet.

Other sources provided additional and relevant information. According to those documents, radar at Truax Air Force Base picked up an unidentified blip over the Soo Locks in restricted airspace. Since it was unidentified, an interceptor was scrambled. Ground radar vectored the jet toward the UFO. Wilson, the radar officer, said that he was unable to find the object on his radar, so the ground radars continued to vector the jet toward the object that had seemed to be hovering but was beginning to accelerate as it headed out over the lake.

> (R)adar operators at Truax Air Force Base picked up an unidentified return over the Soo Locks area in the Great Lakes region and in what was designated then as restricted airspace.

For nine minutes the chase continued with Moncla able to gain slightly on the UFO and Wilson finally able to get a fix on it. The gap between the jet and the UFO narrowed, closed, and then merged as Moncla caught the UFO out over the lake.

At first no one was concerned about this because the ground radar had no height-finding capability and it was possible the jet had flown over or under the object, but the blips didn't separate. They hung together and then the lone blip flashed off the screen. The jet, apparently, was gone.

Attempts to reach Moncla by radio, including the emergency frequency, failed. Radar operators called for Search and Rescue, providing the last known position of the jet. Through the night they continued to search, later joined by the Canadians. They found nothing. They found no clue about the fate of the jet or the crew. No wreckage and no sign that the crew had bailed out.

An early edition of the *Chicago Tribune* carried a story about the accident with the ground-based radar operator's opinion that the jet had hit something in the sky. While the search continued, the Air Force moved to suppress the idea that the jet had hit anything.

Although a well-coordinated search was conducted, and everyone thought they knew where the jet had been because of the radar tracking, they never found anything. There was no wreckage, no oil slick, no bodies, nothing. The last trace of the jet had been when the two radar blips merged.

In 1976, after the Air Force had declassified the Project Blue Book files, I had a chance to go through them at Maxwell Air Force Base. One of the first files that I asked to see was that on the Kinross case. I knew the date and location and the archivist brought the file into the small reading and study room that I was using as a base to review the material.

The file contained only two sheets of paper. One of them was a single sheet that suggested that Moncla and Wilson were lost chasing a Canadian aircraft. It was just the briefest summary and added nothing to what I already knew.

Later, in one of the reports about the progress of the UFO investigation, there was more information. According to this report:

This incident was not reported to ATIC as a UFO sighting and therefore we have no case file. Due to the great amount of public interest in this incident, ATIC contacted the Flying Safety Division at Norton AFB, California for information pertaining to this aircraft accident. It was determined from Norton AFB that the F-89 was scrambled to intercept an unidentified aircraft which was successfully accomplished. The aircraft was reported in as a Dakota (Canadian C-47). From the time that the F-89 started to return to the base nothing of what happened is definitely known. It is presumed by the officials at Norton AFB that the pilot probably suffered from vertigo and crashed into the lake. The wreckage has never been recovered. This case is carried in Air Force Accident Records.

What is interesting here is that the writer of this document said, without equivocation, that the unknown was identified as the Canadian aircraft and that the F-89 was returning to base when it crashed into the lake because the pilot suffered vertigo. It is interesting that the writer of the short report said that what happened was not definitely known but then suggested pilot error, or rather an episode of vertigo, caused the loss of the aircraft. In other words, in that short paragraph, he seemed to contradict himself.

The Menzel Solution

Dr. Donald H. Menzel had little of relevance to say, but a galley from one of his UFO books was also included in the Project Blue Book case file. He went even further with his analysis of the case than did the Air Force. Following the Air Force line, he wrote, "The jet successfully accomplished its mission and identified the unknown as a Dakota, a Canadian C-47. On its return to base, however, the Air Force jet crashed into Lake Michigan and, as often happens when a plane crashes into deep water and the exact place of the crash is not known, no wreckage was ever found."

> "It was determined from Norton AFB that the F-89 was scrambled to intercept an unidentified aircraft which was successfully accomplished."

Without critical thought, Menzel has bought into the Air Force explanation. And then he adds to it. He wrote, "As the ground radar at Kinross had tracked the returning jet, the scope picked up a phantom echo in the neighborhood of the jet; the two blips had seemed to merge just as both went off the scope."

There is no indication that anyone thought that the blip was a phantom, and in fact, it was the unidentified blip that had initiated the interception. Menzel was inventing an explanation to satisfy himself but without benefit of evidence. This is something that he would do repeatedly as he attempted to explain all UFO sightings in the mundane. He was incapable of admitting that there might be something anomalous in a case that wouldn't necessarily invoke the extraterrestrial.

He continued in that vein: "Since the crash was not reported as a UFO incident and did not involve any question of unidentified flying objects, ATIC was not asked to investigate."

This is, of course, the Air Force explanation, but it is in error. If there had been no unidentified flying object, there wouldn't have been an interception. The identification of that object, which the Air Force, and Menzel, said was a Canadian aircraft, does not mean there was no initial UFO sighting. And since the identification of it is disputed by the Canadians, it remains as unidentified. The Air Force dodged the truth by claiming this was an aircraft accident and claiming that there had been no UFO.

But it is clear that Menzel was making up answers and while it might be difficult to prove on this specific case, it is not when looking at the report filed by Clyde Tombaugh, the astronomer who discovered Pluto.

In 1949, at 10:45 P.M., Tombaugh, his wife, and his mother-in-law saw something strange in the night sky. The full report is now housed at the J. Allen Hynek Center for UFO Studies in Chicago, and I have held the original report in my hands.

Tombaugh wrote, "I happened to be looking at the zenith ... when suddenly I spied a geometrical group of faint bluish-green rectangles of light.... As the group moved south-southeasterly, the individual rectangles became foreshortened, their space of formation smaller ... and their intensity duller, fading from view at about 35 degrees above the horizon.... My wife thought she saw a faint connecting glow across the structure."

Menzel, the UFO debunker and critic of anyone who suggested that any UFOs are anything other than misidentifications or hoaxes, was able to solve the sighting quickly. He suggested that "a low, thin layer of haze or smoke reflected the lights of a distant house or some other multiple source."

Tombaugh, who saw the objects, replied to Menzel, who didn't see them, writing, "I doubt that the phenomenon was any terrestrial reflection, because in that case some similarity to it should have appeared many times ... nothing of the kind has ever appeared before or since."

Eyewitnesses to Kinross?

While I was studying at the University of Iowa, I had the opportunity to speak with an Air Force officer who had been assigned to Truax Air Force Base at the time of the incident. He remembered because you don't forget an incident in which two aircraft crewmen and their fighter disappear off the radar screen to never return.

> He said that there had been a number of UFO sightings in that area during that time frame, which, of course, is not part of the Blue Book file.

He told me there were two schools of thought about the disappearance of the aircraft. The first, smaller school, was that something had happened to Moncla or to the aircraft and it had crashed straight into the lake. If the airplane did not break up, or if the crash site was small enough, then searchers the next day might never have found the evidence.

But, the second, larger school, was that whatever it had been, whatever Moncla and Wilson had chased, it had "taken" them. He repeated that the two blips had merged and that they never separated. To some of those, on the scene that November night, it meant that Moncla and Wilson had been "kidnapped."

He added something that is relevant. He said that there had been a number of UFO sightings in that area during that time frame, which, of course, is not part of the Blue Book file. In fact, not long after Moncla and Wilson were lost, a small flight of fighters found themselves being paced by another UFO in that area. The UFO did nothing but stay close to them. Finally, the flight leader said that on his command, the flight would turn into the UFO to see what it would do. He was fully aware of what had happened to Moncla and Wilson but gave the order anyway. As they turned toward the UFO, it shot away in a burst of speed.

Here's where the story gets interesting. He knew that I was on my way to Maxwell Air Force Base to look at the Blue Book files. He said that they had filed a number of UFO reports from the base and he wondered what conclusions had been drawn. There were no listings for any UFO sightings in that area at that time and the Kinross Case was marked "INFO ONLY," which meant it wasn't a case at all.

The Aircraft Found?

That's where the story ended for decades. The Air Force had downplayed the UFO report claiming it was an unidentified aircraft so it wasn't reported as a UFO. Those in UFO groups suggested that this was another case in which Air Force officers had been killed during a UFO investigation; the others included the two officers killed during the Maury Island hoax and Thomas Mantell killed chasing a UFO in Kentucky.

But then, in 2006, an outfit known as Great Lake Dive Company claimed they had found the wreckage of the aircraft sitting on the bottom of Lake Superior in about five hundred feet of water. On their website, www.greatlakes-dive.com, was a photograph of an aircraft that could be the missing F-89. It was in surprisingly good shape considering it had crashed into the lake in 1953.

If this was the missing jet, then one question had been answered. We would know what happened to the aircraft. If Great Lake Dive succeeded in getting down to the aircraft and could verify that it was the missing jet, then they might be able to suggest something about the fate of the two men on board.

There were some, inside the UFO community, who cautioned that we should wait for more information before making any sort of judgment about the case. Finding the wreckage of an aircraft that could be an F-89 doesn't automatically mean that it was the one flown by Moncla and Wilson. What we had was the possible solution to a mystery.

Or rather it seemed that way, but like so much else in the UFO field, there was another side to the story. Gord Heath wrote to *UFO* magazine in November 2006 reporting on his investigation of the claims by Great Lake Dives. He posted the same to UFO UpDates in January 2007. Following is his letter.

Dear Editor,

I read your article on the alleged discovery of the missing F-89 in your November issue and was quite surprised to note that it contained no mention that this discovery is now widely believed to be a hoax. Also, contrary to the brief follow-up comments by Dirk Vander Ploeg in the December issue of UFO magazine, there seems to be nothing of the story which can be verified. Many individuals have checked into this story and it seems that no one has yet been able to verify even the most basic information. I am sure that your readers would be interested to know the findings of the investigation by James Carrion, international director of MUFON, into the claims of Adam Jimenez. I will briefly summarize the findings:

1) No one has yet been able to verify the existence of "Great Lakes Dive Company" (GLDC) which Jimenez claimed to be an incorporated company or LLC in the state of Michigan.

2) No one in the Great Lakes shipwreck searching community or dive community seems to have any knowledge of Great Lakes Dive Company as an organization actively involved in the searches they mentioned on their web site.

3) No one seems to have any basic information about Adam Jimenez to validate he is who he claims to be, such as an address or current phone number.

4) While the GLDC web site was operational, no photographs of team members, boats or sonar equipment were ever posted to the website to document their alleged discovery.

5) Some experts in the field of side scan sonar believe the alleged sonar images may be fakes.

6) The initial story quoted in an email that was forwarded to the UFO Updates list appears to be faked as an Associated Press story from a Port Huron, Michigan publication.

It should be noted that Adam Jimenez claimed to have video recordings obtained from an ROV survey of the alleged F-89. He claimed that the tail code was visible in the video and that the canopy of the craft was intact, implying that the crew were still inside. Despite these claims, he never shared any of this evidence with any of the family of the missing pilot, Lt. Gene [most reports suggest his name was Felix] Moncla.

It is unfortunate that persisting questions surrounding the mysterious disappearance have largely been side-stepped in your coverage of what seems to be an elaborate hoax. I have spent many years researching this incident and my findings are published on the UFOBC website at www.ufobc.ca/kinross. I am sure your readers will be quite interested to know that parts from a military jet aircraft were found in the bush near the eastern shore of Lake Superior back in October 1968. A photograph of the tail stabilizer is shown with an Ontario Provincial Police officer and USAF officer on the front page of the Sault Daily Star newspaper, accompanying articles about the discovery. It appears that the identity of the mystery jet was never released to the public and the Canadian government claims they have no file records of this discovery. Were these parts from the missing F-89?

The article in UFO Magazine also reprints a map which erroneously places the last position of the F-89 in the accident report as being at coordinates 45 degrees 00 minutes north at a location near Sturgeon Bay, Michigan. The actual coordinates are printed in several locations such as the Search and Rescue report prepared by the RCAF and in several telexes. All state the last coordinates were 48 degrees 00 minutes north and 86 degrees 49 minutes west, north of the US Canada border over Lake Superior.

In closing, I wish to bring to your attention the photograph which you published in your magazine of Lt. Moncla contains no caption mentioning this photograph was provided to me by his sister, Leonie Shannon and his cousin, Carol Campbell. I don't know where you obtained the photograph but I know it has been published several times on the web since we first posted it in an article printed in the UFOBC quarterly and now posted on our web page devoted to the missing pilot www.ufobc.ca/kinross/persons/personsMonclaMain.htm.

I enjoyed reading many of the other articles in your November issue, but I couldn't restrain myself from responding to your articles referring to the missing F-89.

Yours truly,
Gord Heath
UFOBC

It should be clear from this that the missing F-89 has not be found. While the most probable explanation is that the aircraft is at the bottom of the lake, we don't know that for certain. There is always the possibility that it was "taken" by the UFO and is now on display on some distant planet as an artifact from a primitive world.

Walesville, New York, 1954

According to various UFO writers and researchers, including Donald Keyhoe (*Aliens from Space,* pp. 26–27), on July 1, 1954 "an unknown flying object was tracked over New York State by Griffiss AFB radar. An F-94 Starfire jet was scrambled and the pilot climbed steeply toward the target, guided by his radar observer. When the gleaming disc-shaped machine became visible he started to close in."

Keyhoe continued, "Abruptly a furnacelike heat filled both cockpits. Gasping for breath, the pilot jettisoned the canopy. Through a blur of heat waves he saw the radar operator bail out. Stunned, without even thinking, he ejected himself from the plane."

Keyhoe then noted, "The F-94, screaming down into Walesville, N.Y., smashed though a building and burst into flames. Plunging on, the fiery wreckage careened into a car. Four died in the holocaust—a man and his wife and their two infant children. Five other Walesville residents were injured, two of them seriously."

If all this could be factually established, that is, that the jet crashed as a result of the actions of a UFO, then we have big news. UFOs aren't just harmless lights in the sky, but can result in tragedy on the ground.

Keyhoe wasn't alone in his belief of a UFO attack on an Air Force interceptor. Otto Binder, writing in *What We Really Know about Flying Saucers* (1967), suggested that it was the radar officer who saw the UFO and pointed it out to the pilot. The pilot turned the aircraft to get a better look and when the cockpit filled with heat, both men bailed out. Binder claimed that both men were interrogated at length by Air Force investigators who concluded that they were not responsible for the crash. According to Binder, there was only one source for the heat and that was the UFO. Binder said that his account was based on Air Force Records, which is true, to an extent. There was also a great deal of interpretation in Binder's account.

J. Allen Hynek and Jacques Vallee, in *The Edge of Reality* (1975), discussed the case. Vallee suggested that there had been a dense cloud cover and that the UFO had been picked up on radar. Two jets were scrambled, one that remained in the clouds and the second that climbed to a higher altitude. When it broke through into clear sky, the pilot saw the UFO coming at him. The cockpit filled with heat and both men believe the aircraft was about to burst into flames. They bailed out and landed safely, but the aircraft crashed into Walesville, creating the tragedy.

An engine from the F-94 that crashed in Walesville, New York, after a heated encounter with a UFO in 1954.

Hynek said the case wasn't documented but Vallee said, "Yes, it is documented. It was even mentioned in the *New York Times* the next day."

So, what are the facts in this case? According to both news and official sources, there was a UFO sighting over Rome, New York, on July 2, but in the evening, hours after the jet crash. The *New York Times* for July 3 reported:

UTICA. N.Y., July 2 (AP)—A silvery, balloon-like object floating over the Utica area tonight sent residents rushing to their telephones to make inquiries of newspapers, police and radio stations.

The Utica Press estimated that more than 1,000 calls about the object jammed its switchboard between 6 and 10 P.M. It was reported by residents in a twenty-five mile radius extending from Rome on the west to Frankfort, east of Utica.

Col. Milton F. Summerfelt, commandant of the Air Force Depot at Rome, said the object appeared to be a plastic balloon about forty feet long and partially deflated. He theorized that it was making a gradual descent and said that if it was still in the area tomorrow morning a plane would be sent to investigate.

A Mohawk Airlines pilot estimated the altitude of the object at about 20,000 feet. He said he saw a light apparently shining from it.

For some reason, Keyhoe and some of the others have given the July 1 date for the balloon sighting and sometimes for the jet crash as well. A confusion of the two events might explain how the description of a disc-shaped object originated. Since both incidents were reported in the same general area and on the same day, the confusion is understandable.

The Project Blue Book files tell the jet-crash story in a slightly different way from that given by Keyhoe, Vallee, and others. Neither incident is part of Blue Book's official record. The index for Blue Book, which does list the accident, also notes it is "info" only, and lists the "witnesses" as Len Stringfield and others. I suppose I should point out that Stringfield, living in Ohio, did not make an on-site investigation and didn't witness the incident. He reported it in his privately published newsletter and that is what made him a "witness" in the Air Force file.

> When it broke through into clear sky, the pilot saw the UFO coming at him. The cockpit filled with heat and both men believe the aircraft was about to burst into flames.

According to the "Summary of Circumstances" which is part of the official Air Force file on the case:

> The F-94C took off at 11:05 AM EST for an operational training mission out of Griffiss Air Force Base, New York on 2 July 1954. The aircraft was only a few miles out when the Griffiss control tower operator called the pilot to advise that he was being diverted to an active air defense mission. A vector of 60 degrees and 10,000 feet altitude was given to intercept an unidentified aircraft. The pilot experienced some difficulty finding this aircraft and the controller informed him of a second unidentified aircraft in the area. This aircraft was [subsequently] identified [by the pilot] as an Air Force C-47, tail number 6099. At this time there were no indications of F-94 malfunctions as stated by the pilot and the C-47 pilot.

What this tells us is that the unidentified object was later identified as a C-47. The F-94C was not, in fact, scrambled to intercept a UFO as suggested by some, but was already airborne when diverted to the active mission. However, it is true that the aircraft was asked to identify an unknown target, which, in layman's terms, is a UFO.

Once the C-47 was identified:

> The ground controller gave the F-94C pilot a heading of 240 degrees as a vector back to the first unidentified aircraft. The F-94C was at 8,000 feet, flying about the tops of broken clouds, so the pilot started to descend below the clouds. It was evident that the unidentified aircraft was going to Griffiss Air Force Base. During the descent there was intense heat in the cockpit and the engine plenum chamber fire warning light came on. The pilot shut down the engine and the light re-

mained on. Due to critical low altitude and the fire warning, the pilot and the radar observer ejected and were recovered without injury.

Clearly, based on this, the other UFO, the one the pilot couldn't find at first, was in the traffic pattern for the Air Force base. The identity, though not established by the pilot, was by the tower crew and the mission had ended. The UFOs were both military aircraft.

I think this is where the idea there were two jets involved came from. There were two attempted intercepts but by only one aircraft. I have seen notations suggesting a second jet, but the evidence in the case file doesn't bear this out.

> The Air Force report says nothing about the aircraft being scrambled, a disc-shaped UFO, or a heat ray, as alleged by some UFO writers.

The other point that needs to be made here is that there was not a dense cloud cover. The term "broken clouds" relates to the portion of the sky obscured by clouds. This means there were some clouds but they did not obscure the whole sky, and given the various altitudes for those clouds, it could have meant that from the cockpit, little of the sky was hidden. In other words, the clouds might not be relevant.

The report ended by saying, "The aircraft traveled about four miles from the point of ejection and, while on a heading of 199 degrees, crashed into the Walesville intersection at 11:27 AM EST. The aircraft struck a dwelling, killing a housewife and injuring her daughter, then struck an auto at an intersection, killing all three occupants."

The Air Force report says nothing about the aircraft being scrambled, a disc-shaped UFO, or a heat ray, as alleged by some UFO writers. There is, in fact, no reason to suggest that this case has anything to do with UFOs, other than the assumptions made by Keyhoe in the 1950s and those who followed after that.

Keyhoe, in fact, gets the identities of the civilians killed wrong. According to the *New York Times* for Saturday, July 3, 1954, "Those killed were Stanley Phillips, 38, his wife, Florence, 32, and their son Gary, 11, all of neighboring Hecla, and Mrs. Doris Monroe, 28, occupant of one of the houses."

The Air Force conducted an investigation into the accident, but this report was sealed for many years. Given that the Air Force-sponsored University of Colorado UFO study, that is, the Condon Committee, had access to many official documents, it may not be surprising they did not create a UFO file for this incident because there was no UFO involved.

With or without a UFO, there is the question of what caused the heat in the cockpit. Was there a fire on the F-94C, and if so, what caused it? Was the malfunction of the aircraft in any way mysterious?

Until years after the crash, these questions could not be answered definitively because the accident report was still in the government archives. But upon the request of Jan Aldrich, the report was declassified and released. The general details of the accident are basically the same as reported by Keyhoe and the others. The key finding in the accident investigation is in paragraph three of the summary statement:

> Investigation revealed the primary cause of the accident to be a malfunction of the aircraft fire detector circuit. The cause of the malfunction could not be determined. The pilot's decision to abandon the aircraft was consistent with the emergency instructions contained in the F-94C Flight Handbook.

A thorough examination of the plane's air conditioning and pressurization system indicated no evidence of smoke, fuel, or oil, which would have been generated by a fire. The pilot had flown the aircraft on a previous flight that same day and had found it necessary to adjust the cockpit temperature manually several times. The air vents were set so that pressurized air was being directed into the cockpit.

The report suggests that "Inasmuch as the pilot acknowledged changing the engine power settings and flight altitude during his attempted second interception, it appears that the pilot interpreted a normal, non-automatically controlled temperature rise as an overheat cockpit condition. Since there was no evidence of an inflight fire, the fire warning indication received was probably due to a malfunction of the fire warning circuit."

This accident then became a terrible bit of bad luck as the malfunctioning of the fire warning occurred just as the cockpit was being heated from normal aircraft operations. Following procedures, after the warning continued, the pilot shut down the engines and he and his radar observer bailed out, leaving the pilotless plane to crash in Walesville. As a relevant aside, another conclusion of the report was that the Air Force's inspection requirements for the F-94C fire and overheat warning circuits were inadequate.

The accident report was completed on August 17, 1954, before Keyhoe wrote *Flying Saucer Conspiracy*. If he had been given access to the document, or at least was provided with the relevant conclusions by Air Force spokesmen, the confusion over Walesville might never have happened. Instead, given the understandable confidentiality requirements of military accident investigators, Keyhoe and other writers were left to speculate about the cause of the heat in the cockpit and the cause of the crash.

In any event, the Walesville case, like that of the death of Thomas Mantell in 1948, should be removed from the UFO files. There was no UFO involved in this tragedy, though there certainly were momentarily unidentified aircraft.

Fawcett and Greenwood in their book, *The UFO Cover-up* (which originally was titled *Clear Intent*) wrote, "Without the full details of the crash, it is impossible to determine what caused the jet to malfunction."

Kevin Randle.

Then they go on to write, "In the *Encyclopedia of UFOs*, edited by Ron Story (Doubleday Dolphin, 1980), an entry by Kevin Randle attempts to explain away the Walesville crash as nothing more than an engine fire which poured heat into the cockpit. His "documented evidence" is a news clipping from the *New York Times*. If the author of the entry had truly been interested in documented evidence other than a newspaper clipping, he would have noticed that the accident report on Walesville contained the following conclusions: 'Investigation of the wreckage disclosed no in-flight fire. *The cause of the malfunction in the fire warning system could not be determined.*'(Emphasis in the original.)"

Of course, had they bothered to read what I had written, they would have realized that I was quoting Jacques Vallee. The sentence in question is, "Jacques Vallee claimed that the case was documented, and it was even reported in *The New York Times*."

Documentation available today suggests, as noted earlier, there was no fire anywhere on or in the aircraft, but there was a malfunction in the fire warning system that suggested a fire. The pilot, identified as Lt. William E. Atkins in various sources, thought that because the cockpit was extremely hot, and because of the warning light, that the aircraft was on fire. Fawcett and Greenwood wrote that "he [the pilot] alerted the radar operator, Lt. Henry Condon [identified in some sources as Coudon], placed the throttle in the idle position, waited four seconds, then stop-cocked the throttle. After waiting another four seconds, Atkins and Condon successfully bailed out."

They then added, "So, while we have no specific evidence that the aircraft was attacked by a UFO, the cause of the crash remains unknown to this day. Is it merely coincidence that the jet developed a fault during a UFO chase or …?"

Except everything points to the UFO, or UFOs, being identified as aircraft or the partially deflated balloon. These resolutions were reached independent of the Air Force investigation. There is no UFO in the classic sense involved in this case. The cause of the accident is the malfunctioning fire warning light and the only thing not explained is the sensation of extreme heat in the cockpit that suggested to the pilot, along with the warning light, that the aircraft was on fire.

Unlike the Kinross case, this is a tragic accident that resulted in the deaths of four civilians on the ground. The Air Force got this one right. It isn't a UFO case, but an aircraft accident.

The Metcalf Sighting, 1955

Kinross is certainly not the only case of disappearing aircraft in UFO history. Eugene Metcalf, from Paris, Illinois, reported that he had seen a fighter disappear as it chased a flying saucer. According to an affidavit signed by Metcalf:

> On March 9, 1955, at approximately 5:50 P.M. I witnessed the "plane-napping" of a jet plane while standing in my backyard at Paris, Illinois. The plane was coming toward me from the southwest and was traveling in a northeasterly direction. As I stood watching this plane, an odd-looking craft came from behind the plane and just swallowed it. The U.F.O. had an opening that was in my line of vision, and through the opening it took the plane. After this, the U.F.O. hovered and pulsated and churned up and down. Then it seemed to whirl and lift upwards.
>
> While going through these gyrations, vapor came from porthole-like openings around the bottom part. The plane and U.F.O. were in perfect view, and stood out clearly against the sky. The object was bright silver and I heard no noise. The U.F.O. was very big and bell-shaped.

The affidavit was signed by Metcalf on April 2, 1957, in Edgar County, Illinois. Signing an affidavit, in and of itself, does not prove that the witness is telling the truth, but it does suggest a certain level of belief in the tale. Metcalf was going to a lot of trouble to prove to others he had seen what he had described.

Other documentation suggested that Metcalf "sent letters describing this action to the following: The Chicago *American* newspaper: comment, none. *Newsweek*: comment, would like to print letter if room is found; Civil Air Patrol, comment, first said was American craft, then said they didn't know. Who does? Federal Bureau of Investigation: they thanked me for my information, so maybe some one of them will get their eyes opened."

A similar statement by Metcalf appears in the Project Blue Book files about the case. He added some detail to it by writing:

> A very curious sighting. I have tried in vain to find out more about all this but have been unable to do so. My actions were not for publicity nor I still do not want it. However, I would like to know more about this, your help will be appreciated. I have observed this craft for several years. In fact, I was wondering about them before the first publication on flying saucers. I still see either this craft or one similar quite frequently. I could write several pages and still not mention all I have seen of these phenomena.

He signed it with his name, which the Air Force redacted when the Blue Book files were made public in 1976.

What is more interesting is a letter from the Air Technical Intelligence Center, on their official letterhead, and directed to the Commander of the 4602nd Air Intelligence Service Squadron at Ent Air Force Base in Colorado. In it, they are asking for the 4602nd to investigate the case. According to the letter, the sighting was "given prominence by the Telonic Research Center, a private UFO research organization with a fairly wide membership."

It was also noted, in that letter, that "with reference to Mr. Metcalf's statement of the observed UFO 'swallowing an aircraft,' your investigation should include the determination if any bomber-jet parasite 'pick-up' tests were conducted in the vicinity of the alleged sighting."

At the bottom of the second page of the letter was the response from the 4602nd. It was brief and said, "As requested, a complete investigation has been made by Flight 3-A, 4602d AISS.

"2. Results of this investigation strongly indicate that the source is completely unreliable."

> The problem here is that anyone who said he or she had seen a UFO on more than one occasion was considered unreliable by the Air Force.

This was signed by Major John D. Taylor, Jr., who was the adjutant of the squadron.

This means, quite clearly, that the Air Force got involved, but there is nothing in the file to suggest they searched for any "parasite" pickups, or that they did much of anything, other than respond that Metcalf was unreliable. The problem here is that anyone who said he or she had seen a UFO on more than one occasion was considered unreliable by the Air Force. Their term for that was repeater.

Len Stringfield, a very trusted UFO investigator who lived in Cincinnati, Ohio, added something to the case after his investigation in 1956. According to his investigative notes, which were dictated on August 26, 1956, Stringfield asked a friend, identified only as Fitch in Cleveland, to investigate Metcalf.

Fitch, unlike the Air Force, believed that Metcalf was sincere and that he, Metcalf, believed to have seen exactly what he claimed to have seen. Stringfield also had a note in his files that he thought of Fitch as reliable and intelligent.

In 2000, I received an email from a fellow in Cleveland who believed that the Fitch mentioned by Stringfield was his grandfather. The letter said that his grandfather "and a friend saw something that neither could ever explain. From what he told me, he would never have believed the stories if he had not seen for himself."

This doesn't tell us much, but does suggest that Fitch was predisposed to believe UFO tales, even one as wild as that told by Metcalf. And, of course, provides for no new corroboration of Metcalf's claim. This is an interesting story told by a man who provided nothing in the way of proof for what he had seen.

The Schaffner Disappearance, 1970

This is a story which, when superficially examined, seems to mirror that of Felix Moncla, Jr. and R. R. Wilson. It is about a fighter pilot, Captain William Schaffner, who, while on an intercept of an unknown object, disappeared after witnessing a brilliant flash of blue light. Radar stations watching the intercept reported that the blips merged and then the lone blip disappeared and the aircraft was gone.

But the facts of the case paint a slightly different but no less tragic version of events. It was only after the classified files of the case and the investigation were released that this case could be understood fully.

The story, as told in UFO circles, is quite dramatic and seems to provide solid evidence that something strange, something alien, had visited on the evening of September 8, 1970. It started, according to some sources, at 8:18 P.M. when radar on an island north of the Shetland Islands picked up an object as 37,000 feet, traveling at 630 miles an hour. Nothing extraordinary about that as it could have easily been a commercial airliner. It then changed direction turning toward the south and picked up both speed and altitude. It was clearly no longer a commercial airliner, but was not operating outside the limits of a military jet, especially some of the secret reconnaissance craft available to various air forces.

Two jet fighters were launched from RAF Leuchars in eastern Scotland but the object reversed direction, now heading north, and shot off the radar screen. Its speed was believed to be about seventeen thousand miles per hour, much too fast for any military aircraft.

Over the next hour, the object, or one similar to it, reappeared on various radar screens, and according to UFO researchers, intercepts were attempted. Two F-4 Phantoms were scrambled from Iceland, but they were unable to find the UFO.

According to the stories that were published later, radars as far away as Cheyenne Mountain, the NORAD Headquarters in Colorado, tracked the UFO. There were more attempted intercepts; the object was tracked, flying twice the speed of sound and flying at various altitudes.

Finally, at 10:06 P.M., Captain William Schaffner of the United States Air Force on detail to the 5 Squadron of the Royal Air Force took off from Binbrook to intercept the UFO. He was flying in a Lightning, tail number XS894. He carried two Red Top air-to-air missiles. He was told the UFO was now flying at 6,000 feet at 530 miles per hour and parallel to the coast east of Whitby.

According to the UFO researchers, he was able to intercept the object and flew alongside it. He is reported to have said the object was conical in shape with an intense blue light on it. He also said that a glass ball was flying alongside the UFO.

The radar operators saw the blips of the interceptor and the UFO merge. The single blip slowed to five hundred miles per hour, finally hovering for two minutes. It then accelerated and the two blips separated, one accelerating to twenty thousand miles per hour while the other flew at six hundred miles per hour, descending.

Radio contact, which had been lost, was re-established with Schaffner complaining that he was dizzy and there were shooting stars. He said that his instruments were not working properly. He was told to ditch the aircraft, though he had enough fuel to return to base.

> (Captain William Schaffner) is reported to have said the object was conical in shape with an intense blue light on it.

A Shackleton, a four-engine, twin-tailed, British aircraft that was patrolling in the area, reported that Schaffner's aircraft was down. The crew of the Shackleton saw it on the ocean before it sank.

While this seems to mirror the Kinross case, this is where the similarity ends. The aircraft was found sitting, intact, on the ocean floor. The canopy was closed but there was no sign of the pilot. Divers were able to recover the aircraft and it was taken to Binbrook for the accident investigation.

Everything about the investigation was classified then. However, in accident investigations by the U.S. Air Force, everything is always classified. It is believed that classifying the information will facilitate the flow of needed information. Junior officers will feel free to express themselves if they do not believe there will be retribution by their superiors. For the Air Force, learning what caused the accident has the highest priority.

Decades later, that information was declassified, and the UFO was removed from the report. According to the documentation, the UFO was, in fact, the Shackleton reconnaissance aircraft. It was part of an exercise in which Schaffner was participating that evening.

Unlike the Kinross case, there were witnesses besides the radar operators. According to the documentation in the accident report, a Lightning pilot who had completed an earlier practice intercept, and the Shackleton crew, reported they had seen Schaffner flying far below them, close to the surface of the ocean. Contact was lost with him a moment later and it is believed that it was then he hit the water.

What is interesting is that the report shows that the aircraft's ejector seat had not been properly serviced and that it failed to fire. Schaffner apparently then manually opened the cockpit as he attempted to escape from his now sinking aircraft. This suggests that he was able to successfully ditch, that he was conscious, and that he had gotten out of the airplane. Once clear of the aircraft, he apparently lost his survival gear and that he succumbed to the freezing temperatures in the water. This, of course, explains why his body was not found in the cockpit, but it doesn't completely explain what had happened to him.

It also explains why the cockpit canopy was closed. Since the ejector failed to fire but was opened manually, the canopy was not "blown clear" of the aircraft. As it sank, the hydraulics that had opened it and held it open slowly eroded and the canopy closed again.

This, then, was a tragic accident. Schaffner did as he was told when he attempted to bail out of the aircraft. He successfully ditched, but when the plane sank, he was left in the freezing waters. In such circumstances, the pilot would have survived less than an hour and had probably lost consciousness much faster. It was an accident and not a UFO event.

Frederick Valentich, 1978

On October 21, 1978, twenty-year-old instructor pilot Frederick Valentich took off from Moorabin, Victoria, Australia, heading for King Island, Tasmania. He was flying a Cessna 182 designated as Delta Sierra Juliet, which was part of the aircraft registration number. The flight following was with the Melbourne Flight Service Unit, and the controller there was Steve Robey.

Just after 7:00 P.M., Valentich contacted Melbourne and asked if there was any other traffic, or more specifically, was there any other aircraft near him below five thousand feet. Following are transcripts of the official communications between Valentich and the Flight Service Unit as published by the Australian authorities:

19:06:14 DSJ [Valentich]: Melbourne, this is Delta Sierra Juliet. Is there any known traffic below five thousand?

FS [Robey]: Delta Sierra Juliet, no known traffic.

DSJ: Delta Sierra Juliet, I am, seems to be a large aircraft below five thousand.

19:06:44 FS: Delta Sierra Juliet, what type of aircraft is it?

DSJ: Delta Sierra Juliet, I cannot affirm, it is four bright, and it seems to me like landing lights.

19:07:31 DSJ: Melbourne, this is Delta Sierra Juliet, the aircraft has just passed over me at least a thousand feet above.

DSJ: Er-unknown, due to the speed it's travelling, is there any air force aircraft in the vicinity?

FS: Delta Sierra Juliet, no known aircraft in the vicinity.

19:08:18 DSJ: Melbourne, it's approaching now from due east towards me.

FS: Delta Sierra Juliet.

19:08:41 DSJ: (open microphone for two seconds)

A bright and highly luminous UFO pursued Frederick Valentich's Cessna 182 in 1978.

19:08:48 DSJ: Delta Sierra Juliet, it seems to me that he's playing some sort of game, he's flying over me two, three times at speeds I could not identify.

FS: Delta Sierra Juliet, roger, what is your actual level?

DSJ: My level is four and a half thousand, four five zero zero.

FS: Delta Sierra Juliet and you confirm you cannot identify the aircraft?

DSJ: Affirmative.

FS: Delta Sierra Juliet, roger, stand by.

19:09:27 DSJ: Melbourne, Delta Sierra Juliet, it's not an aircraft it is (open microphone for two seconds).

19:09:42 FS: Delta Sierra Juliet, can you describe the—er—aircraft?

DSJ: Delta Sierra Juliet, as it's flying past it's a long shape (open microphone for three seconds) cannot identify more than it has such speed (open microphone for three seconds). It's before me right now Melbourne.

19:10 FS: Delta Sierra Juliet, roger and how large would the—er—object be?

19:10:19 DSJ: Delta Sierra Juliet, Melbourne, it seems like it's chasing me. What I'm doing right now is orbiting and the thing is just orbiting on top of me also. It's got a green light and sort of metallic like, it's all shiny on the outside.

FS: Delta Sierra Juliet.

19:10:46 DSJ: Delta Sierra Juliet (open microphone for three seconds). It's just vanished.

FS: Delta Sierra Juliet.

19:11:00 DSJ: Melbourne, would you know what kind of aircraft I've got? Is it a military aircraft?

FS: Delta Sierra Juliet, confirm the—er—aircraft just vanished.

DSJ: Say again.

FS: Delta Sierra Juliet, is the aircraft still with you?

DSJ: Delta Sierra Juliet; it's (open microphone for two seconds) now approaching from the south-west.

FS: Delta Sierra Juliet.

19:11:50 DSJ: Delta Sierra Juliet, the engine is rough-idling. I've got it set at twenty three twenty-four and the thing is (coughing).

FS: Delta Sierra Juliet, roger, what are your intentions?

DSJ: My intentions are—ah—to go to King Island—ah—Melbourne. That strange aircraft is hovering on top of me again (open microphone for two seconds). It is hovering and (open microphone for one second) it's not an aircraft.

FS: Delta Sierra Juliet.

19:12:28 DSJ: Delta Sierra Juliet. Melbourne (open microphone for seventeen seconds).

That was the last that anyone heard from Valentich. That last seventeen seconds, according to some, were the sounds of metallic scraping but no voice. After that just silence. When Valentich failed to arrive at King Island, other light aircraft began a visual search of the flight route but they found nothing. Although the aircraft was equipped with a radio survival beacon, it was not activated, or it had failed because no signal was detected from it.

The Royal Australian Air Force (RAAF), using an Orion long-range reconnaissance aircraft, followed Valentich's flight route but found nothing other

Lenticular clouds have, on occasion, been mistaken for flying saucers.

than an oil slick. Samples of the oil were recovered by surface vessels but turned out to be marine diesel fuel and not aviation gas. Clearly the slick was not caused by Valentich's aircraft.

After several days without results, the search was suspended. Although they had found debris in the general area, it was identified as the remains of packing crates and plastic bags. It had nothing to do with Valentich.

Australia's Bureau of Air Safety released a report in May 1982, some three and a half years after Valentich vanished, saying, in essence, they really knew nothing about it. They were unable to find a location for what they identified as the "occurrence," they didn't know what time it had happened, even with the records available, they believed the accident was fatal, though they had found no body or wreckage, and they had no opinion why the aircraft disappeared. In other, more precise words, they knew nothing of relevance and their investigation added nothing to the case.

Over the years there have been many explanations for this event. Bill Chalker, an Australian UFO researcher, interviewed A. Woodward, who had signed the official Aircraft Accident Summary Report. Woodward made it clear that he believed this to be an aircraft accident and suggested it was possibly caused by pilot disorientation ... or it was suicide ... or the aircraft had been struck by a meteorite and knocked out of the sky. He didn't know and was just wildly speculating as the comment about a meteorite was suggested.

Harley Klauer, another Australian UFO researcher, had two ideas about the case. He believed that Valentich had either been knocked down by drug runners or by an electrical discharge from a lenticular cloud. This would be, I presume, lightning.

Later he would abandon the drug smuggler theory but did say that he had some direct evidence from a series of photographs taken at sunset on October 21. Klauer said the pictures revealed that the aircraft had exploded. The only problem was that the pictures were taken prior to Valentich's last radio transmission and an explosion would have left debris scattered over the water.

Unfortunately with something like this tragedy, there are those who come up with strange explanations. Valentich was supposedly spotted in the former Soviet Union in 1982. In documents that surfaced in 2003, a man identified only as Nikolay D. claimed that he had seen smoke some distance away in a remote region of the Soviet Union. When he and other officials approached, they found a man who Nikolay said was about forty years old.

Taken into custody, the man soon revealed that he was Frederick Valentich and that he had been captured by a UFO. He said that he was offered the chance to become a pilot of one of their (alien) craft. He continued with other extraordinary claims which, of course, were never proved.

Valentich was also spotted at Plaza Del Charco in the Canary Islands in 1990. To prove that he was really Valentich, he showed his Australian passport. He told those around him that he had been "recruited" by the aliens, joining a larger group of other humans also recruited by aliens. He didn't seem to explain what they were supposed to have been recruited to do, only that it had been by aliens.

There were also reports, in 1982, that his aircraft had been found. An independent film producer, Ron Cameron (not to be confused with Jim Cameron), said that two divers had told him they had found Valentich's aircraft in deep water while they were on a salvage search. For ten thousand dollars, they would provide the location of the aircraft and other documentation to prove their story.

But nothing ever came of this. The Australian Department of Aviation said that they would have a role in any salvage operation because it was an open case. They wanted to maintain a low profile, however, because they thought it might turn into a media circus.

At that point the divers disappeared. Maybe they feared they would be charged with fraud if they couldn't provide the evidence. Although Cameron tried to find them again, they had vanished as completely as Valentich.

In the End ...

In the end, just as seen with the Kinross disappearance, there is no solution. Maybe he flew into the ocean, maybe his aircraft exploded or failed him in some other fashion, though he was in radio contact when he disappeared.

It should be noted that both Moncla and Wilson, and Valentich, disappeared over water. The lakes and oceans can hide a great deal. Searches of the area that were quickly mounted failed to provide any clues. And in the decades since, no answers have surfaced.

These are tales of aircraft disappearances that are related to UFO sightings. Some of the documentation is more persuasive than that of others. It can also be shown that the government, whether American or Australian, can be less than candid in their attempts to explain UFO sightings.

And, after all is said, a hoax cannot explain the disappearance of an aircraft … not in these circumstances.

The Condon Committee

Beginning about 1960, the Air Force decided they wanted to drop the public investigations of UFOs. There are documents that prove this. Their solution, according to those documents, was to find a university that would study the question of UFOs, determine that national security was not an issue, and then recommend that the Air Force no longer investigate them. The outcome of this was the University of Colorado study, popularly known as the Condon Committee.

Air Force Loses Interest

Contrary to what the Air Force might claim, what the news media might report, and what most people might believe, by 1960 the Air Force was no longer interested in the investigation of UFOs. They found themselves in a position they did not like. By regulation and expectation, they had to investigate UFO sightings, but they had long ago determined that UFOs did not pose a threat to national security and their continuing investigation presented them nothing more than a public relations nightmare. No matter what they said, no matter how they spun the information, no matter how many cases they solved, the public continued to believe they were hiding information about alien visitation.

In fact, after the Levelland, Texas, sightings of November, 1957, Richard Horner, then an Assistant Secretary of the Air Force, in a broadcast, said, "The Air Force is not hiding any UFO information. And I do not qualify this in any way."

But documents circulated internally by the Air Force proved that this was not the truth, the whole truth, and nothing but the truth. Project Blue Book, while known to the public, gathered information and then classified it routinely as "secret." That is, in fact, hiding information because those without a security

Lonnie Zamora.

clearance, and a need to know, would not have access to it. Horner knew this when he made the statement, but then, he was attempting to protect the project and the research being conducted and wasn't worried about what might be learned about the project and classifications at some future date. He wasn't worried about the accuracy of what he said other than it was basically accurate.

While this hinted at an attempt to derail the UFO investigations, other documents that surfaced after the Project Blue Book files were made public in 1976 suggested that the Air Force wanted everything explained. In December, 1958, an officer assigned to the UFO project said that he had found "certain deficiencies" that he believed "must be corrected." He was referring to Air Force Regulation 200-2 that had been revised on 5 February 1958, which ordered the following, " ... to explain or identify all UFO sightings."

Essentially, the Air Force was ordering its officers to investigate UFO sightings and then explain them. If the sighting was of some mundane object, then that explanation was offered immediately. If it wasn't easily identified, then possible explanations were to be accepted as the real thing and those should be offered to the public.

After the sightings of the mid-1960s, which included the Lonnie Zamora landing trace case from Socorro, New Mexico, the Air Force embarked on a search for a university or some other "neutral" entity that could investigate UFOs to provide a scientific framework for the evidence. While they suggested they wanted an independent study, the documentation made it clear that what they really wanted was someone to study the questions and then find the answers the Air Force desired.

This, then, was the study undertaken by the University of Colorado with a half a million dollars of taxpayer money. Chosen to lead the investigation was Dr. Edward Condon, a well-respected scientist, according to some of the advanced publicity for the study.

This seems an odd choice, at first, given his entire background. He was a scientist who favored the free exchange of ideas, theories, and information inside the scientific community, even with colleagues in the Soviet bloc. He had worked on the Manhattan Project, but only for weeks, quitting over what he believed to be overzealous enforcement of the security regulations. He was given security clearances and had them revoked a number of times. He worked in government, worked in private industry, and had taught at the university level.

There is nothing in his background to suggest that he was disloyal or that he would have shared secrets with those not authorized to have them if he was entrusted with them. It didn't seem to matter if the secrets were government or industrial. He chaffed at having the information restricted to a few but he didn't seem to have shared anything that he had learned during those periods. His record was cleared a number of times, but in the end government bureaucracy overcame good sense and decency and his clearances were finally revoked.

> "It is my inclination right now to recommend that the government get out of this business."

So, that the Air Force would select him to lead their UFO investigation seems strange. The Air Force said that it was his lack of a stated policy or opinion on the subject that led to his selection. But then, some eighteen months before the final report was due, with the investigation still underway, Condon told scientists in Corning, New York, on January 26, 1967, "It is my inclination right now to recommend that the government get out of this business. My attitude right now is that there is nothing in it. But I am not supposed to reach a conclusion for another year."

But the case for conclusions existing before any work was done by the scientists on the Condon Committee, as it became known, is much stronger than a simple statement made in front of colleagues who might wonder about his involvement with flying saucers. On January 16, 1967, before the real work began and ten days before Condon would tell his Corning audience his opinion, Lieutenant Colonel Robert R. Hippler of the Science Division, Directorate of Science and Technology, part of the HQ, USAF in Washington, D.C., wrote to Dr. Edward U. Condon. The letter was received by the committee on January 23.

Hippler wrote:

This is an informal letter expressing some thoughts on our round-table discussion on the UFO program, and does not constitute the formal letter requested by John Coleman.

There are two items which leave me a little uneasy. The first is the Wertheimer Hypothesis, and its corollary that one cannot "prove" the negative on extraterrestrial visitations. The second is an apparently obscure understanding of what the Air Force wants. Since I will discuss this second item, you will see why this is an informal letter expressing my own opinion—and hence is not binding on you.

On the first item, I wish to present a slightly different approach. When we first took over the UFO program, the first order of business, even before approaching AFOSR, was to assure ourselves that the situation was as straightforward as logic indicated it should be. In other words, we too looked to see if by some chance the intelligence people have information other than what exists in Blue Book files. There were no surprises. While there exist some things which may forever remain unknowable in the universe, certainly an extraterrestrial visitation must fall in the "knowable" category. An alien would not come light years merely to pick up surreptitiously some rocks, or melt holes in reservoir ice (à la Edwards). He would have long since gone through the geologic bit, and would be fairly knowledgeable of the make-up of stars and planets. You have stated that President Truman was unaware of the Manhattan Project until he became President. In that same time period, physicists not connected with the project were aware of the possibilities and knew that something was going on.

No one knows of a visitation. It should therefore follow there has been no visitation to date. As you are aware, if UFOs are an Air Force "sacred cow," the other services in the usual competitive spirit would not be constrained by this "sacred cow." Nor is the "fear of panic" holding anyone's tongue. No one is reticent about the horror of an ICBM attack. Words such as "end of civilization" have been used many times.

This brings us to the second item. When you have looked into some sightings and examined some Blue Book records and become acquainted with the true state of affairs, you must consider the cost of the Air Force program on UFOs, and determine if the taxpayer should support this for the next decade. It will be at least that long before another independent study can be mounted to see if the Air Force can get out from under this program. If the contract is up before you have laid the proper groundwork for a proper recommendation, an extension of the contract would be less costly than another decade of operating Project Blue Book.

Hippler signed his name.

In his response, which is not reproduced in its entirety simply because some of the things said, "Yes, you're right," Robert Low wrote:

Maybe we will find that extraterrestrial visitations have occurred, but there's no way to demonstrate that they haven't. This is a logical problem that can't be skirted, and I'm sure, if we were to miss the point, the National Academy would set us straight....

We don't know what technology exists on other planets. I think one can assert, however, that for a spaceship to get to the earth from a planet outside the solar system, it would be necessary to employ a technology far more advanced than we enjoy. Since we have no knowledge of that technology, speculation on it brings one right into science fiction, and once one has crossed that boundary the sky is the limit. He can argue anything, and the rules of scientific evidence and methodology have been abandoned. So there is no point in stepping across the boundary, except to engage in idle speculation! Such speculation isn't useful in helping to close in on an answer to the problem of whether there have been extraterrestrial visitors or not. And probability won't help.

You mention that the fear of panic is not holding anyone's tongue. That's an extremely good point; I had not thought of it. On the second page, you indicate what you believe the Air Force wants of us, and I am very glad to have your opinion. In fact, you have answered quite directly the question that I have asked—you may remember that I came back to it a couple of times—at our meeting on Thursday evening, January 12.

Low then signed off, after suggesting that he and Condon would be in Washington, D.C., and they could "perhaps" get together.

The language in both Hippler's and Low's letters can be seen as benign, but it can also suggest an attempt by Hippler to tell Low what they were to find and what recommendation the Air Force wanted. End the study of UFOs by the Air Force. Get the Air Force off the hook for UFO investigations. Suggest that National Security was not an issue, and let that be the end of it.

All of this was part of the original plan as discussed on January 12, 1967, in what was called "Air Force Advisory Panel Briefing," that included Hippler, Major Hector Quintanilla who ran Project Blue Book at the time, and a number of civilian scientists who held various positions with the Air Force, including John W. Evans, Myron B. Gilbert, John Howard, and Kenneth E. Kissell.

The meeting was called to figure out just how they were going to proceed with the investigation of UFOs. In fact, at the onset, Condon said, "At this meeting we would like to discuss our progress and future plans with you, and especially we hope to benefit from your opinions on where the emphasis should be placed with respect to policy questions the Study must deal with."

Condon then noted that one of the problems was going to be field investigations. He said that he knew of no problem in physics in which the data were obtained by interviewing the citizens. He said that nearly all a physicists' research was done in the laboratory and the problem they faced was the transitory nature of UFO sightings. The appearance of the UFO could not be predicted and the sightings were relatively short-lived so that one of their investigators would have no chance of getting there to make independent observations and measurements.

Arrey, New Mexico, April 24, 1949

While it is true that sightings can't be taken into the lab for study, it is also true that scientists have been involved in UFO sightings themselves. Charles B.

Moore, of Project Mogul fame, had his own UFO sighting on April 24, 1949, near the White Sands Proving Ground which is near Arrey, New Mexico. It is a report that is still classified as "Unidentified" in the Project Blue Book files, and is one that the Condon Committee should have reviewed as part of their study. It had multiple witnesses that included a scientist and involved instrumentation in the observation. In other words, here was a scientific observation of a UFO.

According to the documentation, Moore, who was working with General Mills and had manufactured the balloon they were using in their research, along with a crew of four Navy-enlisted men, had set up their equipment to record local weather data to prepare for a Skyhook balloon launch. They were near Arrey, and had "released a 350 gram balloon about 1020 MST and were following it with a standard ML-47 David White Theodolite."

Moore had made a reading at 1030 and then gave up the theodolite to watch the balloon with his unaided eyes. Moore said:

> We thought we had the balloon when we picked up a whitish spherical object right along the direction the theodolite was pointing. The object was drifting east rapidly but we had thought to encounter similar winds on the balloon. When the distance between the theodolite and the supposed balloon became apparent, I took over the theodolite and found the true balloon still there, whereupon I abandoned it and picked up the object after it came out of the sun.... The object was moving too fast to crank the theodolite around; therefore one of the men pointed to the theodolite and I looked. The object was ellipsoid about 2 to 1 slimness ratio; length about .02' subtended angle. White in color except for a light yellow of one side as though it were in shadow. I could not get a hard focus on the object due to the speed at which the angles changed. Therefore I saw no good detail at all.

> The azimuth angle continued to decrease as the object continued on a north heading, growing smaller in size.... The object then disappeared due to distance after a total time of observation of about sixty seconds. The object was not a balloon and was some distance away.

Donald Menzel believed that he could identify the object. Menzel, after talking to Moore, said that he knew what Moore and his crew had seen. Menzel said that it was not an object but a mirage, an atmospheric reflection of the real balloon, making it seem there were two objects in the sky when there was but one. He told Moore about it.

But Moore, who described himself as an atmospheric physicist, and who considered himself qualified to discuss this with Menzel as a peer rather than as a layman, said that the weather conditions were not right for the creation of a mirage. Since Moore was on the scene and Menzel was safely ensconced

Edward Condon, a highly respected physicist who also once headed the National Bureau of Standards, led the committee that bears his name in debunking UFO reports.

in his classroom in far-away Massachusetts, Moore's opinion carried more weight. When Moore talked with Menzel, Menzel didn't want to listen to what Moore had to day. The Air Force sided with Moore and marked the case as "unidentified."

In August 1949, the information about the case leaked into the press. One of the officers who was at White Sands that month mentioned the flying saucer sightings that had been made there. Articles were published in various newspapers, including those in El Paso, Texas, and Los Angeles, California, saying that there were flying saucer reports happening at military bases in New Mexico.

The main article, written by Marvin Miles of the *Los Angeles Times* and published on August 30, 1949, said, "Flying saucers or at least mysterious flying 'objects' have been sighted by service personnel at this vital [White Sands Proving Ground] center of America's upper air research."

According to Miles, "One officer believes, sincerely, that the objects seen are space ships and declared that a ballistic formula applied to one observation through a photo theodolite showed the 'ship' was 35 to 40 miles high, an egg-shaped craft of fantastic size and traveling at incredible speeds of three to four miles a second!"

That officer was probably Commander Douglas C. McLaughlin, a regular (as opposed to Reserve) Navy officer. McLaughlin said that "objects had been sighted at least six times," and that two of the objects, or discs, had flown along a V-2 rocket.

In the March 1950 issue of *True*, McLaughlin went into greater detail. He wrote:

Shortly after the balloon was aloft, west of the observation point, the theodolite operator swung his instrument rapidly to the east.

A strange object, seen by everyone present, had crossed the path of the balloon. The instrument man, confused, had followed it. Swiftly, one of the scientists [Moore] grabbed the theodolite and began tracking the missile.

An accurate plot of the object's course was recorded. Analyzing this data later, I [meaning McLaughlin] can state definitely that:

1. The object, viewed in cross section, was elliptical in shape.

2. It was about 105 feet in diameter.

3. It was flying at an altitude of approximately 56 miles. (This was determined by a ballistics expert. An object at a lower altitude on this particular bright day could not have fitted the data taken. For security reasons, I cannot go deeper into this method of calculating altitude [though it seems that the object would have been extremely difficult to see that high above the ground].)

4. Its speed was about 5 miles per second.

5. At the end of its trajectory, it swerved abruptly upward, altering its angle of elevation by 5 degrees—corresponding to an increase of altitude of about 25 miles—in a period of 10 seconds. A rough calculation indicates that a force of more than 20 G's (20 times the pull of gravity) would be required to produce this elevation in this time.

6. The object was visible for 60 seconds.

7. It disappeared at an elevation of 29 degrees.

Miles, in his original article, concluded, "In all, some five reports have been made in the last six months." He said his source for this was an unnamed officer and that this officer mentioned other officers who had reported seeing UFOs.

Since all the information, in 1949, was classified, and because it seemed that classified information had leaked, the Air Force Office of Special Investigation was called in. A number of agents from the AFOSI District Office #17 at Kirkland Air Force Base in Albuquerque conducted the investigation. This investigation, however, concentrated on the possible compromise of classified information and not on the sightings themselves.

What was learned was that there had been other sightings at White Sands, and Moore might have known about them, but never said a word if he did.

But the real point here is that the Condon Committee had been lamenting the fact that UFOs weren't brought into the lab, couldn't be brought into the lab, the sightings were relegated to civilians without scientific training, and that the reports were usually brief.

> This investigation ... concentrated on the possible compromise of classified information and not on the sightings themselves.

Information picked up in the Project Blue Book files showed that there had been sightings from Los Alamos on May 3, June 2, 11, and 20. All were identified as mundane objects, mostly meteors. It would seem that scientists would be able to recognize meteors when they saw them. But if nothing else, here was a series of mundane sightings that the Condon Committee could have used to develop information about the psychological reactions of those who saw UFOs and learn something about their inability to identify meteors.

Back to the January Briefing

Condon then said, "From there [meaning the transitory nature of the sighting] I don't necessarily draw the conclusion that one should not make the effort. One or two good field incidents which we ourselves can observe with a camera or spectrograph or radiometer under our own control would be very good evidence. When one considers what is implied in attempting to do this, however, the feasibility is considerably reduced."

But then, in October of 1968, there was a sighting which would have allowed the time for a team to get to the location, they would have had the opportunity to interview many firsthand witnesses, they would have been given a photograph of the object in the air, and because the event took place over several days, they could have made their own observations of some of the residue from the case.

The Lack of Investigation—Shag Harbour

As it turns out, the Condon Committee didn't want to do much in the way of fieldwork. This is demonstrated by the Shag Harbour UFO crash in October 1967.

Although the Condon Committee had been commissioned to review the UFO evidence, and although they had received a report that something had crashed into Shag Harbour, Nova Scotia, their entire investigation of the incident was a telephone call or two to the Royal Canadian Mounted Police. They were alerted to the event by Jim Lorenzen, then the International Director of APRO. Given that information, they launched their "investigation" using the telephone.

Dr. Norman E. Levine provided the information for the Condon Committee and it was reported on page 351 and 352 as Case No. 34, labeled as North Atlantic and dated as Fall 1967. Levine wrote:

> He [Jim Lorenzen] stated that the original report had come from two teenagers and that the Navy was searching for wreckage. No aircraft were reported missing in the area.... A corporal of the RCMP [apparently Victor Werbicki] stated that the first report had come from five young people, 15–20 yr. old, who while driving near the shore had seen three or four yellow lights in a horizontal pattern comparable in size to a 'fair-sized' aircraft.... They observed the light while they drove about .25 mi., then reported the incident to the RCMP detachment.

Chris Styles and Don Ledger, two Canadian researchers who have between them decades of experience in UFO investigations, provided me with a thick file on the case. Just a quick reading of that information certainly suggested that something quite unusual had happened. According to them, the events began on the night of October 4, 1967, near the small fishing village of Shag Harbour. Something, estimated to be about sixty feet in diameter, descended to the surface of the water about a half mile from shore. On it were four bright lights that flashed in sequence.

Newspaper articles, one of them published in the *Halifax Herald*, reported that Laurie Wickens, with four others, spotted something above and in front of them at about 11:00 P.M. that night. It was a large object that had four flashing amber-colored lights; the object was descending, as opposed to falling, toward the harbor.

As it struck the water, there seemed to be a bright flash and explosion. Wickens decided to contact the police and drove through one village and into another trying to keep the object in sight so that he could provide precise information. They entered the parking lot of the Irish Moss Plant. All five of them, Wickens included, ran to the water's edge when they could see what they would later describe as a dark object floating or hovering just about the water. Now the flashing lights were gone and only a single, pale yellow light that seemed to be on top of the object could be seen.

Wickens decided that he would report the sighting to the Royal Canadian Mounted Police, but rather than driving back to the detachment outpost, he would drive west to Wood's Harbour in search of a telephone. There he contacted Corporal Victor Werbicki, who wasn't very impressed with the report. Instead of asking him anything about the crash, Werbicki asked him if he had been drinking. Werbicki then told Wickens to hang up but to wait by the telephone.

Several other witnesses, some of them thinking that some sort of aircraft had crashed, called the same RCMP detachment at Barrington Passage. Mary Banks, who was on Maggie Garron's Point, which is near the harbor, told Werbicki that she had seen an airplane crash into the sound. A third call came in from two women who were about thirteen miles away and who had seen the same thing. A man, in a fourth call, said that he had also heard a whistle and a bang. Although they all talked in terms of an aircraft accident and others mentioned only bright flashing lights, no one suggested that this was a UFO, meaning alien craft.

> As it struck the water, there seemed to be a bright flash and explosion.

It was now apparent to Werbicki that something had happened out there. He called Wickens back and told him to meet him at the Moss plant. Three of RCMP officers made it to the shoreline and one of them, Constable Ron Pond, said that he had seen the lights from his car and that he'd seen the object, or the lights, or whatever, dive toward the water. He thought he saw a shape behind the lights which certainly changed the dynamic of the sighting. In other words, Pond saw not only the lights, but believed those lights had been attached to something solid.

Standing on the shore with the Mounties were a number of other witnesses. These included Wickens and his four friends, and the occupants of a pickup truck that pulled into the lot. Norm and Wilfred Smith had seen the object in the air before stopping for a better look. Although Werbicki didn't see anything until Wickens pointed it out to him, all could see the pale yellow light that floated about a half mile from shore. Through binoculars, they could see that whatever floated on the surface was creating a foaming, yellow wake as it moved. Because the object was in the water offshore, the Coast Guard was notified and fishing boats were called in to look around. Although the cause of the yellow foam disappeared before the boats arrived, they could still see some evidence of its passing. The Coast Guard cutter arrived too late to see anything and by three in the morning the search was suspended but would resume the next day.

This is the situation as it stood when Jim Lorenzen notified the members of the Condon Committee. Levine, in his preliminary statement, suggests that the first reports were made by teenagers and he seems to be suggesting that others saw lights on the water, but nothing in the sky. Levine went on to write:

> Two officers [RCMP constables Ron O'Brien and Ron Pond] and the corporal [Werbicki] had arrived about 15 min. later, in time to see the light on the water. It persisted about five minutes longer. Ten minutes after it went out the two officers were at the site in a rowboat; a Coast Guard boat and six fishing boats were on the scene.

They found only patches of foam 30–40 yd. wide that the fishermen thought was not normal tide foam....

The site of the presumed impact was in between an island and the mainland, about 200–300 yd. off shore. Apparently, no one actually saw anything enter the water [though I must point out that a number of people saw the object descend to the water, which is, essentially, the same thing]. However two young women driving on the island reported that a horizontal pattern of three yellow lights had tilted and descended, and then a yellow light had appeared.... The RCMP corporal stated that the light on the water was not on any boat, that Air Search and Rescue had no reports of missing aircraft in the area, and an RCAF radar station nearby reported no Canadian or U.S. air operations in the area at the time, nor any ususal radar object.... A search by Navy divers during the days immediately following the sighting disclosed nothing relevant.

Five days later the Naval Maritime Command advised the project [that is, the Condon Committee] that the search had been terminated. The watch officer read a report from the RCMP indicating that at the time in question a 60 ft. object had been seen to explode upon impact with the water.... A captain of a fishing boat that had been about 16 mi. from the site of the earlier reports, reported to the project that he and his crew had seen three stationary bright red flashing lights on the water, from sundown until about 11 P.M. The ship's radar showed four objects forming a six mile square; the three lights were associated with one of these objects [so now we see that Levine is contradicting himself with radar reports and people seeing the object descend]. At about 11:00 P.M., one of the lights went straight up. The captain had judged that the radar objects were naval vessels and the ascending light a helicopter; he had attached no significance to these observations until he had heard on the radio of the sightings; he then reported the foregoing observations.... However, since the position he reported for the objects was about 175 n. mi. from the original site, the two situations do not appear related.

No further investigation by the project was considered justifiable particularly in view of the immediate and thorough search [that had failed to find anything which would suggest that the Condon Committee should be interested in the case] that had been carried out by the RCMP and the Maritime Command.

This shows that the on-the-scene investigation by the Condon Committee was a telephone call and then a dismissal of the case. This was a case of multiple witnesses, certainly more than just the teenagers that Levine mentioned, and there was a possibility of physical evidence, but they declined go to Canada.

Levine seemed to believe, or at the very least claimed he believed, that the sightings had been thoroughly investigated by others on the scene, that nothing of interest was found, and that the search had been called off.

Years later, an investigation by Canadian researchers Chris Styles and Don Ledger uncovered not only additional witnesses, a photograph of the object in the sky, but also documentation and testimony from high-ranking Canadian officials. Styles, in writing about the case, would say that he had met with a former general who had served with the DOPS section of the Canadian Forces Headquarters. The officer was annoyed with Styles for finding him but did supply some interesting information about the case.

> (A)n investigation by Canadian researchers Chris Styles and Don Ledger uncovered not only additional witnesses, a photograph of the object in the sky, but also documentation and testimony from high-ranking Canadian officials.

According to Styles:

> The story told to me in Ottawa by the Brigadier contained all the verifiable bits and earlier partial stories of ships sitting over a submerged U.F.O. off C.F.S. Shelburne's government point. The Brigadier's source was [sic] men who were loyal to him that were commandeered by NORAD and the navy to play the role of identification team if they found something physical. Apparently, they did and according to the Brigadier the men claim that 'There was no doubt.' It was not a conventional aircraft or spacejunk [sic] originating from either 1967 superpower. They told their regular Canadian C.O. that 'There was activity down there.' In fact incredibly they say that there was a second craft. In the Brigadier's own lingo, 'It was standing nines for the damaged saucer.' The basic outline of the story ends when a russian [sic] sub enters the then 12 mile offshore international limit. The small flotilla sails toward the intruder to offer challenge. This is after a weeks [sic] observation by sonar and T.V. remote over the U.F.O.'s resting place. It is at this point that both U.F.O.'s [sic] begin moving under the water back towards the Shag Harbour area. Once they clear open water in the Gulf of Maine they surface and fly away. The Brigadier closed our meeting by stating that he doubts I will find any paperwork on this operation in Canada.

That Styles and Ledger were able to uncover the documentation and testimony from the event suggests that this was something that the Condon Committee should have done as well. It happened on their watch, would have provided them with a very interesting case that hinted at the extraterrestrial, and met the criterion for an investigation with the exception of it happening in Canada. Even with that problem, there were American military forces involved, and the scientists could have arrived before the conclusion of the incident, but they were content to ignore it as a prank by teenagers.

Continued Notes from the January 12, 1967, Meeting

There were some other interesting, if not disturbing, aspects of that meeting. They discussed the crop of UFO sighting reports that had been gathered, concentrating on the Air Force but not ignoring the civilian organizations. What was said was, "Briefly, he [Michael Wertheimer from the Department of Psychology] has hypothesized that regardless of how many reports we received and how many we are able to dispose of, we are almost certain to find a residue of unexplained ones. The existence of the residue, however, does not prove that anything is coming from outer space. To prove that, one needs direct evidence that some objects are really from outer space and that they are intelligently guided; the existence of a residue of unexplained sighting reports does not constitute such proof."

Condon, at some point, said that he would accept as evidence of an alien visitation the recovery of a spaceship. He said, "I wouldn't be satisfied with anything other than actually getting a vehicle, with or without occupants, so under my control that I could take it and exhibit it to something like this committee so that all of you saw it, or take you to a place where I had it 'captured.' Anything less than that I wouldn't believe."

Observation, then, even by those who were trained, and the committee had suggested pilots, both military and commercial, as trained observers, and by scientists, would not be sufficient. They didn't discuss the indirect evidence as being sufficient, even if that evidence was supported by multiple-witness observation. Landing traces, radar returns, photographs, and other measurements wouldn't build a sufficiently strong case to convince Condon that there was alien visitation, which in and of itself isn't as disturbing as some of the other things that Condon said.

Wertheimer, in a long section, discussed reaction to various types of stimuli and then said, "Unfortunately, I think it is becoming clear that the fundamental question that the public wants answered is simply unanswerable. The assertion that at least some of these are actually caused by objects of intelligent extraterrestrial origin is neither proof nor disproof, nor made less likely by the existence of cases in the X class [meaning those cases that have no suitable explanation, or in other words, the 'unidentifieds' in the Project Blue Book files]."

Wertheimer was suggesting at this point that they had no hope of learning if UFOs were extraterrestrial in nature. He believed that they couldn't possibly come to any sort of conclusion about this, which is, what the public expected and what it was suggested this scientific study would do. Scientists would review the data and the evidence, investigate new cases, and in the end come to some sort of a conclusion.

But as noted, in reality, all they were supposed to do was say something positive about the way the Air Force had handled the UFO investigations and say they did not threaten national security. Wertheimer, in fact, said during the meeting, "Here is an excerpt from a memorandum I sent to the UFO Study:

> I think the Blue Book attempts have been superb—that the Blue Book personnel are badly overworked, that considering the small amount of time and staff available they have done a superb job. Chances are that a substantial proportion of the cases, though, that are now explained in the files would on closer examination not be very convincing after all. There are probably some also which are now unexplained which more careful analysis might find a fairly plausible explanation for. But I am also convinced that, however, much time we or any other group spend studying these detailed reports, there will still remain some that are unsatisfactorily explained.

In other words, the Blue Book team had done a good job with the little support and resources they had available to them. And, if better information had been provided originally, then some of the unidentified cases might be resolved to the satisfaction of everyone.

Condon's Change in Tone

At the beginning of the "investigation" Condon seemed to be having some fun with UFOs. He attended UFO conventions, and interviewed and had his picture taken with some of the more outrageous characters to dot the ufological field. But this attitude began to slowly change, as if he had begun to fear UFOs. The general theme of the discussions, after the summer of 1967, was that UFOs were harmful. Not that seeing them was harmful, or getting close to them was harmful, but the idea they might be of extraterrestrial origin was harmful to children.

> "Air Force officers (concluded) ... that none of the things seen, or thought to have been seen, which pass by the name UFO reports constituted any hazard or threat to national security."

In the summary of the report that would be published in 1969, Condon wrote, "We strongly recommend that teachers refrain from giving students credit for school work based on their reading of the presently available UFO books and magazine articles. Teachers who find their students strongly motivated in this direction should attempt to channel their interests in the direction of the serious study of astronomy and meteorology, and critical analysis of arguments for the fantastic propositions that are being supported by appeals to fallacious reasoning or false data."

In 1969, the committee released its findings. They found, as had all the previous official and, supposedly, unbiased investigations, that UFOs posed no threat to national security. Condon wrote, in the "Section I, Recommendations and Conclusions" that "the history of the past 21 years has repeatedly led Air Force officers to the conclusion that none of the things seen, or thought to have been seen, which pass by the name UFO reports constituted any hazard or threat to national security."

After suggesting that such a finding was "out of our province" to study and that the committee members would pass any such evidence on to the Air Force, Condon wrote, "We know of no reason to question the finding of the Air Force that the whole class of UFO reports so far considered does not pose a defense problem."

Condon went on and wrote in the recommendations that "it is our impression that the defense function could be performed within the framework established for intelligence and surveillance operations without the continuance of a special unit such as Project Blue Book, but this is a question for defense specialists rather than research scientists."

With that, Condon had taken care of most of the requirements of the study. He had said some positive things about the way the investigation had been conducted, he had determined that it was not a national security issue, and he had recommended the closing of Project Blue Book because other military organizations could perform the investigative functions without having a dedicated project.

But to make sure the general public was not fooled by the UFO researchers or the writers of popular literature, Condon wrote, "It has been contended that the subject has been shrouded in official secrecy. We conclude otherwise. We have no evidence of secrecy concerning UFO reports. What has been miscalled secrecy has been no more than an intelligent policy of delay in releasing data so that the public does not become confused by premature publication of incomplete studies or reports."

The Bolender Memo (Again, Briefly)

Although Condon seemed to believe that there was no secrecy involved in UFO investigation, other than for the time it took for the Air Force to properly research a case, documentation proved this wrong. He'd already seen a stack of Project Blue Book files that were marked "secret" long after any investigation had been completed and the solutions found. He might have been privy to other documents contained in the Blue Book files including a long list of studies, papers, and briefings that, in 1969, were still marked as "secret" even though they had been made, written, and briefed a decade or more earlier.

And, in 1969, Air Force Brigadier General C. H. Bolender wrote, "Moreover, reports of unidentified flying objects which could affect national security are made in accordance with JANAP (Joint Army, Navy, Air Force Publication) or Air Force Manual 55 11 and are not part of the Blue Book system."

And then Air Force Regulation 200-2, which guided the investigations of UFOs by the Air Force, made it clear that reports of UFOs were to be investigated by the 4602d AISS (Air Intelligence Service Squadron) after 1953 rather than being sent directly to Project Blue Book. (This was after the Robertson Panel study, which had also been classified, and in 1969 had only been released in a limited way.) The regulation ordered, "For those objects which are not explainable, only the fact that ATIC will analyze them is worthy of release, due to the many unknowns involved."

Or, in other words, the reports were to be made to various military organizations, but that information was to remain with those organizations and would not be released into the civilian world. This was the secrecy that Condon had failed to find.

This all seems to lead to the conclusion that the Condon Committee was not an unbiased investigation of UFOs, but a carefully designed study to prove that UFOs were not worthy of study and to discourage research. That they were reaching for solutions is proved by the study itself.

Labrador, 30 June, 1954

According to the firsthand account of a commercial airline pilot as printed in the Condon document:

> I was in command of a BOAC Boeing Strato cruiser en route from New York to London via Goose Bay Labrador (refuelling [sic] stop). Soon after crossing overhead Seven Islands at 19,000 feet, True Airspeed 230 kts, both my co-pilot and I became aware of something moving along off our port beam at a lower altitude at a distance of maybe five miles, in and out of a broken layer of Strato Cumulus cloud. As we watched, these objects climbed above the cloud and we could see one large and six small. As we flew on towards Goose Bay the large object began to change shape and the smaller to move relative to the larger....

> We informed Goose Bay that we had something odd in sight and they made arrangements to vector a fighter (F-94?) on to us. Later I changed radio frequency to contact this fighter; the pilot told me he had me in sight on radar closing me head-on at 20 miles. At that the small objects seemed to enter the larger, and then the big one shrank. I gave a description of this to the fighter and a bearing of the objects from me. I then had to change back to Goose frequency for descent clearance. I don't know if the fighter saw anything, as he hadn't landed when I left Goose for London.

The description in the final report of the Condon Committee noted that the UFO was "an opaque, dark 'jelly–fish–like' object, constantly changing shape," which to them was suggestive of "an optical cause." But they noted that

> (T)he Condon Committee noted that the UFO was "an opaque, dark 'jelly-fish-like' object, constantly changing shape," ...

very little meteorological data are available for that date and that "the presence of significant optical propagation mechanisms can be neither confirmed nor ruled out. Nevertheless, certain facts in the case are strongly suggestive of an optical mirage phenomenon...."

But the argument for some kind of mirage, or against it, is not what is important in this specific example. It is clear from the back and forth, that is, a mirage, not mirage arguments by the committee members, left them with no real answer for the case. And that there seems to be no report from the fighter pilot is also significant. His observations would certainly have provided weight to one explanation or another because he would have seen the UFO from another perspective.

In the end, the Condon Committee did solve the case, at least to their satisfaction. On page 140 of the Bantam paperback of *The Scientific Study of Unidentified Flying Objects*, the author of the Goose Bay report wrote, "This unusual sighting should therefore be assigned to the category of some almost certainly natural phenomenon, which is so rare that it apparently has never been reported before or since."

The End of Blue Book

Condon did the job he had been hired to do. He attempted to bury the questions about UFOs under a blanket of scientific jargon, biased and incomplete investigations, and supposed objectivity. The final report was structured the way Condon wanted it structured and the case book that was supposed to accompany the report was scrapped because it might have led to embarrassing questions.

The other thing that Condon did that was deceptive was produce an "executive summary." This was a short volume that supposedly included all the relevant information from the much thicker formal report. The problem is that the executive summary, which is about all the members of the news media and that many of the scientists outside the committee read, is not accurate. While Condon is suggesting that he had finally put the idea of UFOs as alien craft to rest, the statistics in his main report do not confirm that.

None of that makes any difference because today this report is held up as an example of scientific research into UFOs. To skeptics and debunkers, it proves there is nothing to the theory that some UFOs represent alien spacecraft and alien technology. The report accomplished its mission because, on December 17, 1969, the Air Force announced the closing of Project Blue Book. Investigating UFOs would be left to local law enforcement or civilian UFO groups. The Air Force was no longer interested....

Or so they said.

Project Moon Dust

For nearly fifteen years after the Condon Committee made their recommendations and the Air Force announced the termination of Blue Book, there was no hint that any U.S. agency was involved in UFO research. If a civilian called an Air Force base to report a flying saucer, he or she was told that if they felt threatened to call a local law enforcement establishment. Some of those law enforcement agencies had the telephone numbers of UFO researchers and that citizen would be passed on to them. It seemed that no one in authority had any real desire to investigate UFO sightings. There was simply nothing to them.

But that wasn't quite the situation as it existed inside the government. There were provisions for gathering and investigating UFO data. A secret project, which had a classified code name and an investigative responsibility, existed. According to documents released, accidentally, under the Freedom of Information Act, it was suggested that this was Project Moon Dust.

Robert Todd, a UFO researcher and what some might have called a rabid skeptic, using Freedom of Information, filed dozens, maybe hundreds, of requests for UFO information. He didn't just target the Air Force, but followed leads into other government departments, including the Department of State. In what some suggest was a mistake, he received a number of microfiche that contained the code name "Project Moon Dust." These suggested that the gathering of UFO material from around the world had continued, though other government organizations suggested otherwise.

Clifford Stone, a researcher living in Roswell, New Mexico, decided to follow the path that had been discovered by Todd, and requested his own copies of the documents contained on the microfiche with similar results. He learned not only of Moon Dust, but of Operation Blue Fly, which seemed to be the logistical support for the Moon Dust teams.

Stone, in fact, supplied me with a document that seemed to outline all of this. According to that document, dated 3 November 1961, the purpose is "to provide qualified personnel to AFCIN intelligence teams." There is a deleted segment and then in paragraph 2, subsection C, it said, "In addition to their staff duty assignments, intelligence team personnel have peacetime duty functions in support of such Air Force Projects as Moon Dust, Blue Fly, and UFO, and other AFCIN directed quick reaction projects which require intelligence team operational capabilities (see Definitions)."

Under "Definitions," it said:

e. Unidentified Flying Objects (UFO): Headquarters USAF has established a program for investigation of reliably reported unidentified flying objects within the United States. AFR 200-2 delineates 1127th collection responsibilities.

People who see UFOs are now supposed to contact law enforcement, not the FBI or military.

f. Blue Fly: Operation Blue Fly has been established to facilitate expeditious delivery to FTD of Moon Dust or other items of great technological intelligence interest. AFCIN SOP for Blue Fly Operations, February 1960, provides for the 1127th participation.

g. Moon Dust: As a specialized aspect of its over-all material exploitation program, Headquarters USAF has established Project Moon Dust to locate, recover and deliver descended foreign space vehicles. ICGL #4, 25 April 1961, delineates collection responsibilities.

What makes this document important is that it spells out the collection of UFO-related materials, but it does not mention Project Blue Book. As General Bolender said in his memo, "Moreover, reports of unidentified flying objects which could affect national security are made in accordance with JANAP (Joint Army, Navy, Air Force Publication) or Air Force Manual 55-11 and are not part of the Blue Book system." This is the proof of that.

Of even more significance, it spells out the way in which that material is to be collected and has set up a special operation, Blue Fly, to get the material into the hands of those who could exploit it. And while descended foreign space vehicles suggests, in this case, the Soviet Union, and later anyone who was launching vehicles into space, it could also mean material of an extraterrestrial nature. The term "descended foreign space vehicles" covered a range of possibilities.

It becomes even more specific on page 3, in paragraph C, which said, "Peacetime employment of AFCIN intelligence team capability is provided for in UFO investigation (AFR 200-2) and in support of Air Force Systems Command (AFSC) Foreign Technology Division (FTD) Projects Moon Dust and Blue Fly. These three peacetime projects all involved a potential for employment of qualified field intelligence personnel on a quick reaction basis to recover or perform field exploitation of unidentified flying objects, or know Soviet/Bloc aerospace vehicles, weapons systems, and/or residual components of such equipment."

Although this document was labeled as a draft and it was never put into operation in this form, it is clear that it was implemented in some fashion because other documents released through Freedom of Information showed that there had been attempts at gathering the data. Released documents mention the recovery of a cone-shaped satellite in Sudan on August 17, 1965, four objects that fell in Nepal on March 25, 1968, objects that were seen to "de-orbit" over New Zealand on April 7, 1972, and a very interesting one from Bolivia on May 6, 1978.

Stone, in his attempts to verify some of the information, eventually contacted New Mexico Senator Jeff Bingaman, who queried the Air Force about Moon Dust and Blue Fly. Lieutenant Colonel John E. Madison of the Congressional Inquiry Division, Office of Legislative Liaison wrote, "There is no agency, nor has there ever been, at Fort Belvoir, Virginia, which would deal with UFOs or have any information about the incident in Roswell. In addition, there is no Project Moon Dust or Operation Blue Fly. Those missions have never existed."

The problem, of course, was that these projects and operations did exist and there were a number of documents with the proper provenance to prove it, including several messages from the Department of State. While it might be argued that Madison didn't have the proper clearances to have access to the information, it can also be argued that someone should have told him the truth about it.

Bingaman went back to the Liaison Office with copies of the documents that mentioned Moon Dust and Blue Fly. Now Colonel George M. Mattingley, Jr., wrote, "This is in reply to your inquiry in behalf of Mr. Clifford E. Stone on the accuracy of the information we previously provided your office. Upon further review of the case (which was aided by the several attachments to Mr. Stone's letter), we wish to amend the statements contained in the previous response to your inquiry."

So the Air Force, through Mattingley, was now suggesting that the earlier letter had been in error which might have just been a mistake on the part of Madison or it might have been a deliberate distortion of the truth. Mattingley continued, writing, "In 1953, during the Korean War, the Air Defense Com-

U.S. Senator Jeff Bingaman.

mand organized intelligence teams to deploy, recover, or exploit at the scene downed enemy personnel, equipment and aircraft. The unit with responsibility for maintaining these teams was located at Fort Belvoir, Virginia. As the occasion never arose to use these defense teams, the mission was assigned to Headquarters, United States Air Force in 1957 and expanded to include the following peace-time functions:

a) Unidentified Flying Objects (UFOs), to investigate reliably reported UFOs within the United States;

b) Project MOON DUST, to recover objects and debris from space vehicles that had survived re-entry from space to earth;

c) Operation BLUE FLY, to expeditiously retrieve downed Soviet Bloc equipment."

We have moved from the project and operation didn't exist to they existed. This suggests that the information in the draft proposal was accurate, even if, as the Air Force claimed, that the proposal was never put into operation. It shows that the Air Force, to cover up the operation, no matter the reasoning, was not above supplying a United States senator with faulty information. But it goes further than that.

Mattingley wrote, "These teams were eventually disbanded because of a lack of activity; Project MOON DUST teams and Operation BLUE FLY missions were similarly discontinued."

But this isn't the whole truth either. These missions were deployed as several of the Moon Dust documents showed. For example, on the night of March 25-26, 1968, four objects fell in the area of Nepal. The American Embassy in Kathmandu, in a secret memo dated July 23, alerted the 1127th USAF Field Activities Group (which once had been the 4602d and the 1006th at Fort Belvoir) that they expected full cooperation with the government of Nepal and the subject of the message was "Moon Dust."

On May 6, 1978, three engineers with the Banco Minero Boliviano, along with a number of natives of the area, watched an elongated object, said to be about four meters in diameter, pass overhead. It crashed into the side of Cerro Taire with a huge explosion.

In a secret telegram sent to the Department of State, it was claimed, "[The case] has been checked with appropriate government agencies. No direct correlation with known space objects that may have reentered the earth's atmosphere near May 6 can be made. However, we are continuing to examine any possibilities."

According to "State Airgram A-6343 of July 26, 1973, which provided guidance for obtaining additional information, "In particular any information pertaining to the preimpact observations, directions or trajectory, number of objects observed, time of impact and a detailed description including markings would be helpful."

All this suggests that contrary to Mattingley's statement, the teams were used. Worse still is the response to another FOIA request by Todd. On July 1, 1987, the Air Force explained that the "nickname" Project Moon Dust no longer officially existed.

According to Colonel Phillip E. Thompson, deputy assistant Chief of Staff, Intelligence, "It [Moon Dust] has been replaced by another name that is not releaseable. FTD's [Foreign Technology Division] duties are listed in a classified regulation that is being withheld because it is currently and properly classified."

What that says is that Moon Dust was not abandoned as the Air Force suggested. It was the same old trick of changing the code name so that it could be said, truthfully, that no such project now exists. It is a way to disguise the truth. It was what they had done when Project Sign evolved into Project Grudge and when Grudge evolved into Project Blue Book. Those operations were not ended, merely renamed.

Although the Roberston Panel had suggested in 1953 that the Air Force quit investigating UFOs, that recommendation was not accepted. Although there is documentation that many had tried to end the investigation because they believed nothing would come of it, they failed. Only after the Air Force and the Condon Committee conspired to ignore evidence did the official, public investigation of UFOs by the Air Force, Project Blue Book, end.

But it was not the end of the investigation as the documents, letters, and investigation showed. As late as 1987, there was still an investigation, but it was properly classified and there was no release of any information related to the investigation of UFOs.

The Air Force said they were done with it, but clearly they were not. They just buried it more deeply.

UFO Conspiracy Today

The nature of UFO investigation, and the nature of the UFO conspiracy as it exists today, is quite different from that of thirty and forty years ago. In the past we could point the finger at the government, at the Air Force, and at those unseen men and women working behind the scenes at high levels. Today much of the conspiracy can be set at the feet of the UFO community as they work to keep admitted hoaxes alive or create thousands of documents to prove their case of alien visitation and reject scientific methods and objectivity.

Hoaxes That Persist

While we attempt to find the truth, there are others who care little for it. They invent their tales of UFO sightings and government coverups. Others, seeing or hearing of a UFO sighting, begin to suggest they were involved in it. They spin wild tales, and while those tales are often spectacular, they are often not true. What they do is hide the real phenomenon in the middle of their lies. It makes it easy for the media, for science, and for others to ignore UFOs, believing that anyone reporting one is lying or deluded or both.

I have touched on some of the cases that are almost universally considered to be hoaxes, but that reappear with frightening regularity. For example, the History Channel started a program called *UFO Hunters* and the first thing they investigated was the Maury Island hoax, though they didn't come at it from that direction. Instead they began from the point of view that there was something unusual about it that deserved further investigation. They seemed to be unaware of all the controversy around it, that the two prime witnesses were less than reliable, the physical evidence the two men presented to Air Force officers was shown to be worthless slag, and that there was no solid evidence about the case to suggest anything other than hoax. Worse still, two Air Force officers were killed in an aircraft accident that some have suggested as mysterious, maybe caused by aliens attempting to keep the mystery metal from being analyzed or by a fire started by that very same metal. Because of aircraft accident, Ed Ruppelt called it the dirtiest hoax in UFO history.

The Florida Scoutmaster Case, Briefly

There are a few others like this tale. In 1952, at the height of that UFO sighting wave, a Florida scoutmaster claimed that he had seen a UFO, approached close to it, and had been injured when a mysterious ball of fire came from the craft and superficially burned him. The Air Force did investigate and learned that the man had a history of telling tales, that he had claimed to have been a flying sergeant with the Marines in World War II, but in reality, had been dishonorably discharged in 1944. He hadn't been a flying sergeant.

The culture of UFO conspiracists persists, with the help of a large community of believers all over the world. The UFO-Fureaikan museum in Ino-machi, Japan, is one of many such museums around the world.

To friends he told a tale of being dropped on a Japanese-held island to spy on the enemy and had a story of a hairy rescue. But the man had never risen above PFC, and secret missions behind enemy lines require someone with special skills and special training, neither of which this man had. In the end, the story must be rejected, but it still pops up occasionally in UFO books or on UFO blogs and websites.

As we moved into the end of the twentieth century, there were some fascinating new cases, each of which deserve some review. One of these new cases is most probably a hoax, one is a series of interesting sightings that have yet to be satisfactorily explained, and one is a combination of inexplicable observations and probable explanation.

Gulf Breeze, November 1987

On November 11, 1987, Ed Walters, a self-described prominent businessman, was working in his home office in the early evening hours. He thought he saw something glowing behind a thirty-foot pine tree in the front yard. He stepped outside to get a better look and saw a top-shaped craft with a row of dark squares and smaller openings around the midsection. There was a bright, glowing ring around the bottom.

Realizing that this was something very unusual, Walters reached into his office and grabbed an old Polaroid camera. He stepped back out and took a photograph as the craft moved from behind the tree. In all, he would take five pictures that night as the UFO, about a hundred and fifty feet away, continued to drift northeasterly.

Just six days later, Walters visited Duane Cook, editor of the *Gulf Breeze Sentinel*. He showed Cook the pictures, but claimed, initially, they had been taken by someone else. Walters gave Cook a letter allegedly written by the anonymous photographer explaining the situation. Two days later, on November 19, 1987, the letter and the pictures were published in the newspaper.

The next day, on November 20, as Walters returned home and as he walked in through the door, he heard a humming in his ears. At first he hardly noticed it, but it grew in pitch until it was nearly unbearable. He walked through the house, followed by his wife, Frances, and then back outside. According to Walters, the hum was the same as what he heard during his first encounter. They saw nothing in the sky.

After his wife and son left the house, Walters picked up his camera and walked out the front door. Outside, he said, "I hear you, you bastard." There was a rush of air, and the internal voice said, "Be calm. Step forward."

High overhead there was a speck of light that fell rapidly toward him. He took a picture of the UFO as it hovered above a power pole. While the voices were still speaking to him, the UFO shot to the right and Walters took a second picture. About that time, the first voice told him to take a step forward so that he could enter the craft. Walters told them they had no right to do what they were doing, and the voice said, "We have the right."

The female voice added, "You must do what they say. They haven't hurt us and we are going back home now."

As the first voice said, "We will come for you now," images of naked women filled his mind. Walters took a third picture. The UFO moved forward and then shot upward, into the sky, vanishing almost instantly.

He next saw the UFO on December 2, when he was awakened by the sound of a baby crying. Although there were no babies in either of the neighbors' houses, or his own for that matter, Walters was upset. He then heard the voices, speaking Spanish, and talking about the crying baby. Accompanied by his wife, Walters, carrying a .32 caliber pistol, checked the house and the yard. Out back, he saw the UFO descending rapidly. It stopped briefly about a hundred feet above the pool, then drifted a short distance before stopping again.

Walters retreated to the house to join his wife, who was seeing the craft for the first time. Once again Walters grabbed his Polaroid camera and took it, along

As the first voice said, "We will come for you now," images of naked women filled his mind.

with his pistol, out the door. Near the pool in his backyard, he took another picture, but when the flash went off, he felt exposed. He ran back into the house. From the kitchen, he, along with his wife, saw the UFO vanish. When it was gone, the hum inside his head faded.

Back in bed, Walters said he heard the dog bark once, which he said was unusual. Walters again got up, and carrying both his pistol and camera, walked to the French doors, sure that he would see the UFO once again. Instead, when he opened the curtains, he saw, just inches from him, a four-foot humanoid with big black eyes. It was wearing a helmet with a bit of transparent material at the eye level that apparently allowed it to see.

Walters, who seemed to have remained calm enough through his other UFO experiences to take multiple photographs of the craft, who disobeyed their commands not to photograph the object, forgot about the camera in his hand. He screamed in surprise, jumped back, and tripped. Walters raised his pistol, thinking he would fire if the creature tried to enter the house, but never thought to take a picture.

Walters finally got to his feet and then struggled with the lock on the door. He put down his pistol and camera. The creature retreated, but was no more than twenty feet away. Walters was sure that he could capture it. But as he opened the door and attempted to step out, he was struck by a blue beam. It seemed that his foot was nailed to the floor. As the beam lifted his leg, Walters grabbed at the side of the doorway for balance. Frances grabbed at him and pulled on him. Both saw that the UFO was about fifty feet in the air, above the backyard.

With the UFO hovering over a nearby field, Walters, now free of the blue beam, again grabbed his camera and shot a picture of the UFO. He didn't manage to photograph the alien being, but had the presence of mind to take still another picture of the craft. He saw the object shoot out another blue beam, and Walters believed this was to pick up the creature.

By December 17, he had taken seventeen photographs of the object. By the end of December, Walters had figured out that videotape would be more impressive than still photographs. On December 28, he made a videotape that ran just over a minute and a half. According to Walters, his wife, son Dan, and daughter all saw the object.

Over the next couple of weeks, Walters would see the UFO again and take additional pictures of it. He would see more of the alien creatures, but strangely took no photographs of them.

On January 21, Walters was now working with friends to corroborate his sightings. He was in communication on a walkie-talkie with Bob Reid who was staked out a block away with a camera. Reid saw the lights that Walters reported, but he identified them as a small aircraft. Walters said that Reid was not looking in the right direction to see the real UFO.

At the end of February, the Mutual UFO Network provided Walters with a special camera that had four lenses to take three-dimensional photographs. The camera produced four negatives for each picture. It should have made it possible to gather a variety of technical information about the object, based on measurements from the negatives. That evening, Walters took more pictures of an object, or at least took pictures of lights in the distance in the night sky. Strangely, none of those pictures matched the spectacular nature of the other photographs that Walters had taken on other occasions using his Polaroid, meaning here that rather than an obvious structured craft, he had only taken pictures of distant lights.

On March 8, Walters returned to a Polaroid camera, now using a newer model. Again he took a picture of the UFO, this time hovering about three hundred feet beyond two pine trees. It was much better than the pictures of distant lights he had taken with the special, sealed camera, which could have provided precise technical data.

At the beginning of May, Walters, again alone, was in the park with a SRS camera when he heard the faint hum. This time he shouted, "Here I am! I want you out of my life!" As he attempted to photograph the object yet again there was a blinding flash and Walters lost all sensation except for a feeling that he was falling. About an hour later, he regained consciousness at the edge of the water. This was the last alien encounter that Walters would report.

Because of the nature of the case, the number of sightings, potential corroborating witnesses, and the existence of so many photographs, a number of investigations were launched. Researchers from the J. Allen Hynek Center for UFO Studies, including Robert D. Boyd, were convinced, almost from the beginning, that the case was a hoax. Boyd felt that Walters did not react as someone who'd had six months of self-proclaimed horrifying UFO experiences would react. In fact, it was noted by Center investigators, that the only cases in which a witness claimed repeated encounters with multiple photographs were either known hoaxes or strongly suspected to be hoaxes.

Bruce Maccabee of the Fund for UFO Research.

On the other hand, the Mutual UFO Network's investigators, including Don Ware and Charles Flannigan, were convinced that this was one of the best cases to have been reported to date. Bruce Maccabee of the Fund for UFO Research was also convinced, based on his professional examination of the photographs, that Walters was telling the truth and that the pictures showed a real craft from another world.

There were hints about the reality of the case. One of the first to suggest that there was more to the Walters case than had been published was Tommy Smith. Around the first of January 1988, Smith told family members that he had seen a UFO and showed them a series of pictures he claimed to have taken. But about a day later, Smith confessed that the photos were part of a prank that Ed Walters, also known as Ed Hanson to those in the Gulf Breeze area, was playing.

According to an investigation conducted by Carol and Rex Salisberry, Smith told his family that Walters had given him the photos and told him to take them to the Gulf Breeze *Sentinel*. There, he was to claim that he had taken them. He also said that he had seen two UFO models at the Walters' home and that he had seen Ed Walters photograph one of them. According to the report prepared by the Salisberrys, Smith said that Walters' wife, son, and another teenager named Hank Boland were all involved in the hoax.

Smith told family members that he didn't know what to do, but his father, Tom Smith, Sr., asked his law partners and then-Gulf Breeze Chief of Police, Jerry Brown, what his son should do. They all decided that the best action, at the moment, was no action. They believed, that since many people in Gulf Breeze already knew the pictures were part of a practical joke, the interest in them would die quickly.

Of course, that didn't happen. Interest in the photographs continued to spread with national television audiences having a chance to see them. On June 19, 1988, Gulf Breeze mayor Ed Gray called a press conference. Tommy Smith's account was substantiated by sworn testimony and independent interviews conducted with the principals.

Smith was given a number of tests in an attempt to verify his veracity. According to the Salisberrys, a recording of one of the interviews was made. It was the opinion of a number of professionals that the recording could be used in a voice stress analysis. In a report dated October 10, 1990, Dale Kelly, in a signed statement for the Gulf Breeze Chief of Police, wrote, "At the request of and under the authority of Chief Jerry Brown of the Gulf Breeze Police Department, I analyzed a tape of a person known only as Chris [Tommy Smith] to me. The subject matter was the taking of photos of 'UFOs' and if the photos were faked. Based on the test results, it is the opinion of this examiner that 'Chris' was telling the truth when he described how he was told how the photos were faked. In answer to all questions put to 'Chris,' in my opinion he was telling the truth."

In a second report dated October 18, 1990, Ed Halford, in a signed statement for the Gulf Breeze Chief of Police, wrote, "I ran a test for the chief of police in Gulf Breeze, Fl., to determine the truthfulness of a statement made by a male identified as 'Chris' [Tommy Smith].... In my professional opinion, the answers to all the questions asked of this person were truthful. I used the Mark II Voice Stress Analyzer to arrive at this conclusion."

According to the massive report prepared by the Salisberrys, after their intense and exhaustive investigation, Craig Myers, a staff writer for the Pensacola newspaper, told of how a model of the UFO seen in the photographs was accidentally found. Walters had sold the house from which he had repeatedly seen the UFO. Myers, according to a statement in the report, went to interview the new owners on June 4, 1990.

Myers wrote, "During the interview Myers asked if they had ever seen or heard anything unusual, found any darkroom materials, models, etc. The Menzers said they had found what may be construed as a UFO model, and loaned it to the *News Journal*. During the next several days the model was used in an exhaustive series of photographic experiments."

Further down in the statement, Myers wrote, "Using the model we were able to re-create photographs very similar to those Ed Walters printed in his book. Walters and his supporters have stated that the photographs are not the same because most of his UFOs had two rows of windows. However, a second row of 'windows' can easily be re-created by drawing them on the lower portion of the model."

In what is an important point, Myers wrote, "On Saturday, June 9, 1990, *News Journal* Managing Editor Ken Fortenberry interviewed Walters in Fortenberry's office. Metro Editor Joedy Isert and reporter Nathan Dominitz witnessed the interview in which Walters denied any knowledge of the UFO model, but refused to take either a lie detector test or a voice stress analysis conducted by independent experts. Walters did, however, sign a sworn statement denying any knowledge of the model. Walters said the model was obviously 'planted' in his former residence by debunkers, and intimated that the government may have been behind the debunking plan."

> "Based on the test results, it is the opinion of this examiner that 'Chris' was telling the truth when he described how he was told how the photos were faked."

It would seem, then, with the testimony of Tommy Smith, with the discovery of the model, and the misleading statements made about the case, the only conclusion to be drawn is that the Gulf Breeze photographs and the accompanying story was little more than a hoax. But the supporters had their own version of the events. They insisted that there was a conspiracy to destroy the case. Solid investigation, corroboration from additional witnesses, and the shady background of those suggesting a hoax would prove to believers there was no hoax.

There were parallel events. Walters hadn't just taken pictures of UFOs, but had also taken pictures of ghosts during teenage parties held at his house. These photographs taken during those parties is illustrative of the mindset of Ed Walters. Again, according to the investigation conducted by the Salisberrys, "They said that Tommy [Smith] was aware of Ed's tricks and even was Ed's accomplice in a stunt.... In one instance of the stunt being played, a girl's name (obviously preselected) was also made to mysteriously appear on a board when a match was struck. According to several witnesses the girl was so scared by this that she ran from the room in tears. (Ed told Charles Flannigan, Rex, and myself that he had chosen Tommy to be in on the stunt because Tommy was so quiet that no one would suspect him of being an accomplice.)"

Salisberry, attempting to corroborate these parties, investigated further and learned, again according to her report, "I asked one young woman if she had ever gone to a party at the Walters' home. Her reply surprised me. 'It was no party; it was a seance! I'm a Christian, and I was offended by what happened there and I never went back again.' She explained that there was a pentagram or star on the floor and that Ed had 3 girls sit in the middle of a circle surrounded by the other guests. Then he read the 23rd Psalm backwards, having the kids recite after him. (Summoning the ghost for the Polaroid pictures of 3 individuals, one of which would be the chosen one. The chosen one would have the ghost in the picture with her.) This girl's brother, who was also present at this party, and some of the others I interviewed verified this.... The kids, now all graduated from high school, said that they couldn't figure out how Ed did the pictures or some of his other tricks. Those interviewed considered Ed to be very clever and that he seemed to know a lot of tricks and games.... Several of these witnesses who knew Danny ... said that they thought it was unusual that Danny never spoke about the numerous UFOs that appeared at his house...."

There is also the testimony of a number of other teenagers who were there when some of the jokes were played or who saw the results of the trick Polaroid pictures. Some were offended by Walters' seances, and others participated in his practical jokes. In other words, there was a great deal of corroboration for the fact that Walters played practical jokes and created pictures of ghosts using a Polaroid camera.

There is very good evidence, then, from a number of people, that Walters used a Polaroid camera in the jokes he played on others. He created photographs of ghosts to fool the teenagers at these parties. A Polaroid camera was used to produce evidence that the seance had been real and that there were ghosts in the room. This is all the result of double exposures, which demonstrate that Walters knew how to do it with spirits and means he could have done the same thing with UFOs.

Proving that Polaroids can be used to fake photographs, those on *Fact or Faked: The Paranormal Files* demonstrated a method of doing just that. While none of the faked pictures on the show matched the detail of those taken by Walters, the point is that the closed Polaroid system can be defeated.

Carol Salisberry concluded, "Based on the information given in peer group interviews, it seems that the Walters had a variety of parties and also small group gatherings at their home. The same teens did not always attend the gatherings. All the parties did not involve a mock seance or spooky tricks but there seems to have been several parties in 1986-87 where these things did take place and a ghost photo was taken. Most of the interviewed teens and parents stated that when the UFO pictures first came out in the paper they thought it was just another of Ed's jokes."

> All the evidence seems to weigh against Walters. He stands alone against a large number of witnesses....

All the evidence seems to weigh against Walters. He stands alone against a large number of witnesses to his love of jokes, his ability to fake photographs with Polaroid cameras, and his attempts to induce others to join in the jokes. All of this makes a great circumstantial case suggesting the story is a hoax, but the diehard believers are always going to say it doesn't prove it beyond a shadow of a doubt. Find real evidence that the pictures are faked.

That final test comes from an examination of the photographs that Ed Walters claimed to have taken over a period of several months. Some had suggested that if one was proven to be a hoax, then it could be claimed that all were a hoax. That seems to be a valid theory. After all, if a man is taking photographs of a real object on a number of occasions, what purpose could be served by faking one? Instead of having twenty such pictures, he has only nineteen, which puts him way ahead of everyone except contactees.

One of the Ed Walters' pictures has been proved to be faked. Photograph No. 19, which Walters claims to have taken from his truck, which clearly shows the hood of the truck, part of the road, and the UFO, is a hoax. The photograph itself also shows a darkened sky, a treeline, and some other detail, seen at twilight. Several disinterested photographic analysts have used that picture to prove the point.

Early on in the investigation of the photographs, Bob Boyd tried to warn the MUFON investigator, among others, that there were problems with some of Ed Walters' pictures in general and Photograph No. 19 in particular. On March 7, 1988, he wrote, "The photographic evidence reveals certain inconsistencies which cause suspicion. One example is the state highway 191 B photograph [this is Photograph No. 19, which was taken as the object hovered over the highway] of the object a few feet above the road. The reflection below the object on the pavement does not conform to proper physical features consistent with such reflections."

More importantly, Ray Sanford said that he had examined Photograph No. 19 that had been "light blasted and enhanced for detail as published in Walters' book." He noticed that he could see the reflection of the treeline on the hood and believed that the reflection from the UFO illumination should also be visible, especially when it is remembered that not only was there a light ring under the UFO, but porthole lights around the center and some sort of light on the top. Even if the light ring was too low to reflect in the hood of the truck, though there is debate about that, those other lights should have been reflected and they were not.

That led to the suggestion that another analysis be performed. The best of the various independent analyses was completed by William G. Hyzer, with an assist from his son, Dr. James B. Hyzer. Their investigation of Photograph No. 19 revealed, "There was no UFO present and the photo is a product of multiple exposure techniques."

To put all this in context without resorting to minor detail that is unimportant, it must be said that a number of experiments were performed on the road. The Salisberrys, among others using various light sources, distances, and a truck similar to the one owned by Walters, established an "envelope" of distances, heights above the road, and deflections right or left of the truck. Inside the envelope there would have been a reflection in the truck's hood. According to all the information available, the UFO, as well as the lights on it, fell inside the envelope. In other words, given the location, time of day, and evidence as available on Photograph No. 19 itself, there would have been a light reflection on the hood of the truck if a UFO had been hovering over the road. That there was not was the conclusive evidence that Photograph No. 19 was a double exposure and therefore a hoax.

Hyzer, in his report, wrote, "It is this author's professional opinion that the results of this study are conclusive: if the UFO-like object in photograph number 19 had been real, reflections of luminous sources associated with the dome and dome light at the top of the object would have to be visible in the truck's hood; but they are not."

The conclusions for the case are obvious to all but the true believers. Ed Walters, playing a somewhat admitted practical joke, found himself the center of attention, and he loved it. The fact that there was nothing to the sightings meant nothing to him. He grabbed the spotlight as quickly as he could, and has done everything possible to stay in it. But his story, from the very beginning, was a hoax.

The Belgium Sightings, 1989

So, it seems that the Gulf Breeze sightings and photographs taken by Ed Walters are a hoax. But there have been other, very good sightings in which there is no evidence of a hoax. The events are real. It is the interpretation of those events that is in dispute.

All the accounts of the Belgium wave of UFO reports begin by mentioning the first sightings of a triangular-shaped object on November 29, 1989. Keep that in mind because the triangular shape will become important in another series of sightings. More than 120 people, including 13 police officers, were among the witnesses around Eupen, Belgium. The object, with shining lights, was seen at close range. Although it was multiple witness, it was little more than nocturnal lights. It did, however, mark the beginning of a series of sightings that would produce some interesting and impressive evidence.

Just two days later, Francesco Valenzano was driving through Ans in Liege province when his daughter shouted that he should look up. In the sky above them was a large, triangular-shaped object that drifted along slowly, just above the buildings of the town square. Finally it flew off toward another village.

Valenzano, it should be noted, was an Air Force meteorological specialist. On December 11, a Belgian army lieutenant colonel, Andre Amond, while driving with his wife spotted a slow-moving, strangely-lighted object at low altitude. Amond stopped the car so that he could get a good look at the object. It flashed a beam of light at him and began to approach. His wife began to shout, wanting to get out.

Amond said that the object then departed rapidly. He later told investigators that he had been impressed by the slowness with which the object moved originally, and then its speed as it flashed away in moments. The object made no noise as it maneuvered.

The day after Amond's sighting, and in response to the growing wave, the Eupen police and SOBEPS (Belgian Society for the Study of Spatial Phenomena) held a press conference in Brussels. Also at the press conference were Belgian Air Force officers who would be investigating the sightings and Guy Coeme, the Belgium Defense Minister.

> In the sky above them was a large, triangular-shaped object that drifted along slowly....

No solutions for the sightings were offered. The purpose of the conference was to inform the media about the sightings and let them know what was to be done. It was the first time that anyone with the Belgium Ministry of Defense had spoken out on the topic of flying saucers.

Not long after the press conference, one of the daily newspapers in that area printed a story suggesting the UFOs were actually American-flown F-117As. The article suggested that these were secret test flights and that the explanation had come from Washington. Although the F-117 bore a slight resemblance of the triangular UFO, it could not drift along slowly and the pattern of lights reported didn't match those on the aircraft.

Augste Meessen, a professor of physics at the Catholic University at Louvain, investigated the explanation, learning that it hadn't come from Washington as the reporter had claimed, but from Finland. A writer for *Het Laatste*

Nieuws said that he had just read an article about the F-117 and had wanted to inform his readers about the strange aircraft. To make the article interesting, he had suggested that the recent UFO sightings in Belgium might have been caused by the Stealth Fighter. He had no inside knowledge, just his wild speculation. Other newspapers grabbed the explanation and ran with it rather than checking it first, which in the world of flying saucers isn't all that unusual.

Lieutenant Colonel Wilfried De Brouwer, the Chief of Operations of the Belgian Air Force, told Meessen that they had sought help from the American Embassy in an attempt to find solutions for the sightings. Had the F-117 been the culprit in the sightings, De Brouwer would have been told about the flights prior to them being made. The U.S. Air Force does not routinely invade the airspace of a friendly, foreign nation without alerting that nation to its presence.

On December 12, 1989, despite the negative press, a man was awakened by a throbbing sound that he at first believed to be a circulation pump. He grabbed a flashlight and headed out toward the boiler. When he shut down the pump, he could still hear the noise.

As soon as he stepped outside, his attention was drawn to an oval-shaped object between two fir trees. In the bright light of the moon, he could see the object clearly. There were small lights around the perimeter that changed color from blue to red and back to blue. The object was metallic looking. At the front was a window or porthole of some kind.

After a few minutes, the object rose slightly and the sound coming from it changed in pitch. Drifting toward a meadow, it began shining searchlight-like beams under it. The object then disappeared behind a house but a moment later a well-defined, bright light shot into the sky. The witness was too frightened to investigate. Instead he returned to his own house.

Unlike so many others who saw the strange objects at that time, this man reported his sighting to the police. A search of the fields conducted by the police, and the Belgium army, turned up a giant circular area looking as if the grass had been cut by a lawn mower. There were also traces of some sort of yellow material on the grass.

There were others who later claimed they too heard the noise from the craft but who didn't go out to investigate. A reporter, living in the area, said that he had been awakened by a bright light outside but thought it was one of his own lights and rolled over to go back to sleep.

The most spectacular of the sightings, and the ones that received the widest press decimation, occurred on the evening of March 30 and the early morning of March 31, 1990. It had been suggested that when there were reliable sightings of the triangular-shaped object, the Belgian Air Force would respond with American-made F-16 fighters. When several police officials and a host of other civilian witnesses reported seeing the object, the fighters were dispatched.

According to one published account, though the fighter pilots made no visual contact with the UFO, the onboard radars did "lock on" to a target. It moved slowly, only about twenty-five miles an hour, but then would accelerate at fantastic speeds. It was reported to have dropped from an altitude of 7,500 feet to 750 feet in about one second.

The fighters locked on to the target three times that night, but each time the UFO evaded them. Eventually both the UFO and the fighters left the area. SOBEPS representatives are still unsure of what happened that night, but did express praise for the Belgian Air Force for its honesty in reporting the incident.

> The fighters locked on to the target three times that night, but each time the UFO evaded them.

A month later there was a close approach of an object near Stockay, Belgium. On May 4, 1990, a respected archaeologist walked outside to close his greenhouse door and heard the dogs in the neighborhood howling. As he returned to the house, he saw a huge object with a clearly defined outline in a field about five hundred feet from him.

He tried to alert his neighbors, but they were not home. Instead he told his wife and together they saw, at the front of the house, a cone-shaped object with a top that was mushroom-like in appearance.

After watching it for a number of minutes, his wife returned to the house. He went with her and then decided to take another look. He walked along his field and saw the object was only 100 to 150 feet away.

The object made no noise. The bottom was bright and opaque, the center was white, and the edges were yellowish. The craft seemed to be twenty-five to thirty feet in diameter at the base and was about fifteen to eighteen feet high.

The mushroom tip, at the top of the object, detached and began to climb. As it did, it turned a bright orange. After a few moments, the mushroom descended, reattached itself at the top, and the colors returned to their original shades.

Unable to find any other people to witness the event, the archaeologist returned to his house where his wife waited. They watched the UFO for a few more minutes, then went back inside.

Their son went to to spot of the encounter the next day. He found, and videotaped, four circular ground traces in a rectangular shape about twenty-five by thirty feet. The grass in each of the circular marks was twisted and depressed. A fine, yellowish powder was found on the blades of grass.

In October 1990, with the stealth explanation ruined by uncooperative Belgian and American officials, a new explanation was trotted out by a French magazine. Now, it wasn't a stealth aircraft, but some other experimental aircraft, flown by American pilots without notifying the Belgian Air Force that such flights would take place. Of course, there is absolutely no evidence that any

American aircraft, stealth, experimental, or otherwise, were involved in the Belgian sightings. The French were just not willing to let go of what, to them, was a good explanation for the sightings. Besides, they got to blame the Americans as an added bonus.

In fact, in October 1990 there were more and better sightings taking place. On Sunday, October 21, two residents of Bastogne were returning home late when two lights appeared, descending toward them. Echoing the words shouted by another Belgian witness, one of them screamed, "They're coming for us!"

They lost sight of the object for a few moments, but it reappeared, now behind a hedge bordering the right side of the road. They thought it might be a reflection on the car window, but when the window was cranked down, the light was still there, no more than fifty feet from the car.

As they drove along, the object seemed to pace them, staying with them. As they slowed and stopped, so did the object. When they accelerated, the light did the same. When they reached the end of the roadside hedge, they stopped. They could see a dark mass, more than forty-five feet in diameter. It climbed rapidly and silently into the sky. On the bottom was a ring of seven or eight lights.

Less than forty-eight hours later, at about 5:30 in the morning on October 23, a young woman identified only as Regine was awakened by her alarm clock. Through the window of her residence on the outskirts of Athus, near Luxembourg, she saw two bright lights hovering over a hill about a quarter of a mile away. Between the two bright lights was a smaller, dimmer blue light.

Ten minutes later, the lights rose into the sky and began drifting toward her silently. The lights passed over her house and she ran into the dining room where she could again see the object. She noticed that there was a small red light on the lower part of the object.

The lights kept moving in the direction of Athus. They then veered to the left, in the direction of Luxembourg, and disappeared. There were apparently no other witnesses to the event.

Later that same day, that is, October 23, four teenagers saw an object that came from behind a hill. It was about a quarter mile away and had a number of extremely bright lights on the lower part of it that were directed toward the ground. Centered among these lights was a smaller, dimmer light. They believed that the object was taking off because of the low altitude when they first spotted it.

This craft was shaped like a pyramid with the apex pointing to the front. At the base were two more red lights. The object was in sight for about thirty seconds and disappeared behind another hill.

Another sighting was made of a craft quite close to the ground. On November 22, 1990, at the village of Fluerus, a young woman was lying in bed when an intense light penetrated the room. She got out of bed, wiped the frost from the glass, and saw that the bright light was coming from behind a neighbor's wall. Although the light wasn't more than a hundred feet away, it was just behind the wall and in an abandoned field. As the light dimmed, she noticed blue flashes from that area. When a train rumbled through, the last of the lights dimmed and vanished.

The sightings continued. On December 9, more than a year after the first of the reports, another couple traveling by car saw an object. At first it seemed to be a glowing triangle. Then, watching through one of the car's windows, they saw a huge, circular plate over the tops of a group of trees. Around the edge were bright white lights. There were also four spokelike lines that were a glowing brass color.

The UFO was about one hundred and fifty feet in the air. Although they wanted to stop the car, because of traffic, they were unable to do so. They lost sight of it quickly.

> The UFO was ... about two hundred fifty feet long and forty to fifty feet high. The underside bulged outward and was dark gray.

The end of 1990 brought no respite. On January 6, 1991, two separate groups of witnesses saw a low-flying circular plate. The first group also reported they had seen a cupola on the top. There were many lights on the object.

Minutes later, another group reported they saw three lights to the left of the road. They, at first, believed it to be the lights from a soccer field. They noticed, however, that the lights were on something hovering over a quarry.

The UFO was, according to one witness, about two hundred fifty feet long and forty to fifty feet high. The underside bulged outward and was dark gray. Fifteen portholes on the side were lighted. The rear was flat and seemed to have some fins.

The press lost interest in the sightings as they continued. The stories were all becoming the same. Witnesses were seeing brightly lighted, mostly triangular-shaped objects, floating silently above the ground. There were no real examples of physical evidence left behind and the few photographs taken provided no proof of the visitation and contained no real detail.

SOBEPS reported that the reports were not just lights in the night sky. These sightings were of objects quite close to the ground with the witnesses, in many cases, not far away. They were receiving good, detailed descriptions. The only difference was that the media were no longer interested in the reports.

One Belgian newspaper recklessly suggested that Washington had "confirmed" the reports of stealth aircraft in the skies over Belgium. Clearly there was no such confirmation. The reporter should have checked those facts, rather than accepting them as true because that is what he wanted to believe.

The one thing that came from the Belgian sightings was the governmental cooperation. Rather than bury the details in a classified study that would be released in parts over the next decades, the Belgian Air Force was quite candid. They assisted researchers trying to find explanations for the series of sightings.

The real point here, however, is that we had a wave of sightings in Belgium in the early 1990s. Hundreds saw the craft and reported it. Belgian Air Force fighters attempted one intercept. The evidence for the sightings is the same as it has always been, witness testimony. Can the judgments of these witnesses be trusted, or is there something that creates a mob psychology so that normally rational people believe they are seeing flying saucers in the night sky.

The sightings, according to SOBEPS, have slowed and virtually disappeared. There are a few still made, but not with the regularity of the early part of the decade. What is left is a core of interesting reports that suggest something invaded the airspace over Belgium, and other countries, but there is no evidence that the craft were real or extraterrestrial.

The Phoenix Lights, 1997

The first of the reports began just after eight o'clock on the evening of March 13. A former police officer said that he and his family had seen a strange cluster of lights in the night sky near Paulden, Arizona. It looked to be a "V" formation of red-orange balls of light. During the next several days, dozens of others reported to have seen the same thing about the same time.

Similar reports were also made from the Prescott and Prescott Valley areas, about fifty miles north of Phoenix. The witnesses there saw very bright white lights in a triangular-shaped formation. There were those who suggested, however, that they, too, had seen red lights in a triangular formation.

Others reported those lights as they moved from northern Arizona to southern, a distance of about two hundred miles in about thirty minutes. Simple calculation showed that the object, objects, or lights were moving at about four hundred miles an hour. That certainly is not outside the realm of conventional aircraft and is a fact that might become very important as the investigation continued.

And that might be the solution to, or perhaps part of, the problem. An amateur astronomer interviewed for the *New Times* by Tony Ortega, an independent newspaper in Phoenix, said that he had seen the lights in the sky and trained his telescope on them. Tim Printy, a skeptic who specializes in UFO reports (now that Phil Klass is no longer with us), saw that article, and according to what he posted on his website:

> In May of 1997, I contacted one of the Phoenix area astronomy clubs and received a report that one of their members saw the formation in his telescope and noted they were distant, high-flying aircraft. I had no other data to go on until an article showed up in the Phoenix Newstimes [sic]. This identified Mitch Stanley, a young amateur astronomer, who saw the light formation through his telescope that night.

In part the article, which was titled *The Great UFO Coverup*, stated, "Mitch Stanley, 21, spends several nights a week in his backyard with a 10-inch telescope, exploring the night sky. He's owned the telescope for about a year, and has learned the sky well. With its 10-inch mirror, the telescope gathers 1,500 times as much light as the human eye. And with the eyepiece Stanley was using on the night of March 13, the telescope gave him 60 times the resolving power of his naked eye.

"That night Mitch and his mother, Linda, were in the backyard and noticed the lights coming from the north. Since the lights seemed to be moving so slowly, Mitch attempted to capture them in the scope. He succeeded, and the leading three lights fit in his field of vision. Linda asked what they were. 'Planes,' Mitch said.

"It was plain to see," he says. What looked like individual lights to the naked eye actually split into two under the resolving power of the telescope. The lights were located on the undersides of squarish wings, Mitch says. And the planes themselves seemed small, like light private planes.

"Stanley watched them for about a minute, and then turned away. It was the last thing the amateur astronomer wanted to look at. 'They were just planes, I didn't want to look at them,' Stanley says when he's asked why he didn't stare at them longer. He is certain about what he saw: 'They were planes. There's no way I could have mistaken that.'"

Printy found one other witness, not associated with Stanley, who had seen much the same thing. Printy interviewed him as well and posted the results to his website. He wrote:

The first witness was a man named Rich Contry who was driving west that evening on I-40 north of Prescott. His statement was in the March Postings of the Area 51 message boards and is completely ignored by the investigators. The date of his e-mail is 17 March and he states, "I was on my way from Flagstaff to Laughin Thursday when I saw the light formation reported on the radio the other night. I'm a pilot and was in the u.s. air force 4 years. Being in the mountains on highway 40, the night was clear and still. As the formation came towards me I stopped my car and got out with my binocs to check out what this was. As it came towards me, I saw 5 aircraft with there running lights (red and green) and the landing lights (white) on. They were also flying fairly slow and in the delta formation. As they went over me I could see stars going between the aircraft so it could not have been one large ship. The flying was like that of the Blue Angels or the thunderbirds demo team. Also as they went by their jets were not very loud because of the low throttle setting for flying slow but I did hear the jets as they went away towards the south.

However, there was another set of sightings that took place in and around the Phoenix area and which resulted in a videotape. These lights were not a group of planes; they seemed to be flying by in a rigid formation until they began to wink out one at a time. These were the lights, and the videotape, that inspired the investigations.

The videotape, shown on national television, was analyzed using a number of impressive computer arrays and some very sophisticated software. The conclusions drawn by those analysts and supported by their computers was that the lights seen over Phoenix were not natural and did not exhibit any of the features of manufactured lights. In other words, they were unique.

> There were those who claimed to have seen a triangular-shaped object, and others who claimed to have seen individual lights in a trianguler....

The Air Force was queried about it and the official spokesman said that the Air Force no longer investigated UFO sightings. Most people in Phoenix didn't accept that as an answer. They believed that the Air Force was hiding the truth, but this is the standard Air Force response. They haven't investigated UFO sightings since 1969.

Others, including private researchers, began collecting the stories of the lights that had moved across Arizona, some of those investigators believing that the sightings were all related. There were those who claimed to have seen a triangular-shaped object, and others who claimed to have seen individual lights in a trianguler, or "V"-shaped formation. Some thought the lights were white, others red, and still others saw faded colors in the lights.

Couple the hundreds of witnesses to the formation of lights that were videotaped over Phoenix and an impressive case begins to emerge. Then, eliminate most of those sightings because of Air Force confirmation of night flight activities over Arizona on March 13, and the report from the amateur astronomer, Mich Stanley, and Rich Contry. Officers at Luke Air Force Base, near Phoenix, reported they did track a flight of high-flying jets over the Phoenix area at the times in question. That tends to corroborate the observations of the amateur astronomer. Suddenly everything is back to, and surrounding, the Phoenix videotapes.

The analysis of the tape, performed by Village Labs in Arizona, suggested that the lights were not flares. But the analysis conducted had little scientific legitimacy. It was, in fact, little more than smoke and mirrors, which looked impressive, but that meant nothing.

Other analysis, however, suggested that the lights were flares. Although the local Air Force units said they had nothing airborne on March 13 that would drop flares, they weren't the only units using the firing ranges. A squadron from the Maryland Air National Guard was using the range that night, and their planes did drop flares. The confusion came about because they were not located in Arizona and it was several days before anyone thought to ask them about flares.

In fact, most of this comes from asking the wrong questions. Investigators and reporters called the local Air Force base and asked if they had anything flying that night. They answered that they did not, which was the truth. Those local spokesmen or women didn't know what other units might be doing, might not have even realized that Maryland Air Guard was there, and certainly were not involved in the Air Guard's training mission.

Later, when further inquiries revealed the presence of the Air Guard aircraft, the right questions could be asked. Yes, the Air Guard dropped flares over the firing range to the southwest of Phoenix.

Those at Village Labs, as well as others, said they had observed flare drops on other occasions but this didn't match. There was even an impressive bit of computer analysis that broke the wavelength of light into a basic spectrum, or so it was claimed. A graph showed the differences between flare light and those images on the videotape. To some this proved that whatever had been videotaped over Phoenix was not flares.

Others did simpler comparisons. A Phoenix television station videotaped flares and compared them to the Phoenix lights. They could find no differences in the two tapes. Maybe not the most scientific of analyses, but one that did suggest an explanation.

But those with the knowledge of the technology used to analyze the flare said that all that was being charted was the difference in brightness between the flares on the videotape of the UFO and a videotape of a flare drop. In fact, using a different point on the videotape of the UFO provided differences in the graph. In other, less complicated words, it was a difference in brightness and not a difference in composition as claimed. The analysis proved nothing other than that different points on the videotape would give differences in brightness.

The problem with the flare theory, according to many, was that the lights appeared to be over Phoenix, and not over the range. Certainly the Air Force wouldn't be dropping flares over the city, where they could start fires and kill people. Witnesses said that the objects were in front of the mountains, not beyond it.

Another analysis, this one using a bit of videotape taken in the daylight, provided what might be the final clue. Looking across the valley, there are a number of mountainous ridges. Beyond those mountains are the ranges used for gunnery practice and for dropping flares. Those ranges were to the southwest of Phoenix, just as were the lights on the videotape.

When the videotapes are superimposed, so that the mountains are "visible" at night and the UFO's lights are seen to be hanging in the sky before they wink

> A Phoenix television station videotaped flares and compared them to the Phoenix lights. They could find no differences in the two tapes.

out, an interesting thing is revealed. The lights, apparently descending very slowly, disappear behind the mountains. They don't burn out or wink out until they fall behind the mountains.

What this means, clearly, is that the objects were flares, dropped on the range. It was the mountains, invisible at night and invisible on the videotape, that caused the lights to fade one at a time.

That is the explanation for the best of the videotapes made that night. There are, however, others. Five others. The objects on these tapes are not as sharp or as bright. These tapes were made between 8:30 and 10:00 when the flares were dropped.

What this means is that there were other things seen that night. The slow-flying aircraft observed by Stanley and Contry and the flares filmed later do not account for these other tapes. Each show multiple objects. Unfortunately, the tapes are of poor quality, which is probably a reflection of the brightness of the lights and the capabilities of the cameras. If we had better evidence to work with, we might be able to explain those tapes as well.

Phoenix Lights, Part II, 1999

Jim Kelly, of the Arizona MUFON group based in Phoenix, has investigated a number of spectacular UFO reports that began with the mass sightings of March 13. As often happens in UFO research, some of those cases, under proper investigation, have been solved as natural phenomena or as conventional aircraft. Others have defied careful scrutiny and remain unidentified.

One of the best of the unidentified, according to what Kelly told me, involved two police officers in a helicopter who had seen a strange green light in the distance on October 12, 1999. They said it was about twice the size of Venus, very bright, and might have been as much as four miles away from them. They did not see an object behind the light, but they made some intriguing observations. The officers were surprised and upset by what they saw because neither had seen anything like it before that night.

The light seemed to respond when they turned the helicopter upward toward it. The light climbed suddenly, stopped, and then hovered. Both officers could see that it was rotating in some fashion. The smooth maneuvers performed by the light suggested to the officer that they were watching something under intelligent control rather than a natural phenomenon.

The pilots wondered if they were picking up a reflection from the instrument panel, but quickly eliminated that explanation by observing the light through the open doors on the side of their aircraft. This gave them a clear view without the obstruction of the plexiglass windshield or flashing of the rotor blades.

As they watched the light, the officers tried to contact other helicopters in the area and people on the ground. They wanted to find additional witnesses with different perspectives that would give them valuable information about the light. Unfortunately, the individuals they reached couldn't see what they saw.

The light maneuvered a number of times, seemed to reverse its course more than once, climbed, and descended. Kelly ruled out a balloon-borne flight, as there was virtually no wind that night, according to weather records. Had the light been attached to a balloon, it might have risen slowly or seemed to hover, but it would not have maneuvered up and down the way police officers described.

Kelly, being as thorough as possible in his investigation, contacted the local FAA searching for reports of radar contact with the light, but according to the limited information he was able to gather, there was no reported contact. However, in today's world the lack of radar contact means nothing. Stealth technology has rendered the radar argument moot.

The police officers believed that the light was several miles from them but they couldn't be sure. They were looking up at it, with no reference points around it. That means, simply, the light could have been much closer and much smaller than they thought, or it could have been much farther away and much larger. They really had no way of knowing.

They were dispatched to a police call and had to leave the area. When they returned, the light had disappeared. According to Kelly's report, the officers watched the light for ten to twelve minutes. That provided them with ample time to identify it, if there had been a mundane explanation for it.

Clearly, the officers saw something, and that observation disturbed them. But in the final analysis, all they saw was a bright light that seemed to react to them, spinning several miles away. This is the classic nocturnal light and nothing more than that.

Needles, California, May 14, 2008

If there is a case that leads to various conspiracies, this reported UFO crash close to Las Vegas is the one. That is, if you define a conspiracy as two or more people working together. There is nothing evil about it, as far as I can see, but it does demonstrate the world in which we live.

According to various eyewitnesses, none of whom have been seriously challenged as unreliable or delusional, early on the morning of May 14, 2008, they had seen a flaming object, traveling relatively slowly, fall from the sky, cross the river, and crash into vacant land.

One of the witnesses, known only as Bob, said that a glowing, turquoise-blue-green object appeared high in the sky and headed toward him. It passed over his houseboat and he thought it might be on fire. He said that he saw it hit the ground on the far side of the Colorado River and heard the sound of the impact.

George Knapp.

Frank Costigan, who lives about three miles east of the river, said that he had gotten up about three in the morning to let the cat out. He saw the glowing object flash overhead. He said the colors were turquoise and blue and green. He said that he didn't hear it hit and he had lost sight of it when it disappeared behind a hill.

Not long after the object disappeared, Bob said that five helicopters, flying in formation, including a large one he identified as a CH-54 Sky Crane, flew over toward the crash site. The crane picked up the object, still glowing, and took it away, heading toward Las Vegas. According to Bob, the helicopters arrived within twenty minutes of the crash.

George Knapp, an investigative reporter for a Las Vegas TV station, got involved, interviewing the witnesses. He spoke with Bob, and said that he, of course, knew Bob's full name. He talked to people at the Needles airport and learned that a number of black aircraft had been on the tarmac there. He was also convinced that what fell near Needles was not an alien craft, but some sort of test vehicle.

Needles is not all that far from Las Vegas, and Las Vegas is not all that far from Area 51. Area 51 is, at the very least, the place where the next generation of military aircraft is tested. There have been some stunning sightings around Area 51, but then, some of the aircraft, when finally unveiled, are stunning. From certain angles, for example, the F-117 can look like a domed disc, and the B-2 bomber is anything but conventionally shaped.

What fell near Needles is most likely something that was being tested and somehow that test roamed off the ranges and test areas. It was clearly being watched by someone because of the quick response of the military; the fact that there is no one else who could have responded that quickly with that array of aircraft suggests this. It is a conspiracy to keep the object, aircraft, whatever it was, hidden from the public and that is not always a bad thing, especially when it is a test of a new technology.

But Knapp talked of another aspect of this. He, with his crew, were driving the highways around Needles when they spotted a convoy of black vehicles traveling together. These were large SUVs and clearly all belonged to the same agency, whether governmental or someone else. Knapp and his boys followed them to see what would happen.

What happened was one of the vehicles pulled over and when Knapp and his crew pulled in with them, they learned most of the truth. It was a government convoy, they were operating under the authority of the government, and deadly force was authorized. But they had nothing to do with the object that fell. Their mission was something else.

Not long after that Knapp received a telephone call from the Department of Energy and was invited by the agency to see some of its facilities and training. He learned that the mission was nothing all that nefarious. The dark vehicles are often on the roads around Needles and they have nothing to do with UFOs.

So there was the second conspiracy. A Department of Energy mission that was vaguely defined, but to the satisfaction of Knapp. They do travel around on their classified missions.

Conspiracies Continue

As we have seen, there are all sorts of conspiracies. There are those by government agencies to keep information hidden, often with good reason, and there are those that keep information hidden for no apparent reason. There have been projects and plans to hide information and there have been others who have conspired to release it.

The one truth here is that there have been conspiracies on all sides. The government continues to deny and hide, and UFO researchers to promote a particular point of view. There have been conspiracies to trick people into releasing information and conspiracies to prevent them from telling.

About the only solid truth is that conspiracies exist. Most are benign. Most are little more than a few people working for what they believe is a good cause. But there are some that have much more nefarious purpose, and these all need to be exposed.

As you move around, think about this. We can prove the government hid information about UFOs. It is spelled out in the documents. It is underscored by the various projects. Why are they doing it? What do they hope to gain by it?

The one truth here is that there have been conspiracies on all sides. The government continues to deny and hide, and UFO

Sign that was posted outside of Area 51 warns people to keep away.

researchers continue to promote and expose a particular point of view. There have been conspiracies to trick people into releasing information and conspiracies to prevent them from telling all that they knew.

About the only solid truth is that conspiracies exist today. Most of them are benign. Most are little more than a few people working for what they believe is a good cause or in the national interest. Some are by people who shouldn't be trusted at all and who are working only in their own self-interest. But there are some conspiracies that have much more nefarious purposes and are much more wide-ranging. These need to be exposed for the benefit of all.

As you move around in this bizarre world, think about this: We can prove the government hid information about UFOs. It is spelled out in the documents. It is underscored by the various projects that were once classified and some of which that are still hidden. We can prove there has been a manipulation of the data, sometimes in not very clever ways. We can prove that some government officials have lied about what they knew.

The questions are these: "Why are they doing it?" "What do they hope to gain by it?"

We could also ask, "What harm is this secrecy doing?" and "Can we do anything about it?"

When we figure out the answers, we often realize there is very little that we can do, and sometimes very little we should do. Maybe the best solution to all this is to just go out and have a good time. At least that way we get some benefit out of what we are doing.

BIBLIOGRAPHY

"A Celestial Visitor," *Nebraska State Journal* (8 June 1884).

Air Defense Command Briefing, January 1953, Project Blue Book Files.

Air Intelligence Report No. 100-201-79, "Analysis of Flying Object Incidents in the U.S.," 10 December 1948.

Alberts, Don E., and Putnam, Allan E. *A History of Kirtland Air Force.*

Base 1928–1982. *Albuquerque: 1606th Air Base Wing, 1985.*

Alexander, John B. *UFOs: Myths, Conspiracies, and Realities.* New York: St. Martin's Press, 2011.

Allan, Christopher D. "Dubious Truth about the Roswell Crash," *International UFO Reporter* 19, 3 (May/June 1994), 12–14.

Anderson, Michele. "BIOSPEX: Biological Space Experiments," *NASA Technical Memorandum 58217,* NASA, Washington, DC, 1979.

Anderson, Ted. Alleged diary for July 1947.

"A Relic of a By-Gone Age," *Scientific American* (June 7, 1852): 298.

Asimov, Isaac. *Is Anyone There?* New York: Ace Books, 1967.

ATIC UFO Briefing, April 1952, Project Blue Book Files.

"The Aurora, Texas Case," *The APRO Bulletin* (May/June 1973): 1, 3–4.

Baker, Raymond D. *Historical Highlights of Andrews AFB 1942–1989.* Andrews AFB, Maryland: 1776th Air Base Wing, 1990.

Barker, Gray. "America's Captured Flying Saucers—The Cover-up of the Century," *UFO Report* 4, 1 (May 1977): 32–35, 64, 66–73.

———. "Archives Reveal More Crashed Saucers." *Gray Barker's Newsletter* (14 March 1982). 5–6.

———. "Chasing Flying Saucers." Gray Barker's Newsletter 17 (December 1960), 22–28.

———. "Von Poppen Update." *Gray Barker's Newsletter* (December 1982): 8.

Barnett, Ruth. Personal diary, 1947.

Baxter, John, and Atkins Thomas. *The Fire Came By.* Garden City, NY: Doubleday, 1976.

Beckley, Timothy Green. *MJ-12 and the Riddle of Hangar 18.* New Brunswick, NJ: Inner Light, 1989.

Berlitz, Charles, and Moore, William L. *The Roswell Incident.* New York: Berkley, 1988.

"Big Fire in the Sky: A Burning Meteor," *New York Herald Tribune* (10 December 1965).

Binder, Otto. *Flying Saucers Are Watching Us*. New York: Tower, 1968.

———. "The Secret Warehouse of UFO Proof." *UFO Report*, 2,2 (Winter 1974): 16–19, 50, 52.

———. *What We Really Know about Flying Saucers*. Greenwich, CT: Fawcett Gold Medal, 1967.

Bloecher, Ted. *Report on the UFO Wave of 1947*. Washington, DC: privately printed, 1967.

Blum, Howard. *Out There: The Government's Secret Quest for Extraterrestrials*. New York: Simon & Schuster, 1991.

Blum, Ralph, with Judy Blum. *Beyond Earth: Man's Contact with UFOs*. New York: Bantam Books, 1974.

Bontempto, Pat. "The Helgoland Crash: A Dissection of a Hoax." Privately printed, 1994.

———. "Incident at Heligoland." *UFO Universe* 5 (Spring 1989): 18–22.

Bowen, Charles, ed. *The Humanoids*. Chicago: Henry Regency, 1969.

Bourdais, Gildas. *Roswell*. Agnieres, France: JMG Editions, 2004.

Braenne, Ole Jonny. "Legend of the Spitzbergen Saucer." *International UFO Reporter* 17, 6 (November/December 1992): 14–20.

Brew, John Otis, and Edward B. Danson. "The 1947 Reconnaissance and the Proposed Upper Gila Expedition of the Peabody Museum of Harvard University." *El Palacio* (July 1948): 211–222.

Briefing Document: Operation Majestic 12, November 18, 1952.

"Brilliant Red Explosion Flares in Las Vegas Sky," *Las Vegas Sun* (19 April, 1962): 1.

Britton, Jack, and Washington, George, Jr. *Military Shoulder Patches of the United States Armed Forces*. Tulsa, OK: MCN Press, 1985.

Brown, Eunice H. *White Sands History*. White Sands, NM: Public Affairs Office, 1959.

Buckle, Eileen. "Aurora Spaceman—R.I.P.?" *Flying Saucer Review* (July/August 1973): 7–9.

Bullard, Thomas E. *The Myth and Mystery of UFOs*. Lawrence, KS: University of Kansas Press, 2010.

Burleson, Donald R. "Deciphering the Ramey Memo," *International UFO Reporter* 25,2 (Summer 2000): 3–6, 32.

———. "Levelland, Texas, 1957: Case Reopened," *International UFO Reporter* 28, 1 (Spring 2003): 3–6, 25.

Buskirk, Winfred. *The Western Apache: Living in the Land before 1950*. Norman, OK: University of Oklahoma, 1986.

Cahn, J. P. "The Flying Saucers and the Mysterious Little Men," *True* (September 1952): 17–19, 102–12.

———. "Flying Saucer Swindlers." *True* (August 1956): 36–37, 69–72.

Cameron, Grant, and Scott T. Crain. *UFOs, MJ-12 and the Government*. Seguin, TX: MUFON, 1991.

Candeo, Anne. *UFO's The Fact or Fiction Files*. New York: Walker, 1990.

Cannon, Martin. "The Amazing Story of John Lear." *UFO Universe* (March 1990): 8.

Carey, Thomas J. "The Search for the Archaeologists." *International UFO Reporter* (November/December 1991): 4–9, 21.

Carey, Thomas J., and Donald R. Schmitt. *Witness to Roswell Revised and Expanded*. Pompton Plains, NJ: New Page Books, 2009.

Carpenter, Joel. "The Senator, the Saucer, and Special Report 14." *International UFO Reporter* 25, 1 (Spring 2000): 3–11, 30.

Carpenter, John S. "Gerald Anderson: Disturbing Revelations." *The MUFON UFO Journal* 299 (March 1993): 6–9.

———. "Gerald Anderson: Truth vs. Fiction." *The MUFON UFO Journal* 281 (September 1991): 3–7, 12.

Cassidy, Jadyn. "Australia UFO Crash: Meteor of Extraterrestrial Craft?" All News Web (www.allnewsweb.com/page646948.php) (20 June 2009).

Catoe, Lynn E. *UFOs and Related Subjects: An Annotated Bibliography*. Washington, DC: Government Printing Office, 1969.

Chaikin, Andrew. "Target: Tunguska." *Sky & Telescope* (January 1984): 18–21.

Chamberlain, Von Del, and David J. Krause. "The Fireball of December 9 1965—Part I." *Royal Astronomical Society of Canada Journal* 61, 4.

Chariton, Wallace O. *The Great Texas Airship Mystery*. Plano, TX: Wordware, 1991.

Chavarria, Hector. "El Caso Puebla." *OVNI*: 10–14.

Chester, Keith. *Strange Company: Military Encounters with UFOs in WW II*. San Antonio, TX: Anomalist Books, 2007.

Citizens against UFO Secrecy. "Conversation with Dr. Sarbacher." *Just Cause* (September 1985).

———. "Confirmation of MJ-12?" *Just Cause* (June 1987).

———. "The MJ-12 Fiasco." *Just Cause* (September 1987).

———. "MJ-12: Myth or Reality?" *Just Cause* (December 1985).

———. "MJ-12 Update." *Just Cause* (June 1989).

———. "More On MJ-12." *Just Cause* (March 1989).

Clark, Jerome. "Airships: Part I." *International UFO Reporter* (January/February 1991): 4–23.

———. "Airships: Part II." *International UFO Reporter* (March/April 1991): 20–23.

———. "A Catalog of Early Crash Claims," *International UFO Reporter* (July/August 1993): 7–14.

———. "Crash Landings." *Omni* (December 1990): 92–91.

———. "Crashed Saucers—Another View." *Saga's UFO Annual 1981* (1981). 44–47, 66.

———. "The Great Crashed Saucer Debate." *UFO Report* (October 1980): 16–19, 74,76.

———. "The Great Unidentified Airship Scare." *Official UFO* (November 1976).

———. *Hidden Realms, Lost Civilizations and Beings from Other Worlds*, Detroit: Visible Ink Press, 2010.

———. "Mystery Aeronauts in Texas," *International UFO Reporter*. 33, 3 (December 2010): 4–7, 21.

———. *UFO's in the 1980s*. Detroit: Apogee, 1990.

———. *The UFO Encyclopedia*. Detroit: Omnigraphics, 1998.

———. "UFO Reporters. (MJ-12)." *Fate* (December 1990).

Clarkson, James. "The Westport UFO Crash Retrieval Event." In *6th Annual UFO Crash Retrieval Conference*. Broomfield, CO: Wood and Wood Enterprises, 2008.

Committee on Science and Astronautics, report, 1961.

Cohen, Daniel. *Encyclopedia of the Strange*. New York: Avon, 1987.

———. *The Great Airship Mystery: A UFO of the 1890s*. New York: Dodd, Mead, 1981.

———. *UFOs—The Third Wave*. New York: Evans, 1988.

Cooper, Milton William. *Behold a Pale Horse*. Sedona, AZ: Light Technology, 1991.

Cooper, Vicki. "Crashed Saucer Stories." *UFO* 6, 1 (1991): 15.

———. "The Roswell Case Revived: Was It an Alien Saucer?" *UFO* (January/February 1991): 25–29.

Corso, Philip J., and William J. Birnes. *The Day after Roswell*. New York: Pocket Books, 1997.

"Could the Scully Story Be True?" *The Saucerian Bulletin* 1, 2 (May 1956): 1.

Crary, Dr. Albert. Personal diary, June–July 1947.

Creighton, Gordon. "Close Encounters of an Unthinkable and Inadmissible Kind." *Flying Saucer Review* (July/August 1979).

———. "Continuing Evidence of Retrievals of the Third Kind." *Flying Saucer Review* (January/February 1982).

———. "Further Evidence of 'Retrievals." *Flying Saucer Review* (January 1980).

———. "Top U.S. Scientist Admits Crashed UFOs." *Flying Saucer Review* (October 1985).

Davies, John K. *Cosmic Impact*. New York: St. Martin's, 1986.

Davis, Richard. "Results of a Search for Records Concerning the 1947 Crash Near Roswell, New Mexico." Washington, DC: GAO, 1995.

Davison, Leon, ed. *Flying Saucers: An Analysis of Air Force Project Blue Book Special Report No. 14*. Clarksburg, VA: Saucerian Press, 1971.

Dawson, William F. "UFO Down off Shag Harbor." *Fate* 21, 2 (February 1962): 48–53.

"The Day a UFO Crashed inside Russia." *UFO Universe* (March 1990): 48–49, 62.

Dennett, Preston. "Project Redlight: Are We Flying the Saucers, Too?" *UFO Universe* (May 1990): 39.

"Did a UFO Blast a Hole in Russia?" *The New UFO Magazine* 13, 4 (November/December 1994): 8–9, 46–49.

Dobbs, D. L. "Crashed Saucers—The Mystery Continues." *UFO Report* (September 1979): 28–31, 60–61.

"DoD News Releases and Fact Sheets," 1952–1968.

Dolan, Richard M. *UFOs and the National Security State: The Cover-Up Exposed, 1973–1991*. Rochester, NY: Keyhole Publishing, 2009.

Douglas, J. V., and Henry Lee. "The Fireball of December 9, 1965—Part II." *Royal Astronomical Society of Canada Journal* 62, 41.

Earley, George W. "Crashed Saucers and Pickled Aliens, Part I." *Fate* 34, 3 (March 1981): 42–48.

———. "Crashed Saucers and Pickled Aliens, Part II." *Fate* 34, 4 (April 1981): 84–89.

———. "The Scam That Failed: Fred Crisman and the Maury Island Incident." *UFO* 24, 1 (October 1, 2010): 12–13, 65.

———. "The Scam That Failed: Fred Crisman and the Maury Island Incident, Part Two." *UFO* 24, 2 (January 2011): 12–13.

———. "The Maury Island Hoax, Part Four and Conclusion." *UFO* 24, 4 (October 2011): 38–52.

Eberhart, George, *The Roswell Report: A Historical Perspective*. Chicago: CUFOS, 1991.

Ecker, Don. "MJ-12 'Suspected Forgery,' Air Force Says." *UFO* 8, 3 (1993): 5.

Editors. "Flying Saucers." *Look* (1966).

Edwards, Frank. *Flying Saucers—Here and Now!* New York: Bantam, 1968.

———. *Flying Saucers—Serious Business*. New York: Bantam, 1966.

———. *Strange World*. New York: Bantam, 1964.

"Effect of the Tunguska Meteorite Explosion on the Geomagnetic Field," Office of Technical Services U.S. Department of Commerce, 21 (December 1961).

Eighth Air Force Staff Directory, Texas: June 1947.

Endres, Terry, and Pat Packard. "The Pflock Report in Perspective." *UFO Update Newsletter* 1, 5 (Fall 1994): 1–6.

Estes, Russ, producer, "Quality of the Messenger." *Crystal Sky Productions*, 1993.

"Experts Say a Meteor Caused Flash of Fire," *Deseret News* (April 19, 1962): 1.

Fact Sheet, "Office of Naval Research 1952 Greenland Cosmic Ray Scientific Expedition," October 16, 1952.

Fawcett, Lawrence, and Barry J. Greenwood. *Clear Intent: The Government Cover-up of the UFO Experience*. Englewood Cliffs, NJ: Prentice-Hall, 1984.

Final Report, "Project Twinkle," Project Blue Book Files, Nov. 1951.

Finney, Ben R., and Eric M. Jones. *Interstellar Migration and the Human Experience*. CA: University of California Press, 1985.

"Fireball Explodes in Utah," *Nevada State Journal* (19 April 1962): 1.

"Fireball Fame Comes to Lapeer," December 10, 1965.

First Status Report, Project STORK (Preliminary to Special Report No. 14), April 1952.

"Flying Saucers Again." *Newsweek* (17 April 1950): 29.

"Flying Saucers Are Real." *Flying Saucer Review* (January/February 1956): 2–5.

Foster, Tad. Unpublished articles for Condon Committee Casebook. 1969.

Fowler, Raymond E. *Casebook of a UFO Investigator*. Englewood Cliffs, NJ: Prentice-Hall, 1981.

———. "What about Crashed UFOs?" *Official UFO* 1, 7 (April 1976): 55–57.

ALIEN MYSTERIES, CONSPIRACIES AND COVER-UPS

"Flying Saucers Are Real," *Flying Saucer Review* (January/February 1956): 2–5.

Friedman, Stanton. "MJ-12—Secret Document Proves Govt. Has Crashed Saucers and Alien Beings." *UFO Universe* 1, 2 (September 1988): 8–12, 68.

———. "Roswell and the MJ-12 Documents in the New Millennium." In *MUFON Symposium Proceedings* (2000): 193–220.

———. *Top Secret/Majic*. New York: Marlowe & Company, 1996.

Genesee County (Michigan) telephone directories, 1945–1950.

Gevaerd, A. J. "Flying Saucer or Distillation Machine?" *Brazilian UFO Magazine* (November 2006).

Gillmor, Daniel S., ed. *Scientific Study of Unidentified Flying Objects*. New York: Bantam Books, 1969.

Goldsmith, Donald. *Nemesis*. New York: Berkley Books, 1985.

———. *The Quest for Extraterrestrial Life*. Mill Valley, CA: University Science Books, 1980.

Good, Timothy. *Above Top Secret*. New York: Morrow, 1988.

———. *Alien Contact*. New York: Morrow, 1993.

———. *The UFO Report*. New York: Avon Books, 1989.

Gordon, Stan. "After 25 Years, New Facts on the Kecksburg, Pa. UFO Retrieval Are Revealed." *PASU Data Exchange #15* (December 1990): 1.

———. "Kecksburg Crash Update." *MUFON UFO Journal* (September 1989).

———. "Kecksburg Crash Update." *MUFON UFO Journal* (October 1989): 3–5, 9.

———. "The Military UFO Retrieval at Kecksburg, Pennsylvania." *Pursuit*, 20, 4 (1987): 174–179.

Gordon, Stan, and Vicki Cooper. "The Kecksburg Incident." *UFO* 6, 1 (1991): 16–19.

"Great Lakes Fireball," *Sky & Telescope* (February 1966): 78, 79, 80.

Graeber, Matt. "Carbondale UFO Crash Chronicles No. 10—Case Closed." www.roswellfiles.com/AARE/Carbondale.htm, 2009.

———. "The Reality, the Hoaxes and the Legend." Privately printed, 2009.

Greenwell, J. Richard. "UFO Crash/Retrievals: A Critique." *MUFON UFO Journal* 153 (November 1980): 16–19.

Grenfell, E. W. "First Report on a Captured Flying Saucer," *Sir!* (1954).

Gribben, John. "Cosmic Disaster Shock." *New Scientist* (March 6, 1980): 750–752.

"Guidance for Dealing with Space Objects Which Have Returned to Earth," Department of State Airgram, July 26, 1973.

Hall, Michael. "Was There a Second Estimate of the Situation," *International UFO Reporter* 27, 1 (Spring 2002): 10–14, 32.

Hall, Richard. "Crashed Discs—Maybe." *International UFO Reporter* 10, 4 (July/August 1985).

———. *Uninvited Guests*. Santa Fe, NM: Aurora Press, 1988.

———. ed. *The UFO Evidence*. Washington, DC: NICAP, 1964.

Hanrahan, James Stephen. *Contributions of Balloon Operations to Research and Development at the Air Force Missile Development Center 1947–1958*. Alamogordo, NM: Office of Information Services, 1959.

———. *History of Research in Space Biology and Biodynamics at the Air Force Missile Development Center 1946–1958*. Alamogordo, NM: Office of Information Services, 1959.

Hastings, Robert. *UFOs and Nukes*. Bloomington, IN: Author House, 2008.

Haugland, Vern. "AF Denies Recovering Portions of 'Saucers.'" *Albuquerque New Mexican* (23 March 1954).

Hazard, Catherine. "Did the Air Force Hush Up a Flying Saucer Crash?" *Woman's World* (February 27, 1990): 10.

Hegt, William H. Noordhoek. "News of Spitzbergen UFO Revealed." *APRG Reporter* (February 1957): 6.

Henry, James P., and John D. Mosely "Results of the Project Mercury Ballistic and Orbital Chimpanzee Flights," *NASA SP–39*, NASA, 1963.

Hessmann, Michael, and Philip Mantle. *Beyond Roswell: The Alien Autopsy Film, Area 51 and the U.S. Government Cover-up of UFOs*. New York: Marlowe & Company, 1991.

Hippler, Robert H. "Letter to Edward U. Condon," January 16, 1967.

"History of the Eighth Air Force, Fort Worth, Texas" (microfilm), Air Force Archives, Maxwell Air Force Base, AL.

"History of the 509th Bomb Group, Roswell, New Mexico" (microfilm), Air Force Archives, Maxwell Air Force Base, AL.

Hogg, Ivan U., and J. B. King. *German and Allied Secret Weapons of World War II*. London: Chartwell, 1974.

Houran, James, and Randle, Kevin. "Interpreting the Ramey Memo," *International UFO Reporter* 27, 2 (Summer 2002): 10–14, 26–27.

Hughes, Jim. "Light, Boom a Mystery. *Denver Post* (12 January 1998).

Huneeus, J. Antonio. "A Full Report on the 1978 UFO Crash in Bolivia." *UFO Universe* (Winter 1993).

———. "Great Soviet UFO Flap of 1989 Centers on Dalnegorsk Crash." *New York City Tribune* (14 June 1990).

———. "Roswell UFO Crash Update." *UFO Universe* (Winter 1991): 8–13, 52, 57.

———. "Soviet Scientist Bares Evidence of 2 Objects at Tunguska Blast." *New York City Tribune* (30 November 1989): 11.

———. "Spacecraft Shot out of South African Sky—Alien Survives." *UFO Universe* (July 1990): 38–45, 64–66.

Hurt, Wesley R., and Daniel McKnight. "Archaeology of the San Augustine Plains: A Preliminary Report." *American Antiquity* (January 1949): 172–194.

Hynek, J. Allen. *The UFO Experience: A Scientific Inquiry*. Chicago: Henry Regency, 1975.

Hynek, J. Allen, and Jacques Vallee. *The Edge of Reality*. Chicago: Henry Regency, 1972.

"Ike and Aliens? A Few Facts about a Persistent Rumor." *Focus* 1, 2 (April 30, 1985): 1, 3–4.

"International Reports: Tale of Captured UFO." *UFO* 8, 3 (1993): 10–11.

"It Whizzed through the Air; Livonia Boys Find Fireball Clues," *Livonian Observer & City Post* (16 December 1965).

Jacobs, David M. *The UFO Controversy in America*. New York: Signet, 1975.

Johnson, J. Bond. "'Disk-overy' Near Roswell Identified as Weather Balloon by FWAAF Officer," *Fort Worth Star-Telegram* (9 July 1947).

Jones, William E., and Rebecca D. Minshall "Aztec, New Mexico—A Crash Story Reexamined." *International UFO Reporter* 16, 5 (September/October 1991): 11.

Jung, Carl G. *Flying Saucers: A Modern Myth of Things Seen in the Sky*. New York: Harcourt, Brace, 1959.

Keel, John. "Now It's No Secret: The Japanese 'Fugo Balloon.'" *UFO* (January/February 1991): 33–35.

———. *Strange Creatures from Space and Time*. New York: Fawcett, 1970.

———. *UFOs: Operation Trojan Horse*. New York: G. P. Putnam's Sons, 1970.

Kean, Leslie. "Forty Years of Secrecy: NASA, the Military, and the 1965 Kecksburg Crash." *International UFO Reporter* 30, 1 (October 2005): 3–9, 28–31.

Kennedy, George P. "Mercury Primates," *American Institute of Aeronautics and Astronautics* (1989).

Keyhoe, Donald E. *Aliens from Space*. New York: Signet, 1974.

———. *Flying Saucers from Outer Space*. New York: Henry Holt, 1953.

Klass, Philip J. "Crash of the Crashed Saucer Claim," *Skeptical Inquirer* 10, 3 (1986).

———. *The Public Deceived*. Buffalo, NY: Prometheus Books, 1983.

———. *The Real Roswell Crashed-Saucer Coverup*. Amherst, NY: Prometheus, 1997.

———. "Roswell UFO: Coverups and Credulity." *Skeptical Inquirer* 16, 1 (Fall 1991).

———. *UFOs Explained*. New York: Random House, 1974.

Knaack, Marcelle. *Encyclopedia of U.S. Air Force Aircraft and Missile Systems.* Washington, DC: Office of Air Force History, 1988.

LaPaz, Lincoln, and Albert Rosenfeld. "Japan's Balloon Invasion of America." *Collier's* (17 January 1953): 9.

Lasco, Jack. "Has the US Air Force Captured a Flying Saucer?" *Saga* (April 1967): 18–19, 67–68, 70–74.

Lester, Dave. "Kecksburg's UFO Mystery Unsolved." *Greenburg Tribune-Review* (8 December 1985): A10.

Library of Congress Legislative Reference Service, "Facts about UFOs," May 1966.

"Little Frozen Aliens." *The APRO Bulletin* (January/February 1975): 5–6.

Lore, Gordon, and Harold H. Deneault. *Mysteries of the Skies: UFOs in Perspective.* Englewood Cliff, NJ: Prentice-Hall, 1968.

Lorenzen, Coral, and Jim Lorenzen. *Encounters with UFO Occupants.* New York: Berkley Medallion Books, 1976.

———. *Flying Saucer Occupants.* New York: Signet, 1967.

———. *Flying Saucers: The Startling Evidence of the Invasion from Outer Space.* New York: Signet, 1966.

Low, Robert J. "Letter to Lt. Col. Robert Hippler," 27 January, 1967.

Maccabee, Bruce. "Hiding the Hardware." *International UFO Reporter* (September/ October 1991): 4.

———. "What the Admiral Knew." *International UFO Reporter* (November/December 1986).

"The Magical Meteor," *Nebraska State Journal* (10 June 1884).

Mantle, Phillip. "Alien Autopsy Film, R.I.P." *International UFO Reporter* 32, 1 (August 2008): 15–19.

———. *Roswell Alien Autopsy.* Edinburg, TX: Roswell Books, 2012.

Marcel, Jesse, and Linda Marcel. *The Roswell Legacy.* Franklin Lakes, NJ: New Page Books, 2009.

Matthews, Mark. "Armageddon at Tunguska!" *Official UFO* (May 1979): 28–30, 58, 60.

McAndrews, James. *The Roswell Report: Case Closed.* Washington, DC: Government Printing Office, 1997.

McCall, G. J. H. *Meteorites and Their Origins.* New York: Wiley & Sons, 1973.

McClellan, Mike. "The Flying Saucer Crash of 1948 Is a Hoax." *Official UFO* 1, 3 (October 1975): 36–37, 60, 62–64.

"McClellan Sub-Committee Hearings," March 1958, August 1958.

McDonald, Bill. "Comparing Descriptions, An Illustrated Roswell." *UFO* 8, 3 (1993): 31–36.

McDonough, Thomas R. *The Search for Extraterrestrial Intelligence.* New York: Wiley & Sons, 1987.

Menzel, Donald H., and Lyle G. Boyd. *The World of Flying Saucers.* Garden City, NY: Doubleday, 1963.

Menzel, Donald H., and Ernest Taves. *The UFO Enigma.* Garden City, NY: Doubleday, 1977.

"Meteor Explodes in the City." *Dublin Press* (20 June 1891).

"Meteor Lands in Utah, Lights Western Sky." *Los Angeles Times* (19 April 1962).

Michel, Aime. *The Truth about Flying Saucers.* New York: Pyramid, 1967.

Moore, Charles B. "The New York University Balloon Flights during Early June, 1947," privately printed, 1995.

Moore, Charles B., Benson Saler, and Charles A. Ziegler. *UFO Crash at Roswell: Genesis of a Modern Myth.* Washington, DC: Smithsonian Institute Press, 1997.

Moore, William L., and Jaime H. Shandera. *The MJ-12 Documents: An Analytical Report.* Burbank, CA: Fair Witness Project, 1991.

Moseley, James W., and Karl T. Pflock. *Shockingly Close to the Truth.* Amherst, NY: Prometheus Books, 2002.

Mueller, Robert. *Air Force Bases: Volume 1, Active Air Force Bases within the United States of American on 17 September 1982*. Washington, DC: Office of Air Force History, 1989.

Murphy, John, "Object in the Woods," WHJB Radio, radio broadcast, December 1965.

National Security Agency. Presidential Documents. Washington, DC: Executive Order 12356, 1982.

Neilson, James. "Secret U.S./UFO Structure." *UFO* 4, 1 (1989): 4–6.

"New Explanation for 1908 Siberian Blast." *Cedar Rapids Gazette* (25 January 1993).

NICAP, *The UFO Evidence*. Washington, DC: NICAP, 1964.

Nickell, Joe. "The Hangar 18 Tales" *Common Ground* (June 1984).

Nickell, Joe, and John F. Fischer. "The Crashed-Saucer Forgeries." *International UFO Reporter* 15, 2 (March/April 1990): 4–12.

———. "Further Deception: Moore and Shandera," unpublished paper, privately printed, 1993.

"No Reputable Dope on Disks," *Midland [Texas] Reporter Telegram* (1 July 1947).

Northrup, Stuart A. *Minerals of New Mexico*. Albuquerque: University of New Mexico, 1959.

Oberg, James. "UFO Update: UFO Buffs May Be Unwitting Pawns in an Elaborate Government Charade." *Omni* 15, 11 (September 1993): 75.

O'Brien, Mike. "New Witness to San Agustin Crash." *MUFON Journal* 275 (March 1991): 3–9.

Oldham, Chuck, and Vicky Oldham. *The Report on the Crash at Farmington*. Lansdowne, PA: privately printed, 1991.

Olive, Dick. "Most UFO's Explainable, Says Scientist." *Elmira [NY] Star-Gazette* (26 January 1967): 19.

Packard, Pat, and Terry Endres. "Riding the Roswell-Go-Round." *A.S.K. UFO Report* 2 (1992): 1–8.

Papagiannis, Michael D., ed. *The Search for Extraterrestrial Life: Recent Developments*. Boston: Springer, 1985.

Peebles, Curtis. *The Moby Dick Project*. Washington, DC: Smithsonian Institution Press, 1991.

———. *Watch the Skies!* New York: Berkley Books, 1995.

Pegues, Etta. *Aurora, Texas: The Town That Might Have Been*. Newark, TX: privately printed, 1975.

Pflock, Karl. "In Defense of Roswell Reality." *HUFON Report* (February 1995): 5–7.

———. "Roswell, A Cautionary Tale: Facts and Fantasies, Lessons and Legacies." In Walter H. Andrus, Jr., ed. *MUFON 1995 International UFO Symposium Proceedings*. Seguin, TX: MUFON, 1990: 154–168.

———. *Roswell in Perspective*. Mt. Rainier, MD: FUFOR, 1994.

———. *Roswell: Inconvenient Facts and the Will to Believe*. Amherst, NY: Prometheus Books. 2001.

———. "Roswell, the Air Force, and Us." *International UFO Reporter* (November/December 1994): 3–5, 24.

Plekhanov, G. F., A. F. Kovalevsky, V. K. Zhuravlev, and N. V. Vasilyev. "The Effect of the Tunguska Meteorite Explosion on the Geomagnetic Field." *U.S. Joint Publications Research Service* (21 December 1961).

Press Conference—General Samford, Project Blue Book Files, 1952.

"Press Release—Monkeynaut Baker Is Memorialized," Space and Rocket Center, Huntsville, AL, 4 December 1984.

"Project Blue Book" (microfilm). National Archives, Washington, DC.

Prytz, John M. "UFO Crashes." *Flying Saucers* (October 1969): 24–25.

RAAF Base Phone Book, Roswell, NM, August 1947.

RAAF Yearbook, Roswell, NM, 1947.

Randle, Kevin D. *Conspiracy of Silence*. New York: Avon, 1997.

———. *Crash: When UFOs Fall from the Sky*, Franklin Lakes, NJ: Career Press, 2010.

———. "The Flight of the Great Airship." *True's Flying Saucers and UFOs Quarterly* (Spring 1977).

———. *A History of UFO Crashes*. New York: Avon, 1995.

———. "MJ-12's Fatal Flaw and Robert Willingham." *International UFO Reporter* 33, 4 (May 2011): 3–7.

———. "Mysterious Clues Left Behind by UFOs." *Saga's UFO Annual* (Summer 1972).

———. *The October Scenario*. Iowa City, IA: Middle Coast Publishing, 1988.

———. "The Pentagon's Secret Air War against UFOs." *Saga* (March 1976).

———. *Project Moon Dust*. New York: Avon, 1998.

———. *Reflections of a UFO Investigator*, San Antonio, TX: Anomalist Books, 2012.

———. *Roswell Encyclopedia*. New York: Avon, 2000.

———. *Roswell Revisited*, Lakeville, MN: Galde Press, 2007.

———. *Roswell, UFOs and the Unusual*. Kindle eBooks, 2012.

———. *Scientific Ufology*. New York: Avon, 1999.

———. *The UFO Casebook*. New York: Warner, 1989.

Randle, Kevin D., and Anthony Bragalia. "Two Roswell Witnesses, Reconsidered." *International UFO Reporter* 32, 3 (July 2009): 6–8, 24.

Randle, Kevin D., and Donald R. Schmitt. *The Truth about the UFO Crash at Roswell*. New York: M. Evans, 1994.

———. *UFO Crash at Roswell*. New York: Avon, 1991.

Randle, Kevin D., and Robert Charles Cornett. "Project Blue Book Cover-up: Pentagon Suppressed UFO Data." *UFO Report* 2, 5 (Fall 1975).

———. "Siberian Explosion, Comet or Spacecraft?" *Quest UFO* 1, 1 (1977): 10–15.

Randles, Jenny. *The UFO Conspiracy*. New York: Javelin, 1987.

Ramsey, Scott, and Suzanne Ramsey. *The Aztec Incident: Recovery at Hart Canyon*. Mooresville, NC: Aztec 48 Productions, 2012.

Redfern, Nick. *On the Trial of the Saucer Spies*. San Antonio, TX: Anomalist Books, 2006.

———. *The Real Men in Black*. Pompton Plains, NJ: New Page Books, 2011.

———. "Tunguska: 100 Years Latter [sic]." In *6th Annual UFO Crash Retrieval Conference*. Broomfield, CO: Wood and Wood Enterprises, 2008.

"Report of Air Force Research Regarding the 'Roswell Incident,'" July 1994.

"Rocket and Missile Firings," White Sands Proving Grounds, January-July 1947.

Rodeghier, Mark. "Roswell, 1989." *International UFO Reporter*. (September/October 1989): 4.

Rodeghier, Mark, and Chesney, Mark. "The Air Force Report on Roswell: An Absence of Evidence." *International UFO Reporter* (September/October 1994).

Rosignoli, Guido. *The Illustrated Encyclopedia of Military Insignia of the 20th Century*. Secaucus, NJ: Chartwell, 1986.

Ruppelt, Edward J. *The Report on Unidentified Flying Objects*. New York: Ace, 1956.

Russell, Eric. "Phantom Balloons over North America." *Modern Aviation* (February 1953).

Rux, Bruce. *Hollywood vs. the Aliens*. Berkley: Frog, 1997.

Sagan, Carl, and Thornton Page, eds. *UFO's: Scientific Debate*. New York: Norton, 1974.

Saunders, David, and R. Roger Harkins. *UFOs? Yes!* New York: New American Library, 1968.

Sanderson, Ivan T. *Invisible Residents*. New York: World Publishing, 1970.

———. "Meteorite-like Object Made a Turn in Cleveland, O. Area." *Omaha World-Herald* (15 December 1965).

———. "Something Landed in Pennsylvania." *Fate* 19, 3 (March 1966).

———. "This 'Airplane' Is More than 1,000 Years Old!" *Argosy* (November 1969): 33–37, 74, 76.

———. *Uninvited Visitors*. New York: Cowles, 1967.

Schaeffer, Robert. *The UFO Verdict*. Buffalo, NY: Prometheus, 1981.

Schaffner, Ron. "Roswell: A Federal Case?" *UFO Brigantia* (Summer 1989).

Schmitt, Donald R. "New Revelations from Roswell." In Walter H. Andrus, Jr., ed. *MUFON 1990 International UFO Symposium Proceedings*, Seguin, TX: MUFON, 1990, pp. 154–168.

Schmitt, Donald R., and Randle, Kevin D. "Second Thoughts on the Barney Barnett Story." *International UFO Reporter* (May/June 1992): 4–5, 22.

Scully, Frank. *Behind the Flying Saucers*. New York: Henry Holt, 1950.

———. "Scully's Scrapbook." *Variety* (12 October 1949): 61.

Shandera, Jaime. "New Revelation about the Roswell Wreckage: A General Speaks Up." *MUFON Journal* (January 1991): 4–8.

Simmons, H.M. "Once upon a Time in the West." *Magonia* (August 1985).

Slate, B. Ann "The Case of the Crippled Flying Saucer." *Saga* (April 1972): 22–25, 64, 66–68, 71, 72.

Smith, Scott. "Q & A: Len Stringfield." *UFO* 6, 1 (1991): 20–24.

Smith, Willy. "The Curious Case of the Argentine Crashed Saucer." *International UFO Reporter* 11, 1 (January/February 1986): 18–19.

Special Report No. 14, Project Blue Book, 1955.

Spencer, John. *The UFO Encyclopedia*. New York: Avon, 1993.

Spencer, John, and Evans, Hilary. *Phenomenon*. New York: Avon, 1988.

Stanyukovich, K. P., and V. A. Bronshten. "Velocity and Energy of the Tunguska Meteorite." *National Aeronautics and Space Administration* (December 1962).

Status Reports, "Grudge—Blue Book, Nos. 1–12."

Steiger, Brad. *The Fellowship*. New York: Dolphin Books, 1988.

———. *Project Blue Book*. New York: Ballantine, 1976.

———. *Strangers from the Skies*. New York: Award, 1966.

———. *UFO Missionaries Extraordinary*. New York: Pocket Books, 1976.

Steiger, Brad, and Sherry Hanson Steiger. *Conspiracies and Secret Societies*. Detroit, MI: Visible Ink Press, 2006.

———. *The Rainbow Conspiracy*. New York: Pinnacle, 1994.

———. *Real Aliens, Space Beings, and Creatures from Other Worlds*. Detroit, MI: Visible Ink Press, 2011.

Steinman, William S., and Stevens, Wendelle C. *UFO Crash at Aztec*. Boulder, CO: Privately printed, 1986.

Stone, Clifford E. *UFO's: Let the Evidence Speak for Itself*. CA: privately printed, 1991.

———. "The U.S. Air Force's Real, Official Investigation of UFO's." Privately printed, 1993.

Stonehill, Paul. "Former Pilot Tells of Captured UFO." *UFO* 8, 2 (March/April 1993): 10–11.

Story, Ronald D. *The Encyclopedia of Extraterrestrial Encounters*. New York: New American Library, 2001.

———. *The Encyclopedia of UFOs*. Garden City, NY: Doubleday, 1980.

Stringfield, Leonard H. "Retrievals of the Third Kind." In *MUFON Symposium Proceedings* (1978): 77–105.

———. "Roswell & the X-15: UFO Basics." *MUFON UFO Journal* 259 (November 1989): 3–7.

———. *Situation Red: The UFO Siege!* Garden City, NY: Doubleday, 1977.

———. *UFO Crash/Retrieval: Amassing the Evidence: Status Report III* Cincinnati, OH: privately printed, 1982.

———. *UFO Crash/Retrieval Syndrome: Status Report II*. Seguin, TX: MUFON, 1980.

———. *UFO Crash/Retrievals: The Inner Sanctum Status Report VI*, Cincinnati, OH: privately printed, 1991.

Sturrock, P. A. "UFOs—A Scientific Debate." *Science* 180 (1973): 593.

Styles, Chris. "Sag Harbor in Perspective." In *MUFON Symposium Proceedings* (1996): 26–52.

Sullivan, Walter. *We Are Not Alone*. New York: Signet, 1966.

Summer, Donald A. "Skyhook Churchill 1966." *Naval Reserve Reviews* (January 1967): 29.

Sutherly, Curt. "Inside Story of the New Hampshire UFO Crash." *UFO Report* (July 1977): 22, 60–61, 63–64.

Swords, Michael D., ed. *Journal of UFO Studies, New Series,* Vol. 4. Chicago: CUFOS, 1993.

———. "Too Close for Condon: Close Encounters of the 4th Kind." *International UFO Reporter* 28, 3 (Fall 2003): 3–6.

Tafur, Max. "UFO Crashes in Argentina." *INFO Journal* 75 (Summer 1996): 35–36.

"Target: Tunguska." *Sky & Telescope* (January 1984): 18–21.

Tech Bulletin, "Army Ordnance Department Guided Missile Program," January 1948.

Technical Report, "Unidentified Aerial Objects, Project SIGN," February 1949.

Technical Report, "Unidentified Flying Objects, Project GRUDGE," August 1949.

Templeton, David, "The Uninvited." *Pittsburgh Press* (May 19, 1991): 10–15.

Thompson, Tina D., ed. *TRW Space Log.* Redondo Beach, CA: TRW, 1991.

Todd, Robert G., "MJ-12 Rebuttal." *MUFON Journal* (January 1990): 17.

Todd, Robert G., Mark Rodeghier, Barry Greenwood, and Bruce Maccabee. "A Forum on MJ-12." *International UFO Reporter* (May/June 1990): 15.

Torres, Noe. *Ultimate Guide to the Roswell UFO Crash,* Edinburg, TX: Roswell Books, 2010.

Torres, Noe, and Ruben Uriarte. *The Other Roswell.* Edinburg, TX: Roswell Books, 2008.

Trainor, Joseph. "UFO Crashes into Dam in New South Wales." *UFO Roundup* 4, 34 (16 December 1999).

"Tunguska and the Making of Pseudo-scientific Myths." *New Scientist* (March 6, 1980): 750–751.

"UFOs and Lights: 12 Aliens on Ice in Ohio?" *The News* 10 (June 1975): 14–15.

U.S. Congress, House Committee on Armed Forces. Unidentified Flying Objects. Hearings, 89th Congress, 2nd Session, April 5, 1966. Washington DC: U.S. Government Printing Office, 1968.

U.S. Congress Committee on Science and Astronautics. Symposium on Unidentified Flying Objects. July 29, 1968, Hearings, Washington, DC: U.S. Government Printing Office, 1968.

Vallee, Jacques. *Anatomy of a Phenomenon.* New York: Ace, 1966.

———. *Challenge to Science.* New York: Ace, 1966.

———. *Dimensions.* New York: Ballantine, 1989.

———. *Revelations.* New York: Ballantine, 1991.

"Visitors from Venus." *Time* (January 9, 1950): 49.

War Department. Meteorological Balloons (Army Technical Manual) Washington, DC: Government Printing Office, 1944.

Weaver, Richard L., and James McAndrew. *The Roswell Report: Fact vs. Fiction in the New Mexico Desert.* Washington, DC: Government Printing Office, 1995.

Webb, Walter N. "An Anecdotal Report of a UFO Crash/Retrieval in 1941, Part I." *International UFO Reporter* 21, 4 (Winter 1996): 20–28.

———. "An Anecdotal Report of a UFO Crash/Retrieval in 1941, Part II." *International UFO Reporter* 22, 1 (Spring 1997): 28–32.

Webber, Bert. *Retaliation: Japanese Attacks and Allied Countermeasures on the Pacific Coast in World War II.* Corvallis, OR: Oregon State University Press, 1975.

Wenz, John. "Nebraska May Have Its Own Roswell in 1884." *Daily Nebraskan* (19 March 2007).

Whiting, Fred. *The Roswell Events.* Mt. Rainier, MD: FUFOR, 1993.

Wilcox, Inez, personal writings, 1947–1952.

Wilkins, Harold T. *Flying Saucers on the Attack.* New York: Citadel, 1954.

———. *Flying Saucers Uncensored.* New York: Pyramid, 1967.

Wise, David, and Ross, Thomas B. *The Invisible Government.* New York: 1964.

Wood, Robert M. "Forensic Linguistics and the Majestic Documents." In *6th Annual UFO Crash Retrieval Conference*. Broomfield, CO: Wood and Wood Enterprises, 2008, pp. 98–116.

———. "Validating the New Majestic Documents. In *MUFON Symposium Proceedings* (2000): 163–192.

Wood, Ryan. *Majic Eyes Only*. Broomfield, CO: Wood Enterprises, 2005.

"World Round-up: South Africa: Search for Crashed UFO." *Flying Saucer Review* 8, 2 (March/April 1962): 24.

Young, Kenny. "A UFO Crash in 1941?" Privately printed, 1 May 2000.

Young, Robert. "Old-Solved Mysteries: What Really Happened at Kecksburg, PA, on December 9, 1965." *Skeptical Inquirer* 15, 3 (1991).

Zabawski, Walter. "UFO: The Tungus Riddle." *Official UFO* (May 1977): 31–33, 59–62.

Zeidman, Jennie. "I Remember Blue Book." *International UFO Reporter* (March/April 1991): 7.

Zigel, F. Yu. "Nuclear Explosion over the Taiga (Study of the Tunguska Meteorite)." *U.S. Department of Commerce, Office of Technical Services, Joint Publications Research Service* (8 September 1964).

INDEX

Note: (ill.) indicates photos and illustrations.

A

Abbey Mine, 22
abductions, alien, 39–40, 40 (ill.)
Adam, 20
Adamski, George, 15, 50, 50 (ill.), 207
Aerial Phenomena Research Organization (APRO), 144, 189, 206, 284
Agassiz, Professor, 20
Agobard, Archbishop, 12–13
Agricola, Emperor, 6
Air Intelligence Service Squadron (AISS), 237, 266, 291
Air Technical Intelligence Center (ATIC), 91–92, 177, 254–55, 266, 291
AiResearch, 142
Aldrich, Jan L., 201, 263
Aldrich, Lynn C., 85, 87
Alien Autopsy: Fact or Fiction, 119
Alvarez, Jose, 240, 245
Alverez, Luis, 157–58
Amond, Andre, 309
Anatomy of a Phenomenon (Vallee), 5, 12, 14, 51
ancient aliens, 1–57, 2 (ill.), 7 (ill.), 8 (ill.), 11 (ill.), 16 (ill.)
Andrew, Lucile, 94–95
Andrews, Colin, 114
Andrus, Walt, 45
Angelucci, Orfeo, 207, 207 (ill.)
Annals of Thutmose III (Thutmose), 9
Antikythera computer, 24–26, 25 (ill.)
APRO (Aerial Phenomena Research Organization), 144, 189, 206, 284
Aquarius Briefing, 193, 197

Aquarius Telex, 178, 187–190, 193
Archer, J.J., 78
Archimedes, 25
Area 51, 195, 203, 315, 320, 321 (ill.)
Arnold, Kenneth, 16, 59–66, 69–76, 91, 177, 227–28
artifacts, ancient alien, 17–33
ATIC (Air Technical Intelligence Center), 91–92, 177, 254–55, 266, 291
Atkins, Lieutenant William E., 264
Atomic Energy Commission, 99
The Aztec Incident (Ramsey and Ramsey), 142
Aztec UFO crash
about the, 135–154
and alien bodies, 108
images relating to the, 112 (ill.), 136 (ill.), 137 (ill.), 139 (ill.), 147 (ill.), 152 (ill.), 153 (ill.)
and the MJ-12 conspiracy, 207

B

Bad Archaeology, 21
Baird, Vernon, 78
Baker Jr., Robert M.L., 161, 164–66
Balthaser, Dennis, 103–5
Baltimore, David, 204
Banks, Mary, 285
Banpo Museum, 3
Barnes, Patrick, 44
Barnett, Barney, 203
Barnett, Jack, 115
Barth, Sergeant Norman P., 237, 239–242, 244–48

Bass, Donald, 150
Beam, Lieutenant Colonel James C., 86
Behind the Flying Saucers (Scully), 135, 137–38
Belgian Society for the Study of Spatial Phenomena (SOBEPS), 309, 311, 313
Belgian UFO hoax, 308–14
Bennewitz, Paul, 188–190
Bequette, Bill, 61
Bergier, Jacques, 10
Berkner, Lloyd, 157–58, 167
Berliner, Don, 201–2
Binder, Otto, 259
Bingaman, Jeff, 295, 296 (ill.)
Black, James A., 186
Blackwell, Quinton A., 220–21
Blanchard, Colonel William C. "Butch," 83, 99–101, 103, 105
bodies, alien
about, 93–133
images of, 95 (ill.), 108 (ill.), 110 (ill.), 114 (ill.), 126 (ill.), 130 (ill.), 131 (ill.)
Body Snatchers in the Desert (Redfern), 152
Bogne, C.J., 68
Boland, Hank, 304
Bolender, General C.H., 173, 290, 294
Bollen, Constable Lloyd, 244
Bourdais, Gildas, 103
Bowen, Colonel John W., 109–10
Bowra, George, 145
Boyd, Lyle, 237
Boyd, Robert D., 303, 307